DEMOCRACY

DEMOKRATIA

Second Edition

By Tim Damianidis

This eBook was published in 2025 by

Tim Damianidis

Hillarys WA, 6025

Second Edition

Revision 2.06

DIGITAL EBOOK, ISBN-13: 978-1-7637431-4-4

PAPERBACK, ISBN-13: 978-1-7637431-5-1

HARDCOVER, ISBN-13: 978-1-7637431-6-8

Acknowledgements

Perseus Digital Library, available through Tufts University, provided a gateway to most of the quoted texts in this book. All reproduced material is believed to be in the public domain. Perseus Digital Library is available at www.perseus.tufts.edu.

In addition, Project Gutenberg provided an alternative source. All quoted material from Project Gutenberg is believed to be in the Public Domain. Project Gutenberg is available at www.gutenberg.org.

All other material used in quotes or generally from others is believed to also be in the public domain.

Dedication

For the love of each other

Prologue

In a world without Democracy, the truth becomes a lie, and a lie becomes the truth. The irrational and incoherent outnumber the rational and coherent; madness prevails over sanity, and as the people compete against each other, the Monarchies and Oligarchies are within their elements to rule over them all. Furthermore, democracy requires unity, not the type coerced at the point of a sword or weapon, but through the will of the people; and unity can only come when the truth is known and when the people are rational enough to deduce that truth, and coherent enough to communicate that truth to others, and sane enough to place righteousness before selfishness and act righteously in all matters of their state and lives. Only then can a people begin the process of establishing a Democracy. When righteous people are united by a desire to lead themselves, they will form a holding of power, a state, a nation, a democracy.

Why write this philosophy?

You may wonder what motives there are for writing this philosophy; if it is not political, then what? The purpose is purely philosophical. Also, if you want to pick up a book filled with "facts" that give you concise figures and statistics, you are most certainly reading the wrong book. Those books are often referred to as educational textbooks and are entirely different genres. They aim to deliver as many facts as possible about a subject, even without proof. It is commonly found that many people want to know the truth, but they often rely on pre-established facts that are presented to them. It is like the saying, "If you give a person a fish, they will feed themselves for a day, teach them how to fish, and they will be fed all their life." Similarly, the preceding common phrase can apply to learning and philosophy. The skill of acquiring knowledge and processing it wisely is closely related to the purpose of philosophy. Instead of telling you in point form several facts, of which you will have no idea how or why they were derived, philosophy relies on making the reader think deeply and with interest and concern. Philosophy is more than learning pages of numbers and facts; rather, it is an in-depth investigation into the origins of all facts. This philosophy is about investigating a subject solely to establish the truth. Unlike modern textbooks or educational books, philosophy is a way of thinking and analyzing the subject. We will apply this approach to the specific topic of Democracy.

The process of creating the book

Many books, journals, and literary works from renowned universities worldwide were researched in preparation for this philosophy. During the research, materials were analyzed from various world projects that considered themselves promoters of Democracy. Additionally, contemporary journals and old, decaying books were included in the mix of sources. Yet the only quotes you are most likely to find are from Plato, Aristotle, Socrates, and a few others from the Classical Age, perhaps even some historical footnotes. We can't reference other authors or their works without risking ruining the philosophy entirely.

On a tangent, research into Democracy has revealed a deliberate effort to distort its true meaning. Those academics paid by the world's universities and commercial sector have a purpose, but it is not to find the absolute truth. If we mention something here, most likely, the majority will turn to these "academics" and their work to find their opinions and "truths". Yet, I am not sure we can call them academics and scholars; perhaps profiteers is a more suitable term. While writing this, I have come to realize that very little of old academia remains today. Many so-called scientists and academics write what they are paid to write about. It is because of caution and safeguarding the concept of Democracy that we omit many otherwise valid and contemporary contributors to the field of Politics and Democracy. There must be an attempt to be cautious because the author cannot discern every person's hidden agenda. In other words, quoting another person places the author at risk of inadvertently supporting the agenda of the person they mention.

Furthermore, even words and phrases that have become part of common usage do not immediately reveal their origins, and we often use them without much consideration. For example, Communists popularised the words 'Community' and 'Society'. Yet it should be preferred that the words Church or Koinonia, and also polity, be used. Church originally meant the congregation of people or the Assembly of people. Koinonia implied unity without a specific assembly or congregation and was introduced into widespread usage during the Christian era. Other terms, such as 'Civilization,' have also been avoided; instead, the term 'Politeia' is used.

Furthermore, if an author disagrees with anyone, it would cause friction among many people. For instance, a well-known university published a book called Democracy that detailed the "Democratic Sultanship", which, to even the least educated, would seem like an oxymoron. We could, perhaps, quote them to highlight their weaknesses, but again, this would likely lead to conflict and wasted time. The same university tried to rewrite the Bible, and all these things make a mockery of Academia because it is stealing and manifesting propaganda within Academic studies to serve themselves. Then again, their monarch was also their religious despot. It is much like the rewritten Bibles that serve the agenda of thousands of Christian denominations. So, instead, references have been carefully selected to provide the best possible sources of information and additional reading.

That does not mean, for example, that there is an outright acceptance and agreement with Plato's Republic. Just because there is a reference to a particular author does not immediately imply that everything they write is accepted. However, in the previous example, for the most part, there is agreement on how Plato's critical thinking shapes thought.

Also, the work known almost universally as Plato's Republic is a misnomer; his works were known as Politeia (Civilization). The original Greek meaning of the word implied issues related to city life. Socrates, through Plato, did not claim that the Republic was a better system; he primarily highlighted the relationship between an Oligarchy, a Republic, and a Democracy. He tried to bring to people's attention that authority and our trust in authority lead to the perversion of Justice and Democracy. He goes on to define justice by addressing its many aspects. Plato was a Democratic person but was seeking a way to curb a potential Ochlocracy and the Oligarchy that took the life of his best friend, Socrates.

Both Socrates and Plato lived during a time when it was easy to shift a Democracy into an Ochlocracy or an Oligarchy. It was almost fearful that their system could flux between the two. That is why Plato and Socrates needed to define justice so that, whichever system presented itself, justice would at least prevail. It was a separate subject yet integral to understanding government. If we conclude that justice is an essential part of government, we must treat it as a different part.

On Speaking the truth

What if your conclusions drastically differed from what you were taught or what others believed? Imagine trying to convince others of that view or conclusion. Many people were scorned, laughed at, and even exiled from society — or worse — for differing views. Even the sane and innocent were sentenced to death for speaking the truth. There is little merit or initiative to talk about the truth when others do not want to listen to it, even less when it leads to your persecution, imprisonment, or worse. Those who know the truth and its fate often avoid embracing it. Few believe it is better to have uttered the truth only once in our lives and face the consequences than to speak a myriad of lies daily and live a long life.

In many ways, the regime or power structure in a nation or polity determines the fluidity of an idea, its ability to spread, and its potential to promote change. Many people are open to the truth and willing to compromise what they know for it. Many would assume it is unusual to find individuals who prefer to listen to lies rather than the truth. However, it occurs when we have a false positive, and people mistakenly believe the lies are true. These false positives are the illusions we prefer to believe for comfort, security, and well-being, rather than facing the harsh reality of the opposing truth. In such situations, where people become devoted to the lies, they find it hard to initiate change. Many, in turn, challenge any form of change with great conviction. Change for the sake of the truth and the bettering of human life does not seem influential to the majority. The majority tends to prioritize short-term needs and quick fixes. Rarely are steps taken purely out of principle and without some incentive.

Oppressive rule by a minority is least likely to allow change despite the majority's will. The power to change rests with those who govern. The ease with which change can be permitted to appease the majority's will is most likely found in a Democracy rather than in any other system. The key factors are that the majority want the change, and since they are in power, they can implement it. If the truth were found in the majority and that majority wanted to change, then democracy would be the better-suited system to deliver the truth. However, if the truth lay with the minority and they wanted to implement change, oligarchies, aristocracies, monarchies, or autocracies would deliver it most effectively. Therefore, change is not necessarily determined by who speaks the truth, but by who controls the system of administration, also known as government.

If the majority believes something to be true, but it is a lie, it will be harder to convince them of the contrary because of their numbers. False positives – where what everyone believes is true is a lie – are difficult to change in a Democracy. But if power rests with a few people, they need only delegate orders, which will eventually be carried out. We assume that the truth was the primary target of both systems. Based on that unrealistic assumption, there is merit in a Pyramid of power where a few, or a monarch, rule over the majority, but those merits can also be flaws —a double-edged sword. If the lie rests with the minority and is forced on the majority, then Pyramidal structures excel at spreading lies. Sometimes, in the case of feints, bluffs, and military strategies, lies are sought as much as the truth. But what strategists do and what governors do are separate matters. Because a lie, feign, or bluff may be of benefit on a battlefield, it has no place in a court seeking justice or in the laws that are to be upheld and applied.

If power is with the people or the majority, lies and the truth are harder to spread. That is because when people are in power, they must decide what is true or false, and to do so, they require facts and information they trust. The process is far lengthier, as it requires a majority vote and a willingness to change one's mind.

In some modern societies, the law of the few has such a powerful enforcement mechanism that it can compel people to wear or not wear a particular hat, helmet, or mask. They can make certain things in life legal or illegal. On this point, some believe that governments control information to such an extent that they can make people believe they have walked on other planets and touched their stars and moons. These societies often frown upon those who speak the truth, making them appear foolish or of poor repute. They blame madness or other things to ridicule and dismiss what they have to say. The word 'conspiracy' is often used in place of 'madness,' as if to discredit anything that contradicts the norm. But that norm is not initiated by the people but by those in power, and those in power are typically the few.

For change to occur within a democracy, it initially requires expressing and discussing ideas. In some cultures, free speech or public speaking was and is met with violent, authoritative actions; in other places, people were and are selectively imprisoned. In most modern nations, governments tend to control the media. Controlling information means controlling what people know to be true or false. Change is impossible if the people are content with very little, know only what their masters have told them, and are too docile to take affairs into their own hands. "Free Speech" allows people to say anything they want until others start listening, at which point it may become a problem. Many of the most influential philosophers became proclaimed political threats or enemies to their states. Plato was a guest in the palace of a Sicilian King for over a decade. In India, Gandhi became a political threat and martyr. From the days of Christ until the modern era, we know that free speech is only free up to a point. All Christ's disciples except John died for what they believed at the hands of those who initially didn't believe the Truth. All were martyred, yet John was the only one to survive.

Change, therefore, is most straightforward when the minority that rules decides to change. Such was the case when Constantine declared Christianity the faith of the Roman Empire, but of course, the people were already Christian at the time. Equally,

Diocletian, the emperor before Constantine, wanted to preserve the faith in the Olympic or Pagan Gods and began a long-term persecution of Christians. Speaking the truth has minimal incentive when we live under systems governed by the few. Even in systems that put on a façade of kindness and caring, their methods become more subtle, but the outcomes remain the same. In some places, there will be bans. In other areas, they will increase the prices to achieve the same effect as a ban. They may filter searches on global search devices and control things by subtle means. Completely forbidding something can cause problems, but making it inaccessible or unfavorable can achieve similar or better results. By these methods, they often make nudity and other immoral things seem favorable and enticing, and they make the truth appear bland to encourage disinterest.

Communicating the truth

Additionally, for a democratic system to communicate the truth, a medium must be used to convey it. However, giving control of that medium to a small group of people will lead to problems. That is why, in some countries, every major political party has its own newspaper or news source. They provide news that aligns with their agendas. In schools, the information children learn is almost always skewed by the political party in power. So, how can we provide the information needed for change or any other action? The information source and the medium must remain Democratic. Trusting one person, group, or source over another is an issue the majority must deal with. It is better to have multiple sources of information and communication channels. Allowing the few to control information and rely on them to gather and deliver it on behalf of the people is problematic. While there may still be a need for reporters and free media, the entire news industry would need to operate on an equally democratic basis. The precautionary rules that preserve democracy would apply to any industry closely tied to how people make decisions.

Change can't occur where the freedom and the ability to express an idea are minimal. Most places in the world that undergo systemic changes do so through the will of a minority. Very rarely are the majority in a position to initiate anything other than a display of occasional frustration, temporary chaos, or riots. Throughout the world, issues such as taxes, budgets, military composition, laws, and all facets of life are controlled not by the people but by a minority. In such places, the change would not require expressing or discussing an idea, because the minority only needs a method to compel the majority to comply with the enforced change. We must also be aware that, just as the ease with which truth and lies can spread within a Pyramidal power structure, rights, freedoms, and all matters of life diminish to a state controlled by the few. The truth, much like all other attributes of a polity, becomes manipulated or influenced by the minority. Free speech, or the ability to communicate with others, is no different. Since the minority controls the most effective mediums by which information can travel and spread, the few restrict the truth, free speech, and all facets of communication to the broader polity.

Lost freedom to spread the truth

People often stood on street corners in the past and loudly spoke their ideas. It was a tradition dating back to the Athenian Democracy. The Athenians called these speakers Orators, who often bent the truth and gave speeches to persuade people. Their importance was paramount for spreading ideas; many modern and old cities continued the tradition even during the 19th and early 20th centuries. Towards the late 20th century and early 21st century, after Christ, the Orators began to be seen as entertainment. Orators soon became too few compared to the city's population, and their effectiveness on public streets became negligible. When a city has an Orator for every street and speaks of the same thing, the news will travel much more rapidly than a handful of Orators for the entire city. The decrease in the number of orators or public speakers relative to the city's population can partly be attributed to modern technology. The modes of transport in the 20th and 21st centuries have also changed from pedestrian or slow-moving transport to fast-moving enclosed vehicles. Therefore, the effectiveness of direct contact and communication by street-side speaking has become almost entirely redundant. The bulk of modern technology purchased by the public is anti-social and is geared to suit the individual. It shuts people inside a sphere or world that relies on being part of "the system." It creates dependencies beyond water, food, and shelter. Instead of playing and enjoying the world, children are often confined to machines and toys that entertain them while leaving them disconnected from reality. It becomes an escape of sorts for them. Verbal communication with large numbers of people has become redundant due to numerous technological and cultural changes.

Among many other side effects, today's technology creates a generation gap between parents and children because children are playing with things that did not exist when their parents were children. The process is partly one of Domestication, Assimilation, and Separation.

Women in industrialized societies tend to flock to shops in large numbers every day. Gone are the small, individually owned shops; in their place, large corporate entities sell large volumes of low-quality produce to primarily women and children. For comparison, men also shop, but their psyche tends to be negative toward shopping malls and centers where multiple shops are under one roof. Some men and women prefer specialized stores rather than large chains under a single landlord. As you may realize, this dilution of freedom for small business owners is not the only thing, but one of many small things that contribute to the entrapment and control of society. Let us elaborate further: In the generation immediately preceding the time of writing this, men went to a barber to cut their hair, but such are the men today that many shave their beards and go to where women cut their hair. But it is not purely the choice of the men; it is because the choice was taken from them. Likewise, we are accustomed to enjoying various types of meat, not all of which come from large animals. Many people experienced this, particularly if they were partially or wholly raised in an agricultural environment. However, the specialist butchers who once traded such meats have almost all closed their doors. Instead, large companies force beef, lamb, and pork into people's diets. Gone are rabbits, geese, turtles, eels, pigeons, quails, and many more from typical household menus. These meats were considered commercially viable products before the 19th-century Industrial Revolution. When men shopped for meat at small butcher shops, they came home with various kinds of produce. The choices are reduced considerably, and only a few novelty stores offer alternative meats. But all that is cultural and will change from place to place and with time. Some do not eat pork, and some do not eat beef, and there are a variety of other dietary issues that are related to religious or cultural biases. It may not be clear at first, however, a cultural shift is typically based on numerous detailed reasons, all of which are symptoms of Pyramidal power and its application to society's commerce. No one elected to stop using barbers, butchers, or any other specialized stores. The choices were removed due to commercial or business-related factors. Some claim "competition" forces these changes in the business. However, when such things occur, we recognize that it has happened due to the will of a few.

The same can be said of information, news, and all mechanisms used to deliver the truth. Media and large publicity organizations now replace the Orators. Media and publicity organizations are established to bridge the gap in disseminating messages and ideas. Of course, in almost every nation, the government controls the media through various financial or legal tactics. Even in privatized systems where a corporation may own a large network of media outlets, the government stipulates what can and cannot be shown. Beyond the law are the guidelines and negotiations that control what the people know and what they do not. Again, the Pyramidal structure of the merchant class dictates the products and services we use, as much as all other facets of our lives. A minority ruling class often engineers our choices.

The more dependent we become on a system, the more we lose control over every freedom. It is proposed to you that so long as a structure of Pyramidal scope is active, the few at its pinnacle will dictate everything that makes up our lives. If that pyramidal structure exists among growers and farmers, they will determine what food is available, provided another minority does not control them. If a merchant controls which products and services are available, then they select what we can choose from. Some think there is a relationship between supply and demand, but no one questions how the demand or supply was established in the first place. The demand is created by the same people who supply, much like creating people with an addiction and then feeding their addiction.

Lost power over the government

Since we have raised the influence of government, media, and other parts of a polity, the next question should be: who owns and controls the government? If systems of varying nature mute the effectiveness of conveying an idea by conventional speech, then who controls the mechanisms by which ideas can be communicated? Often, most people cannot answer such questions with any philosophical accuracy. Some will remark on the private industry, the government, or other sources.

Each government system is unique, and each location has its own set of laws. There is undoubtedly an interplay between those who invest financially in delivering the news and those who control the news and information through legal means. As we proceed, these questions will be addressed in more detail. It is worth recognizing that monetary ownership does not automatically imply control or power; similarly, the government and elected leaders do not automatically imply that they have power or control. Systems skewed to serve the interests of the few exist everywhere and have been a part of human history since the advent of the written word. These systems do not necessarily have to be government systems, and, as we know, the term "monopoly" has also become an issue in the business and financial worlds. Groups of people own monopolies that possess sufficient economic power to influence the buying and selling of nations and their respective governments. For our purposes, it is best to highlight that formal institutions such as the government and the private business sector, along with other interests and power sources, influence media owners.

Within the context of government systems, the Athenian Democracy was preceded by an Oligarchy and, before that, a Monarchy. The Oligarchy tried to come back many times, as did the Democracy. There was a perpetual antagonism between the Oligarchy and the Democracy. At any given moment, power and control were contested between the majority and the few who sought to control them. Conflicts between merchants and politicians, as well as between farmers and merchants, often escalated into power struggles. In ancient Egypt, for example, while the Pharaoh had assumed a role akin to that of a god on Earth, the priests advised the Pharaoh. The ancient Greeks often sought advice from the temple of Delphi.

In 21st-century modern societies, following the Industrial Revolution, large financial institutions and extremely powerful merchants controlled and influenced many of the world's politicians and governments. A government cannot become subject to any other entity, as that would forfeit its legitimacy. It becomes an illusion to appease those it aims to control.

Democracy and the truth

At this point, we need to acknowledge a few more facts about Democracy. Democracy is one of those subjects that gets a lot of media attention. It has become almost an international standard for the most undemocratic places to propagate within their society the falsehood that they live within a Democracy. As an idea, it has in every supposed Democratic nation some attached propaganda, skewed definition, and political motive. There are people willingly trying to redefine it, turn it into something else, and manipulate it to serve a purpose. If they can't redefine the term "Democracy", they lie about their government system and call their Oligarchies and Dictatorships Democracies. Those who contradict them are scorned, persecuted, ridiculed, and, in some countries, far worse.

Some pressures are preventing all of us from speaking the truth. If you are prevented from reading this philosophy, all I ask is that you question why. If what you know of this philosophy came from others, you should then assess and analyze it for yourself. What is written should not be taken for literal meaning alone, but for the encouragement or inspiration it may give to analyze and assess the subject of Democracy. Philosophical arguments are available for everyone to expand upon and utilize. Ultimately, everyone will have an opinion, but your opinion will be the most important to you. Therefore, it would serve you best to ensure that your opinion was formed from the philosophical truth rather than the random hearsay or opinion of others. Rather than dismissing a philosophy before it has been read, you should keep an open mind until the end. At this point, neither of us knows how this philosophy will be concluded.

To proceed with any philosophy requires the reader to read the argument without prejudice. Understanding a political subject like Democracy entirely depends on an individual's ability to approach it honestly and truthfully. If you have come here disgruntled by hearsay or other streams so that you may learn what is said here merely to contest or attempt to ridicule the content, then you are as bad as those who came to absorb every matter and mimic it. That is to say that embarking on a journey to read this philosophy with a prejudice, either pro or against it, is equally faulted. An open, clear mind, ready to absorb the truth, is far more valuable than a closed, prejudiced one. With all its variations in knowledge and wisdom, each person's mind is a far greater asset to this and every philosophy. Ultimately, those who approach the subject with an open mind and learn before speaking also become the most outstanding teachers.

Since we hold democratic principles so high in value, every person's philosophical views should be considered more valuable than anything any single teacher can offer. Amongst us are people who know many things, yet no one knows everything. In the same way, we do not accept the opinion or idea of any one person as the absolute truth without analysis and assessment. The same should apply to all those traditional conveyors of information. Do not rely on public media as a primary source of information, and do not consider authority a source of information. Do not even let the educators of any system be the primary source of information. Instead, consider what has been stated: this changing world has changed many things, including the definition of words, ideas, and even Democracy. Here, we are interested in truth from logic and wisdom.

To begin a topic like Democracy, we need common ground — a platform and a premise from which to discuss and establish its philosophy. People considered far greater philosophers than I have already established a more robust base or framework for discussion. It would be foolish to talk about the subject without mentioning their views. The subject may be old, and it is over two thousand five hundred years old at the time I am writing this, but do not be fooled into thinking that old things should be taken for granted. We may have the technology today, such as high-speed calculating machines, but how many older technologies have we forgotten? In many ways, as we forget our Heroes and their battles, we also forget the meaning of many things, including the value and significance of freedom and democracy. If we study Democracy, we must consider the views of those great minds who not only wrote about the subject but also witnessed and lived in the only truly democratic state the world has ever seen: Athens, Greece. Only then can we expand it and attempt to establish a modern philosophy.

Who is the author?

The first thing to clarify is what will be addressed and by whom. Before we begin, though, there is the matter of explaining who I am and why I am writing. I am not a king, an oligarch, a wealthy merchant, a paid writer, or anything similar. I describe myself not so much as a prologue, but someone who has learned that they know very little. It is probably better to define myself, and in doing so, I will express my reasons for writing. By knowing who I am, I hope you will come to understand what this philosophy truly represents. At least that way, you will be able to assess my writings and gauge their relevance in the years to come. After all, a sign of truth is that something remains true and doesn't change.

Additionally, you may ask yourself, 'Who is this person?' And why is he writing? If he is intelligent, why write down his thoughts for all to see and read? Why choose Democracy as a subject? So, to set aside all these questions briefly, I will explain them in a manner I feel is both the simplest and most definitive. I am a husband and father who lives in poverty. I have nothing of significance to give my children or their children. All I have are some wise words. I shared these words with them before writing this philosophy, yet I felt compelled to write what I told them so they would remember them.

Additionally, my life is not what I had hoped it would be when I was a child; it is far from it. I never sought materials nor had a passion for material wealth. I am at a loss for secular words without saying I only hoped one day God would give light to these eyes. Despite the vivid magnificence and splendor of the world around me and the light that flooded my childhood eyes, I was still blinded to many things through ignorance and innocence. That is who I was: a person from the lowest socio-economic status, a person that most people look down upon from a socio-economic point of view. Yet, as fathers and all fathers, which of us does not defend with our last breath the justice deserved by our family?

During my childhood, I wanted to change things for the better; I wanted a world better than the one I had found. But I had no power or strength to change it by traditional means. My father passed this urge on to me because he was an orphan who worked from the age of 5 to feed a family of eight. He always wondered how much better the world would be if people helped each other instead of looking at each other like marks ripe for the plunder. He was known in our local polity as a man who always wanted to help. He helped in the hope that those he helped would, in turn, help others. This low socio-economic background molded me into a father who sought to create a better world by replanting the ancient seeds of Democracy. That was, and is, my bias, but I do not wish you to think that this bias will affect what I say. I know all too well that humans can never achieve the absolute truth, yet here I am, trying to be as honest and truthful as possible. I also know that it is foolish to write something and give it to others to read, because often what we write, believe, and say changes as we mature and gain a better understanding of things. As accurate as it is to say that even the Saints have sinned, their lives also describe a path towards the truth. Similarly, even though I may be flawed in some of what I say, I hope I have the opportunity to correct it and place this argument on the path towards absolute truth.

I hope to write about my philosophy on democracy because it has been on my mind since childhood. Additionally, the subject of Democracy needs to be revisited. Perhaps it is because I am searching for a system that my children, yours, and the world could inherit. Maybe it could bring humanity happiness once again. After the Industrial Revolution, many of us work our lives away to build mini empires, wealthy homes, assets, and lifestyles beyond what we need. Wars perpetually plague the planet, yet I look over the horizon to visualize humanity in the future, and I can't see anything better than what we have today. I see my children growing up in a world with little light and little chance to improve. Therefore, in pursuit of a better system, some of us have devoted nearly our entire lives to reading and discussing democracy. I feel ready to part with what I have learned from others. I am neither a politician nor a writer, and I do not receive payment for my writing. As I have already said, I am a simple man who, since childhood, saw the possibility of a far better world. I used to ride my bicycle in my neighborhood, telling people there is a better way of life. I am a mature man saying the same thing, but I hope with far more eloquence and knowledge.

Despite my passion for Democracy, I must emphasize that my aim is not political. I aim to clearly and methodically explore all facets of the Democratic system. I will neither hide its faults nor elevate its status. This philosophy will try to remain as neutral as possible. Although I attempt to write generically, references to the current system refer to the state of things at the time of writing. It is a manner of speech that the term "today" may be used instead of "at the time of writing". Also, writing about an old subject like Democracy will seem redundant to many people. Some may be educated on the subject, thinking my writing is obvious or rhetorical. Other people will know something about Democracy. Some others may think they do, but they don't. Whichever the case, I assure you that when you read this philosophy, you will all know you are reading the truth.

Table of Contents

1. Justification for democracy

"Knowing what divides us will help bridge the unity needed for a democracy."

The world and its people are constantly changing in many ways. Within a lifetime, people often compare various cultural changes. Most of the changes and differences we notice are visible across generations. Some take so long to manifest that they go unnoticed. Only those who have experienced the change can compare it truthfully. We can, however, approximate the understanding of the change when there are sufficient historical accounts. For many generations, the word Democracy has been used to describe many state administrative systems that do not resemble democracies. Could we have regressed so much that we cannot accept that our political systems are not Democracies?

When writing a philosophy, we need to acknowledge the great diversity that sets us apart. Not for the sake of scrutiny or to judge each other, but to ensure that the philosophy being developed is more than a misguided generalization, and is a universal or absolute truth. Various people find it difficult to comprehend that others can resolve or solve the same problem in different ways. While mathematics assumes that there is one absolute answer, almost all mathematical problems can be solved differently.

We uniquely approach each problem and situation. Some of us are doing what we were told, others may be copying someone or something, and others are trying to find a solution. Much of how we approach problems and situations is based on our knowledge, experiences, and predicaments. Some believe that work, a job, and building a financial foundation are the most essential things in life. Sometimes, wealth and power become so crucial that people lose moral boundaries. Some strive for personal excellence in the arts or for pious living.

Our outlook and the way we perceive things are part of who we are. These characteristics include the intrinsic memory of our genetics, experiences, intelligence, wisdom, spiritual, metaphysical, and somatic fitness. Our mood, emotional state, cognitive processing, and general psychosocial stressors can affect our outlook and perceptions. Along with the perception, there is the delivery of information. Our delivery's particular characteristics are audio-visual, written, or verbal. Each has its merits and disadvantages. However, all of this depends on variables such as volume – both auditory volume and the amount written – or delivery length. Several variables determine and maintain interest in the topic by revealing and providing discovery along the pathway. What we know is also dependent on external factors affecting these things. Our differences in learning are a blend and combination of these things and how they interface with our state. As a result, there will be differences in delivery, perception, and our environment, including our intellectual and dynamic states. All these contribute to understanding something different from other people.

Before describing a democracy, it is essential to establish that what is presented here is, in good faith, an attempt to explain the philosophy of a Democracy as thoroughly as possible. Everyone is expected to have a different view of what is presented, so we should discuss and share what we know to be true.

The world and its current state require review. But that will be done briefly later on. For now, the reason we can justify a Democracy is that it is possible to establish a;

- Fair distribution of wealth,
- Elimination of poverty,

- Truthful education,
- A balance between classes,
- Fair judgment process,
- Fair lawmaking process,
- Fair enforcement process.

But more than that, our differences—the segregation and partitioning of society—must be addressed first. As mentioned earlier, it will help define what a Democracy should be. It will also highlight that these divisions are intrinsic to systems worldwide at the time of writing. That is truer if the differences raised can be resolved democratically. Therefore, it is worth mentioning and investigating the common divides for this purpose.

1.1 The biases of life experience

Many people judge the value of philosophy, and some believe that reading it is a waste of time. Yet most of us enjoy learning something new and discovering something we did not have the time to think about in detail. Since there is diversity and change between us, so too has the concept of Democracy changed. Over many generations, our perceptions of Democracy have changed. That is why, for any philosophy to have any sense of truth, it needs to go beyond our personal views or biases. It needs to be a universal idea removed from the daily influences of the writer and the audience. That is why we are not here to judge the greedy or the poor, the good or the bad. This philosophy is not biased towards any particular individual or group. Its scope is intended for the general public. This philosophy is applicable to everyone, regardless of their education and background.

Within a single family, there is always a multitude of unique experiences, ideas, and knowledge that each member possesses. We can't seek the truth and be limited by the biases of our own experiences. If we rely solely on our own experience, we forfeit the experiences of others. If we always slept through the night, we would need someone to stay awake to tell us about it. Something as simple as that can't be described, because the person who has experienced being awake at night has experienced it firsthand, and the person who hasn't is trying to understand it without having experienced it. It is the same when we describe the loss of loved ones to those who have not experienced it. The same can be said about trying to explain a Democracy when none exists in the world at the time of writing this. Therefore, when considering a philosophy, the purpose is not to give an opinion based on experience but rather to present a collection of ideas that, if we place them in the correct order and analyze and assess them, we can derive a fact or truth.

As we progress, we must be willing to discard what we discover to be false and retain what we discover to be true. Even in situations where we have lived a lifetime thinking we knew the truth of something, a reasonable person must be willing to accept the argument results and the established truth. We should no longer hold onto lies or such things. People fear failure and what they perceive as failure. That is a normal experience; fear is common among people. When we prove something wrong or discover that we have been mistaken, we must work to accept a change in our views. People who fear appearing foolish may prevent receiving a correction to their argument. These reactions could be allowing their ego to steer them away from the truth. That is why, before a person can accept the truth, they require an open mind. By this, I mean not open to everything but to what is proven true. That is very important to remember when reading any philosophy, and even more so when reading one with many political opinions, such as Democracy.

1.2 The wealthy and the poor

The blame should never be placed on the wealthy or the poor, as some do; however, it is essential to highlight a prevalent division in many societies. It is probably the most significant divide in situations lacking Democracy. That is the division of the poor and the wealthy. The socioeconomic divide affects politics in many different places. It can also lead to a conflict between the rich and the poor.

A child pampered from a young age will establish certain entitlements and expectations for a particular lifestyle they perceive as expected. When one of these children is deprived of that lifestyle or is no longer entitled to what they had, it causes anxiety that can manifest in many severe behavioral issues. It is this anxiety, or future-based anticipation, that causes many to seek more selfishly.

The poor seem to be in a constant battle and overly preoccupied with earning money in currency. That can be a numismatic or a power-based currency, such as control over a resource like water. The children of those who are overly poor suffer significant deprivation. That can lead to complex lives that strive for the same things their parents desire; more. It is clear, then, that many wealthy seek more, and many poor seek more. If those with nothing and those with abundance seek more, what is the difference other than a subjective view?

Wealth is a subjective or relative term. A person holding two seemingly worthless stones is wealthier than one who has one, and the person holding one stone is more affluent than those with none. From our point of view, the stones may be of little value in terms of currency, but if they were a form of currency, they would gain a particular subjective value. It is the same with other things; water can become the most valuable form of currency for a desert society. However, it is given less significance in places where water is abundant.

In modern societies, people serve with ambition and scope to attain what they want and/or need. Their servitude is a means to an end. The more they aspire to have what others offer, the more they limit and reduce their freedom. Often, we overlook the fact that the value of something derives purely from its scarcity, and that scarcity is sometimes intentionally engineered. Therefore, a person who controls the flow of wine or water can also control those who seek these things. Often, people become overly preoccupied with their lives, chasing an incentive, a limited resource, or some currency. It is, therefore, the same problem whether it is numismatic or otherwise; the currency can be anything that others require, want, or need. In pursuit of what they want or need, people often enslave themselves.

It is also commonly perceived that people experiencing poverty lack the power and authority to lead; therefore, they are often controlled. In some systems, capital and money afford certain freedoms; in others, they become less relevant to power and authority. The purchase of freedom is an old idea that does not necessarily entail receiving a receipt and a certificate of freedom. It can be a subtle thing where the enslaved believe they are free but behave in almost all matters as slaves. Not knowing that a person is an enslaved person may last many decades or even a lifetime. It is more challenging for people to lead when they are oppressed or suppressed. Therefore, it is not a measure of leadership or of characteristics, traits, or qualities that prevent people living in poverty from leading. To engage others in an activity, they must initially want to participate. The qualities that promote participation are the courage to lead, truthfulness in communication, and one of three things: mutual gain, common interest, or an act of love.

If people are governed, it means there is a dominant entity defining many aspects of society. When a political ideology becomes closely associated with a specific government, it enforces that ideology through the governing system and then influences the culture of the people. It is a top-down flow of cultural attributes. Within a system where the few govern the majority, the direction of cultural forces tends to be more from the government to the people. When the few lead, they are expected to determine what the law is and what is not. Those laws will lay down the foundation to which a polity's ethics will adhere. It makes no difference what type of government is operating. It only matters that they have codified cultural attributes that distinguish them from others and other polities. So, it is not simply apathy or lack of power that prevents people experiencing poverty from significantly impacting a government system. There is far more proof to suggest that how a government system is structured and operated also determines, to some degree, who will have the most political impact within the governing system. For example, many unusual types of government and administrative systems have existed historically. While examining the three basic types of government – Monarchy, Aristocracy, and Democracy – we can balance these with cultural, political, age, religious, monetary, and/or class distinctions, making the basic model unique. Therefore, it is not surprising that we find, in historical contexts, that prosperous farmers were often leaders of society, as seen in India, and that priests held significant leadership roles in ancient Egypt. Then we also had military generals establish dictatorships and so on. Each system was essentially a Monarchy or Oligarchy, but the distinction emerged because one occupational group had more power than another.

When writing this, several people referred to capitalist systems as kleptocracies, plutocracies, and more. Capitalism had evolved into a system that allowed corporations without personal identities to wield powers akin to those once held by farmers or priests. These issues will be addressed later, as they relate to class balancing, not the administrative structure. Class balance focuses on the equality and fairness available to administer, make, judge, and enforce those laws. Not merely from an individual perspective but from groups preoccupied with some work, be they soldiers, merchants, tradespeople, professionals, or farmers.

A competing ideology embedded in an Oligarchic structure is that of communism. Communism aims to establish a system in which all the commune's assets and belongings are shared equally and are at the disposal of those within it. However, the fundamental problem is that once an oligarchy forms within a commune, it determines how the resources are spent. Then the poor or neglected seek reprieve, but their arguments are typically never heard, so long as those enjoying surplus continue to enjoy the surplus. That was one of the reasons communism lost substantial support over the decades. However, it is more than this alone that causes both capitalism and communism to fail. Both systems use the currency spoken of earlier. Therefore, the limiting reagent—the limiting factor—is determined by one question: who controls the currency? In answering this question, if it is not the majority of people, then it must be the few —the Oligarchs. That leads to the assertion that those who control the currency also control those seeking it.

As stated, the poor tend to envy the wealthy, and the needy envy those with a surplus; as such, envy creates a problem of its own. As with the previously mentioned historical accounts, the people seem to have little to no power, yet in most cases, they can achieve the power to govern. In other words, there are few powers a system gives people experiencing poverty to change the system. However, the majority can change the government if they want to. Historically, people experiencing poverty have not had easy access to changing laws. Wealth is a relative term, and wealth levels vary across a population. As already stated, who we call poor and wealthy is relative or subjective, and in one instance, a person can be both poorer and more affluent than others. Therefore, recognizing that financial status or wealth can often act as a bias becomes essential. The poor, for instance, may desire what the rich possess, and the wealthy may be unwilling to part with it. If our poverty is so intensely affecting our lives, then it is understandable to have a bias towards finding an easier way to survive. Similarly, those who are adamant about maintaining their wealth and power will do everything in their power to retain it. These biases must be set aside to appreciate this philosophy fully.

Biases borne from hunger, although understandable, do not establish the truth. Neither do the forces of wanting a decadent and soft life. To attain the truth, we must consider all the people within our philosophy, even those without occupation. The truth is not prone to bias but remains consistent across all people. When we read a philosophy, these divisional biases and those like them should not exist. Our views are often influenced by the importance we attach to wealth, so we must be cautious not to judge a philosophy based solely on our personal perspectives. Few people, for instance, seek spiritual wealth over material wealth; yet, some do. Therefore, it is essential to clarify that this philosophy is not exclusive to the rich or the poor. The things mentioned here are intended to establish the truth about a democratic system. In no way must such a philosophy favor anyone in particular. Otherwise, if we start favoring the elite and the extremely wealthy, we lay the foundation for an aristocracy or an oligarchy. If we favor the poor, many wealthy people would fear losing their wealth, and that in itself is a sign that a democracy is becoming an ochlocracy. Indeed, wealth — and its lack — will influence how we think. That is granted, but not here, not when trying to achieve the truth.

If we are to discuss the success of democracy, it is clear that it requires boundaries—rules and guidelines—for it to function effectively. Otherwise, things like a lynching mob professing to be the people's voice would create the lesser or degraded Democratic entity we know as an Ochlocracy. There must be some moral boundary between what benefits the individual and what benefits all the people. While significant, our interests must also take into account the enormous diversity of other views. A governing system that favors the poor or the wealthy cannot sustain itself. That is because currency can't be an effective motivator for issues like justice, ethics, and basic somatic needs. Eventually, the immorality of consistently pursuing money will clash with people's moral expectations. That is true for any government that uses currency as the principal motivator.

1.3 Poverty and class distinction

As mentioned, poverty and the poor are critical issues in discussing a political system. While the wealthy face numerous problems, the unfortunate reality is that the impoverished and those without the means to survive, let alone establish a stable lifestyle, face serious issues that are, in part, systemic to the existing system at the time of writing this. It excludes them from participating in political affairs.

For a long time, people from the lower socioeconomic class have been overlooked in most of the literature available to read. Few gave voice to the impoverished. Their difficulty in participation in almost any system has been, for the most part, undocumented. Children of people experiencing poverty are more likely to be taken by forces of the underworld and dragged down into an undertow.

What would the middle socio-economic class and beyond know about having to patch torn and worn clothes? What would they know of weaving, sewing, or knitting your clothes? What would the middle socio-economic class and above know about not affording the books and stationery that other children have? What would they know about not having shoes to wear? Truancy forced through the shame of presenting without uniform, attire, shoes, or cleanliness? What would anyone know of sharing a single meal between an entire family? How many of us lit candles or tiny fires to keep warm? How many didn't have warm water for a bath or shower?

Some argued that communism would give to the poor and take from the rich. But from what we know of communism, under an oligarchy, is that so long as the oligarchy exists, no one in a commune will be free, let alone treated fairly. The selfishness of the few in power will always outweigh any argument in favor of those experiencing poverty. Communism controlled by an Oligarchy creates a form of Tyranny.

People opposing communism often believed that economic systems, such as capitalism, could be closer to attaining freedom. However, within that system, the same oligarchy controls the monetary system. Thereby, whoever controls the money controls the system and everyone in it. It becomes apparent that the mechanisms for self-sufficiency have been deliberately controlled and made unviable. That was done to entice people to look for work and jobs, and to buy items at a lower price than they could produce. Those who lead at the pyramidal apex, called the Oligarchs, will never let anyone accumulate enough money to achieve anything they don't want. In this way, Capitalism controlled by an Oligarchy creates a form of Tyranny.

The poor are known by many names, such as enslaved people, workers, servants, etc. We understand the sensitivity of the word "slave". The phrase often implies that imperial slavery was found throughout the 1700s - 1800s and up until the 21st century. Yet when I speak of slaves, I am not speaking of ethnicities or skin colors or any variation of humans. When I speak of slaves, I refer to the meaning of the word itself: "doulos," from its Greek origin, means a servant, worker, or someone working for another. The other word, sklavos, from Koine Greek, refers to a captive or forced laborer. The latter was the type of slaves that were predominantly made of people caught or trapped during the years of the 1700s - 1800s slave trade. These two words form a stark and extreme view.

Without chains, whips, and mistreatment, and without direct captivity, can a person still be enslaved? Things change and shift, and we can't be stuck with old views that limit how we see things for what they are today and into the future. Nothing can take away the fight of the people whose ancestors were trapped and traded like livestock. We add that they tilt the platform at a different angle while still playing the same game. What is the difference between a free-range rooster and a caged rooster? They are both captives. Yet, one has some choices available. One can choose to eat the supplied meal, whatever is available, or whatever is abundant. The free-range rooster can also decide where to move on the owner's property. The caged rooster is bound to stay in one place and lacks choices. But in the end, almost all the non-breeding roosters are slaughtered. Are they not enslaved to fulfill one particular function alone? There are some differences, but both, in my eyes, are strikingly similar. That is how we are these days. We are given free range without chains or whips, with plenty of choices, but none to be free.

There was never a system in the world that gave a voice to people experiencing poverty other than a Democracy. A democracy doesn't help you attain wealth or material things, but it empowers the people. Democracy empowers the people to ensure they all live well and comfortably. The wealthy, powerful, and even middle class feared losing their possessions. However, under the systems of government we had at the time of writing this, ownership was an illusion. The State can take anything held in our hands under myriad laws.

Democracy also requires that everyone participate because, without participation, there can't be democracy. The impoverished are disadvantaged and limited in participation due to currency or other resource shortages. In that way, impoverishing the majority intends to prevent democracy from occurring. Democracy isn't for the lazy; it's for those who want to take an active part. That said, once people become comfortable, they tend to stop participating, and from then on, others take over. That contributed to the fate of Athenian Democracy thousands of years ago, but, more importantly, it remains the main reason Democracy often fails today.

1.4 Innocent criminals and justice

Innocent individuals wrongfully convicted of crimes often endure unimaginable suffering, both physically and psychologically. The impact is wide-reaching and is shaped by social stigma, employment opportunities, and restrictions on participation in the government and public sectors. Most people are unaffected by this and so have no proper understanding of the emotional trauma that comes with innocently being convicted. It should be considered because it is a part of systemic discrimination. Had alternative views existed, there would not be a systematic processing of individuals who are stigmatized for life. The stigma is real and deeply hurtful to an individual. In some countries, they are stripped of their rights to participate in various functions, such as serving on juries or voting. They are left unable to exercise their full rights and privileges as citizens.

Often, the state administration system, the government, makes criminals of people by penalizing their attempts to escape poverty. That is a symptom of the system known as wage slavery. Where people work from one payday to the next and only seem to afford to survive by paying basic living costs. They can't have options to increase their pay based on their living demands and, therefore, are stuck in a caste or category of people enslaved by laws and financial hardship.

Many people in this position resorted to all types of efforts to escape from the shackleless of enslavement that forced them to live utilizing their earnings. Most of their efforts are usually confronted by myriad opposing laws. It was once illegal for a person to play a musical instrument in the streets without a license. Or conduct a business without first registering the business. Usually, when people resort to street entertainment for profit, they are at a very low point. If the people had the money to buy a license or register a business, they would most likely have used their funds. But in most cases, people try to play music regardless of the law and end up in more debt from fines. Some activities of people experiencing poverty are not typically unjust; it is that they are judged by unfair laws that force them to behave and act in ways that risk their good names and forsake currency to buy basic things like food.

It is essential to understand that some people make mistakes, like fathers defending their families. Fathers who were eager to bring about justice sought to enforce it themselves. They ask themselves questions that infuriate them with each answer, such as 'why' and 'how' they could do that. They become emotional over the treatment of those they love, and often that is the basis on which many people commit an act against the perpetrators. Yet doing so makes them criminals through unfair laws. In ancient Athens, it was lawful to execute someone with sufficient witnesses to specific crimes. But of course, as with all such things, a fair trial was necessary first.

Also, as with any system, the corrupt may give false witness for a higher cause. In the process, they unknowingly testify falsely and falsely bury a person. As a consequence, the victim is often falsely charged and sentenced. Many situations arise like this, especially when the false witness intends to protect someone they love, care about, or have something in common with, or when bribery and/or utility are involved. That is why, throughout history and in religious texts, it has been repeatedly stated that giving false testimony is unethical. Such people are more likely to be criminals than anyone they choose to convict.

Undoubtedly, many crimes that lead to imprisonment are related to love, family, and friends; this is why it is essential to choose wisely those you call friends. Additionally, there are many reasons for inadvertently or unintentionally being on the wrong side of the law. Often, people look down on those with a criminal record. Some use the biases of the judgments to exclude them from specific functions. That is why creating a stigma around those with a past is an unfair way to deal with things. Sincere repentance for those released back into society may have led to a change in personality and qualities. But these are not shown on a criminal record. Therefore, we should not judge those who have committed crimes. We must view someone who has repented with a new, clean slate. However, to do so requires a truly repentant person. If they repeat their mistakes and continue making them, they should not be given a fresh appraisal. Therefore, it is clear that when a conviction is justified, a repentant person must be allowed to rejoin society as a full citizen. When a person is falsely convicted, they must also be given full citizenship.

1.5 Ethnicity

Another widespread political division is ethnic identity. As discussed elsewhere, citizenship eligibility often requires birth in a particular city or state. However, the complexity of ethnicity or nationality deserves a particular in-depth mention. It impacts identity, discrimination, disunity, and more.

Group Identity politics occur when specific groups become self-aware of their ethnic identity. Usually, but not consistently, individuals who join such groups or sub-groups within a city achieve a sense of belonging. In ancient times, a similar thing existed in Athens. They were known as tribes.

The tribal element matures and grows; however, it often lacks a voice in certain settings, such as under monarchies and oligarchies. For example, if one ethnicity forms a group within a city and individuals find that this group defines their identity, it would be expected that the tribe should have a voice and the power to govern itself. However, where it impacts other tribes, democracy shines because it gives more than a voice; it also provides power, justice, fairness, and much more to every tribe or deme.

Political fragmentation of ethnicities occurs when a topic of importance is supported by the majority of one ethnicity and opposed by the majority of another within the same system of administration or governance. Most likely, the system is again a monarchy or oligarchy because, within a democratic system, fragmentation is handled through arguments and countered or supported by more than two opposing forces. There were typically 12 or more tribes in a city, and while two groups may argue a matter, it was up to the arguing tribes to convince the others to support or oppose a particular case. There was a catchment for political fragmentation in a Democratic system. The pluralism found uniquely in democracies recognized, affirmed, and constructively incorporated ethnicities into their systems. However, it remains a problem in monarchies or oligarchies. It is impossible to force ethnic diversity and acceptance by the few over the majority without causing political ramifications of fragmentation and disgruntlement. In a Democracy, it was common to settle political fragmentation issues internally. Historically, many new cities emerged when they split away from their home city. It happened enough times to consider fragmentation of this type a problem unique to Democracies.

Marginalization and Discrimination are more than mere political fragmentation. They are extreme views that often cause detrimental outcomes to those being marginalized or discriminated against. In some situations, a minority view may be presented to the general public in an attempt to change their views. Some individualistic characteristics of sexuality, disability, appearance, age, religion, education level, etc, are also relevant. Ethnicity is one of the larger categories. Marginalization and discrimination based on ethnicity will affect a large proportion of the population. Other large groups are age and gender categories. Therefore, to ensure self-representation, cohesion, and equal power, a democratic system seeks to include as many tribes or ethnicities as possible within its model. The number of the smallest tribes should always be used to determine the quorum, provided they meet specific criteria to determine whether they exist as an ethnicity. Therefore, the smallest tribe will determine the expected numbers for assemblies, juries, etc.

1.6 Religion

Religion can create the same types of issues found in other factors that segregate people. However, it should be noted that under a Monarchy or Oligarchy, one religion is usually favored over others. The latter is how unity is perceived: one state and religion must exist. However, in a democratic state, the religion of each tribe is accepted within the overall assembly of the people; as such, each religion and system of belief is given freedom to exist. Each tribe typically has its own religion, but not always. Some want a separation of powers. However, religion can not be entirely separated from the system of governance. Society, community, and organization develop based on the religion—or religions—of the constituent people. Many people place the order of acceptance of others as follows: religion or lack thereof, ethnicity, tribal or national identity, and all the other matters we have raised.

Tension between religion and State: because many people put religion above all else, it can create specific tensions within any State. These tensions are not entirely or specifically unwanted, detrimental, or harmful. Depending on the religion and the state, religious morals and ethics can drive changes in state laws. Alternatively, some laws may conflict with religious rules or laws. Conflicts arise when tribes of different religions that have come together may find fragmentation or difficulty cooperating. Therefore, as described elsewhere, the chances are that fragmentation and splintering colonization may occur. Under a Monarchy or Oligarchy, the problem arises that the laws do not intend to reflect the religious stance of the tribes or groups within society. Instead, Monarchies and Oligarchies tend to advance their interests through laws, thereby creating enslavement by law. Often, the religions conflict with the government and oppose such self-interested motives. That is concurrent with Christianity and similar faiths within monarchies or oligarchies.

Therefore, democracy shines as the only system that effectively manages religious and state tensions, protects faith, maintains a separate state and faith, ensures values common to the population, and tolerates and respects religious diversity within its system. In all other cases, religion causes many to consider it a prevailing power in politics, often against the purpose of monarchs and oligarchs, but not always. On the contrary, monarchies and oligarchies have used religion to rally people into wars and other actions that they probably wouldn't have otherwise considered. Such is its importance.

1.7 Individualism and the pack

The diversity and differences within a population operate at three significant levels: the individual, the group, and the majority population. The groups we have relationships with are typically family and friends, but in some instances, they can also include teams or other groups. The attributes, qualities, or characteristics that we consider to define individuals, groups, and a polity or majority population are interactive. Individuals influence groups; groups influence individuals; individuals can influence a majority population; groups can influence the majority population; and the majority can influence individuals and groups. Every possible relationship among the three entities — individuals, groups, and the majority population — will determine the potential meetings and communication exchanges among people. Within this network or web, our differences and commonalities manifest into influences that affect us all.

An individual and their actions may seem minor within the context of the majority population. Just as they affect themselves, they also impact others, whether close family and friends, group members, a couple, or even the majority population. Usually, however, a trickle-down effect spreads an idea within a community, especially when the population is enormous and many people are strangers to one another. The trickle effect usually flows linearly from individuals to groups to the majority, in either order. In summary, one person can have an idea that spreads to others, who then pass it along from person to person. Then, groups will do the same because the individuals comprising those groups may know of the original idea. Eventually, these actions will make a majority aware of that idea. The process is lengthy, prone to distortion, and often does not progress far unless it can withstand scrutiny from everyone who becomes aware of the idea.

Conversely, a majority can enforce their cultural values similarly through groups and individuals. There are many more ways to communicate an idea, and we have merely described one. In modern times, utilizing a widely available medium to disseminate information has become a common means for governments to communicate with their citizens. Unlike word of mouth or the trickle-down effect, the filter system in mass media prevents specific ideas from gaining widespread popularity. Suppose most people, for example, are listening to a speech. In that case, there is no real indication that the speech was questioned or tested by the people or the majority before its delivery. In contrast, when spreading information through the trickle effect or word of mouth, each person can filter out the parts they deem less valuable and highlight the parts they consider valuable to know. We should mention that, for decades, schools have taught people not to trust the trickle effect or word of mouth, so people have come to rely on the authorities' controlled communication channels instead.

Some people cannot think beyond the day and how they will attain food and shelter. They have little interest in properties or material value, and at the start, they lead uncommon lives. Perhaps to them, the perfect system would guarantee that they will never worry about food or shelter. The truth is that a Democracy can make many wonderful things happen, just as it can make many horrible things occur. The people and their opinions become the power that drives a Democracy, and it can be both a blessing and something to fear. However, a democracy fails when the people have no interest in the everyday things that usually form the foundation of a polity. Many people do not participate in actions that benefit themselves or others for various reasons.

Looking back at our division based on wealth, disparity, or differences, some people will come from exceedingly wealthy backgrounds, thinking it is a waste of time to read or implement a philosophy that offers nothing to the elite. On the other hand, a philosophy that empowers the elite would be considered tantamount to empowering tyrants or autocrats. In other words, there will always be bias and opinion. Self-interest is very hard to set aside, and asking someone to diminish their power is unlikely to succeed. By mentioning the differences created by our financial status alone, we can see that what often benefits the impoverished does not always benefit the wealthy and vice versa. We all have different biases that influence our behaviors and perspectives on the same idea. However, the critical point about any philosophy is that most of our attitudes and biases also shape what we perceive as true. They also affect the polity in general, from the type of system operating to its operational structure and functions. Those biases represent people's daily wants and needs. But here, in this philosophy, it is essential to note that what is written is not explicitly intended for the wealthy or the poor, the communist or the capitalist, the religious or the atheist. What is being attempted is the writing down of the truth.

Within the context of truth, we try not to take the individual's view but rather a view that seems true to most people in a polity. Therefore, a commonly agreed-upon philosophy is more likely to be closer to the truth. However, a philosophy uncommon in its views and not considered the truth by the majority is seen as nothing more than an opinion. That does not mean that a popularity contest determines the truth. I am suggesting that if we thoroughly analyze a subject independently and learn from one another through debate, our logic will eventually become reasonably uniform, and most of us will agree on a given subject or point. That is what this philosophy aims to be, something that most people will agree with.

Every person has ideas, but how true those ideas are depends on how long they have thought about and analyzed them. The quality of an idea is what distinguishes an opinion or idea from a philosophy. It is these matters that will determine an ideology from a philosophy. Therefore, while our tendency may be to follow an easy, beneficial path or an apathetic one, that same path does not always lead to the truth. The easiest and most helpful path will not allow a system like a democracy to function. It is foreseeable that a minority can lead an apathetic majority or a majority that prefers the easiest and most obviously beneficial path. Throw into the argument that there are few brave people; many cowardly people make most decisions. Exceptionally few choose a path that offers more than the easiest, seemingly lowest-risk path. These are not traits that can lead to a Democratic institution. That is why, in the old Democracy, the Heroes were well looked after and remembered for many years through tales, songs, and dance. They wanted to promote the attributes needed for a society to function as a democracy. From what we know of the stories attributed to him, even Aesop wrote that no matter what we do, we can't make the coward brave. However, these qualities are complex matters that I will revisit. The main point is that we must constantly analyze and assess a subject independently. If someone shows us how to do something, we should go back and analyze and assess it ourselves. If we are given facts, we must seek proof. If we face a significant obstacle, we should not always take the most common path, or the easiest, most beneficial, or risk-free one. Doing so leads to gradual apathy and conformity to the status quo. We must distinguish and highlight all the factors that determine whether we are taking a passenger role rather than a driving role. Philosophy requires a person to be both a listener and a speaker, or to share and debate ideas in order to establish and maintain the truth.

Another matter that requires clarification is that the city's infrastructure is laid out in a way that prevents human interaction and communication. People can't be accessed and spoken to in large numbers due to the layout of cities and the way we commute. People often congregate in private shopping centers, so they can't simply start voicing their views or even sharing their ideas with others. People commuting are no longer walking; they are using vehicles, making them inaccessible to orations. Then there is the design of parks, where no large congregation areas, amphitheaters, etc., are provided, and if they are, they are only used during special events. Those special events are not always possible to hold for new and exciting ideas. Therefore, the way society structures itself also affects its ability to be transparent with one another and to relay ideas among them. Private media control the public medium. The problem I present is the inability to communicate effectively with people, so instead, private or even government outlets control what is spoken. Remnants of democratic culture included symposia, bars, and public drinking places. However, the people who visit these places now are attending to have a social and entertaining night. They are not going to these places to discuss and communicate with others. The purpose of these places has become so corrupted that they no longer function as intended. Symposia in the modern age often lack philosophy, politics, and religion, instead focusing on entertainment in other forms.

Individualism, emphasizing personal freedom, autonomy, and self-interest, often appears to be in contrast with society, which highlights communal values, collective goals, and social harmony. However, the discussion and the level of understanding achieved reveal that individualism and society are not mutually exclusive, but rather intricately intertwined concepts that shape and influence each other.

Individualism provides a framework for personal growth and self-actualization. It recognizes the intrinsic worth of each individual and promotes the idea that one's unique talents, aspirations, and perspectives should be acknowledged and nurtured. Society benefits from the unique contributions of individuals when they are encouraged to pursue their passions, cultivate their talents, and express their creativity.

On the other hand, society plays a fundamental role in shaping an individual's identity. It provides a framework for shared values, norms, and cultural practices that foster a sense of belonging and cohesion. Individuals develop an understanding of identity, gain social support, and find purpose beyond their endeavors by participating in social groups, communities, and institutions. Society provides a collective consciousness that connects individuals, enabling them to share experiences, knowledge, and resources, and creating a sense of continuity and belonging across generations.

Individualism and society are not opposed but somewhat interconnected forces that drive social progress. The advancement of societies relies on the collective efforts of individuals working together to address shared challenges, solve complex problems, and create positive change. Collaborative endeavors, whether in science, technology, or social action, demonstrate that combining individual talents and collective effort can lead to remarkable achievements and societal advancements.

While individualism emphasizes personal freedom and autonomy, it is crucial to recognize that society also requires certain limits and responsibilities to ensure its smooth functioning. Individual liberties should be exercised in accordance with social responsibility and ethical considerations. A balance between individual rights and social obligations is necessary to prevent the erosion of social cohesion and safeguard the well-being of all members of society. This balance can be achieved by establishing laws, regulations, and ethical standards that protect individual rights while promoting everyday ethics.

Individualism and society are not mutually exclusive; they exist in a complex, symbiotic relationship. While individualism provides the impetus for personal development, creativity, and innovation, society fosters a sense of belonging, shared identity, and social progress. A harmonious coexistence of individualism and society requires a delicate balance between personal freedoms and social responsibilities. Acknowledging the value of individual autonomy and collective well-being is crucial for fostering a society that celebrates diversity, respects individual rights, and promotes the common ideal.

1.8 The people and freedom

In the world that was evident at the time of writing, there is a stigma against those who do not want to work for others. Their stigma is that of the Unemployed. The word "Unemployed" has many negative connotations, not merely for the youth or middle-aged, but even for the aged and anyone expected to work. There are many acceptable reasons why people do not work. Many are injured, traumatized, and have other physical, somatic, psychological, and other problems. The stigma against the unemployed is prevalent mainly in the industrialized world, where people often frown upon and criticize those who are not working.

Yet, in ancient Greece, the opposite was true. Paraphrasing Plato, he and the philosophers of his time believed that people needed time to invest in their interests. While ancient Athenians worked, the kind of work they did and how they did it differed significantly from modern times. What kept them motivated and energetic in their endeavors is unclear. Still, if working for others was not as common as working for themselves, they must have had a complex incentive system. One thing we do know about Ancient Athens is that they all participated in a system called Democracy. Their first job or primary occupation was to administer their city.

Many in history, and several considered saints, including Saint Kosmas Aetolos (also known as The Aetolian), believed that life on farms and outside major cities was a sign of freedom. In his writings, he highlights the importance of liberating the people and retaining that liberty by staying out of the cities. His comments were historically significant, as Greece was fighting for independence. However, they offer insight into how an individual's self-sufficiency is linked to their liberty. The farmers were considered more self-sufficient and free than the city dwellers. It was also common in those days for each family to live in the city but to have ancestral lands to which they would return for celebrations, family gatherings, and political matters.

In any case, we bring this matter to attention because some people believe they should judge others by their income or lack thereof. Others judge those less fortunate, and so forth. It is not just the monetary divide; people often think they are superior because of income or revenue. Some will listen to the opinion of the extremely wealthy and yet turn their back on the poor. The views of richer countries are often more valuable than those of poorer countries. It has been the case for many generations: monks living humble, impoverished lives have written and spoken many truths about human nature, but hardly anything they say is taken into account by the vast majority. In part, the macro level is influenced by those who control the media. Still, at a micro level, where we sit in private conversations, people often don't respect the opinion of the unemployed, the poor, or the disabled. Such is the nature of society.

Aristotle wrote in paraphrase that two categoric forms of slavery exist, by law and by nature. The distinguishing feature of the two systems was that one form was systemic, and the other was natural. We have covered both forms so far based on what has been said. It should be noted that the natural form of slavery is loosely applied and not often mentioned. That means that when a person puts a child on their back and plays like a horse for the child, they are not only humiliating themselves, but they are also performing work for another voluntarily. The playful fatherly gesture shows humility for the child's enjoyment. But it can't be judged in the same light as when someone is systemically coerced, enticed, or even forced to work in a routine for their entire life. Then again, what of those bound in chains and stolen from their homes? It must be clear, then, that freedom will vary oppositely to that of slavery and servitude.

For an opinion to be considered, people perceive it must come from those they esteem. Such esteem is often falsely attributed to those with higher social and economic status. Sometimes, people place their esteem in authority figures, those like themselves, or those they idolize. Generally, people won't listen to a person they don't like. Historically, disfigurement was a punishment for the elite because, with a disfigured face, they found it more challenging to find allies. For Democracy to work, it requires all of us to see each other as valuable, no matter our wealth or occupations, whether we are appealing, entertaining, or likable or not. For a Democracy to work, we should not judge each other but be prepared to listen to everyone who wishes to speak the truth.

When the topic of Democracy is raised amongst the people, some have argued that it is better to be enslaved and secure than to be free with all the associated risks. Relying on ourselves for safety and security is good for the strong and able, but it also leaves the old, frail, and impaired behind. In some ways, freedom depends on our ability to defend ourselves; when we can't, we rely on those closest to us.

Some view freedom as related to living in the wild or some anarchist institution. In the wild or by nature, as well as in rural or urban life, governance manifests in many different ways. Anarchy is rarely a static state, as every group of people, whether related or not, adopts some form of governance. Governance in which the young and strong manipulate the frail is hardly a system that promotes freedom. We must establish here that freedom does not necessarily equate to an individualized or anarchist existence. While freedom can exist within Anarchy, it does not mean that Anarchy produces or sustains freedom. Anarchy can't sustain itself, let alone be the initiating force behind anything other than Chaos. In all cases where anarchy emerges, chaos occurs within a short period. Chaos emerges from the confusion caused by anarchy. That confusion is created by the wants and needs of all the people within the same locality. Then, typically, after the chaos has subsided, some form of order emerges, and at this point, governance sets in.

Suppose we consider those who can't defend themselves or maintain high self-sufficiency. In that case, we quickly realize that while a young man may feel free within an Anarchist state, there are no rules or systems of leadership to preserve what most of us perceive as fundamental rights for himself, his family, and friends. So that even a young individual, on a day he is ill or unable to be typically strong, will be exposed to similar problems that the weak and aged face. If freedom is to form a part of a governing system, it must be somehow preserved by the system. That is to say, freedom can exist irrespective of any system, but to say that freedom is a part of a system, the system must have the qualities that preserve freedom. If, within Anarchy, there is a moment that we believe we have freedom, we must also understand that type of freedom is very fragile. It will come and go at the random will of those we meet within the locality of the Anarchy. Therefore, it should be stated that anarchy is not only the absence of leadership; it is the absence of any system of governance. Anarchy can't work towards, guarantee, or establish anything because order requires unity as a precursor, and unity requires consultation and cooperation, two of the foundations of governance. Take, for example, a well of water shared by people; how then is it shared if the people do not find some order? Who will use the well first? How much of the well is to be used? What happens if the water runs out while others wait to use it? Should children, the sick, the elderly, or the soldiers be given priority? A free system without laws and order is more prone to chaos. That fairness and equality among the people are skewed in favor of those who can manipulate the given system most effectively. It is essential to note that, in our example, in an anarchistic system, the youth and the strong are often the most capable, whereas in a bureaucratic system, it often favors those who establish the rules and laws, such as the wealthy and elite.

Very few of the possible governing systems can preserve freedom. Yet, among all the government systems that can manifest, the one that allows the individual to live freely, and as they hoped, can only exist in a government system where the same individual and others preserve that right. Such government systems foster a system of reciprocity, where the individual gives to the system and the system reciprocates by giving to the individual. We call this not so much a duty as an obligation. To defend the system, individuals join together to protect it. There will come a time when the system enables the defense of those who have defended it. The system must reward everyone in turn —not just some, but all, because the system's authority, defenders, and executors are the majority. Since the system's authority is composed of each person, every obligation to the system also has a fraction of the obligation to the individuals that compose it. As much as people are willing to commit to the system, they also expect a return on that commitment to the people.

In this way, freedom is preserved because those who control the system are the people, and the majority determines the extent to which they impose their liberty. In every other system, the amount of freedom imposed upon one is determined by the minority. The difference between a democracy and an oligarchy, or any other form of government, is that a democracy directly upholds its citizens' interests. All other systems are like the majority holding their hands in a hot flame, waiting for a small group without their hands in the fire to determine when the majority have had enough. By directly controlling the government, people can preserve their freedom. However, the system alone does not guarantee that their liberty is preserved. Democracy offers a fair and reasonable chance of maintaining freedom more than any other system.

A system of reciprocity establishes democracy and freedom because citizens will always seek to benefit from participating in government affairs. The system, in turn, will benefit from their participation, and both will have a common cause, provided that the majority are not swayed or corrupted. In such situations where people are lazy, they can be persuaded to skew the balance between their obligation to work for their system and the system working for them. For instance, it is foreseeable that some people will expect more than they are willing to contribute.

Concerning the argument of living as a safe enslaved person or an endangered free person, the reality is far removed from such an argument. A slave is dependent and reliant on others in almost all matters. The free person works and commits to what they need and want. It is essential to realize that the system that promotes slavery or servitude can never offer freedom. There is nothing to stop those who control the enslaved people from rounding them up and sending them to war. Those wars often have nothing to do with the needs or wants of the people; they are waged to advance the agenda of their masters. The security felt under oppression or suppression, enslavement, or forced servitude is often an illusion. People thrive on this illusion because it comforts them; therefore, it is one of the hardest to disprove. For instance, the lamb and chickens, the cattle and pigs, all felt safe and secure immediately before their slaughter for sale as meat. I always wonder why my father taught me how to slaughter animals we hand-fed. Then, one day, when I was a young adult and without subtlety, he said, "We are in the same position as those animals." People want such illusions to be true. They refuse to believe there is any danger until it directly affects them.

From 1950 to 1975, historians inform us that the USA, Australia, Canada, Britain, and several other countries united in a war against Vietnam. During that time, using the military draft became a politically sensitive topic. The conscription of citizens into wars in which the people had no vested interest was commonplace throughout those years. The Anglo Sphere, comprising mainly the USA, Australia, Canada, and Britain, had used conscription as a normal way of operating its military. However, public outrage led to the revision of conscription laws in all these countries. Like sheep off to slaughter, the safe and secure would be rounded up and sent to cheap training facilities to be briefly instructed on the equipment they were expected to use, and then thrown into battle within as little as a fortnight. The exact number of deaths in the Anglo-Sphere army during the Vietnam War remains unknown. There are estimates that over four hundred thousand lives were lost. The USA claimed it had lost around three hundred thousand people.

There was an uproar in the politics of these nations against war and military conscription, which forced people into conflict. All the Anglo-Sphere nations abolished the conscription laws, which appeased everyone for some time. However, in each case, their laws had a loophole that allowed for conscription to be raised if needed. The rules typically state that conscription will never be used to recruit for the military; however, a loophole exists that allows a government to vote to legalize it. In other words, there is a prohibition on conscription until they decide to reinstate it. That time will most likely come when the people themselves will forget the history of their fathers and forefathers.

Most people enjoy this type of security within these Oligarchies, not just in the Anglosphere but in all places where Oligarchies and Monarchies exist. That, of course, is only one example, and philosophies that are reliant on one example, or a few, are not entirely philosophical. However, my examples highlight what we know: there can never be freedom while others govern us and our lives. We can never truly be safe or secure based on the assumption that our masters, leaders, rulers, or governors will provide it. However, if a system exists that promotes freedom, it can also promote the security and safety of the people. In other words, the people with freedom must also find a way to secure themselves against aggressors.

Many argue that domestic freedom differs from freedom between nations or polities. Commonly, it is argued that our freedom as a polity or nation depends entirely on the efficiency of the military that protects us. It is considered that a Monarchy or Autocracy, and an Aristocracy or Oligarchy, have intrinsic qualities that enable them to manipulate the military more effectively. Yet, historically, it has been shown that people in a Democratic system can provide security and safety at the domestic and inter-polity (international) levels.

The main advantages of Autocracy and Oligarchy are that they can lawfully mobilize people quickly and across many cities, and do so without much debate. For example, a Democracy usually only works at a city level after lengthy discussion. Therefore, when each city is rallied and engaged in war, it would take considerably longer than when a single person or a group controls many cities. However, there should be no doubt that people can be competent enough to be free, safe, and secure through their leadership. While individuals may lack some skills to give us this confidence, security can be achieved as a community or polity.

We should be cautious when handing out our obligations and duties to others. The moment we, the people, rely on others to provide a service that keeps us safe and secure, or to control the military or governance, then our freedom is guaranteed to be diminished. To lose complete freedom within a system is to lose any authority over the laws, judges, police, and army. We will investigate these issues later to establish a philosophical truth. It is sufficient to note that, while the quality of the military varies and is influenced by numerous factors, some systems are better equipped to wage war than others. It is also true that some systems provide better living conditions than others.

Let us now examine the types of work people do, so we can understand the type of government that promotes them. People typically do two kinds of work. The initial job or work is what allows them to survive. It is the work done out of what most call necessity. The work done to earn an income is not always related to the type of work people do for survival or necessity, but often is. The second and highest value is people's work as part of their learning, interest, pastime, or entertainment. Work can be paid or unpaid, a hobby, a means of survival, or a pursuit for some alternative and higher purpose. Almost always, the first type of work, done out of necessity, involves working for someone else. Many will also work out of necessity but not receive payment or recognition from others. The work we consider a pastime or a vocation is similar to that worked out of necessity. The work may benefit survival, but it may also serve the purpose of understanding, exploration, or any other higher goal beyond the essential needs of survival. It is not the type of work being done but the purpose that matters. So, ultimately, there are only two main avenues for a person choosing to work: the one driven by necessity and the other by personal conviction. Either we have decided to work, or we need to work. Some go fishing to survive, while others fish for relaxation or enjoyment. Some will fight to survive, while some will fight for competition and pleasure. So, the purpose of doing work defines the type of work. It is essential to distinguish this before attempting to understand people's jobs, what motivates them, and how tasks in society are accomplished, because all of these, along with others, impact the ability of a democratic system to operate.

1.9 Servitude

Servitude – the state of being bound by duties or obligations to serve another – has a long and complex history in human societies. From ancient civilizations to modern times, the concept of servitude has taken various forms, encompassing slavery, indentured or contracted servitude, and certain forms of employment.

Servitude, in its most explicit form, can be traced back to ancient civilizations, where slavery was prevalent. Enslaving people was deeply entrenched in societies such as Ancient Egypt and Rome. Slavery served as an economic foundation, with individuals captured during battles who were then traded and forced to labor under harsh conditions. It was a system that forced enemies to build and serve in the cities so their hard work would contribute to the very things that enslaved them. An ironic twist of fate. The legacy of these early forms of prisoner-of-war servitude systems would shape the course of history and leave an indelible mark on societies across the globe.

Indentured or contracted servitude emerged as an alternative form of slavery during the colonial era. Under this system, individuals would agree to work for a specified period in exchange for passage to a new land or to repay a debt. Although different from traditional concepts of slavery, indentured or contracted servitude still entailed significant restrictions on personal freedom, often subjecting individuals to arduous labor and limited rights.

In Western nations and many Eastern countries, homeowners are compelled to pay substantial sums of money each year to the government for various reasons. These payments become part of a base debt set by their government. The base debt value is the minimum amount of money each person needs to exist, not to survive or live. Base debt is typically lowest when a person owns their home and highest when they rent a shelter. Each home is expected to pay a set amount each year for various reasons. Those reasons are typically not based on consumption. Consumption is usually added to the top of this base sum. Also, the base sum is often inflated by various costs associated with the services and/or products the government offers. The result is that for a person to exist, they are placed in debt every year, even when they own their own homes. That, of course, describes the final course of a person's life in the West. The same people are required to earn substantial amounts of money to afford a home initially.

From the base of a pyramidal system looking upwards, we may perceive those few at the pinnacle as unreachable. If we put one much larger pyramidal structure next to that pyramid, we notice that for a smaller pyramid to control a larger one, all that is needed is to control the few at the pinnacle. Our small pyramid can control the larger one because it involves controlling only the pinnacle of each. To preserve the power of those at the pinnacle, those at the base are often manipulated and forced to fight and die for the interests of the few. Of course, if we invert the pyramids, their base at the top would be formidable and far more resistant to the whims of the few. Yet even then, where the majority rules, they must take precautions so that a larger majority does not overpower them. The same can be said within the pyramidal government structure. If the majority is not careful, a minority can tip the balance and invert the pyramid. These are some of the intrinsic dynamics of the pyramidal forms of government.

The European Union, a political and economic union among selected European nations, has dealt a significant blow to what were once considered independent nations. If we are to pretend that Southern Europe recovered from the Germanic invasions of Rome, we could also pretend that the nations that followed their democratic revolutions were free. The pretending need not stop there; we could also pretend that these independent nations had control over their destinies. But the harsh reality is that, for a long time after the Medieval world wars, the East remained under the rule of a Confederate Islamic state, while Germanic monarchs and their aristocracy still led the West. The point here is that Southern Europe has a history demonstrating clearly that a nation can become a slave in the same way an individual can become a slave.

Much was said in history about the Russian Satellite nations during the Cold War of the 1980s. The Russian Satellites were a euphemism for vassal-like states that included Poland, Romania, Hungary, Czechoslovakia, and East Germany. Yet, very little was said about the Germanic hold over Western and Southern Europe, or about the British, French, and Spanish hold and influence over their colonies and former colonies. It is now clear, following the 2020 pandemic, that what may seem to be independent nations can be so heavily politically, financially, and militarily dependent that they ultimately lose their autonomy and/or freedom. Even the Germans in the East became vassals of Russia, losing the Western portion of their nation as vassals to the Allies —the United States of America, Britain, and her colonies. For instance, the German Military in the West was heavily restricted by domestic and international laws following World War II. During this time, their nation had become almost entirely dependent on a foreign military presence from the United States of America and the United Kingdom under the banner of the North Atlantic Treaty Organization (NATO).

Some of the political issues that have been raised may seem current and relevant at the time I am writing, but they will become history by tomorrow. One thing we learn from history is that people often fail to learn from it. From ancient history to the modern era, the events and descriptions are subject to dispute, and there are likely political reasons to question their accuracy. Even though many truths seem to repeat seemingly perpetually, hardly any of those truths are significant to today's people. So, it serves us best to take them as an allegory or parable, because we can't validate all these facts without relying on what others have written, and we don't know whether what they have written is true. It is, therefore, essential to steer this argument back to the individual and how all this relates to the individual citizen.

Nations and people are not too different in the attributes that constitute their character. A Nation's constituents are the individuals who define the state and the larger entity that we call the Nation. Additionally, the nation, as an entity, influences individuals through its systems and culture. Also, there is a relationship between the individual, the people, and the ideology that unites them. The methods that turn nations into vassals or satellites are almost identical to those that entrap individuals. Of course, they are not precisely the same, but they can have similar qualities or attributes. It can be against our will, with our consent, or without a contract or agreement, such as in some wage systems.

What motivates us to work and do things? For some people, the job they want to do also earns them an income for survival. For most others, their work to survive is separate from what they aspire to or want to do. In ancient Athenian democracy, the type of work they considered important was their calling or vocation. However, in many other societies, the type of work considered important is that done out of necessity. This simple shift in what we perceive as essential—what many people call a "real job" rather than a hobby or a fulfilling occupation—has significant implications. The freedom to dabble in activities beyond everyday chores, and especially the lack of need to work for others, enabled the Ancient Athenians to produce some of the world's best scholars. It could be argued that the freedom to pursue one's vocation has such a significant impact that approximately 200 geniuses were born in Athens during the Athenian democracy.

People with the freedom to work on the things they love will produce better results in their field of interest. A person paid to do a task has no incentive to do it for its own sake. A woodworker making an object for the sake of making a wooden object has the incentive to create a finished wooden object. Such creations are often the best because the maker or craftsman is motivated to finish them well. That is because there is an actual love or interest in the art.

The purpose of creating a product or providing a service for an artist arises from the incentive to see the completed product or service. The artist is also incentivized to finish their art because the end product is something they wish to see, hear, or bring to fruition. However, the end product or service differs when someone is given a tangible incentive such as money. A doctor, compelled by the science of medicine and the desire to heal the sick, differs from a doctor who arrives at work to make money. Art or science, the discipline itself, can be performed by vocation or duty. What we are discussing also shapes our view of government. The incentive to govern needs to be for the sake of governing and not for the benefit of governing. No matter which system is considered —whether a king, an oligarchy, or a democratic people — if the leaders are not leading and not governing for the sake of governing, they are governing or leading for the wrong reasons. The latter is the most common form of government. Throughout the world, governments exist, but they are not led by people seeking to provide quality service; they are led by those seeking to profit from such positions.

There are many reasons to work, but people often fail to assess the underlying need to work. The need to work is especially true of cultures that have developed over a long period through a feudalistic history. The need to work can be derived from outright force or from a subtle, almost translucent manipulation. A nation compelled to work to pay its debts or transform its people's labor to repay national debts, outgoings of service or product is subject to the same necessity to work for its master as the people within it.

In countries where feudalism has historically existed and where being a vassal to other countries is deemed a historical norm, we begin to see some acceptance of this pressure to work for others. The research into this subject revealed that many believed that working for others had a historical continuity. Most people could not recognize any other way to survive independently. It was also discovered that this was not a historical norm in Ancient Athens. Also, working for others had almost entirely ceased during the Enlightenment and soon after. However, the same period encouraged using enslaved people to compensate for the loss of local production.

Many have worked by tilling the soil or working in poor occupational conditions. Later in people's lives, they began writing, teaching, or performing higher-level tasks. We know, at least, that the latter is true from several philosophers' accounts. You may have even noticed that many people change direction and occupation because there is often a conflict between how we use our time through employment and what we would rather be doing. Do not think for a moment, as many do, that leadership topics are beyond your abilities or those around you. Just because we are compelled to live our lives in a way pre-designed by others does not necessarily mean we can't sculpt our own lives out of the resources we have. Today, we may perform a duty or job and even be confined to a particular socio-economic level. However, we should never consider anything as permanent. Nor does our occupation define or reflect on our ability to lead and manage our affairs. Yes, working for others leaves us with little time to advance our knowledge, but let that not stop anyone who wishes to learn about Democracy. Each of us can be a capable leader at all levels. We may be like those workers who are blinded to everything aside from their work, but with some free time and essential resources, we can do the things we love better than others. But what good is it to have free time and whittle it away through lethargy or decadence? If people need free time, that free time should be spent as a means to fulfill their obligations to operate their government. After all, a government system that preserves its freedom depends on everyone keeping themselves free. Democracy is a system that offers its citizens the chance to create a degree of freedom beyond anything comparable under a Monarchy or Aristocracy. We will explore this uniqueness in more detail later.

People under a Monarchy or aristocracy cannot have the same freedoms as those living in a Democracy. Even in the most pleasant or the most challenging times, hardships will come and go. During the most difficult periods, the poor will often pay the highest price for the wealthy and those who control the government. However, in a system operated by the people, there is a much higher probability that everyone will go through those same periods of hardship with the least loss.

As stated before, the system I live in considers knowledge paramount. Yet the quality of that information and knowledge has been left to others to determine. In doing so, the governing system provides little information and knowledge that empowers people. People in the street were asked whether knowledge was important to them, and the majority said yes. Yet, despite what the people, media, or orations may say, the quality of that knowledge is not very important to the system we live in because the system and its institutions do not promote questioning and seeking the truth as a valuable part of life.

In summary, this means that most people asked on the streets and those met equated knowledge with a form of power to liberate or elevate an individual. In paraphrase, many would say: "It is not what you know, but who you know." Others would say, "The smarter you are, the more money you make." "The more you know, the more power you have." These views give the false impression that knowledge helps people find work and, therefore, money to survive or live well. But to do all that in servitude is meaningless. The above common statements merely highlight that our lives are in the hands of others. That our lives are in the hands of others is true in all systems of government, but when the few determine our fate, we rely on using what we know to gain leverage to influence them for our benefit.

Therefore, servitude, in all its forms, has profound implications for individuals and society. From a human rights perspective, servitude represents a fundamental violation of every individual's intrinsic dignity and equality. The oppressive nature of servitude denies people agency over their own lives, subjecting them to exploitation, abuse, and dehumanization.

On a societal level, servitude perpetuates inequality and social divisions. It creates a hierarchical structure in which the privileged few benefit from the labor and subjugation of others. The legacy of servitude is often reflected in deeply ingrained social, economic, and racial disparities, which can persist long after the formal abolition of slavery or the end of indentured and contracted servitude.

1.10 Systemic youth control

Youth represents life's most dynamic and transformative phase, where individuals discover their identities, explore the world, and shape their futures. However, societies often exhibit systemic youth control, ranging from cultural norms to institutional policies. While some argue that such control is necessary to maintain social order and protect young people, others contend that it stifles creativity, limits personal development, and perpetuates inequality.

Systemic youth control encompasses the array of social, cultural, and institutional mechanisms that shape young people's behavior, choices, and opportunities. These mechanisms include parental guidance, educational systems, societal expectations, government policies, and media influences. The intent behind such control may vary, ranging from protecting youth from potential harm and negative influences to shaping them into responsible citizens who conform to societal norms, or to the benefit of those who systematically control them.

Proponents of systemic youth control argue that it serves as a guiding force, providing young people with structure, protection, and education. They contend that society can nurture autonomy through responsible control by equipping youth with the necessary skills, values, and knowledge. Education systems, for instance, aim to prepare young individuals for future challenges, instilling critical thinking, problem-solving, and social skills. Furthermore, parental guidance and community support can help young people navigate life choices and foster personal development.

On the other hand, critics may argue that systemic youth control often limits young individuals' potential by imposing rigid expectations and suppressing their roles in a polity. Societal norms and expectations can stifle creativity, discourage unconventional paths, and limit the expression of diverse identities. Traditional educational systems, which prioritize standardized testing and conformity, may hinder the exploration of individual talents, passions, and alternative learning approaches.

Furthermore, systemic youth control can perpetuate social inequalities. Discriminatory practices, such as biased school admissions or limited access to resources based on socioeconomic status, hinder equal opportunities for personal growth and development. In such cases, systemic youth control functions as a barrier rather than a facilitator, reinforcing existing disparities and preventing marginalized youth from reaching their full potential.

Additionally, systemic youth control can safeguard vulnerable youth from harmful influences. Laws and regulations related to alcohol, drugs, and explicit content are implemented to shield young individuals from potential dangers and promote their well-being. Restrictions on certain activities, such as age-based driving restrictions or curfews, can also protect young people from engaging in risky behavior.

From the very first moment children step into mandatory schooling to the time they die, they are led down a pre-specified path. Most don't notice until they are unable to do anything about it. Children are often taken from their parents, not physically, but by replacing their parents as their educators. When Plato wrote about education, he emphasized that education is too important to be left in the hands of a single instructor. We could expand on what he meant by saying that having a single source of education is equally as dangerous. But philosophically speaking, the number of sources does not necessarily matter, but the number of independent sources does.

For a substantial number of generations, children and parents have remarked on a "generation gap". They use this phrase to play down the forces that separate the child from the parent. They utilize technologies, ideas, philosophies, sciences, and various educational matters to make what a child knows distinct from what their parents know. The children grow to think they do not want to be like their mother or father, and they believe they will succeed. That is a remarkable change, considering that in past generations, fathers taught their sons their trade or profession. Family-owned small businesses or operations were often handed down within the same family for generations.

In these modern paedocleptic societies, the children and adults are distanced from their own families, not by choice, not by force, but by the mechanisms of education. These things, of course, could exist in a Democracy and any other form of government. The only difference is in who controls the system of government and to what extent they force this to happen. I say this not only concerns the majority-or-minority governing system, but also what if the actual system of government itself does not have enough power to govern? Then what power does the government have to determine what everyone learns? Are we all to be given the same information and knowledge? Uniformity and conformity, assimilation and subjection before innovation, progress, and freedom?

In our Democratic or ancient Athenian model, productivity, material or otherwise, was a symptom of, or a by-product of, originality, inventiveness, and the pursuit of the truth. These points are how Plato's world would have been. He highlights that he is not a politician by trade but by passion, hobby, or genuine interest; therefore, his genuine productivity rests in his political philosophy. Many have commented on the extraordinary number of geniuses that lived within a two-hundred-year span within a Democratic system. Many historians believe, as I do, that progress —beyond mere productivity or increases in wealth or value — requires a period of focus on learning and on dedicating ourselves to the things we love. The degree of progress and the number of geniuses of that period were entirely indicative of the freedom or luxury people had to pursue their interests and ideals. Of course, chores, work, and self-employment all existed. Still, people balanced these things in ways that maximized learning and accelerated achievement across all areas of what we now know as academia. However, the wealth of their society was not only confined to Academia. It appeared in their music, entertainment, pottery, art, science, and every facet of life. What better system is there than one in which people are self-employed and do the things they love?

The freedom to learn and work in the things we love is unknown to most people. Some say they work for an employer to enjoy themselves on holidays, vacations, or in their spare time. They become content because that is how much people have become institutionalized, like prisoners who become content to live another day, to be served their meals, and to have their free time to watch a show, a play, or some sports. There is nothing wrong with being content with little; Socrates believed that the secret to happiness in life was not a matter of how much wealth was at our disposal, but the ability to be content with the least. People like me are indeed content with the least. Yet I would rather live under a tree and be poor than as an enslaved person in a palace. That is different to those who become content because they give up the fight and, in the process, exchange their freedom for a fistful of coins. Let us not confuse domestication and institutionalism with contentment.

People think that the way things are around us has always been this way. Some insist that there is nothing wrong with the systems in which they live. Often, people remark, "Why change something if it's not broken?" It is a typical response from those who are not so much content as institutionalized. I am probably breaking the innocence of some who, from childhood, thought the purpose of their life was to work and survive. It has become almost institutionalized to work for your family by dedicating the best years of your life to a series of employers or ventures in order to accumulate wealth. In the process, they refer to this as surviving. This work-to-survive ideology was popularized during the Industrial Revolution, which may be why many people follow this code of conduct or way of life.

In the East, people had a solemn outlook on working for the shark, like the Remora fish picking up the scraps of a Shark's meal. Phagoi, or Eaters, is often used to denote the relation between those compelled to work to survive and those who compel them to do so. The Greeks refer to the Phagoi as those who consume humanity to pursue wealth. The Indians have documents describing how a husband was accorded exceptional status in their society and was exempt from military service. They worked solely for their families and had no obligation to serve in the military. Irrespective of view, be it East or West, the way of life around us should not be the basis or foundation of what is correct and true. The contrasting views of the East and West are simplistic comparisons to remind us of the diversity we speak of.

This philosophy is not specific to the place of origin, nationality, religion, or environmental influences. We should approach this philosophy as an exploration of alternative government systems, without being tied to any particular time or place on Earth. Many will refute what is being said, especially the statements made about political issues and the examples provided. Examples can be criticized because they distill or oversimplify, and at best, they generalize.

We can't expect that because we perceive things in a particular form today, others will perceive them the same way tomorrow. The unemployed living in a system that rewards only the employed will have very different views from those who enjoy the luxuries of an employed life. Likewise, the unemployed within a Democratic system would be rewarded for their participation, whilst those tied to their work would not. Above all, we expect that cultural norms or what others call common knowledge will have little to no place in finding the truth. As explained, we are far too diverse to expect anything to have become universal knowledge. We should not consider that we are perfect and that the ideal system suits the individual. Many people often complain that philosophies are long-winded, useless ideals. That they have no purpose in "real life".

To proceed, we must be prepared to move away from propaganda and the standard way people have been informed, and instead rely on our logic. If what is said here initially seems like something you think you know better about, please consider everything I say before contributing your views, just as the opinions of others were the basis for determining whether this philosophy should be written.

To strike a balance between nurturing autonomy and preventing potential harm, it is crucial to rethink and reform the systemic control of youth. Empowering young individuals by involving them in decision-making processes, encouraging their active participation in shaping policies, and providing platforms for their voices to be heard can foster a sense of ownership and agency. Above all else, understanding Democratic principles must permeate the fabric of the system to which they belong.

1.11 The purpose of education

Education is a fundamental pillar of human civilization, serving as the bedrock upon which societies flourish and individuals achieve their fullest potential. It is a transformative journey that transcends classroom boundaries, opening doors to opportunity, fostering personal growth, and cultivating a better future for all. The purpose of education extends far beyond acquiring knowledge; it is a holistic process that empowers minds, nurtures critical thinking, and prepares individuals to navigate life's complexities with wisdom and resilience.

Currently, in most places around the world, and at the time of writing, the emphasis on learning is primarily on securing a job. It is as if learning is done solely to secure work or money, with the highest priority. This type of learning is short-sighted; it serves domestic concerns, not broader, higher ones beyond people's self-interest. The incentive is not the art or the science but the income that it enables an individual to achieve.

Education is seen as a catalyst for social mobility and economic progress. It is thought to reduce inequalities, break the cycle of poverty, and empower individuals to uplift themselves and their communities. Education equips individuals with the skills and knowledge necessary to access better job opportunities, enhance their earning potential, and make meaningful contributions to society. Moreover, educated individuals are more likely to make informed choices, participate in political life, and drive positive social change, leading to the overall development of polities.

Some argue that those educated work hard to achieve what they have, but never for a moment do they consider the thought that what they are doing in life is not entirely their choice. The powers that control our lives can also control what we want. Some argue against this notion, but the massive wealth thrown into advertising and media testifies otherwise. Simply making people aware of something is enough for many to want it. Then, once the seeds are sown, communities driven by jealousy and pretentiousness copy one another. In this way, what was given as a seed to a few is copied by many. Controlling information is essential, but most people can't see its value. Education can also be affected by the media and by political views and biases of the source, as well as those of the recipients.

Education begins with acquiring knowledge and providing individuals with a comprehensive understanding of the world, its complexities, and the accumulated wisdom of past generations. It equips learners with the necessary foundations in mathematics, sciences, literature, history, and the arts. Education empowers individuals to make informed decisions by imparting knowledge, encouraging intellectual curiosity, and laying the groundwork for further learning.

The standard type of learning found in most nations is remarkably different from the kind of learning we do to advance our knowledge or improve humanity. The latter was traditionally known as higher learning. In contrast, the type used to train people for a job was considered different. In Western universities, each job requiring a particular skill and training has an equivalent formal course of study and qualification. That is, every "higher" education leads to a specific job. The concept of "higher" education has been reduced to a few studies conducted for income and employment. While some studies focus on nature, the body, chemistry, and physics, most students enroll in subjects to attain jobs in their field. Additionally, most students undergo extensive job training.

Ironically, the same countries in the West and throughout Europe had a different system a few generations ago. Several generations ago, the Universities of the West had open classes, allowing people to enter as they saw fit, enroll in courses that interested them, and learn what they wanted. They would be given a qualification if a set number of studies were achieved. There were detailed limitations, such as the number of sciences, arts, and other disciplines studied. Even with Medicine, a handful of essential subjects were needed, yet a larger base of electives was offered. The fusion of various disciplines gave us the diversity in medical fields that later flourished in the 1980s.

Furthermore, terms such as "productivity" in an industrialized nation became closely tied to the relationship between production and the services rendered by their workforce. Labor productivity is typically measured as the output or service per employee. But there is little room in an economically driven system to acknowledge how much an employee – or, for that matter, a person– has discovered and learned.

Beyond financial issues, education provides individuals with a sense of purpose, meaning, and fulfillment. It encourages self-discovery, personal growth, and the pursuit of passions and interests. Education fosters self-confidence, resilience, and emotional intelligence, enabling individuals to navigate challenges, overcome setbacks, and maintain mental well-being. Additionally, education fosters a lifelong love of learning, inspiring individuals to pursue knowledge and personal growth beyond formal education.

Education is vital in preparing individuals to thrive in an increasingly complex and evolving world. It equips them with practical skills in employment, entrepreneurship, and active citizenship. Education develops communication abilities, teamwork, adaptability, and resilience, enabling individuals to navigate diverse social, economic, and technological landscapes. By fostering a spirit of lifelong learning, education allows individuals to continuously adapt, grow, and seize opportunities in an ever-changing society.

Regarding education and citizenship, one of the primary objectives of education is to impart political knowledge and awareness to individuals. Education provides the opportunity to learn about the history, governance systems, and democratic values that underpin society. Students understand the rights, privileges, and responsibilities of citizenship through comprehensive curricula. This knowledge enables individuals to make informed decisions, participate in democratic processes, and contribute to the betterment of society. Education instills a sense of political duty and encourages individuals to stay informed about current events, local issues, and global challenges, thereby nurturing an engaged and responsible citizenry.

Education not only imparts knowledge but also cultivates critical thinking and analytical skills. In an increasingly complex and interconnected world, citizens need the ability to critically assess information, discern facts from opinions, and evaluate the validity and reliability of sources. Education equips individuals with the tools to question assumptions, challenge prevailing narratives, and seek evidence-based solutions. These skills are essential for active citizenship as they enable individuals to participate in public discourse, engage in constructive debate, and make well-reasoned decisions that benefit society.

Also, education fosters social cohesion by promoting understanding, empathy, and respect for diverse perspectives and backgrounds. By exposing students to different cultures, religions, and worldviews, education encourages tolerance and appreciation for diversity. It helps dismantle stereotypes and prejudices, fosters community, belonging, and unity. Furthermore, this promotes social harmony and inclusivity, key elements of responsible citizenship. Education provides individuals with opportunities to develop essential skills, including interpersonal skills, empathy, and cooperation, enabling them to engage respectfully with others and contribute positively to society.

Above all, education is a platform for transmitting ethical values and political virtues that are fundamental to responsible citizenship. Individuals may learn about justice, integrity, honesty, and compassion through ethical education. Education cultivates a sense of social responsibility and encourages individuals to act ethically in their personal and professional lives. By understanding the ethical implications of their actions, citizens can make choices that align with the common ideals and contribute to a just and equitable polity.

The purpose of education varies depending on the system responsible for it. Under a monarchy or an oligarchy, the educational system will differ from that of a democratic system. Democracies promote the system of Democracy and all things related to it. At the same time, a monarchy and oligarchy would have it in their best interests to educate their people on how to serve.

1.12 Other divisions in society

In society, people can be classified as ethical or unethical—for example, issues that are created and sensationalized, or those that are pro or against a particular lifestyle. Then, there are the compliant and non-compliant classes. Mandate conforming as opposed to mandating noncompliance or those with criminal records against those without criminal records. Then there are the pros and cons. Examples include the abortion debate, environmental carbon emission, and climate change debates. Finally, beyond ideologies are our belief systems, and their association with one belief system or other factors can place people in different classes. These differences can be categorized into eight broad areas: Socioeconomic Disparities, Political Differences, Personal Lifestyle Inequality, Ethnic and Racial Differences, Religious and Cultural Differences, Generational

Divides, Geographic and Tribal Disparities, and Ideological Differences.

How we have been divided impacts how we think and what we consider true. Some people struggle with the class they have been forced into. It is essential to realize that personal views should not affect the truth. The truth is, humanity has been segregated so that it can be ruled over. Without these segregations being highlighted and forced on people, humanity would have been united. I am not saying 'united' in the sense of Globalized unity, but in the sense of unity at the level of the city we all live in. These divisions are popular in many societies and are the modern ones used to control the masses through the apex of an Oligarchy.

In 1960, approximately 70% of people lived in owner-occupied homes. In 2015-2016, only 30% lived in owner-occupied accommodation. Furthermore, the same study indicated that over 62% had a mortgage (37%) or were renting (25%), while 4% had no place to live. The Australian Bureau of Statistics published this study. (Australian Bureau of Statistics, 2015-2016). These statistics indicate that home ownership has steadily declined. It has reached levels related to a communist or Serfdom lifestyle. Although the USA has also experienced a decline in home ownership, it is not as drastic as in Australia. The figures presented clearly illustrate the disparity between financially affluent individuals and those struggling to make ends meet. Over half the population is without homes to raise their families and must rely on debt slavery, wage slavery, or rental enslavement. In any case, this is a philosophical rather than a scientific report. It is enough to say that a person living comfortably in a home will hold views strikingly different from those fighting with every breath to survive and house a family. Just like all the other divisions, they are there with intent. There is no reason why a system should not afford the God-given right to shelter and house families and people in general.

1.13 Unity

Many people are limited by time and resources; as a result, some great minds never get to express themselves. On the other hand, many of those with the time and resources waste their skills by writing for popular and commercial reasons. They talk and write about the things that immediately attract people to read, listen to, watch, or learn. They speak and write about sexuality, violence, perversions, and an assortment of anomalies. Even when the topic is serious, their methods almost always resort to lies because the bizarre and wondrous seem to attract or entertain people. Even people who claim they have little time seem to find time to dwell on such matters.

Over the years, an educated population has become increasingly exposed to the effects of the media. A person unable to read, write, or comprehend the media can be entirely unaware of what the majority knows. The educated may mock the uneducated, but ignorance is not something to be mocked or associated with inferiority. There is far more to ignorance than merely not knowing. Ignorance is not only a reason to have educators; educators themselves can be ignorant enough to think that what they know is more than what others know. Ignorance can become a valid reason for creating an industry of educators, trainers, philosophers, and other related professions. But who gauges the quality of these educators, and who judges their ignorance? Who decides which subjects to teach their pupils? Because we all know something is true, it does not mean it is. Just like a single person can make an error in what they say, so can groups and the majority. However, the impact of that error is diminished to some degree when a particular view is widely held and has been thoroughly investigated and analyzed by the entire group or population. For example, if children's education were left to a single educator who believed something contrary to the truth, that pupil would also be more likely to accept it. However, if a group of educators considers, analyzes, and studies a subject, they are more likely to discover and pass on that truth. The provision here is that they sincerely investigated the same subject equally and independently and arrived at the same conclusion. When a system churns out young educators, we must question the uniformity of their knowledge and the quality of their education. None of these things typically happens because, in an attempt for society to build a universal educational system for all its children, the blunt reality is that there aren't enough natural teachers in sufficient numbers to be good quality teachers. That, and the fact that many of these universal systems lacked individuals who could question, instead promoting those who could memorize without question. So when you ask a scientist or mathematician, and as Plato made a good point of questioning, "What is one divided in two?" many will answer a half. However, they overlook the crucial fact that there are now two parts that make up one, so we do not have a half, but two halves. When I write this, the mathematical regime focuses on only a portion of the complete truth. People are taught to calculate proportions in every division equation rather than to look at the whole picture. When a whole is divided into ten pieces, the answer is not one-tenth but ten-tenths. The original object is fragmented, but each fragment is a portion of the same object. Many refer to this concept by various terms, including the conservation of matter. That is, whatever was there before is still here now. In the same way, if we reword our mathematical questions, there may be some meaning in solving half the equation, but we are far from the truth without understanding the whole equation.

In addition, many people are taught that atoms are divisible and that sub-atomic particles can exist. Ironically, the term "atom" equates to the smallest particle that nature will allow to exist. That is based on our understanding of finite limits, which most of nature seems to comply with. Just like a mountain can only ever reach a maximum height before it collapses on itself or how many animals can feed from the same trough or how many people can drink from the same glass at the same time, or how many bricklayers can work on the same wall at the same time, or how high a flame can travel or how much smoke can be made, all these things are finite with limits.

Believing in infinity is like believing that your glass will never empty if you drain it hyperbolically. Many use these ideas of infinity to explain the space between stars and the matter beyond our planet. Explaining the void as infinite in dimension is convenient, but in reality, nothing is infinite. Even the void we observe in nature is finite. Only a specific amount of void can exist within the material before either the material breaks apart or separates between the largest area of void and the thinnest parts of the matter. However, these arguments are more suitable for another philosophy. Getting back to the model of the atom, they teach that it has constituents, and by their reckoning, those constituents make up an atom.

However, following their ideology would mean that the most minor component "is" the atom. In the model they teach children, the electron is the smallest part of an atom. But by declaring this, they suggest that the electron is the atom because it is also the smallest particle in nature. The smallest particles are assigned several invented terms in the model that is taught to adults. However, whenever they suggest that these smaller particles constitute the atom, they intentionally pervert the understanding of the atom. In reality, the concept of atoms is that there is a limit to an object's size. The atom represents that limit. So, nature will only allow matter to exist once it reaches a size, dimension, and stability limit. For matter to break down any further than an atom is impossible. All our scientific experiments observe these reasons and are consistent with the fact that matter is always preserved. Now, there is no conclusive proof of what this atom is, and because some nations claim to have performed all forms of scientific wizardry, I cannot reveal the full truth about it without offending various groups.

What may further aggravate some groups is that there will never be proof of the atom. I am not being pessimistic, nor am I like those stubborn old men who refuse to accept that the world is not flat. The scientific literature generally agrees with me, although this is not explicitly stated. The only way to see something so small is to shine a light upon it and to magnify it. At least, these are the only accepted methods we know of for seeing something. When light hits an object, it is reflected, or bounced, off the object, and our eyes or machines perceive the object's image through the reflected light. Many factors, including absorption, refraction, diffraction, energy, and material interference, all play a role in how we view an object. However, the most critical aspect is that the light striking an object must be smaller than the object itself. Just like normal microscopes use visible light of a specific wavelength and amplitude, so too do the smaller waves of the electron microscope view even smaller objects. It is expected, by current reasoning, that to view an object, we require something to bounce off its surface, which can only happen if what is being bounced and measured is smaller than the subject. Even energy forms are thought to have mass, but proof of this has yet to be established, despite much debate. So, since the atom is the smallest limit that nature allows matter to exist, how can we reflect anything smaller than the smallest matter and expect to see it on Earth? I believe that energy preserves mass and that energy is mass in an excited state, as many scientists also believe. Within this energy form, nature will most likely place its minimum limit. So, as hot or excited or stimulated or empowered matter gets, the release of energy or the energy transition is limited by nature's limit on preserving that mass and energy. The phenomenon occurs when scientists burn a substance in a closed vessel; the total mass of the vessel remains the same before and after the burn. The inner parts burn, and the burning object may appear to disappear, but the result is that the object remains the same weight, which means the matter before and after is still in the vessel. That matter, as a solid, gas-liquid, or material-energy form, is still preserved by nature and its limitation by what we know to be the atom. Therefore, the atom is the smallest thing that nature allows to exist. What I have said here regarding science and education is, as you know, the truth. But how can one person's truth outweigh or even have any significant value to the majority?

Plato mentioned the relationship between free time and knowledge. He suggested that their knowledge can't increase significantly once a person is compelled to work or become an employee or servant. A person may learn about their occupation or what it compels them to know, but at the cost of learning other things. People who have committed to learning about one thing or a narrow field tend to have less broad knowledge. Often, specialized workers lose interest in peripheral matters.

Doctors learn a great deal about medicines, their effects, diseases, and treatments. Still, when they come home, they are typically not motivated to learn other subjects, such as poetry, history, or philosophy. Few, very few people, live such lives. The same can be said for all our classes in society; rarely does a musician read about surgery or a mechanic about biology. Each occupation takes up time that people would otherwise use to learn. Also, when they have time, they prioritize what they deem essential.

A polity, whether a city, nation, empire, or any organized body of people, thrives on the foundation of unity. Unity is the binding force that holds diverse individuals together, promoting a sense of shared purpose, common values, and collective well-being. Knowledge and what is considered the truth are variable and based on perception. Unity within this climate is perhaps impossible. However, for thoroughness, it is essential to highlight the values that contribute to political unity.

A fundamental pillar of unity is a shared identity encompassing a collective sense of belonging. This identity may be shaped by nationality, language as part of the culture, history, love, or shared values and aspirations. By recognizing and celebrating this shared identity, individuals within a polity develop a sense of pride and loyalty, reinforcing their commitment to the collective welfare.

A polity must establish common goals and a unified vision, aligning its members towards a shared future. When individuals understand and appreciate the significance of collective objectives, they are more likely to collaborate and work together towards their attainment. A clear and compelling vision provides a sense of direction, empowering citizens to overcome differences and concentrate on realizing the common agenda.

Unity flourishes in an environment of inclusive governance, where every voice is heard and respected. A polity that ensures equal participation and representation encourages a sense of ownership and accountability among its members. Inclusive decision-making processes, transparency, and open dialogue enable the diverse perspectives within a polity to contribute to the common good, fostering trust and cooperation.

A cohesive society where individuals respect and understand one another strengthens the fabric of unity. Promoting social cohesion involves building bridges across different groups, embracing diversity, and encouraging a sense of solidarity. Encouraging intercultural exchanges, organizing community events, and implementing policies that promote equal opportunities for all can help overcome divisions and enhance social integration within a polity.

Socioeconomic factors significantly influence a polity's unity. A thriving economy that ensures equal opportunities, reduces disparities, and provides social justice lays the foundation for a cohesive society. Addressing inequality and poverty and promoting inclusive economic policies not only improves the well-being of individuals but also reduces the potential for social unrest and division.

Clear and effective communication is crucial in building and sustaining unity within a polity. Open and honest communication channels facilitate dialogue, understanding, and individual collaboration. The media also plays a critical role by promoting responsible journalism that disseminates accurate information, encourages critical thinking, and fosters a sense of shared identity and purpose.

As stated elsewhere, education plays a critical role in shaping citizens who actively participate in the Polity. By promoting civic or political education, individuals acquire the knowledge, skills, and values necessary to engage responsibly in public affairs. Education systems emphasizing critical thinking, ethical values, and respect for diversity help nurture a sense of unity and active citizenship.

1.14 Considering democracy as a solution

To study Democracy, we should investigate it for what it is, what it does, and everything related to it. However, we should not impose our views and biases on how we dream, imagine, or feel. The views and opinions of the majority also need to be avoided, because we are not interested in the most common or majority consensus, but rather in the most Orthodox and truthful argument. Ironically, the truth is not always based on the majority's view, yet Democracy almost entirely relies on the majority's opinion. We will come back to this intrinsic part of Democracy. It is enough to say at this point that all of us, regardless of where or how we are raised, can achieve the truth if we set aside what we think we know and instead explore new and old subjects, such as democracy, as if they were uncharted territories. We should do so carefully and meticulously to ensure we learn everything about it.

Democracy is a heavily politicized subject, and many people will already have some knowledge about it. Because it is a political subject, many people have tried to use the term 'Democracy' to mean different things. Most are not true. Others from a generation or two ago wrote books they called "Democratic." In Libya, Gadhafi outlined the "democratic" system he wished to implement in his Green Book. He made his book compulsory reading for everyone to ensure they all knew its content. He was a very vocal supporter of "Democracy" and, ironically, a dictator from 1969 to 2011.

In Asia, before The Green Book, there was another book written by Mao in China called The Red Book. Mao Zedong was not only vocal about "Democracy". He was also the chairman of the Communist Party from 1949 to 1976. Again, that book was mandatory reading for everyone in the country. It expressed the ideas and ideologies the governing regime wanted people to know. Each one used Democracy as an agenda for alternative purposes.

Before those books, there were many other ideological books, and, at the time of writing these, the most influential were Capitalism and Communism. One viewed the world as a place of free trade, while the other viewed it as a place of isolation and almost monastic. Often, Western or Germanic nations would portray Capitalism as part of Democracy, and other Communist nations insisted that Communism was Democratic. It is impossible to attach anything as a prefix or suffix to Democracy without ruining or tarnishing it. To most philosophers, the truth is not always the radical extreme, but most certainly, the truth is upheld by the majority of evidence.

Neither Capitalism nor Communism is a government system but an economic model founded on financial philosophies. Due to the close association of these economic models with particular government systems, many believe these financial ideologies are intrinsic to Democracy. Many modern government systems use one of these ideologies, or a combination of them, as a basis for their economic models. We can have Capitalist systems working within a Monarchy, Aristocracy, or Democracy, just as we can have Communist systems working within a Monarchy, Aristocracy, or Democracy. It is enough to say that neither provided a solution to the world's problems, and neither can be claimed to be more or less democratic than the other. The books and ideologies mentioned earlier were, for the most part, ideologies imposed on people. They have been discussed here so that you are aware of the differences between what others write for political reasons and what is written here for philosophical reasons.

The very structure of a Democracy shields fundamental human rights. The people and their constitution establish these rights, making it much harder for a Democratic system to overstep or undermine them. In a Democracy, citizens have the right to free speech, assemble and meet, express their concerns, change the laws, serve as judges or jury members, and enforce the law. Not all at once, but through their passage, starting with cadetship and moving through to citizenship. Of course, this is what we know of Ancient Athens.

Democracy, according to the Ancient Athenian model, encompasses many tribes and encourages the participation of every citizen. Diversity is celebrated and highly regarded. However, the citizenry is limited to specific tribes. Other ethnicities and foreign participants weren't embraced. However, being a Democracy, those who were shunned had a pathway to becoming full citizens.

Peaceful conflict resolution is another attribute that the Ancient Athenian model presented. It allowed differing views and often conflicting tribes to settle matters fairly and peacefully. The rule of the people's law was deemed blessed by the divine. The ethos was to adhere to the laws and the system.

During the Ancient Athenian democracy, financial distribution and economic fairness were established. The system provided a method whereby the nation's wealth was at the people's disposal. Their ethical standards enabled them not to loot their city but prop it up to support themselves and others fairly. Each had two places of work: the city's administration and the job done for survival, whether exchanging goods and services or otherwise.

Often, people argue that democracy does not last very long, citing the Athenian model, in which an oligarchy and then a monarch took over. However, Democracy, as will be revealed, offered substantial stability and longevity to the system of administration. Unlike the violence found in other systems, Democracy enabled peaceful resolutions within society under strict, enforceable laws. Preceding the system of Democracy was a similar system known as Demarchy. Demarchy was considered a sound system, but often became unethical. Therefore, to change the better of the two systems, the one that fused higher-level ethics to the system and its laws was Democracy. Also, Demarchy meant the leadership of the people, while Democracy meant the holding of power by the people. As will be discussed, there is a subtle yet significant difference between the two systems.

Knowing this much about Democracy suggests it could be a real solution to many of society's problems. In review and to highlight this: 1.1 The biases of life experience are balanced by having a majority in leadership. 1.2 The stark divide between the wealthy and poor is not as dramatic in a Democracy; the people own the national treasury. 1.3 Poverty and Class distinction become more balanced but not perfectly balanced. There will always be one class that benefits more from a situation than others. 1.4 Innocent criminals and justice are placed in the hands of the people. We know that the majority are not always correct. Still, when the majority implements justice, there is less likelihood of perversion or corruption of justice, provided that the system is robust and ensures such measures. 1.5 Ethnicity issues become a redundant term in an actual Democratic state. Purely because the qualification to participate relies on a system of citizenry. Being a citizen overshadows any ethnic origins a person may have. 1.6 Religion and its impact take on a positive measure for all humanity within a democratic state. As noted, a tribe's religious orientation may identify it. Democracy and the systems used facilitate tribes of differing faiths. Democracy not only enables people to tolerate one another but also to work together in a mutually beneficial manner. 1.7 Individualism and the pack raises a concern that in a democracy, the majority is the decisive voice. However, when the individual case is more genuine, does Democracy have the intrinsic ability to propagate that truth? It depends on how the systems regarding assembly and meetings are organized. 1.8 The people and freedom are significant issues; freedom can't be guaranteed or offered; it is fought for and held onto. However, in a moment of indecisiveness, a majority can enslave itself to a minority. Democracy, at best, increases the likelihood of keeping the people free because individualism and minority interests are not adequately addressed or implemented. 1.9 Servitude, under a Democratic system, is to the people and for the people, thereby indirectly satisfying the individual concerns a person may have. 1.10 Systemic youth control will exist in every system, but how they are controlled will depend on the system used. In a democracy, this means that the culture, ideals, and laws of the people will control the youth. 1.11 The purpose of education, likewise, will be scoped by the people and forms a blend of things needing to be taught by parents, teachers, tutors, etc. 1.12 Other social divisions are also less likely to impede a Democratic state. The Democratic state, after all, unifies differences through its very acceptance of tribes and their ways. This review provides a pretext for further investigation, as it seems too good to be true that a Democratic state could solve a significant portion of our societal problems.

2. Defining democracy

"A democracy is a government system held and operated by the people."

To satisfy the eagerness to know what a Democracy is, let us make a preliminary definition for those unfamiliar with what it is. A democracy is a form of government in which power is held and exercised by the people or its citizens. It is a system in which the people form and operate the government's judiciary, enforcement, and legislative components. Every position within it is determined by drawing lots, known as sortition. Every issue is solved or resolved by a majority vote. No law, judgment, or action is permitted unless the people directly empower it. This definition should be taken casually, as it is not entirely comprehensive, and we have yet to prove it. More will be disclosed as we proceed.

Let us first look at the government and its purpose. We can begin by defining key terms. In a world where language evolves and words take on new meanings, it is essential to clarify specific terms. A government is an organized entity that governs and administers the political affairs of a polity. We need to define a few basic terms first, as some people may not be familiar with them. Governing and leading are two different things. Governance refers to an administration with authority over the people, but in a democracy, the people also have authority over the government. Leadership entails initiating a motion or action through others, but not necessarily through government or authority. A polity refers to the people living in a city and all their affairs, authority or powers, and, especially, the aspects leading to a social, organized, and united existence. Polity is almost synonymous with organized people. It typically refers to governance by the people and all matters related to that governance. A Polity is often mistakenly called a Civilization by Latin speakers, and the term Civic usually refers to matters about city dwellers. However, civilization and civic are distinct from the term 'polity'. Polity implies a State or kratos, a holding of power usually held by the people and their affairs. A Polity is the people of a city and its surrounding territories, and implies the issues and affairs of the people within it.

On the other hand, a civilization implies a greater degree of socialization or domestication of humans within a defined boundary. Civilization does not immediately mean the political affairs of city life, nor does it relate to matters revolving around people and their powers to govern and administer their state. Though the terms city and civic derive from the same roots in Latin and refer to city affairs, they do not become synonyms for the people's administrative affairs. These implied meanings of 'Civilization' stem from the term's use for thousands of years. Civilization, at the time of writing, can refer to people within an Empire, Kingdom, or Dictatorship. Polity is a term closely related to ancient Athenian Democracy because it was first used by the philosophers of that time to describe it. The terms Polity and Politeia often imply, but do not necessarily mean, liberty, freedom, and democracy. The association stems from the fact that the democratic city-states of Ancient Greece popularized the terms "polity" and "politeia." Polity usually refers to the physical entity, and Politeia is the dynamics of the people within the Polity. Much like Civics and Civilization, the Polity is the people who govern the Politeia. Polity and Politeia are preferred terms for discussing a group of people operating a Democracy.

When writing this book, most cities belong to a sea of combined cities known as nations. The concept of nations was a compromise between an empire and a city-state. Nations often contained several nationalities or ethnicities and were often composed of multiple city-state models. These united National cities can be part of a larger group commonly termed an alliance, league, union, commonwealth, or empire. It makes it difficult for some to visualize a state, or Kratos, a holding of power over one city by the majority of its people and their surrounding lands.

Furthermore, the level of comprehension most people have of a Polity is that it is an entity called a city-state, with the same autonomy and powers as nations do today. Polity, as described, is the holding of power by the people over a city and its state. Not the empirical manipulation of national entities that are further comprised of multiple cities. Nations initially found themselves in situations where leagues of free city-states formed. Leagues, as historians termed them, were known as combat alliances. However, in modern scenarios, when writing this, the nations formed under an empire are often vassal states that purport to be free and independent but lack the constitutional powers to be self-determining or to control their national entities.

Language, culture, religion, and ethics are arguably the most crucial elements of assimilation and unity within a polity. Also, a polity's geographical and physical conditions may help define it. For instance, a polity could be living on an island, a peninsula, a valley, or any group of people living in close proximity in a cultured and ethical manner. A polity can't be established if there is one member from each of a hundred islands or cities, and each island has a different language, culture, religion, or ethics. To some degree, many people would call this exclusiveness. However, what is being discussed is not racial or in any way related to the individuals' physical appearance. For a polity to exist, a degree of uniformity is required. That uniformity is usually based on cultural and behavioral tolerances. Some of us can love all humans without judging, but most of humanity can't. Most people seem to feel more secure when those around them behave and follow traditions and customs similar to their own. That is why a society is different from a polity. A polity requires the majority to work together; to do that, they must have some things in common. A society merely requires people to tolerate and live side by side with others without the functionality of working together in the self-administration of their city.

A polity requires order and several common cultural attributes. As mentioned, the most critical aspects are language, culture, religion, and ethics. In some colonized parts of the world, where people from diverse origins have migrated to settle within a geographically defined space, a process of assimilation gradually encourages individuals to adopt a common religion, language, and culture. The process is not always monodirectional. Also, certain things sourced from the minority influence the majority. The method that creates unity utilizes assimilation. Assimilation implies that people from different backgrounds adopt characteristics considered normal in their respective areas or regions. This homogeneity is both natural and forced, as its source can be derived from two places. The first force for assimilation is cultural, borne by the people and transmitted not by formal authority but primarily through imitation and conformity with the majority. The second method by which assimilation is created is by authority. That authority can be minority or majority-driven, a government formed by the people, or a minority governing the people. When a government enforces assimilation, it typically enacts laws and codes of conduct to implement this policy.

Without government, the people only have their opinions instead of the rule of law, and this often leads to forcing minorities into submission or assimilation by unjust force. The lynch mob mentality, or Ochlos, can emerge. Authorities typically impose their preferred language and cultural aspects on others. However, what they enforce is not limited to language, nor does it have to be good or worthy. Historically, racial, discriminatory, prejudiced, and some very obscure views were often forced onto minority groups and the majority within a city, nation, or empire. An Ochlos can be the source of tyranny in a government operated by the people. Yet tyranny can be administered equally well, if not better, by the few or individuals who control government.

In retrospect, cultural shifts and exchanges are typically passive because the most liked parts of a culture are usually absorbed quickly. This form of bi-directional assimilation, which we can refer to as cultural exchange, is the most common. Still, it is the slowest yet most frequently occurring source of assimilation worldwide. It is a powerful aspect of assimilation because it not only assimilates those within a particular boundary but can also assimilate foreign nations or polities. Cultural exchange encompasses fashionable music and art, unique cuisine, and other aspects of a foreign culture that become integrated into another culture. It may also be that youth culture influences the older culture locally. These changes are widespread worldwide. The most resistant are the isolated tribal cultures, which almost entirely isolate themselves from the influences of those around them.

What has been described accounts for the development of a pulsing, changing, and dynamic cultural shift. At its onset, a

Democratic state may involve the acceptance and love of many tribes. Eventually, these tribes will become indistinguishable if authority and culture reach a state of equilibrium. Sometimes, the tribal names are only symbolic; at others, they remain true to their original intent of preserving the tribe's identity and interests. The interests may be for the love of certain things, the utility value of certain things, or the commonness and similarity with their customs. The final phases of cultural exchange create an equilibrium. That equilibrium is not always balanced and may be skewed one way or another; this provides a reason for greater cultural exchange, and the process continues perpetually.

2.1 Historical assimilation and unity

In past and present empires, a similar effect of bi-directional assimilation occurred. Over time, an empire's chaos or dysfunctional sprawl eventually balances out through various assimilations, including language, religion, and culture. Yet, ultimately, whatever creates languages, culture, and identity is still functional within an empire. As new entities emerge, all empires eventually fragment. Therefore, regardless of how uniform the inhabitants are initially in terms of language, culture, and religion, all empires will eventually collapse.

This may occur when various pockets or areas of an empire fall into neglect, lose their communication links, or are not exposed to the empire's influence. Perhaps it is the ability to defend the stated borders. Usually, the extremities of an empire are the first to collapse, becoming not only military fronts but, in some cases, mere appendages without any real governance. Such places find it easy to continue changing their culture through the influence of those they come into contact with.

2.1.1 The Colonies

Immigration, migration, and settlement or colonization are sources of cultural influence. These also affect language and religion. We are aware of dialects and other regional differences between cities within any nation. Sometimes, especially in the new colonies, the language is not a new dialect but is altered locally to give it a distinct accent. These accents eventually evolve into dialects. In the Northern American States, many impoverished people began speaking the national language in what was considered an uneducated form. Historically, it has always been the uneducated who created languages. When people are isolated for a long enough period and form a close-knit relational community, tribe, or polity, they tend to share mannerisms, characteristics, language, culture, and religion. Therefore, over time, the uneducated and the isolated are the most likely to form new identities.

Small tribes often face this problem, as found in the Southern Indian Region, where many tribes wandered with minimal contact with others, and each had its own language. Although they lived similar lifestyles, they had their unique customs. Some tribes were unable to communicate with others living nearby. Additionally, in many cases, their offspring would leave to form new tribes, and over time, these tribes would often differ significantly within a single generation. New tribes created many languages and dialects, and an inability to understand and communicate effectively. Thus, they were limited in what they could achieve. However, large enough populations of specific language groups did exist, despite their constituents being dynamic; they maintained relative similarity across almost all cultural aspects.

Of the three things that tend to be part of the assimilation process, language is the most crucial in establishing a democratic government. Yet, having many people speak a similar language does not define a polity, but it does contribute to its identity and definition. In other words, a polity must work towards a homogeneous society, but some factors of homogeneity are more important than others. Those critical to our discussion would be those that enable the establishment of organization and order, and ultimately, a democratic polity. As much as we love independence, variation, and uniqueness, a polity requires uniformity in language, religion, belief system, and ethics. That does not necessarily mean issuing an official dictionary and enforcing a fixed grammar. Although it may include parts of such things, it should be dynamic. There is nothing worse than policing our language.

2.1.2 The Hellenistic Age

In contrast, the widespread use of Greek (Hellenic) at the time of Christ and after Alexander the Great, for instance, made it the first truly universal language in geopolitics. That universal language was called Koine, the street version of Greek rather than Attic or other distinct dialects. Yet even with a single language and definitive boundaries, the empire still collapsed, and the people's culture, although enhanced, remained unique and endured until the time of writing this.

Historically, this is evident in the spread and sustenance of empires. Of course, some aspects of empires and the military may have helped open borders, but generally speaking, language spreads because people want to learn it, and that desire is usually related to some benefit, such as earning an income. Empires tend not to represent an ethnicity or nationality, but rather a mode of living through assimilated people. It was a way of incorporating good ideas and the best aspects of another culture, embracing those foreign influences as our own, and then inspiring others to do the same. It was a sprawl based on copying each other.

Herodotus describes something similar in much more detail through his works known as the Histories: *"The naming of almost all the gods has come to Hellas from Egypt: for that, it has come from the Barbarians I find by inquiry is true, and I am of opinion that most probably it has come from Egypt, because, except in the case of Poseidon and the Dioscuroi (in accordance with that which I have said before), and also of Hera and Hestia and Themis and the Charites and Nereïds, the Egyptians have had the names of all the other gods in their country for all time"* (Herodotus, 1920, 2.50.1).

It is irrelevant to our investigation of democracy as to who first named the Pagan Gods. The point is that assimilation through copying each other was in motion. First, the Greeks began copying others and adopting their customs, and others did the same. Herodotus, whether he is correct on where the Greeks learned their alphabet or not, or whatever other facts he gives, is of little concern to us in this philosophy. We know that his history mentions copying as a form of uniting cultures, and this was most evident in Egypt at the time, so he spent a significant portion of his history writing about it. Artifacts of similar characteristics are also found from that period, and, according to many archaeologists, they represent a widespread Hellenistic culture. Several indicators suggest that much of the ancient world communicated ideas openly during the same period. Historians refer to this period as the Golden Age in Greece. They usually date this period to around 450 BC or 500 BC, and extend it to 350 BC. 350 BC roughly indicates the period just before the rise of Alexander III of Macedon, also known as Alexander the Great.

So, we are not talking about a language forced by military might onto people. Nor are we talking about an administrative language that people learn to advance their careers. Between 500 BC and 400 BC, a unique period in human history occurred, as for the first time, a people, whether deliberately or not, began rapidly spreading innovations such as writing, mathematics, open trade, coinage, agriculture, and more. We know from our archaeologists and historians, many of whom, that there was a seemingly homogenized mode of life during the period known as antiquity. Each historical period had its fashions, music, and traditions. However, during the Golden Age, these things reached a pinnacle, not just in Greece or Athens but everywhere that came into contact with the sprawling universal culture. Giving that culture a name is unimportant, but we are speaking of Hellenism and the Hellenistic period for clarity. Civilization was used to describe it, but Politea was preferred in Athens.

Alexander did not spread Hellenism alone; it was already spreading, and he merely facilitated its further spread. Many polities were highly tolerant of foreigners, fostering cultural fusion across the East. We know this because the Greek-speaking Celts, or Gauls, populated Galatia in Anatolia, as the New Testament epistle to the Galatians referred to them. We know that before the rise of the Roman Empire, the Celts produced the Athenian Owl and other Greek-style coins in places like Marseille in France, extending to Britain. Although largely undocumented, many of these coins have been cataloged in various academic databases. Needless to say, the Diadochi or Alexander coins are found throughout East and Southeast Asia. The coins indicate that assimilation and unity often involve a common or similar currency.

The Greek philosopher Aristotle believed education played a crucial role in shaping individuals and societies. His writings emphasized the importance of educating citizens on shared values and virtues, thus contributing to their assimilation into a common cultural framework. Early attempts to educate significantly impacted academia and language usage, facilitating synchronization with surrounding political entities.

The Library of Alexandria, established in Egypt during the Hellenistic period, symbolized intellectual exchange and cultural assimilation. Scholars from different regions congregated there, translating texts into Greek and disseminating knowledge across diverse cultures, fostering assimilation through the exchange of ideas. Further, the Egyptian example was personified by Ptolemy of Egypt, one of Alexander's former generals and Archon of Egypt, who ordered the translation and compilation of the Hebrew scriptures, which became known as the Old Testament or Septuagint.

The Greeks also used language as part of culture, religion, ethics, and law to perpetuate a drive towards the assimilation of surrounding peoples by creating a holistic synchronicity. It was a mixture of cultural and authority-based influences; however, the Greek example demonstrates that the population was driving the assimilation.

2.1.3 The Roman Example

Uniformity and assimilation beyond a certain point can be suppressive, and these are characteristics of Empires more than Polities. Within an empire, many ethnicities, cultures, and languages exist. Yet for a very long time during the Roman rule, people of varying ethnicities identified themselves as Roman. People who would be considered to be of a different ethnicity by nationalistic standards maintained that their ethnicity was Roman. The Romans adopted a "Pax Romana" (Roman Peace) policy to integrate diverse territories and cultures into a unified Roman identity. This assimilation was achieved through various means, including the establishment of a standard legal system, promoting a lingua franca, and spreading Roman customs and traditions.

A Roman philosopher, Cicero, emphasized the concept of natural law, asserting that all human beings share a standard set of moral principles from a divine entity. This idea provided a philosophical basis for the Roman Empire's assimilation efforts. If it wasn't pagan, it was the Christian state religion. Furthermore, the Roman Empire emphasized the inherent unity and equality of all individuals. However, a significant disparity arose during the lifetime of the Roman Empire.

Scholars believe the Roman Empire collapsed because the various ethnicities that came to be part of the empire eventually began to form their own national identities. However, in retrospect, what we call ethnicity depends on the methods we use to define or measure it. Understandably, people wanted their language, culture, religion, and state and cities to govern themselves. So, when uniformity and assimilation were decided on the results of bloody swords, it backfired to some degree. This period of nationalization came towards the end of the Roman Empire, demonstrating that it could no longer offer the protection and security it once did. The city's identity and territory were Greek, as evidenced by snippets about the final siege of Constantinople, which marked the end of the Roman Empire. The term Roman was no longer considered a universal or uniting identity. The Chronicle of Theophanes the Confessor presents a different account. By the mid-700s, Constantinople had lost its original identity. Instead of using one of the several Greek historians to cite, a modern Italian source has been chosen to remove the chance of bias: Thomas the Eparch, an East Roman government official, and Joshua Diplovatatzes, a nobleman, wrote, according to Pertusi,

"Innanzi tutto si deve ricordare come e in che modo la grande e nobile e potentissima città imperiale che si trova in territorio greco col nome di Costantinopoli sia stata conquistata e. presa dall'imperatore turco: questo si trova scritto qui, e avvenne il 28 maggio 1452, cioè il quarto giorno dopo sant'Urbano? " (Pertusi, 1976, p. 234)

In paraphrased translation, "First and foremost, we must recall how the great, noble, and most powerful imperial city located in Greek territory and called Constantinople was conquered and taken by the Turkish emperor. This is found written here, and it happened 28 May 1452, that is four days after the feast of St Urban;..." (as translated from Pertusi, 1976, p. 234). As a note, the cited date, 28 May 1452, is often recalculated as 29 May 1453.

We know that the histories of the West that survived were primarily composed in Greek, with some Italian sources. This modern work shows even more clearly that Greek was probably the language of choice, although both languages were widely spoken in the city. Thomas the Eparch and Joshua Diplovatatzes, as translated by Pertusi, lead us to believe that the city was nationalizing.

Several indicators demonstrate that the empire was nationalizing, such as the emergence of newly independent nations within the former Eastern Roman territory. It makes sense that as the Roman Empire collapsed, it fragmented into smaller political entities, known as nations. Nations themselves are a collection of cities. It is sufficient for us to highlight that commonality and assimilation towards a seemingly common culture were achieved through methods proven to be both culturally and authority-based.

2.1.4 The Former Yugoslav States

Jumping ahead by a millennium, the wars that tore apart the Southern Slavic nations in the late 1990s were perfect examples of how, within a seemingly homogenous state, Yugoslavia, there were enough differences to nationalize the existing populations. The seemingly homogenous state collapsed and then reformed into smaller national entities. So, this raises the question of whether there is ever truly a homogeneous state. It may work toward homogeneity on many fronts, but the reality is that a population is as unique as its individuals. People from one generation differ from those of another. We all have differences, which are reflected in the characteristics of the political entities we form. Even with a common language, heritage, culture, and even a similar religion, something can always distinguish, separate, or even tear apart a political entity. The wars in the southern Slavic regions of Europe led to the formation of nations based on religious or denominational affiliations.

There are large populations that speak a single language, even across oceans and around the world. They formed pockets of large populations with a common language, culture, and, to a lesser extent, religion. At the time of writing, the largest linguistic groups were Arabic, Latin, Germanic, Mongolian, Cyrillic (including Russian and Slavic), and Hindi. Among the Germanic languages, English is the most prominent. Chinese-Mandarin is the largest language group among Mongolians, and among the Cyrillic languages, Russian is the largest. If we were to tabulate the religions and cultures of these places, they would be, to some extent, entwined culturally but distinguished by their languages and religion: Arabic and Islam, Latin and Catholic Christianity, Germanic and Protestant Christianity, Mongolian and Atheism, Cyrillic and Orthodox Christianity, Hindi and the Hindu faith.

2.1.5 Academia

It is essential to recognize that, without an empire or army, the world's people have already shared and achieved academic success. There was no need for an empire or an army to force people to speak one language, to wear certain clothes, or to be anything that a minority forced upon them. So much literature was being written and read that knowledge became very accessible, as much as the advent of modern technologies that provide information on personal electronic devices. Except in those days, it was not a popular company, business, or government providing the information. It was the people writing for the people. Before printing was invented, people handwrote books and sold them at markets or in the agora. Also, in those days, people considered learning a language beneficial, and Greek was just another language they added to their list.

It was not only the academic subjects but also religion and mythologies that began to merge and spread. Once religions and mythologies began to merge, similar ethical principles would inevitably emerge. Gone were the days of cities being founded upon sin, as described by the Septuagint regarding the cities Sodom and Gomorrah. Accurate, symbolic, or metaphorical, the story describes a period when people founded unethical cities. They were so unethical that they were destroyed entirely. These unethical cities symbolize a historical reference to the Ochlos, a form of corrupted democratic rule. There were also common ethical principles in these places where civilization and polities had begun to emerge. Just like everything else, humanity began incorporating the best attributes of other cities, including their ethics. Similar faiths, codes of conduct, laws, and other things seemed to emerge to guide them.

Because we have entered an area that may seem tangential to the topic of Democracy, let me emphasize that the link between all these previous things is that they help define us. Since we have established that a Polity requires a certain amount of similarity among its citizens, we also need to determine whether these historical groupings of people into religious, linguistic, and cultural groups constitute the Political entity, or whether it is the Political entity that creates the uniformity.

We can try to define or unite ourselves around the foods we eat, but not everyone will have the same taste for them. We can define ourselves by the clothes we wear, but not everyone will wear the same clothes. Historically, we have united around our ideals because the poorest and the richest can understand a concept or idea. An idea is not limited to a material exchange, so that everyone can afford it. Religion and the language used to deliver it create a partnership. Language and religion, or the lack thereof, form ideals that spread easily and are readily followed. We can't build a culture based purely on the accumulation or consumption of material goods. For instance, you can't limit citizenship to someone who owns a certain amount of wealth or possesses a particular material or item. However, it remains questionable whether the citizens must also have some knowledge and experience of what a democratic state is. It is a system dependent on our understanding, and if we know what a democracy is or should be, then we can operate and participate accordingly. However, it is more than this; operating a democracy also depends on knowledge of diverse ideas and information.

Ideas or skills may define us, such as keeping warm in the ice, surviving using the oceans or waterways, or living in places others can't. These types of things become cultural, and all these cultural ideas eventually define us. By cultural idea, I mean an idea passed from generation to generation so that it becomes intrinsic to the group of people who have passed that idea down through the generations. However, unlike the ideas that define our physical existence, other things, such as ethics, religion, and language, serve a higher purpose and, ultimately, form a stronger bond.

While physically important cultural aspects can help define us, especially in specific geographical locations, such as the skills of Mediterranean mariners and the skills of Yupik ice dwellers, they alone will not define the Yupik people living in the Mediterranean or the Mediterranean people living in the ice. Our environment plays a significant role in shaping our culture, and when we are removed from the environment that has fostered a particular culture, we also change our culture. It seems natural for humanity to adapt by modifying its culture to suit its environment and the pressures of survival. Sometimes, our culture and the people around us influence our lives. How we live our lives can be defined by the system we adopt to govern the polity or group of people. Yet this latter thing is not a physical, cultural matter.

Culture can also be enhanced by the metaphysical relationships we establish. The higher-level things passed on by language and action are usually culture's physical, survival and material aspects. However, among those things are also ethics and religion. We know this from historical accounts. For some peculiar reason, almost everyone has a Creation story, regardless of religion or faith. In some instances, those creation stories were passed down for millennia. Another strange aspect is that they share an unsettling similarity. These verbal histories, whether considered tales or stories, held immense significance for the people and were passed down for many generations. These higher cultural aspects typically form the pinnacle of human ideology as they are common to humanity. The way those ethics and religions are practiced, what they believe, and the details vary immensely. On the other hand, religious communities share similarities despite the details of their particular faiths. Therefore, it stands that for a polity to be united, it does not necessarily matter what the religion, or lack of it, is, as long as they are common enough to be considered stable or reasonably homogenous and compatible.

Similarly, popular ideas are shaped by how they are expressed. They can be difficult to articulate; therefore, few people understand them or agree or disagree with those ideas. However, academically, everything mentioned in this section plays a role in determining how academia influences its students through education and ideas. A minority may pursue academia, but they have the onus to share their knowledge concisely and clearly.

2.1.6 Genetic Attributes

Could we be defined by any different set of attributes that identify us? The Amazons were said to define themselves by a matriarchy. That raises the question: could we unite by gender? Some may see many faults in the idea. After all, we need both males and females. Giving one dominion over the other has been a perennial issue throughout human history, and cultures have dealt with it differently. More than just gender, almost every possible way to unite people has been tried at some point. In ancient times, matriarchy was often associated with war due to its connection to Hera and Athena. There are global equivalent goddesses of war found throughout the world. Christianity produced a form of Patriarchy for a short period. Yet over the years, it seems the West has become a Matriarchal system, while the East has become a Patriarchal system. While many argue that both East and West have predominantly male leadership, it is essential to clarify that a true Matriarchy would require a female to set the laws and govern, which is typically achieved through monarchies ruled by Queens. However, the manifestation of a Matriarchy does not always end with a single female leader. Sometimes, Matriarchy refers to the role of women in a given society. Polities that have women who are free and able to participate in all facets of society are usually called Matriarchies. In such places, their men shave their beards to look feminine or transgender. This has been the case for over a thousand years. Suppose we intend to segregate and separate by gender. In that case, the population assumed to be a matriarchy would liberate women and give them seemingly the same powers as men. In contrast, the Patriarchy would not provide any liberty for females and instead would elevate the males.

The phenomena of Matriarchy vs. Patriarchy are found at the time of writing between the West and the East. It is typically done to preserve boundaries, borders, and the self-interests of the few. The laity usually has no idea why their males are expected to shave. The reason some military men shaved their beards in ancient times is no different from today. They, too, had a period of flux between the matriarchal and patriarchal systems. In some generations, women had more liberty; in others, less. As these things fluctuated, so too did the culture or fashion. In the late 1800s, most European men depicted in photographs typically wore beards. Yet, in the 1900s, most men were depicted as shaven. When considering war photos, many European armies follow a tradition of shaving. That represented the matriarchy. Europe, particularly Greece, had a tradition of Patriarchy and bearded men, as well as soldiers, but this also fluctuated and changed. Therefore, although gender-specific views can unite, the two opposing views seem to have dominated society throughout history. A polity would need to decide which of the two systems it requires. In other words, gender-based assimilation can be used for many purposes and is limited in its use to unite. It has a place in distinguishing one culture from another, but rarely serves any practical purpose. In a mixed system, it could be argued that women were restricted from the Athenian assemblies for safety and security but enjoyed rights similar to those of men.

The topic of gender is often raised in political issues, and yet it belongs in a category of issues that are genetic and unchangeable. From what we know of history and what we see in other cultures, the worst possible selection of things to unite a people are those that relate to unchangeable physical attributes, such as a person's skin, hair, or eyes, or their intellect or deformities. Gender, height, and weight are generally fairly stable, so they have been used to unite people. Because if we find that the majority are of a given height and a tiny minority are giants or dwarves, the minority can be targeted and blamed like scapegoats.

Throughout history, some leaders have blamed various minority groups based on their genetic attributes. We know that, eventually, many of those minority groups were persecuted.

However, alliance and uniformity based on most genetic features fail because people vary too much, and we are far too complex to be united solely by our physical attributes. A white nation or a black nation, a tall nation, a blonde nation, or a dark nation? All these things were tried in ways that united people in various places. Yet what happens when a tall person falls in love with a short person, or an overweight person falls in love with a petite person? What happens when a blonde person marries a dark-haired person? Over time, these characteristics evolve, and the population and its gene pool (genetic composition) change accordingly. But it is more than this. The basis of unity based on superficial genetic characteristics has repeatedly proven to fail.

The same can be said of our mental or cognitive abilities. Some assume it is correct to say that one person is more intelligent than another, but in reality, we learn different things. Those differences do not make one person more intelligent than another. Most of us are generally of the same intelligence. The only valuable thing that helps distinguish our minds from others is not the mind's ability or the use of terms like learning ability, logic, and intelligence, but the amount of truth contained by that mind. Since wisdom represents the truths that we know, it is somewhat more valuable in a democracy than the ability to learn or memorize. Therefore, what we know seems far more important than how we look, primarily when operating a government or Kratos.

2.1.7 Laws

In almost all political structures, the government system implemented makes it mandatory to perpetuate that same system. For example, an Autocracy will enforce laws that promote the idea that the only acceptable system of governance is the Autocracy. The same can be said of any existing constitutional system. These are called restrictive constitutions that define the type of government. Almost all governments at the time this was written had restricted Constitutions. That is very different from the Athenians, who had an open constitution. It didn't stop anyone from implementing an Oligarchy or a Monarchy instead of a Democracy. Although some restrictions were imposed, there was a fluctuation and a shift, with unclear boundaries between Democracy, Aristocracy, and Oligarchy.

Aristotle first noted that there were several pathways to enslavement. As described elsewhere, slavery by law is similar to the concept that laws and their application can also promote assimilation. Subtle laws may not give the impression of being enslaved; however, these are subjective matters, and a person forced to learn religion, language, or culture may feel trapped and enslaved. Over-reaching with the intent of the law can have opposite outcomes. It is, therefore, essential to establish that although the law can facilitate assimilation, the extent to which it restricts the momentum of others must be balanced.

2.1.8 Citizenship

In the Ancient Athenian model, one thing united people in the democratic assemblies: Citizenship. However, Citizenship was restricted by age and gender. Although women could participate in court and use public services, they were excluded from military service, police duties, and governance. That raises another set of questions: for example, can a polity be united by ideals other than those that govern it? Can we claim equality while limiting governance by age or gender? Can one set of rules and ideals apply to one facet of a population and another set of ideals to another part of that population? Do double standards and variations of our ideals fail a philosophically correct system? While the Athenians resolved some of their issues of unity by introducing the concept of citizenship, what defines that citizenship becomes essential. The purpose of Athenian citizenship was to produce unity by qualification. Citizenship was not a qualification explicitly acquired, but rather one that defined a typical Athenian male. They also had to be of age to be considered candidates for citizenship and leadership.

Excessive pressure upon a people to maintain a particular view, culture, religion, or ideal is usually seen in oppressive states. The reverse pressure of people forcing their will on the government can, amongst other manifestations, manifest as anarchy, instability, and chaos. Typically, we observe that chaos emerges when government oppression or suppression reaches an unacceptable level. There are, however, passive resistances that are equally or more successful over time. Martyrdom, for example, became a big thing in past societies as they used the death of believers as a testimony of faith. While the Romans were busy feeding Christians to lions, they were inadvertently creating martyrs of the faith. Authority may force certain behaviors upon people and perhaps even change their minds over time, but people can also change their culture over a long period.

Only when the government system, or the mechanism by which governance is structured, does not allow the will of the people to manifest, does violence and chaos truly arise. Also, we consider Power difficult to relinquish, and those with the most power find it hardest to relinquish. When people wish for a part of that power or seek to interfere with it, it almost seems as if all forms of philosophy aside from those of military tactics are excluded. You see, arguments are often won by armies, not by the genius of a few or eloquent speeches. In many circumstances, words can strengthen arguments, prolong peace, advance agendas, and have significant value. However, the scariest thing to consider is that the person with the biggest stick wins an argument. The clout in a democratic system derives from the population. The people may be passive and peaceful, but their numbers alone constitute significant power. The virtue of temperament of the people will conclude their arguments. The argument's outcome will also be good if the people are good. Suppose a population count contributes to the outcome, as through a vote, the majority, usually but not always, favors peace, wisdom, and words over war and punishment. However, that is not always the case; therefore, it is vital to have specific guidelines for what is expected of a citizen. These guidelines should be systematic and entrenched within the overall culture and system. Whatever attributes are given deep concern and regard amongst the majority will determine what is expected from the citizens' attributes. As such, we hope these attributes will be manifested, propagated, and nurtured in such a system.

It is better to resolve matters by words alone, leading to polities that live freely and openly. Also, it is disturbing to speak of, but deserves mention, the brutality of a polity or society within a war should never be used to form a cultural citizenry plan. In those environments, philosophy is often pushed aside, and zeal, hatred, and all the most negative emotions run high. The least educated are often zealous for war, yet the oligarchs often determine and wage it. In any case, armies can sometimes inadvertently cause harm to their masters as well. Armies may win a battle or argument by force, but the repercussions of their actions are never known immediately following the battle. Only after the war do we begin to realize the significance of each battle and its effects.

In most cases, wars have been fought for misguided reasons, and their outcomes have created a world marked by animosity, suspicion, and even paranoia. Force, therefore, while seemingly potent in resolving differences, is a detriment to unity because it instead creates communities that are unable to function openly and freely. The most crucial lifestyle attribute for people is the ability to operate openly and freely. The type of culture within a polity can enhance the need for openness and freedom. Therefore, citizenship can unite, as the Athenians did; however, the scope of the qualification is not to create an exclusive club or an oppressive, overtly forceful populace. However, it did aim to exclude several categories of people, and two types of citizenship were considered: residents, such as those held by women, and the official citizenry, as already discussed. The scope of citizenship for unity is to unite like-minded people while simultaneously requiring them to meet the qualifications as citizens under the state's laws. More will be discussed later. For now, we establish that citizenship is a key concept in defining the governing system. Therefore, it is pivotal in forming and establishing unity within a population.

2.1.9 Customs

Cultural equilibrium manifests within a population through various mechanisms. If we look at a mixed population within a particular city, the inhabitants can begin learning each other's customs. Those that are transferable will often transfer first. The ones based on survival are among the transferable skills or customs. However, certain foods may be forbidden in some cultures and religions, yet the city or polity may rely on those foods for survival. That suggests that not everything can be easily transferred between two people from different cultures. However, when transferability can occur without imposing much on existing cultural or religious norms, these things will transfer between the populations involved. That transfer of culture is usually associated with passive assimilation, and it occurs in every society or polity. Usually, the majority sets an example, but in some instances, the minority can have a particularly significant impact. However, let's highlight that passive assimilation is not entirely true. All forms of assimilation are, to some extent, forced or coerced, yet some occur with minimal effort towards change or resistance. For example, some societies offer seductive assimilation, like those where material and liberal customs entice others and tempt them to partake. Such cultures are not truly passive. They have installed mechanisms to seduce people into a particular way of life. Therefore, the first type of assimilation is one in which either population within a society adopts the customs of the other, driven by perceived need or essential adaptation. Those needs or essential adaptations usually center on what is perceived as important for survival and well-being.

The transfer of skills, such as diving into the ocean or sea, moving through snow, fishing, hunting, gathering, and farming, defines essential cultural exchange. However, for clarity in some polities, the ability to look and find work becomes part of the crucial cultural exchange. In prisons such as detention camps, prisons of war, and the like, certain behaviors become common for both inmates and the authorities.

In modern times, the study of organizational culture has emerged to understand and describe the micro-cultures within large business operations. Many organizational cultural attributes are similar to those in other hierarchical systems, particularly where workers have the least say. In those examples, the force that shapes organizational culture comes from those who lead the operation.

In some instances, however, people try to mimic those in power or wealth and engage in behaviors they perceive as similar to those of their organization's leaders. Youth are the most vulnerable to this mentality, as they often consider authority to be the most credible. Mimicry of the people or those in power both contribute to what has been referred to as passive assimilation. It is becoming clear that a complex combination of factors and aspects of a polity will lead to a passive, non-forced transfer of culture. What makes a person behave like another person is incredibly varied, but the crux is that there is some benefit. Based on cultural exchanges such as Artistic and Creative, Culinary, Language and Literature, Religious and Spiritual, Education and Academic, Tourism and Travel, and Technology and Media, an exchange may occur, for the most part, passively. If it is not a personal gain or benefit, it can also be a gain of political identity and a role within the respective polity.

2.1.10 Ideals

Another type of cultural exchange typically involves exchanging things that cannot be easily changed, such as ideals, religion, and language. Usually, these more static aspects of culture are more difficult to adapt to. When two groups speak different languages but live in the same city or region, they tend to assimilate more slowly. Because the change process is slower, it usually takes several generations to realize a high level of assimilation. Being of Greek ancestry, I have seen an entire Greek population almost fully assimilate into its surrounding culture within one generation. Culturally, different populations create subgroups within the population, but these subgroups are not indefinite. Among the most challenging aspects of transferring in any society are the ideals of the people and the authority. When ideals and ideologies transfer, the process usually requires force, whether subtle, systemic, or violent. A society can fragment into various factions, causing physical and/or verbal harm when these restricted or static cultural aspects are altered by force.

When passively enacted, unity through ideals leads to greater unity among people, as they aspire to something that remains relatively unchanged across generations. It constantly influences how certain things are done, including unity and assimilation. It is difficult to accept different ideals; however, this does not mean the transfer is always forced, as observed in many situations. The assimilation of people with a particular religion has been fully assimilated into secular and alternative faith systems. One of the most underestimated forces is that of marriage. Many individuals change their faith or ideals through marriage to fulfill the requirements of marriage.

Another form of assimilation occurs through submission, often when one group is much larger than any other group within the city. The type of effect is derived from a lack of tolerance. It is a case of aggressive, minimal, or forced assimilation. Similarly, we have little tolerance for the injustices of a system; therefore, we tend not to tolerate people behaving unjustly. However, love for humanity may transcend all faults; yet some behaviors make coexistence difficult. That is true for those who practice heinous crimes of the worst type as part of their subculture. In such cases, the majority become enforcers of the righteousness expected and take whatever actions they can to force assimilation into the righteous situation. Usually, the outcomes are not very successful, and there is an attempt to aggressively or forcibly apply the laws or righteousness upon others. The result is typically minimal assimilation. The perpetrators of injustice often hide, lie, conceal, and evade detection to continue committing their injustices.

2.1.11 Authoritative Influence

Authoritative assimilation and unity were prevalent in the new colonies, where they allowed various immigrants to enter but predominantly favored one group. When immigrants come from an unfavoured group or one culturally very different, there is a degree of hostility towards them by the populace and, to some extent, by the lower executive arms of authority. Many new cities require mandatory language skills and often give preference to certain religions and nationalities. This is done to maintain a common language and religion. Therefore, there is a high extent of authority-based assimilation.

Additionally, the new colonies lacked many things that could attract people voluntarily to settle there and mimic the local populace. Aside from the material culture and the physical aspects of their polities, there is little in terms of behavior or tradition that attracts newcomers. Most people enter for security, wealth, and financial gain, but few, if any, enter to truly embrace the culture. Many people from older cultures migrate to the new colonies and feel that many aspects of their lives are missing. Often, this creates a traveling syndrome in which people travel vast distances to be with their families for a moment, experience their customs, undertake religious pilgrimages, or rejuvenate their well-being, among many other less popular reasons. Eventually, when those colonies mature, they will evolve and develop customs and cultures that others will want to adopt. But for now, those attracted to it have lived in the colonies for at least a generation and ultimately know no other way of life. It has been described as a blank canvas, and the people decorate it. However, many subtle government impositions, along with a few influential actors, shape outcomes.

In addition to the tendency to create a passively homogenous polity, a Polity is exposed to many authoritarian forces. This includes the tendency to unite globally under one oligarchy, economic incentives and developments both abroad and locally, migration levels and sources, Government policies and laws, conflicts, and their impact. All these factors and more are utilized to create the impression that rule by an oligarchy is legitimate.

Imperialism, globalization, or any tendency to create an umbrella system over a polity's government can affect a polity's course. The impacts of such imperialism can place immense changes upon a people and their polity, to the extent that the arms of enforcement will detain and treat their citizens without any consideration of otherwise local political rights. It is a recurring pattern observed in the history of Rome, from ancient to modern times. Where a single authoritative culture is forced upon the subdued, in some cases, the subdued are unaware they have been suppressed; therefore, imperial influences permeate.

Typically, in a world dominated by a few individuals, the economic and currency systems are also controlled by the same oligarchy. In this way, economic factors, such as one country receiving preferential treatment for certain benefits, may attract others who have no connection to the oligarchy but possess sufficient power and wealth to take advantage of the situation. For example, when a particular country becomes a manufacturing hub for oligarchs, others may take advantage of it. That creates an incentive to use specific economic benefits. That is used when speaking to coerce the population into accepting and purchasing certain technologies for economic reasons.

At the time of writing, migration levels and the source of those migrations are usually controlled by oligarchic policies. The composition and number of them influence the overall impact they have on a polity. For example, so long as the majority of the migration is from the parental nation, which speaks the same language, shares the same customs, and has the same religion or lack thereof. The majority will passively impact the minorities. However, the government's subtle tweak at the inlet determines the impact on the polity. In everyday use, there are systems of migrant vote harvesting where the oligarchs admit minority groups into their colony, and the government at the time is seen as a savior and receives the migrant vote. At first, these groups appear out of place with the rest of the population; however, strict authoritative influences systematically create a cultural shift.

Government policies and laws are the weapons used against a polity under a Monarchy or Oligarchy. Where the few administer government, laws are rarely written expressly for the benefit of the people. Some laws, such as criminal codes, may appear on the surface to protect the weak; however, not all crimes defined in this manner serve that purpose. The trespass law, for example, tends to protect landowners. However, some laws regarding aggressive theft and other serious crimes apply to both the Oligarchs and those they subdue.

Conflicts and their impact can be local or abroad. The elite who form the global oligarchy take it upon themselves to wage wars every 20 or so years. They have a significant major war every fifty years. These usually last five years, and the system is reset to one of reprieve until the next minor war occurs every twenty years. In the lead-up to this time, the elite staged a pandemic crisis to replace war. In the lead-up to the pandemic, we had the 1920s' WWI, the 1940s' WWII, the 1950s' Korean War, the 1970s' Vietnam War, the 1990s' Gulf War, and the 2000s' Iraq War, and then we were due for war in 2020, but instead, they chose to stage a pandemic. It was, perhaps, an attempt to cause havoc and have the same impact as the post-war eras of the past. However, the effect was not as expected, and the same elites contemplated a 2030 War incident to reset the system and bring about the changes they wanted. At the time of writing, the Near East had begun a war, and another war was already underway in the Ukraine.

Economic factors, such as inflation, are linked to almost every war. Inflation, where one thing costs more than the previous year, is not as market-driven. A global oligarchy drives it. The Oligarchs determined many generations ago that if they could reduce the monetary value, then anyone who, by chance, accumulated enough wealth to threaten their system would lose value every moment. The Oligarchs controlled the making of the currency and were immune to things like inflation. This system works well for the Oligarchs. For example, a person with around 35 English Pounds or around 70 Australian Dollars could buy a city block of land, approximately an acre in size, in the 1930s (The West Australian, 24 December 1932). At the time of writing, they were selling properties that were 1/12 the size of those in the 1930s, or approximately 390 square meters. They cost about 6,429 times as much on average and are 40 kilometers or more from the city. Surprisingly, people still purchase these micro-properties, no matter how absurd the situation may be. They perceive it as an opportunity rather than as a form of enslavement. Generally, they are mimicking their parents and peers. Therefore, in this way, those with something of material value undergo a diminishing of that value as the years progress. Inflation is a systematic trickery of the few over the many.

Central banks, government policies, market forces such as making only micro properties available within workplace distances, oligarchic direct influence, corruption by demanding more for the cost of living, rent-seeking behavior, and economic structure are all significant contributions to inflation, and these also happen to be mainly under the control of the Oligarchy. If the state were democratic, the same would be said of democracy. That is, the people in a Democracy would ultimately control these factors. However, as stated while writing this, there is no Democracy or demarchy in the world at the time of writing. The impact of oligarchical and monarchical rule is evident at the time of writing, and the influence of authority is seen as a significant catalyst for a cultural shift on many fronts.

2.1.12 Assimilation and The Polity

As stated, many people who share a common language, culture, and religion do not constitute a polity on their own. Even with the surrounding territories, the term Polity becomes obsolete once those regions encompass another city. Polity is very much centered on the people of one city and the area they need to survive, including villages, hunting grounds, and other essential resources. But two cities can't exist in a city. The ancients, such as Socrates, Plato, and Aristotle, considered a Polity to be the people of a polis and their affairs. The term matured to imply a city-state or one city, its surrounding region, and the people who lived within it. Indicating that a polity exists across more than one city is like suggesting that a person lives in two cities simultaneously. The polity and citizenship are very much tied to the city-state.

Also, it was mentioned earlier that bringing people from many different cities together on the same island does not create a polity. There is no contradiction to the fact that we also mention that land and territory play a part in defining a polity. I will explain promptly. Unless the individuals all share essential attributes that allow them to form an order, express their desires, communicate their ideas, and administer their governing system, then a Polity cannot form. Therefore, while the social system creates pressure towards a homogeneous state, the State must also be clearly defined in the minds of those within it. Otherwise, individualism, minority groups, fragmentation, and lack of unity arise. Some attributes of people must unite them so that they wish to work together and form the idea of a kratos, or state or condition of power and authority. If there are ten families on an island, each with its own language, culture, and religion, they will most likely not be able to assimilate or unite initially. Instead of one polity forming on the island, ten polities will form. These emerging polities will have a boundary; otherwise, they will feud over resources. We know this from human history and how tribes and nations define their territories.

We also know that sometimes arbitrary, artificial, and imperial borders cause as many problems as, or more than, the absence of borders or defined territory. A third-party or foreign party placing borders on a Polity can lead to enormous problems. For instance, if an artificial border created by a third party crosses a part of a territory that a particular ethnicity or polity considers its own, then problems arise. The island of Cyprus was, and still is at the time of writing, torn in two by such a border during its partial occupation by Turkish forces from 1974 until the time of writing and possibly beyond. The Green line dividing the island is an arbitrary border or neutral band running the island's length. The "Green Zone", as it is officially known, has within it a ghost city named Famagusta. When I visited the island, I could see vehicles from the 60s and 70s left as they were on the day of the invasion and evacuation. They have since been removed.

In the newly colonized nations, the way the states were divided honored very little of the tribal boundaries that formed around geographical features. Nor did those boundaries follow specific geographical features, as they bore no resemblance to tribal or indigenous pre-existing boundaries. In such cases, tension has existed between states regarding how other states handle specific parts of the land and resources within their boundaries. It should also be noted that while the boundaries are drawn on maps, these do not represent the fluctuating tribal boundaries within these new colonial entities. The tribes push and shove to ensure access to resources. The tribal boundaries in the new colonies were constantly shifting and dynamic, while the more heavily defended boundaries of the imperial colonial entities had rigid, unmoving borders.

Controversially, there are currently examples of border or artificial border conflicts between Israel and Palestine. Additionally, the fragmented states of the former Yugoslavia have artificial borders that were created during the conflict. In the case of Yugoslavia, its formation was as artificial as that of the states that emerged from it. The region had a diverse ethnic composition because it was part of the Roman world. During the last thousand years of the Roman Empire, the priority for citizenship shifted from ethnicity or language to religion. While a person was considered Christian, they were also considered Roman. Similarly, the Israeli state has homogenized its citizenry to be predominantly Jewish while Palestine remains predominantly Islamic, yet both areas have a high concentration of Christians.

Specifically, the boundary—the land that encapsulates a collection of people—must be seen as belonging to them all equally to create a sense of cohesion or unity and, most importantly, a sense of lineage to that land. While the borders they define and accept are comprehensible, the borders others impose are not. Natural boundaries, although characterized by human perception, serve a purpose beyond a military agenda and may also encompass military or defensive objectives. For instance, people reliant on waterways, through their culture, can't be landlocked by a border imposed on them. Such an action would, as a consequence, modify their way of life. For most people in the world, borders are shaped by a sense of lineage. Usually, one generation passes down hunting grounds, fertile plains, and knowledge of these borders to the younger generation. We can call this lineage by many names. Still, we are well aware that, among all the people in the world, traditional lands are viewed as a shared resource and birthright among those who feel a lineage or affinity to a particular territory or land. While primitive people may feel a stronger bond with their land, even the most isolated people learn the importance of those borders via subjects like geography. In every instance in human history, we know that the greatest disgruntlement, friction, and hostility came from not recognizing the territory of a Polity, mainly when many generations have been accustomed to those territories and borders.

In many historical cases, many wars have been waged to protect borders. Still, in rare cases, the coexistence and symbiotic sharing of land and waterways have also occurred. This latter point may seem archaic, as few examples exist to support it today. Still, when the earliest cities were forming, people were divided into two broad groups: the nomadic, who roamed vast areas, and the sedentary, who lived in the emerging cities. In those days, nomadic people were not seen as inferior. Instead, they were often seen as wealthy agricultural lords who used unclaimed land to tend their flocks, and they usually served in close union with surrounding cities. However, many of these nomads eventually became semi-nomadic or semi-sedentary. They only seemed to migrate within a given area in regular cycles, usually moving to better pastures.

Regarding sedentary people, we have many archaeological records indicating that the earliest Hellenistic cities in Europe attracted local residents. In Marseille, France, the Greeks coexisted with the Celts, also known as the Gauls. In the east, several cities in Syria feature the coexistence of Greek and some Semitic peoples. According to Strabo, the Greeks founded Rome, and they would never have expected the empire to change identities and sprawl as it did. Even into the late Roman period, the Jewish people were in large numbers in cities and areas around Constantinople.

Furthermore, it seemed that Alexandria, Egypt, also attracted many Jewish people, not only as enslaved people. So, then, when we spoke of pressure towards a homogeneous society, in the case of the earliest cities, the pressure to enter and participate in the city's culture was mostly purely voluntary. No doubt historians are aware of pre-Roman Gaul, where they eventually mimicked Greek coins down to the same Gods the Greeks worshipped. Evidence from early cities indicates that cultures often merged there. Yet they maintained a certain degree of independence and, at the same time, uniformity, particularly in language and religion. The other cultural aspects varied somewhat, but we can never be certain of such a broad subject. We know what it was like to be an ancient Athenian, Spartan, Roman, or Neapolitan, but we do not know exactly what it was like. It is much like trying to describe our modern culture. There will be many differing and equally truthful views within a single city.

Regarding borders and territory, the land surrounding the city was generally considered part of the city's territory. The state was not a massive expanse of land. Instead, the state tried to encapsulate a defendable area around the city. The earliest European settlements typically aimed for a seaport, a small road network, a defendable town center, and additional or unique nearby resources. Often, trees for timber, mines, fruits, especially olives, and so forth constituted the primary resources sought in a particular area around the city. Therefore, it is clear that people of diverse natures became citizens in the early Greek and European colonial cities. Those entering the cities assimilated into the culture of the time. We have so much to defend this view: the coinage, the temples, and the written word.

Additionally, there are biblical references to Abraham and many others who lived nomadic lives until their population became so dense that they eventually rebuilt Jerusalem as the Holy City. It would be foolish to think that borders and territories play little role in defining a polity. Biblically, Abraham was promised a land away from his home that would later become a nation. It would be tied by fate to the founding of an Israelite nation. Later, those related to him would reshape Jerusalem. The nomadic people were slightly different from those living in cities. Nomads tended to be familial. The tendency to assimilate into a tribe would have been more direct and personal than in a large city, such as most Ancient Greek cities. Also, almost everyone within a tribe was related in some way. The frequency of assimilation would have been lower than in large cities. The culture, language, and ethics of a tribe or small city are generally more consistent and uniform than those of larger cities.

The land Abraham sought to use was considered free land, generally used by nomads. In conjunction with tribal and city pressure, there was a tendency for fully nomadic people to become semi-nomadic, migrating to better pastures. Abraham adopted this semi-nomadic lifestyle. Finally, as land, resources, and access to free land became increasingly complex, these nomadic and semi-nomadic people began forming their towns and cities and even entering existing cities. Potentially, this is what eventually led to the fate of Abraham's people.

We know that territories have been an essential part of human lives. But are they important philosophically speaking? As part of that equilibrium towards a homogeneous society, defined borders become part of the push towards a homogeneous society. In the opposite direction are those who would like to sprawl indefinitely or take whatever is on the earth and use it as they see fit. But we know that such childish views are often met with conflict. It becomes especially apparent in places where water is so scarce that the survival of a people depends entirely on securing it. Food and essentials, such as shelter, also play a significant role, and while some of us may turn the other cheek and walk on during a conflict of ownership, most people are not as good. There is an unfortunate perpetual desire for self-satisfaction. Some may call it greed, while others refer to it as self-preservation, defense, or even protection, depending on the situation and the perspectives of those involved. Is it the attacker of those who drink from a watering hole, the aggressor? Or is it the one that drinks, knowing there will be none left for the attacker's family? Actions of preservation may manifest eventually, not so much as personal ownership but as traditional access. Borders and their ability to encompass people's needs become significant as a tribe or population grows. The land around them must be able to sustain them. As the population increases, the borders need to provide access to the resources that sustain it and enable its growth.

Additionally, having observed the ways of numerous tribes and compared their lifestyles, it is evident that they require far more land in arid and desert environments to sustain a given population than modern farming and agriculture. In some places, the nomadic people have the luxury of abundant food, water, and shelter. However, in arid locations, the area the tribes wander is much larger. A tribe in arid conditions wanders with the seasons over a large expanse of land. In contrast, the agriculturalists who colonized the same place made far more productive use of the land per square meter. The latter, of course, is not self-sustainable, as it has caused many problems, such as the use of artificial fertilizers and over-clearing, and other factors that would not otherwise have existed. However, in terms of sustaining a large population, heavy machinery, highly industrialized equipment, and modern fertilizer technologies have created a system in which less land is needed to support a given population. This technological advancement impacts borders or land requirements. It plays a significant role in places where land resources are rare.

In contrast to sedentary people, nomadic tribes define borders based on what they need. Some resources are shared, and others are not. Because of the arid nature of the land, it is strongly against their culture to use others' land, as it can cause damage. For instance, some berries or fruits from an orchard will not affect those that rely on the orchard for food. But taking the fruit of the only existing handful of trees can effectively starve an entire tribe. Therefore, in this sense, we know that while sharing is always an option when there is abundance, the scarcity of a resource can lead to conflict or even the death of another tribe. Also, as humans have always done, the best solution is to keep our borders aligned with what each city needs to sustain itself.

Historically, we know that early cities used boundaries. It also becomes clear that forming a polity relies on people perceiving that boundary. If people think the entire world is theirs, it would lead to many polemical counterclaims. If people do not know their borders, others can reduce their ability to survive.

Borders can be called assimilative regions, or a set geographical location and a system that gently encourages those who live within and join the polity to conform and meld together. This form of polity, or emerging polity, has the potential to grow, spread, and assimilate foreigners into it. If a territory is formed or claimed, as did some tribal and barbaric people, it is not enough without the homogenous growth of that tribe's culture, religion and language. In other words, the culture and polity can't survive without an element of assimilation. Therefore, a Polity is more than a large group of humans living together or near each other. A Polity must also require a common language and culture; otherwise, a Democracy can't function.

In other forms of government, the necessity of a common culture amongst the people is negated by one that demands obedience or subjection to an Autocrat or an Oligarchy and their laws. A different or systemic assimilation is implemented in those systems. For people to lead themselves, they must be able to communicate effectively, establish a majority vote, and draw lots when necessary. These things can only be derived from people with a broad spectrum of commonness, including language, religion, culture, ethics, and beliefs. A similar or common culture is essential because it partially defines the traditional lands. It can create a region or boundary of entitlement through tradition and culture. Specific stories of mountains and peaks, rivers and mythology, as well as numerous other tales and cultural aspects, along with religious ceremonies such as baptisms or ceremonies near landmarks, all contribute to a sense of connection to the land, its territories, and often its borders. Culture also contributes to ethics and norms. Culture determines the mode of life that the people will have. If they were truly free people seeking freedom, they would be different from those who were merely thinking about freedom.

Some cultures prefer certain foods or drinks over others, and these preferences are often social or non-systematic, yet they can create pressure for others to conform to the majority. Therefore, regardless of the government system, we will observe a degree of assimilation in every polity through the influence of the people, rather than the governing system. This force of culture eventually shapes the laws people adopt and, in some cases, the type of religion, belief system, or lack thereof they may adopt. All these factors will ultimately influence how people unite into a polity and shape the nature of their government, if they were to form one. These factors, including boundaries, territories, and forces of assimilation through culture, language, and religion, form the foundation upon which a polity may arise. It also helps describe what we term the conditions of existence: the mode by which a society or polity wishes to live, the things it considers important, and the things it wants to abolish, limit, or regulate.

A government usually works to create a set of desired conditions for the polity, including maintaining order. The government, often in a Democracy, aims to preserve the Polity's language, culture, and religion. It does these things to ensure the ability to perpetuate order and agreement from the time of voting to the generations that apply these decisions or laws. A government can be an instrument of the people, a minority, or an individual forcing the state into order and governance. The desired conditions for a particular polity are determined differently based on the type of government and the people. In a monarchy, a single individual can determine those conditions.

In contrast, a democracy implies that the people define the desired conditions. By 'desired conditions,' I mean a wide spectrum of things, such as lifestyle, work methods, duties and responsibilities, faith and religion, language, education, and all the factors that may become important to achieve and/or perpetuate by the polity or those who govern it. All polities require organization, order, and a defined language, culture, religion, or belief system. How these things are achieved will vary depending on the type of organization and government that forms the authority of the polity. In ancient Greece, the definition of a polity was that a democratic system united a people, and it described their life within the boundaries of their city. Their polity usually lived in a city surrounded by several villages. The word Polity has also been used to refer to the term civilization. However, the term' civilization' has been used in a wide range of meanings. Civilization has been used to describe everything from meek social beings to empires. Each such civilization has radically different conditions of existence, creating a flexible range of terms for using the term' civilization'.

Even though the diversity of systems and their constituent components may vary, some have remained consistent and common over time and by tradition. In all forms of government, the state seeks to maintain order within a polity. We know that we are uniform throughout all instances of a structured society. Additionally, a government will typically have at least three significant areas of administration that vary slightly depending on the type of government system in use. The legislature is where laws are created, and it varies regarding who makes the laws and how they are made. The Judiciary is formed by those who will judge those brought before the court. Finally, enforcers are organized to enforce the law, get people to the judiciary, and act on behalf of the judiciary and the state. These fundamental components exist in every government that can be considered a polity. Even many tribal societies have these three aspects of government. The underlying purpose of these three component areas is to establish and maintain order.

Order can mean many different things under different systems of government. Order in my time is almost, but not always, synonymous with overly empowered police. Yet, Order is of utmost importance to nearly every polity. We know that some tribes had varying systems of governance in ancient times. Some were led by elders, others by a single leader, and some just followed the strongest man in the tribe. However, these systems shared certain common elements, such as Laws, Traditions, and/or Spiritual codes of conduct. These were a form of early legislature. Doing certain things against the God, or Gods they believed in, had inevitable consequences. Acting in ways deemed inappropriate to the tribe's traditions was also punishable. The enforcers would ensure that the leader or leaders heard those who acted against the norm, law, or tradition. All our governance systems, extending from the very family or tribe system and higher, required some form of order. Order in those primitive polities was established through the same methods as in the most complex and civilized systems. The difference was that earlier forms of government relied on word of mouth to preserve the ethics and traditions that represented their laws. There was a contribution towards forming a ruling class, such as those who could remember the oral traditions, laws, and the like, or at least make others believe they did.

Despite the diversity of governance and polities, all human government systems had a degree of law, judgment, and enforcement to ensure order. The word Order often has a more diverse and profound meaning than it does today. Order means many things and can be subjective in evaluation. Order does not necessarily imply a robotic and controlled life. Order can be a sense of maintaining an ethical and cultural entity. People naturally seek a sense of order in society so all participants within that polity can co-exist and live happily. The opposing chaos divides people and prevents them from uniting around a common purpose, since anarchy lies at its core. A leaderless mob is complex because natural leaders often rise within the anarchy. Although rarely witnessed, people begin to cooperate even amid the chaos and unrest, and the seeming anarchy shifts towards order. Order is often established organically and democratically. We see this in many events that sparked chaos and anarchy in city streets, yet the people march together in force without a head or a leader, only themselves. Some would argue that the leadership brought them to the brink of anarchy or chaos, and the need to demonstrate and rally.

Many people have written about how order is achieved and how a society becomes a polity with a government. Some are under the impression that order comes from domination over the majority. Others believe it is a natural process. That same natural process was considered a trait—a divine characteristic of humanity—much like the order found in a beehive, though our roles were less organized. Unlike bees, we are all born with the same abilities, and very few things distinguish us from one another other than our male and female roles. While some people may run faster than others, and specific differences may occur, we share certain macro abilities common to all of us. We can all be workers, technicians, tradesmen, merchants, soldiers, and professionals, and we can, in theory, also be citizens, oligarchs, and monarchs. Only a few things distinguish us.

Regarding natural order in a small community, there is almost always a trend towards stability and order. It does not require a complex system for people to communicate their ideas, as a small group can gather and discuss; they can be summoned by a yell or a wave to join the discussion. The very small size of a community or polity means the level of organization need not be elaborate, unlike in larger polities. However, as the group increases, anarchy can become apparent because each system has a physical limit to its ability to coordinate. At some point, some people will exist who go unnoticed. They are present yet do not seem to participate. Each system can have such a populace living in the shadows; most anarchy arises from that group. When people feel alienated, lack of acceptance or barely recognize any form of order or organization other than within their own existance, they form bands, gangs, smaller subgroups, power groups, etc. Our natural roles and communication methods were not designed to handle a large number of community members. How can one person be heard amongst a hundred thousand or a million or more? That is why, to some degree, anarchy can arise as populations increase, but only because the population outgrows the mechanisms that maintain order. It can reach a stage where the majority become anarchic, especially if the system fails to appease their expectations. Yet, within the anarchy, there will usually be enclaves of families huddled together in natural order. What may appear to be chaos has seeds of order within it.

The youth, those without responsibility or the desire for commitment, are often seen creating anarchy through what most cultures would consider criminal behavior. But organized groups also profiteer from anarchy and often promote it. There are many springs from which anarchy can derive. It is in these situations that we must assess how order can be established and whether it can be achieved naturally through a polity. If we examine the micro details, there are many ways to achieve order; however, in all situations, it ultimately stems from three primary sources. Firstly, people within the polity can create order by progressively becoming more organized to combat the spread of anarchy and chaos. Secondly, a subgroup or minority group may decide to bring about such order on behalf of the polity, but not necessarily for the benefit of the majority. Thirdly, an individual may be so influential, by a method of wealth or otherwise, that they establish order for the majority through their resources. These three approaches to unity are how the so-called natural order initiates within a polity. Often, people assume that they cannot see God's work in this sequence of events.

Yet, in either case, it is likely that the free will of those initiating orders will have the greatest impact. Let me give you an example of a property manager who sees streets and parks entirely submerged in waste. He buys the properties cheaply and pays for the anarchy in the area. He then recruits idealists and people who innocently wish to champion the cause of cleaning the area and pays them as well. Ultimately, he purchased the property cheaply and sold it at the highest price after a decade. Many people, including politicians and businesspeople, engage in this type of anarchy and order. The majority of people prefer order over chaos. Eventually, using one of several types of formal or informal government, order is restored naturally —and by 'naturally,' I mean through the efforts of those initiating order, often for their benefit alone.

In human history, the order has never led to the emergence of a democratic state outside Athens. It is perhaps essential to take the riots in Egypt from 2011 to 2014 as an example; the people rushed into the streets in large numbers. By showing numbers, they created enough pressure for their leader, Hosni Mubarak, to retire as perpetual president. When he was removed, Mohamed Morsi was placed in power. In 2011, the people created chaos against their government. In 2012, although elections were held, the leader appointed could not maintain peace or order, prompting the people to protest again. According to those who escaped and spoke about the matter, it seemed the people caused the chaos to oust what they considered a dictator. They were unsatisfied when another replaced him. One dictator for another, appointed by the few as a candidate from a handpicked minority. The people, recognizing that they had lost their battle, continued to protest frequently but without the same ferocity as in 2011.

When considering natural order, it is essential to clarify that we are referring to our human prioritization of order and the consequences of our actions in achieving it. We suggest that when the order or lack thereof stems from the people, we perceive it to be natural. Otherwise, when an authority's use sustains order, we no longer have a natural order but a systemic one. That means a system, usually with enforcement and laws, is in place to force order when chaos arises. However, sometimes systemic order arises from the will of the majority, where people act in groups or large groups without a formal system. To distinguish between the two types of order mentioned so far —natural and systemic — both can be part of a system and be organic or naturally occurring. The order of the types that do not require authority, communication, and commands is natural.

In contrast, order obtained through authority, communication, and/or actions that bring order to other people or groups is systemic. The neutrality of our need for order does not imply systematic forms of order or planned exploitations, as already mentioned. "Natural order" means that, if we have a group of people, regardless of their number, they will eventually form an understanding and maintain order without the need for authoritative communication or command. This natural order precedes the ability to organize and create government systems.

Systemic Order typically refers to an organized or structured arrangement of components, elements, or entities within a system. It involves establishing rules, processes, or hierarchies to manage and control interactions and relationships within that system. Natural order refers to the inherent or intrinsic patterns, laws, or principles that govern the behavior, organization, and processes observed in the natural world.

The natural order is easily identified within small groups and among their members, but once several groups, tribes, or families exist, that order no longer seems to apply consistently. Even though the existence of a natural order may seem absent as groups become extremely large and composed of many subgroups, it also appears that a natural order does exist, as evidenced by a brief consensus of peace and tolerance among members of different groups. Yet we already detailed that every person is unique, so every group is unique. Not all groups will achieve natural order, but you may find it even in places least expected, like a den of thieves.

There is no direct cognitive reason why the Natural Order exists, yet it is an integral part of human ecology. It is said to derive from spiritual sources. If we were to describe human beings and how we see and represent animals, we could generally agree that most of humanity lives in small familial groups. The nuclear family, where the biological mother and father and their children live together, is one form of group that we tend to adhere to. However, some societies, especially those impacted by the ideology of Feminism, do not seem to be structured adequately around the nuclear model. However, the nuclear family is highly popular and used worldwide. Defining alternative roles or choices for women and men varies depending on the structure of families. However, the basic ecology of children requiring parental care and parents protecting their children seems reasonably consistent, although not entirely accurate. The culture I live in has approximately a 50% chance of divorce among married people.

That then leads to custody battles and splits the lives of the children between their two biological parents. The birth parents often move on to find other partners with whom they typically fornicate and have more children. That then creates a problem for their biological visiting child, as the dynamics of belonging are superseded when a new partner offers a child to their biological parent.

Meanwhile, the feminist movement and most governments, in response to female voters, appease the female population by feeding into this feminist dynamic that creates divorces and breaks up families. The crux of the matter is that in most countries where women are typically said to be oppressed by feminist opinion, the family unit is the same. Families have followed a very similar ecology to that of the families we know about from the earliest part of human history. Of course, some indeed are very oppressive, and we see females entirely mistreated and certainly do not resemble this ancient natural order that we have referred to.

There are also Maternal and Paternal societies, and perhaps I am raising localized issues related to a shift from Patriarchy to Matriarchy. That is to say that possibly divorces and social issues raised here will disappear when women have reversed their roles or traded their roles in society for male roles of leadership. What does stand out, though, is that the ecology of a human family goes a long way in describing why we seek small social groups as individuals. No matter how a family is structured or what things a person must endure, the natural order remains a compelling drive. It is part of our survival instinct and way of thinking; it comes naturally and does not require formal instruction. For example, circles of friends seem to replace the family for many single people. When single people lack immediate contact with their family, they often gravitate towards existing groups or create their own social circles as substitutes for family members. There is a saying that you can't choose your family, but you can choose your friends. In that sense, many people, especially those experiencing loneliness, solitude, and isolation, and living in a foreign place, seek something to comfort them, often in small groups.

We socialize, conduct business, and operate in various ways, yet most of what we do occurs within small groups. Even our tribal ancestors had both friendly and hostile neighboring tribes. This natural order or tendency to manifest order through cohesion with others is indeed part of humanity. At this point, we can't argue against it. We can't assume that chaos is the natural state of human existence. The ecology that describes a family – the multiple variations in family structure, friends, and group interactions – supports the case that we prefer social order over chaos.

As already noted, Natural Order is not always what brings order. Sometimes, fear, through excessive violence, forces people into a submissive state. Historically, this method was typical of many aggressive, expansionist empires that demanded immediate submission. According to numerous texts and archaeological evidence, the ancient Assyrians would raid hostile or defiant cities and towns, often flaying their inhabitants. They would dig holes and place people in them alive before covering them with the bodies of those flayed. The piles were very high, and burning them was forbidden. This oppressive rule is far from the natural order but represents a drastic, forced systemic order. It will be our natural order that, in most cases, will bring people together. But in the absence of that natural order, and because of our natural willingness or desire for order, it becomes exploitable by individuals with money and power or groups with similar wealth and power.

The previous highlights that several methods can achieve order and that these methods usually precede government. With the order established, people can establish the necessary organization to form a government. Once the government is formed, a systematic Order can be established and maintained. In brief, the previous matters all relate to the things required before a government can be established. These will be discussed more thoroughly later. The next step is determining which types of government can be created.

2.2 The types of government

Let us now examine the types of Government. The most significant contributors to the study of government were Socrates, Plato, and Aristotle. Governments can be of three types. Aristotle's three forms of government are as follows: The first type is Monarchy, the second is Aristocracy, and the third is Democracy. Originally, Aristotle developed the system for categorizing government types. For non-philosophers, these categories probably mean something different from what Aristotle meant.

Let us look at them closely. If we attempt to categorize governments by how they are led, we can do this in various ways. We could look at who is in power. Is it a priest? (theocracy), a military general? (dictator) Or is it led by a representative government? (Republic). We could examine how fair or liberal the laws are to differentiate between totalitarian and liberal states. We can examine various characteristics that appear to be present in most governments and compare them. All these categorization methods are acceptable, but not all have a philosophical justification for proving or quantifying. Although they can be philosophically defined, the process would be arduous since our views vary greatly.

Philosophy is not merely a rambling of words, nor the re-assembly of rhetoric, as some believe, but expresses a truth through reason and logic. Wherever a truth exists, it can be proven. In some cases, proof may be limited to observation; at other times, it can be scientifically quantified. The method used here is similar to that of ancient Greek writers, in that even a subjective issue like ethics can yield scientific truth. Philosophies are not limited to subjective ideals; they extend beyond that. That is why preference should always be given to the quantifiable, measurable, and observable. Our logic or reasoning may lead to quantifiable proof, but where such evidence is lacking, qualitative truth is as important as quantitative truth.

While we may be able to calculate the distance to the sun, we can't describe a sunset with maths alone. Lastly, we should treat our ideas, emotions, feelings, or perceptions as less reliable indicators of the truth. Still, an emotion or feeling can often lead to profound truths, established through qualitative or quantitative means. If a philosophical case has no proof or observation but may have a probability or plausibility, it also has some merit. Of course, Metaphysical and spiritual philosophies have proofs of a different nature. Discussing spirituality would be problematic if we rely on the measurable and quantifiable. If we approach the spiritual argument by placing the quantifiable before the spiritual or probable, then our tactic has a problem. The tangible world around us and ourselves can be measured using physical instruments. A spiritual ruler can only measure things beyond this physical world. Choosing the best truth depends entirely on what we believe about the subject. This is similar to deciding which scale we use for testing. However, in the case of physical and human manipulation, physical measurement is often the most reliable and believable. Since the things we measure physically are observed and measurable, so is the instrument by which we test them. Returning to the point, the systems of government and their categorization are among the things we can quantify. We can't say, for example, that a government is representative unless we know that what the people wish is being represented, and obtaining such data will never be accurate. If we consider a government to be totalitarian, how do we accurately determine if it is truly totalitarian? By whose ethics and whose culture do we judge?

There is also the matter of prefixed Democracy: Liberal-Democracy, Open-Democracy, Representative-Democracy, Direct-Democracy and many such terms. All these are redundant or inaccurate categories. All these modern terms that people use to describe governments are useful in everyday language to express ideas, but philosophically speaking, they can become misleading. With which gauge do we test the prefix? What Aristotle did with his categories was sort them by the number of people leading. That is an easily quantifiable way to categorize governments. We can easily determine whether one person, a few people, or all the people are leaders in a society or polity. Aristotle's government categories are, for the most part, quantifiable and accurate. But he also adds a subjective element to them: quality.

The first Aristotelian category is the Monarchy. Monarchy implies that a single person is leading the majority. The same definition is often applied to the terms Autocrat and Autocracy. The term Monarchy is a subjective appraisal of an Autocracy. Some autocracies that people will be familiar with include kings, emperors, dictators, despots, and warlords. Types with a King, Emperor, Caesar, or Basileus are traditionally considered Monarchies. In all these examples, one person leads over the majority, but a monarchy is supposed to be a better form of autocratic government.

The next Aristotelian category is the Aristocracy. This system implies that a few elite people rule over the majority. A similar definition is given to the term Oligarchy. In both an Oligarchy and an Aristocracy, the number of people leading compared to the population is small. However, the difference is lies in the fact that aristocracy is considered the better form of this type of government. In modern society, we often associate aristocracy with relatives and friends of monarchs or the bourgeoisie. However, this latter definition is not the traditional meaning of the word "aristocracy." When writing this, many government systems used the principle of a few people leading the rest. Some of these include Constitutional Monarchies, Familial Aristocracies, Republics and Theocracies. Some people may assert that their government is an Aristocracy because the better or elite are leading.

On the other hand, many may voice discontent with their leadership and consider the same government an Oligarchy. Oligarchies and Aristocracies can be formed by election, appointment or self-appointment. Aristotle viewed an aristocracy as a form of government governed by the best possible values and methods, and he considered it a higher quality form of oligarchy. Many believed it was possible to establish elite rule.

Democracy in Aristotle's Athenian model is a system in which all the citizens lead and control the city-state. In other words, the Demos or citizenry form the archon of government; hence, they become Demarchons. If this system existed, it would require every citizen to have the legal right to make decisions regarding their polity. Democracy is considered, like the others, again a subjective appraisal of a Pleistocracy. A Pleistocracy is a form of government in which the majority holds power over the state or government. A pleistocracy is subtly different from a Democracy; the majority may administer both, but the Democracy is of greater quality. Saint Gregory once used Pleistocracy to complain against the majority or popular opinion over his specialist or educated opinion. An Ochlocracy is when a mob or crowd leads. Ochlocracy is a subjective or derogatory form of Democracy. A Democracy is when the people lead or are in a position to lead, but it is suggested that they lack power over the state and may or may not be of high moral and ethical standards. Therefore, several terms can be defined that, as part of their definition, include the people or the majority ruling over the majority. Democracy is considered to be the better form of a pleistocracy. It is when the majority of people rule over the majority of people, and they are also fair, just, and wise in their decisions. Again, as with the other categories, Aristotle explained, a subjective element has crept into the definition. We are no longer only interested in the number of citizens ruling but also in the quality of that leadership.

These categories, as explained, are accurately measurable and calculable, except for leadership quality, which will be addressed shortly. Therefore, we only need to count how many people are leading and how many people they lead to determine which type of government exists. But to ensure we have better forms of these governments – a Monarchy instead of an Autocracy, an Aristocracy instead of an Oligarchy, and a Democracy instead of an Ochlocracy – there also needs to be a subjective appraisal of leadership quality. Therefore, it is probably worth exploring these various forms of government in more depth, so that distinguishing among them is clearer.

Situations may arise in which individuals of poor character, thugs, or corrupt officials take control of a government, whether it is a monarchy, oligarchy, or democracy. So, how do we distinguish between an ideal government system and one that is tyrannical or fails to achieve the people's desired function? How do we further determine whether the government formed is fair, just, and wise in its choices? Even if the word Oligarchy, by its definition, means the few ruling over the majority, it is not enough that this alone defines a suitable government system. Similarly, autocracy or pleistocracy does not represent an ideal government. The actual quality of leadership needs to be assessed. Aristotle did not directly apply the term Aristoi to all his categories. Still, he implied that the Aristoi (elite, virtuous or perfect people) are the one individual in a monarchy, a few people in an Aristocracy, or the majority in a Democracy, and are required to raise the system's quality. His definitions have a premise, based on Plato and Socrates, that the best Monarchs were often thought of as philosopher-kings, the Aristocracy was composed of transparent, uncorrupted, wise, and elite men, and democracy was constituted of wise people. These, of course, are the best-case scenarios.

As stated before, we hope to produce the absolute truth. Based on what has been said so far, the correct classification of government systems should be based on a mathematically quantifiable component: Autocracy (one ruling over the majority), Oligarchy (the few leading the majority), and Pleistarchy (the majority leading the majority). But when we introduce the question of which is the better form of these types of Government? Then, there is a need to assess the quality of each system.

2.2.1 The Monarchy

For tradition's sake, we will use Aristotle's ideology that Monarchy is the better form of Autocracy, as Aristocracy is the better form of Oligarchy, and Democracy is the better form of Demarchy. What follows is a brief look at the subtle aspects of a Monarchy, the rule of a singular elite. Also, it is worth noting that noone can be perfect. The probability of having an ideal Monarch is low. Therefore, the flaws of the monarch, as described, will have a profound impact on the system entirely.

The Monarchy has always faced specific problems with Legitimacy and Authority. Some claim that Monarchs have a divine right to rule; therefore, hereditary succession is based on that right. Being considered legitimate by their divine authority, they tend to administer with such absolute authority. The Magna Carta diluted the absolute authority and diminished the idea of

Divine rule. The concept of being an instrument of God or a Divine entity has become almost obsolete. In modern times, we find many different types of monarchies based on several factors: some claimed to be God on Earth, as did the pharaohs, or a Divine entity, as did many conquerors.

Life, liberty, and property were the first fundamental rights sought by the population under monarchies. The idea originated from the concept that the consent of the people and respect for them should prevail. In modern times, we can add that the average person could achieve more in life if they had the freedom to do so. The quality of life and gradual wealth accumulation should be preserved with rights. It is not altogether the materialism of having possessions, but rather that the control and use of possessions should be with the owner, not a surrogate owner. Jean-Jacques Rousseau wrote a critique of the compromise between ideals and the existing system. Living in an era of monarchies, the philosopher wrote "Discourse on Inequality" and "The Social Contract." Both influence much of what is considered a fair Monarchical system. The writer preferred a democratic system; however, he states in paraphrase that the idea of land ownership or property ownership was entirely new for that era (Rousseau, 1754).

In some places, the governing system is a monarchy with elected positions. They call these places Constitutional Monarchies. The hardest part of transitioning Monarchies to alternative governments has been the Monarchs' inability to relinquish power. Methods for including them in a Democracy exist, as will be discussed later. It is enough to note that a Monarchy has had several historical moments in which its powers were challenged and curbed by Barons and aristocrats. Not many confrontations were successful. The challenge of bringing them to the table of the People has, for a long time, been evaded. The notion that monarchies still exist in our modern times is somewhat surprising. Especially since the entire 1700-1800s attempted to install Democracies worldwide, many claim to be democratic despite their Oligarchic structure.

Stability and Order, Accountability and Tyranny, Individual Liberty and Autonomy, Ethical Duties of Monarchs, and many more issues arise that are not covered in detail here. These issues with monarchies have become critical and problematic.

While many can argue that stability and order are higher and of better quality under a monarchy, the form of stability and order tends to be oppressive, forcing people into submission through laws. There is an extreme emphasis on systemic order rather than natural order. Stability, in the sense of the system maintaining and propagating itself through generations, is somewhat arguable. Having reviewed the Histories of Rome, we can conclude that the median number of years a dictator, such as Augustus, or a single monarch ruled was two years. They were then either disposed of or usurped. Yet the Roman system itself was maintained and propagated for a millennium. There was instability at the top as many people vied for it. However, the bureaucratic entities continued to operate and perform their functions.

Accountability and Tyranny are best described by the parable of the Lamb and the Wolf, Aesop. Authority under a Monarchy exists solely with the Monarch. While any system can exist under them at any stage, they can override the system's functions or structure. In doing this, the intervention can sometimes be seen as tyrannical, especially when demands are made on unwilling others. A wolf in the forest saw a lamb with its mother in a nearby paddock. The wolf crossed the stream to get to the lamb and its mother, so scared she distanced herself from the lamb. The other sheep all moved much further away.

> *The wolf then speaks to the lamb, saying,*
>
> *"Someone has trespassed on my stream and muddied the water so I cannot drink."*

The lamb said, "I have no strength in my legs. I have yet to walk for the first time.

The wolf then said, "You drank from the water in my stream."

The lamb replied, "I have only tasted my mother's milk".

Then the wolf, frustrated, said, "I will not be cheated out of breakfast," and ate the lamb.

The story's moral is that there is no point in arguing with Tyrants.

Power that affects others, directly or indirectly, becomes more tyrannical as it increases. It is not merely that the position corrupts the person, but rather that power creates tyranny when left to a few or individuals. The power-grabbing and preserving tactics are apparent in how many monarchs, but not all, conducted themselves throughout human history. From the murderous King Henry VIII back to Ramses of Egypt and his enslavement of the Hebrews. The histories of monarchs are riddled with Autocratic power manifesting as Tyranny over a population. We rarely encounter the Righteous Philosopher King, whom Plato considered a better leader.

Another area of concern is the Individual Liberty and Autonomy of people under Monarchies or Autocracies. As described through the understanding of Order and Tyranny, people living in a monarchy tend not to have rights. The Western system grants privileges to subjects. In some places, the people are confused. While the terms' citizen' and 'rights' are commonly used publicly, the reality is that they have no legal status as citizens or rights. Such was the case when I wrote this in Australia, the land often referred to as the southernmost part of India and Southeast Asia. Therefore, the Liberty and Autonomy of the subjects are somewhat hindered. Voltaire paraphrased stated that freeing a person from the shackles they revere is difficult. For most, the illusion comforts them more than the reality, so they prefer to sleep. In this way, the Tyrant or Tyrants bind them and tyrannize them.

2.2.2 The Oligarchy

Oligarchy is a political system characterized by the concentration of power in the hands of a small, privileged group, often based on factors such as wealth, social status, or family connections.

While most problems faced under oligarchies are similar to those encountered under autocracies or monarchies, some areas stand out more than others. Justice and fairness, especially concerning wealth distribution, are problem areas for Oligarchies. Other areas seen as intrinsically problematic include elitism and meritocracy, manipulation and control, democratic value decay, corruption and accountability, economic inequality, and resistance to and pursuit of change.

It becomes apparent when reading literature that the idea of clarifying who is in charge or controlling things has puzzled many people. Aristotle's categories were the closest we have to narrowing down the choices. When all we have to do is structure the system philosophically, determine the functions, and then count who is at the pinnacle of command.

Like street performers, oligarchs use sleight of hand to hide things in plain sight, like trying to find a ball under several cups. You know there is a ball; it is shown to you at the start. But try to find it under the cups, and you almost always lose. An Oligarchy can exist in practically any and every structure. They prefer to distance themselves, evade detection, and use covert operations more than overt ones. Yet, in some places, even monarchs establish elaborate oligarchies that ultimately serve their interests, but baffle the populace into thinking their government represents them. This system is found both formally and informally in places where this is being written, such as Australia and the United States of America.

In Australia, an operating three-tiered government system forms an Oligarchy. The tiers are Federal, State, and Local governments. Above the three tiers are the tiers of the British government, namely the Lords (Aristocrats) and the Monarch. Such is the five-tiered system that rules over the people. Due to its complexity, very few people look beyond their local national or state governments. After all, most matters of daily life are resolved by the Oligarchs in government.

In the United States of America, they have the same system. However, the ties to the British Monarchy are covert and not openly constituted as in Australia. Western European Monarchies Exert control over the United States of America through clandestine influence over the country's currency and financial systems. In the position of intermediate controllers are very wealthy and powerful pawns that they use. Unsurprisingly, Prince Harry had chosen the USA as a possible temporary home. It is the backyard of the Western Monarchies, like Alexander had turned everything East of Macedon, Greece, into his backyard.

Justice and Fairness are not typically experienced by the populace in such systems. The trick of calling subjects citizens is a sleight of hand. They believe they have rights. There is no left or right wing in politics. These are just illusions and another sleight of hand. People have been channeled into a two-party system (Left and Right) so that when one upsets the majority, the other comes into power. But the process is somewhat more elaborate. Promoting the idea that the government is elected when the choices are given and the same oligarchs control how the votes are counted is another sleight of hand. People go about thinking that they can elect whom they want and oust whom they don't. In reality, they are given choices, and the candidates are selected for them to vote on. The government is a toy for the powerful

Oligarchs to control. The mouthpieces they hire utilize pensions, funds, and a range of entitlements, all of which ultimately contribute to how the Oligarchy controls independent governments. They even dare to show us the ball, called Globalization, they are attempting to have an unelected oligarchy rule the entire planet.

In light of what has been described, through examples of systems existing at the time of writing, the control of departments such as the Legislature, Justice, and Enforcement is all controlled by the Oligarchy. The government oligarchs will select the judges, enforcers, and other officials. Often, the system becomes a mixed system that combines elements of Democracy, Oligarchy, and Monarchy. These mixed systems, however, serve the few rather than the majority. That is to say that they are a form of Oligarchy.

Often, the issues of Elitism and Meritocracy arise within an Oligarchy. In an ideal system, one based on merit or capabilities would determine who performed which task. Opposing this is the installation of the Elite over those with merit. There has been significant debate across various philosophies regarding the system, as oligarchs often consider themselves the best suited to rule. At the same time, a substantial portion of the population is regarded as a burden to the Elite. But this is a very biased and skewed view. Often, it is revealed that social status, familial connections, wealth, and power all play a significant role in determining who is considered Elite. None of these attributes is found in the daily administrative process of government; hence, the meritocracy that the Oligarchs claim to exist does not exist.

Manipulation and control have been described and referenced to explain that some agendas are hidden in plain sight metaphorically. Not much more will be said. The Oligarchy manipulates and controls the majority. It is the only way it can survive and continue to function. From this manipulation and control stem the other problem areas: democratic value decay, corruption and accountability, economic inequality, and resistance to change.

Two significant systems should be mentioned: the tribal circle and the republic. These two are because many people live in new colonies that combine tribal indigenous populations with colonial republican systems. The Aboriginal people in Australia, much like those in other parts of the world, had a system that utilized Elders or Archons and a Tribal Circle or Assembly. The system they used would consider a person's age and accord them the respect they deserved. The circle is a metaphor for a naturally organized congregation. The Aboriginal Elders led through advisory positions. From what I understand, they had a demarchy isolated to one tribal state and tied without classes by order of respect from the youngest to the eldest. As I was informed by several tribes in Western Australia, when inter-clan issues arose, the elders were selected to negotiate on behalf of the tribe. The strongest remained back to fight and protect, whilst the elders were typically sent to meetings with other tribal elders. Sometimes, young messengers were sent with message sticks, similar in principle to those used by Marathon to deliver messages to different tribes.

The Melanesian Big Man, or highly regarded individual in a tribe, did not exist among the Aboriginals. The Melanesians on the surrounding islands adopted the Big Man model, which established hierarchy. However, this role was doubled as a medic and spiritual leader. Because there was a precedent of listening to the doctor, the outcome typically promoted the authority of an individual. The Aboriginals, in contrast, had many people trained, and respect and skills were shared rather than closely guarded. Unlike several others in the New Colonies, the Aboriginal people mark history as possibly the last native Demarchy to exist.

2.2.3 The Demarchy

Characterized by the rule of the majority, a Demarchy is considered a less developed and more primitive form of Democracy. In that, it is the fundamental system upon which Democracy is established through the addition and inclusion of viable and robust ethics, as well as the people's power over government.

While attempting to address the problems found with the Monarchy and Oligarchy, a new set of issues emerged: randomness based on sortition and fairness, merit versus chance, informed decision-making, representation and accountability, citizen engagement, minority rights and protection, practical implementation, and demarchy as a complementary system. These issues will be briefly explained.

Randomness and Fairness are issues that some consider intrinsic to a Demarchy. Much of the system is based on randomized results, from jury selection to other selections. However, the misconception is that Randomness interferes with fairness. Fairness involves a qualitative or quantitative assessment that is inherent in the democratic process. It has shifted from evaluating the few to evaluating the many. If we pick the best possible candidate for a job, then that person would be considered the best choice for the people. However, if the job were filled by random sortition, the argument would fall back to whether it is fair.

Being judged by the best possible judge or by thousands of inexperienced jurors is one of the problems of operating a Democracy. However, choosing the best judge leads to reusing the same person and establishing a seat of power that can become corrupt and biased. Therefore, although the quality may not be as good, a jury tends to be fairer. It is unbiased, incorruptible, and can be as resolved as a professional judge, especially for minor cases. For more serious cases, the jury selected by sortition would also need a sufficient number of experienced judges or magistrates to assist the jury.

Merit and Chance are another area of concern. As mentioned, merit and competence must be balanced with random selection. Specialized knowledge is the key to the issue. Understanding and balancing specialized knowledge permits the system to strike a fair and justified balance. Demarchy permits the purity of sortition in the selection process; however, the selected members can be assisted by an appointed expert if required.

An example is the nomination of candidates for a position who have demonstrated, through merit, that they can perform the role. Then, the actual selection could be carried out through a process of sortition. Such was the case for specialized positions within the Athenian Democracy.

Informed Decision-making is required when making a decision. It has been argued that informed choice is absent in a Democracy. However, the reality is that when many people gather to discuss, the decisions that follow will be informed. Where specialist knowledge is required, the process allows for the engagement of such professionals. Using the sortition process does not guarantee fairness, but it prevents prediction and corruption. For example, among three specialists, one has a biased opinion, and the sortition process has a 1-in-3 chance of selecting the biased candidate and a 2/3 chance of selecting an unbiased one. Therefore, as demonstrated, provided the specialist pool is large enough and the sortition process remains constant for all selections, the information shared can be considered both informed and of high quality.

Representation and Accountability are better achieved through the sortition processes of a Demarchy. Randomly selected decision-makers can effectively represent a broader part of the community. Additionally, it is worth noting that participation in the general assembly for meetings and decision-making is not established by sortition, nor is the citizenry of the decision-makers. Therefore, some inclusive qualifications are usually expressed in terms of citizenship. Representation in the form of the majority and accountability in the form of qualified citizenry exist within Democratic systems. Consequently, balancing the selection of decision-makers across several pathways balances representation and accountability. In this way, the broader community will be represented, and accountability will remain with the decision-makers.

Citizen Engagement: Engaging people may seem daunting because getting people involved can be a struggle. During the Athenian era, it was demonstrated that other areas of life took precedence over governance issues. Attending livestock, working on a project, serving in the army outside the city, and several other problems prevented people from participating. It reached a point where one of the Archons of Athens, Pericles, authorized a payment to the people for participating. It made the citizens professional politicians with an income worthy of that position. The attendance was higher. It is therefore important that citizens engage with the system.

Minority Rights and protection were another area criticized under a Democracy or a Demarchy. Minorities could be outvoted. Without formal rights, laws could favor the majority and put a minority at a disadvantage, leading to prejudice, harm, and other detrimental outcomes. However, from a process point of view, once a citizen is born, even if part of a minority, they can have the opportunity to influence the majority. The democratic system, coupled with a tradition of sortition, affords the minority high esteem and equal standing in the legislature, the judiciary, and the enforcement agencies. In retrospect, even when the minority is outvoted, there is still a chance to debate and change others' minds, leading them to shift in favor of the minority view. Compared with other systems, such as oligarchy and monarchy, democracy or demarchy is the only one that intrinsically preserves and protects the rights of all people equally, including minorities.

Practical Implementation: Some have argued that large cities cannot implement democracy when there isn't enough space to accommodate general assemblies. How could anyone be heard in the large number of people present? Large amphitheater-style arrangements, utilizing the human-built or naturally occurring acoustic properties of landforms, were employed to enable people to address the crowds. The sprawl and population in modern cities are so large that not everyone can fit into a single area. If everyone were to attend, a space would be needed to accommodate millions of people. However, the Ancient Athenians encountered a similar problem, and while amphitheater acoustics helped, there was a practical limit to the size of the congregation. That is why citizenship was made to exclude those who would not participate in running the city. Several exclusions were made to maintain the required numbers. However, a better approach is to subdivide the numbers into smaller divisions and create a network of them. Hence, the term Demarchy at the time of writing also refers to local government in Greece. But the way used here refers to the archaic form of Democracy that existed before Athens. In this way, hundreds of thousands of people forming a tribe could meet with others. Tribes brought together to resolve matters by vote could meet independently, then combine the results from each other's subdivisions or districts. When the separate tribes were required to meet, a select number would attend the Central General Assembly. The number could be chosen by sortition and be the maximum possible number deemed practical. The smallest subdivision forms the limit to the numbers. Therefore, careful planning is necessary to ensure that the sample size is sufficient to represent the population accurately. From a statistical point of view, it has been suggested that a sample size of 10% of a large population is considered a suitable sample size.

Demarchy as a Complementary System has often been considered a system of its own. For example, in a constitutional monarchy or a republican system, elements of a demarchy could be incorporated. However, what constitutes a Demarchy and a Democracy requires clarification first. As noted elsewhere, Democracy is the higher-quality and ethical form of a Demarchy. It is essentially the same thing manifested in two different versions. The Demarchy is not always unethical, but by the standards of a Democracy, it is less ethical. Demarchy has the people leading, while Democracy has the people holding the power. It is a subtle but essential distinction that Aristotle made. A lot could be said about the inclusion of a Demarchy within various systems. The systems could adopt the sortition process to balance bias and corruption in government, provided that candidate selection came from the people and was not selected by the Elite.

Overall, a Demarchy precedes a Democracy by providing the mechanisms by which it will work. It is up to the people to ensure that they have the power to control their state. The slightest apathy on such a matter relinquishes control over the state, and it regresses first to a Demarchy and then to several possibilities, including an Ochlocracy, Oligarchy, or Autocracy.

2.3 Quality of Government

In history, many nations have acted in a way to enslave a minority group or to make outcasts of certain people, such as the disabled, unmarried couples, fatherless children, firstborns etc. Ethnicities have also been targeted verbally and violently. The occurrence of injustices within an autocracy, oligarchy, ochlocracy, or pleistarchy would make such a system appear to have little virtue. An unvirtuous system can arise from an uneducated and unwise leader, leaders, or populace. People can also resort to supporting actions that defy our ethics. There is a high likelihood that when people act unethically, something else drives them to do so. Many misguided and unethical political actions are preceded by misinformation or propaganda. That is important to note because our senses are at the interface between ourselves and everything around us. If our senses were to tell us lies, such as it is cold when it is warm, then we would act peculiarly. In the same way, the information we analyze and assess has to be credible. Otherwise, everything from the analysis and assessment of false information will also be erroneous.

Aspects that distinguish the quality of a government system rest on its structure, its ability to function, and the quality of that function. One of the functions of government is to maintain order. As noted earlier, it is the primary reason for establishing government in the first place. Without order, a government system cannot exist. Therefore, it is a prerequisite to any government system. An order achieved reasonably and justly is of higher quality than one imposed ruthlessly. Humans perceive order in the events in their lives. If high levels of crime or dysfunction persist on the streets, citizens may perceive that order has not been maintained. Therefore, maintaining order in society is considered a crucial factor in determining the quality of a system. However, order and the methods used to achieve it require a reference to quality or virtues. If we look at the fairness of laws to indicate the virtues used to attain order, then those laws that impose the least and are fairest to the freedom and happiness of people will rank the highest in terms of quality. People generally perceive specific laws as fair and just if they work for their interests. If a law imposes on their freedom, liberty, rights, or privileges, it will be perceived as unfair. Therefore, the quality of law-making needs to be considered as part of the appraisal when determining what type of government system exists or is to exist. If the people's interest is to forbid a certain action, but the law adversely affects all citizens in the process, then this can be seen as oppressive. Examples of this method of law-making are displayed on roads and transport systems that monitor vehicle speeds. All citizens are monitored when using the road, and any who break the law, by intent or otherwise, are punished by the law. This form of law is usually met with resentment and discontent. Laws such as these may not focus solely on excessive speed but also address other issues related to the mode of transit. It is often argued that speed and the condition and type of equipment used for transit can affect the safety of those using the same road. When such laws become nuisances or, in some places, oppressive, the law focuses on anyone who may be slightly above or below a certain speed on the road, and enforcement results in severe punishment. Those who typically do not speed but are occasionally fined consider such systems unfair. It is a matter of statistics that, given enough laws governing a particular thing, exposure to them will eventually lead someone to contradict or break them.

Additionally, if sufficiently monitored, those accidental and intentional violations of the law will yield a substantial reward to the government that imposes them. The greater the population monitored, the greater the chance of generating income from accidental and intentional lawbreaking. That then brings us to the issue of the quality of the laws that establish order.

To be established fairly and, more importantly, in a way that a society can be content with, the system must allow citizens to enforce the law themselves. This indeed was the case in early Athenian Democracy. Although there is much to say on this matter, it is worth noting that the youth patrolled the city and enforced the citizens' laws. How can anyone enforce a law they deem corrupt, unfair, or far from ethical? The youth and new candidates for citizenship became accustomed to the laws through their enforcement. If they found anything unfair or required amendment, they did so later in life as citizens and as part of the assembly. This system ensured that the policing was done by the same people as opposed to paid or biased minority groups.

Therefore, the order is usually established because of the natural progression towards it by most of us. At the fringes of society are always some individuals who wish to exploit the system and the people. These individuals, who thrive or profit from chaos, also create a need to police and enforce laws within a city. These people are not always from the streets. Many are, in fact, individuals with specific concerns related to power and self-aggrandizement. We notice, for example, that businesspeople and wealthy individuals often vote for laws that favor them, rather than society. At this point, we may ask, if a law is to be made to establish order, what qualities must it have? As noted, it must be a law that the majority feels protects them and their interests. It must be a law that does not incriminate or coerce people into changing their habits. A law that creates or maintains order must place the natural process of order at its highest priority and not use force or suppression. The natural process is most potent in a Democracy because the order is established by the simple participation of each person at an assembly and their execution of state responsibilities. The other systems struggle to achieve the same natural cohesion of a Democracy because, as our history shows, most such systems require the force of law against the citizenry to maintain order.

Fairness and ethical judgment are the following matters to consider. Once we have established that the laws are enacted in the best possible manner, the way those laws are used to judge individuals also needs consideration. The most ethical judgment method must consider that the law is applied fairly and indiscriminately. Its reasoning and understanding methods must be objective yet simultaneously demonstrate compassion. Judgment made by one individual is not a reliable form of judgment. The same person can hear the same case and judge differently due to many factors in a courtroom. If the judge's mood, biases, and other factors influence the judge presiding over a trial, the trial and its outcomes are also affected. A larger number of judges better achieves fair judgment. That assumes that each is as skilled as the others and selected by sortition. Knowledge of the law, a good understanding of the legal system, and a good idea of what justice is are required of every judge.

To answer the question of what defines the quality of a kratos or government, we must first define a perfect system, as we need an ideal system to compare the rest with. The quality of a system must therefore rest on what we consider ethical. Because ethics and their values change over time, we can't define a single set of ethics that will be regarded as ethical forever. Whatever is considered ethical must be present throughout the system, its processes, and applications. In doing this, the system reflects the higher ideals and virtues of the polity. In an oligarchy or monarchy, there was a tendency for the people's ethics to be skewed to the interests of the few. That created a generation gap in behaviors and attitudes between the generations. Each had its own set of morals and ethics. Therefore, the quality of a democratic government will differ from that of other systems. A Democracy relies heavily on the morals and ethics of the majority. However, having said this much, the quality can still be measured through the three functions of the governing system. That is the law-making, the application of judgment, and the enforcement to start with. Then there are the administrative tasks and the quality measures found in them. These include the time, involvement, efficiency, communication, and consultation, as well as the overall caliber and quality of the individuals within the system.

2.3.1 Making of Just Laws

Making fair and just laws is one of the most important considerations. The consequences and related matters of that law can also measure the value of a law. So, if a law is poorly written, it may have dire consequences. A system that relies on both written and unwritten laws can become corrupt. However, having said this, the unwritten law is typically found where the people have established a particular law through precedent. In many places, the law of precedence is known as common law. However, common law, as found in a system of Oligarchy or Monarchy, may benefit the people. The primary purpose of the common law system was to benefit the people. Where the statutory laws do not favor the people or their systems, or when the statutes are insufficient in considering a matter, justice must rely on the unwritten or non-statutory law through a different avenue.

Common law was initially developed to provide a uniform way of dealing with similar incidents, in which many jurisdictions became interdependent and subordinate to a higher jurisdiction. It may have been statutory law in one place but not in another; yet, the idea was considered one to apply uniformly. That was especially true of the various empires and how they operated their legal systems. It eventually, to some extent, gave voice to the people. The people's voice through the law was established when compensatory and work-related laws emerged to acknowledge the unwritten laws that the people expected to protect them. In a democracy, the rule of law and statutes alone are considered the pinnacle achievement of a polity. Aristotle and Confucius independently held that the quality of leaders and their laws significantly contributed to the overall quality of the system. However, their views emphasized a preferred monarchical or oligarchic system. Applying their principles to the democratic system, where the leaders are the people, the idea remains the same. Therefore, the quality of individuals determines the quality of other aspects of the democratic system.

Source, processing, declaration, and enforceability are key areas to consider when making fair laws. These primary areas determine the overall quality of lawmaking. An assessment of the source of a law or a proposed law is needed. What is that law's intention, and what are its purposes? Will it serve the system's ethos and benefit a majority or minority? If protecting a minority's voice benefits a minority, is it ethical? Therefore, once the source has been scrutinized, the value of the proposed law can be determined. In a democracy, the general assembly, where the population meets, must first read the law. More will be said on the administrative aspects; however, the time to read and process the laws is crucial. Investing more time in reading and understanding the laws to start with is vital to the quality of the process. More values can be described; however, they will be discussed later to avoid repetition. The processing must allow ample time, involve all necessary parties, be efficient, ensure effective communication, and comply with the Constitution and other relevant laws. The people must be educated enough to make these decisions, and an ethical process must be administered.

The law should be made public, and people must be aware of it. In the past, many laws were processed without discussion and, after being tabled, were not publicly declared; instead, they were circulated only among those with an interest. A democratic system would present the proposed law in its final version, review it publicly, and make it available for public access. However, more importantly, the announcement of the law must alert citizens to its arrival and implementation. If the law is not advertised to the public before finalization and is not immediately advertised before finalization, the quality of the declaration process would not be transparent enough to qualify as a high-quality system. The transparency of the laws must be such that the entire process is open to scrutiny, even in the final moments before they are enacted and take effect. Once a law has been declared, it will be ascended or enacted pending a vote from the general assembly. In summary, this briefly covers the qualities required to declare a law.

The next consideration is the enforceability of the agreement. Once a law is in its final stages and has been presented to the people, they must decide how well it will be enforced and the quality of its enforceability. When writing this, they turned the average citizen into a tax collector. Each person was required to declare and submit their tax declarations for what they called an

Income Tax Return evaluation. There were penalties for failing to enforce the taxation requirement on each working adult. In a fair and just system, the enforceability of a law should be left to those who enforce it. The enforcement of the law should be fair and not unreasonable or harsh. However, as more laws became self-enforceable, it became apparent that people were performing duties and roles that would not otherwise have been their responsibility. For example, they placed an onus on the statutes, making the safety of others the duty of both the employee and the employer. It's a soft request that seems logical. However, this meant that extraordinary things had to be complied with, well beyond the average person's knowledge and skill set. Such things included micro tasks like checking electrical cables and power tools every three months. At the same time, those who checked the tools raised their prices to profit from the situation. Thus, the average worker is responsible for checking their tools at their own expense. These laws burdened common people with the duty to act as police officers and bear the associated costs, whether material or otherwise. Indeed, no law should impose any requirement on a free citizen, not even the much-desired participation in the General Assembly. The ethics and morals of the polity should drive them with conviction in the operation of their administration. Using this drive would require making fair and democratic laws that impose the least burden on citizens.

Also, the enforceability of punitive laws is usually a measure of the ability to bring a matter to trial and the outcome of such trials. So, if hundreds of cases are brought to trial but the verdicts always dismiss them, there is an issue of enforceability. In addition, for non-punitive and punitive laws, a measure of enforceability is the number of cases brought to trial and the number of verdicts that do not require further action. These are enforceable indicators if a process requires a retrial, an appeal to a higher court, or an appeal of the verdict or sentence.

2.3.2 Just Judgment

It could be argued that the judgment of a qualified and experienced judge will be worth more than that of a group of uneducated and inexperienced judges. However, it is a daunting prospect to leave life-changing decisions in the hands of a few. If the process aims to deliver an unbiased judgment, then the responsibility could be argued to be left to multiple judges in the form of a jury. The jury has the power to render a verdict, but a magistrate or several magistrates, subject to compliance with the rules, can oversee the entire process.

When writing this, the juries were small, and the judges were few in every case. A jury is typically composed of 12 members, and 1 to 3 judges may preside. However, up to fifty judges may also be involved in cases where the judgment has been reserved. That typically involves candid consultation and group meetings to determine the outcome. The Aristotelian constitution describes thousands of jurors with an administrative team ensuring the quality of the hearing. That would involve discussing the facts, allocating time to each party to speak, and setting specific expectations for the conduct of those in the court.

It would be more reasonable in a fair system for the jury to count at least 300 from each tribe up to the practical limit of the smallest tribe. For 12 tribes, that would be 12 × 300, or 3,600 jurors. For a half court, that would be 150 x 12, or 1,800 jurors. A quarter court would be 75 x 12, which equals 900 jurors. These figures are based on the information we gain from the Bible and the Athenian constitution, which was influenced by the works of Aristotle, Plato, and Socrates. Therefore, we know that historically, the establishment of just judgment has relied heavily on an unbiased jury of judges. The magistrates served as administrative staff to ensure the quality of the process, but never intervened or led the case. Otherwise, their biases would resound throughout the process and influence the result.

The ancient Athenians recognized the need for specialist legal skills and implemented them in higher courts composed of many Archons (magistrates) and a jury. This allowed serious crimes to be dealt with by individuals who understood the law and had experience within the legal system to comprehend the nature of the crimes being judged. It would be a blend of judges and a jury sitting together for crimes such as murder.

2.3.3 Fair Enforcement

When criminal law enforcement bends the law to justify an arrest, or when false witnesses bend the law to promote an arrest, enforcement can be unfair. Many people are falsely judged based on evidence collected by the enforcers. Fair enforcement would mean eliminating the possibility of being arrested and put on trial for the same or almost the same incident. It would mean taking a report from a person capable of understanding the consequences. Fair enforcement would also mean that they are aware that they are giving a statement. The person to protect themselves from particular consequences would have the right to remain silent and not give a statement. However, these and many other matters related to fair enforcement concern specific rights that citizens should have. The process of establishing rights is discussed further in this philosophy. It is enough to say that the main areas of concern are the conduct of the citizen, the enforcers, and the witnesses.

Similarly, non-criminal laws require similar guidelines for their enforcement. It is a matter of how well the enforcing officer performs their duties, the entity under scrutiny, and the witnesses who bring about an arrest; all require quality in their functions. An officer must be unbiased, the entity brought to scrutiny must be compliant, and the witnesses must be honest. Fair enforcement can be elaborated further. Prejudiced profiling, such as that based on religion, race, or lifestyle, all lead to poor enforcement and skewed intercepts and engagements. Unfair handling may include rude or violent handling by the enforcers. Concerning the witness, they may be in poor mental health, have a compromised understanding, or face other hindrances that may affect their ability to give evidence or understand the consequences of the evidence at hand.

A person with the right to remain silent may choose not to exercise it, thinking they can explain the situation. However, this is not entirely possible, particularly if a false witness is present. False witnesses are more common than we think. They are often people who take it upon themselves to purport a particular view, such as protecting older people, minors, or some defenseless group from a perpetrator they deem dangerous. The instinct to protect often leads people to lie to save others. But all they are doing is corrupting a system that requires their honesty. You see if a person lies that a person fired a gun when all they saw was them picking up a weapon. Then, the consequences dramatically differ for the person who held the gun. The prevalence of false witnesses is why our religious texts state that we should never bear false witness. In summary, these factors contribute to the fundamental aspects of fair law enforcement.

2.3.4 Time Investment

The time invested in any art or work plays a significant role in determining its quality. Musicians practice their skills, and it takes time before they can perform. It has been said that a lifetime can pass in trying to perfect a skill. Similarly, although we would like a perfect system, the one we achieve relies on the time we invest.

Therefore, the time invested in educating the system that will be governed is the priority and initial step of the quality assurance process. Then, there is the education and experience gained from working with the Legislature, Judiciary, and Enforcement. These areas of education and training require time and should be overseen by auditors and experts, forming a body of Archons. The Archons were experienced magistrates or individuals with expertise in a particular area of the system. There were military Archons, police Archons, Judicial Archons, and so on. However, they took on the role of overseeing that processes were conducted in accordance with the law. They were a form of compliance officer. Then, the Athenian model had auditors who scrutinized the actions of magistrates and archons.

From a philosophical perspective, the time we invest in any art form will benefit us. Therefore, investing time and effort in an aspect of the system will undoubtedly benefit the system positively. However, time alone does not equate to better quality. It merely allows better quality systems to emerge and develop. If time is invested in the wrong things, they can harm the system's quality. That is why we need to ensure other criteria are in place, such as investing time in the best possible matters, properly timing that investment, allocating sufficient time, and commissioning the proper actions within that time frame.

2.3.5 Involvement

Given sufficient time, another indicator of a democratic system's quality is the level of participation. The level of participation determines many other peripheral factors. These peripheral issues include workforce power, morale and motivation, productivity and performance, better compliance, and adaptation to change. In the legislative process of the Democratic system, meetings held without broad and equal representation are considered unfair. The legislative participation needs are the same in the judiciary and the enforcement. A certain number of people are required before a particular task may proceed with confidence. A jury of only twelve people is not a good indicator of a population. Instead, large numbers are required to balance the representation of the various groups and people within a polity.

The involvement of people has never been quantified, and as a result, some systems claim to have juries when, in reality, they are insignificant in number. In some systems worldwide, having a small jury of 12 people with three judges present and approximately 50 judges behind the scenes making the decisions is acceptable. The process is neither transparent nor a case of a full jury representing the people. In contrast, the involvement of people in the system ensures that large, unbiased juries can be formed. But in systems worldwide, there is no democratic jury.

Concerning law enforcement, again, the ability to bring criminals and perpetrators to decisive judgment depends, to some degree, on the number of law enforcement personnel. As has been done in modern times, each regulatory and criminal law department brings people to court. If the ratio of police officers to the population is so low, their enforcement capacity is significantly diminished.

2.3.6 Efficiency

The system's efficiency is another quality factor. An efficient system reduces costs, increases productivity, optimizes resource use and allocation, enables faster decision-making, provides satisfaction to participants, and produces a better system overall. The factors of time and participation have been discussed, and their role in efficiency is calculable. However, many other things will affect efficiency. These include process efficiency, training and education, technology, communication clarity, performance, delegation systems, time management, continuous improvement, flexibility to shift resources, feedback mechanisms, and monitoring systems.

In the legislature, the main problem in the past has been the time allotted to each person to speak. The time to express views is why many people can derail a process by delaying it or consuming time with inappropriate or intentionally time-consuming questions. The legislature's efficiency comes from all the factors mentioned so far. The legislature's highest priority is the ability to communicate and make informed, effective decisions. Anyone who has participated in regular meetings will know that, unless pertinent, questioning should be kept to a minimum, and the facts relating to a matter should be stated if they haven't already. A time limit for pros and cons should be set to ensure equal presentation time for each party. That is also true of the judiciary.

Regarding the judiciary, aside from what has already been mentioned, several cases must be processed each day, and the trials must be handled as efficiently as possible. The presentation of cases, questioning, and other related facts, as well as all other matters, must be handled efficiently. Indeed, the Democratic process takes longer, is less efficient, and doesn't consistently achieve the majority's will. However, this is only because a Democratic system usually promotes a meticulous interest in the quality of the system. Part of that interest is the efficiency of the democratic system in all areas.

For law enforcement, the process is efficient when the number of arrests does not differ significantly from the number of trials. That is, arrests are successfully brought to trial, judged, and sentenced. When a police officer or regulatory officer brings a person or party to trial, efficiency is achieved when the officer correctly assesses the person's or party's guilt, and the system correctly handles the offense and its penalty or punishment. The enforcer's evaluation has often caused issues with how the enforcers try to bring cases to judgment. However, the enforcement biases can be balanced if the enforcers are in multiples of three, selected by sortition and randomly allocated to work together.

2.3.7 Communication

Communication and consultation are essential to a functioning democratic system. As highlighted elsewhere, uniformity and the need for some level of assimilation for effective communication are critical to any decision-making process. Effective communication among the legislature, the judiciary, and enforcement agencies at all levels is crucial for ensuring that informed decisions are made. Furthermore, communication and freedom of speech facilitate transparency within the system. It facilitates communication of the need for participation and ensures people know when and why they should meet. It encourages debates and allows the decision-making process to accept new facts.

Communication plays a crucial role in protecting free speech, resolving conflicts, fostering social cohesion, safeguarding minority rights, and establishing a sense of legitimacy for outcomes and decisions as they are conveyed and understood by the majority. Communication is essential to a critical thinking model's information, analysis, and assessment process.

2.3.8 Compliance

Compliance with the laws requires auditors, magistrates, and Archons to facilitate the process. Preservation of the law relies on the system's ability to process laws, actions, and their intentions. Some areas that may be monitored for compliance include protecting individual rights and ensuring fair and equitable governance that avoids nepotism and favoritism. Furthermore, compliance lends legitimacy to the system, fosters better social cohesion and unbiased conflict resolution, and even prevents authoritarianism, oligarchies, and monarchies from taking control of the system. It might be possible to elaborate further on every point raised. However, the purpose of this topic is to introduce and highlight the importance of compliance with the law.

Some might argue that the rule of law is paramount. Additionally, ensuring that the governing system upholds these laws is crucial. What good is it to have laws that do not apply to those who govern? If the laws, in theory, apply to everyone, but the judgment of the government never seems to happen, then the chances are that the laws are not being applied to them. It is a common worldwide phenomenon in which governors, typically the few, are considered infallible. Rarely do they have the law applied to them, from the most minor to the most serious of charges, to evade the rule of law. In summary, the matters raised lead us to conclude that forsaking credibility, legitimacy, and authenticity in a democratic model requires balances and checks that uphold the rule of law.

The protection of rights is another significant area that requires consideration. Meeting compliance requirements ensures the protection of the people and their authority and powers. Provided, of course, that they have legislated the requirements to monitor the system under several compliance officers, auditors, and essential members needed to determine if the system is being used the way it should be. That requires a clear and concise constitution, as well as relevant and succinct laws. By ensuring the compliance of the governing system, civil rights and the democratic system are protected.

2.3.9 Quality of the individuals

The qualities of the individual can be separated into three broad areas: the individual, the interface with groups, and the interface with the governing administrative system. More skilled philosophers have summarised the individual's traits. However, we can clarify some of the individual ethics requirements. Courage, Justice, Truthfulness, Fortitude, Diligence, Temperance, Patience, Kindness, and Humility. From a philosophical point of view, these affect the individuals' actions, how they interact with others, and how they interact and work within the governing administrative system. These virtues are also common in that they are found in varying forms in all people. If we began by listing critical thinking as a virtue, it would exclude a significant portion of society, including those with creative and artistic minds. Not that such people are incapable of thinking critically. However, some are more concerned with the art than the science of things and, as such, focus more on the arts in the way they carry themselves in life.

Table 1. A list of common virtues.

Virtues	Effects
Courage	Impacts participation. By encouraging people, participation grows.
Justice	Ensures fair treatment of issues and cases. Fair elections, voting, and decision-making. Honest and transparent systems.
Truthfulness	Accurate information.
Fortitude	To persevere with the work that is required.
Diligence	To ensure fair and compliant elections and processes.
Temperance	To share experience and knowledge. To inform, consult, and cooperate in a mannered way.
Patience	To give change and process management time to take effect.
Kindness	To ensure trust and ongoing sharing of information, cooperation, and consultation.
Humility	A leader isn't always a hero. Leadership usually requires an emotive connection to a person, and the catalyst is usually humility.

However, we would like critical thinking, tolerance and respect for others, open-mindedness, leadership, and many other qualities. However, the ones listed affect all facets of how the individual interacts throughout the system. Ultimately, we can conclude that an individual's virtues and ethics greatly determine the quality of the person. People should rarely be judged by a spectrum we call 'normal behavior'. However, those who intentionally and maliciously act within groups and the system require some form of attention. Again, the rule of law must exist to prevent those who struggle to uphold these ethics from participating in the system. In ancient Athens, people were often ostracised for gaining extreme popularity. That was done to preserve the democratic process. There may be other ways to achieve the same results, and each democratic polity must decide such matters.

An area that deserves more focus is Ethical Administration. That refers to the fact that people must behave in a way considered ethical as a group. If they do not, the consequences for the system are serious. That is why a sense of justice is necessary within individuals, as well as effective leadership, to prevent others from steering groups into a maelstrom of immoral activity. The entire administrative system, therefore, must have an ethical culture developed by the individuals who comprise it.

2.3.10 Ethical laws

The next matter is the ethical law of the culture. Each culture develops its morals or ethics, which are usually expressed as cultural laws. Most cultural laws have little to do with debts, property, contracts, damages, or injury, but rather with traditions. Certain days may be considered holy, for rest, or for a specific purpose. Other cultural laws are observed in matters such as marriage, divorce, and certain other aspects. These laws, along with their ethics and sources, are essential to determining the quality of a government. Morals and ethics within a society influence the government, just as the government shapes the morals and ethics of the people it governs. The correlation between the ethics found in society and those imposed by the government must also be balanced to be perceived as virtuous. If a society believes that no one should be executed, and yet the government executes individuals for breaking specific laws, or vice versa, it means a balance of ethics has not been achieved.

Ethics, laws, and justice are the foundation for order. They are the platform upon which a Democracy can be established. More precisely, justice must be ethical, and it must be uniformly applied to everyone through law. Without ethics, laws, and a system, justice will not be just; ethics lead to better justice. Of course, to apply justice, we need laws that apply to everyone and are enforceable for everyone. Once these things are in place, a polity can transform chaos, disharmony, and anarchy into order and stabilize its system of government. Language, religion, ethics, and culture somehow unite people. However, they must then utilize that loose unity to formalize their system of government. In a monarchy, numerous examples have been seen where the monarch's religion, culture, and language have also become the dominant ones for the majority, often through physical or other forms of coercion. Similarly, a Democratic government that is comprised of uneducated and unethical people can devastate the Democratic institution by reducing it to an Ochlocracy.

In quantifying ethics, they are like matters predisposed to the nature of a central source or spring. All things, in my view, stem from them. It is known that thought precedes an action. We can't act unless we think of acting. Even in reflex reactions, the process, whether noticed or not, involves our nervous system, which has been taught and memorized. The other forms of reflex, such as biologically predetermined responses, include events like stimulating a nerve and eliciting a reaction. However, as true as this may be about how we act, it does not describe the quality of our actions. We often hold athletes or people who excel at a particular skill in high esteem. The display of their skills is wonderful. It also hints that we naturally steer towards appreciating these extraordinary skills. Yet we steer away from what we culturally perceive as less ethically valuable. The art of thievery is not admired or appreciated, nor is that of corruption. What we know about society is that the things we perceive as good, as defined by cultural norms, are the actions we like to see exhibited.

Ethics, therefore, like thought, occurs preceding an action. The thought initiates the action process, and ethics defines the parameters of those actions. Both occurred before we took any action. Just as our reflexes learn to remove our limbs from danger – such as fire – so that the process is almost instant, the ethics we develop and learn become ingrained in various situations. When we are yelled at, some of us learn to cry, others yell back, and others respond with physical violence. Sometimes, any combination of these lesser human qualities occurs. It takes longer, and it is far more complex for people to develop good ethics. Religion-based ethics is why religion has traditionally been the tool or mechanism to deliver those ethics. The history of religion teaches us that it never stands alone as a mechanism to worship a deity. There are always other factors associated with it. I am not talking about one religion but about all religions. It has been traditionally accepted that ethics are variable, and where we might say courage is beneficial in some situations, it often leads to needless deaths in others. The concept of ethics has become too complex to quantify due to this variation, but it can be defined for each instance to which it applies. It is like describing the sun in one sentence. We know every day that it is in the sky and visible aside from the unusual ecliptic events, and at night, it is not visible in the sky on one side of our planet. But if you were to describe it at any point, that description would only be viable for that instant and place on Earth. The sun will appear elsewhere in the sky within a few hours, yet if we wait long enough, it will reappear the next day in almost the same position. The Sun's patterns can be complex; our ethics can have complex patterns. As with everything that defines or describes a situation, our ethics will change in response to many variables.

The laws are then an extension of our ethics; this implies that the laws will change as our ethics fluctuate. The laws define the structures and processes that are allowed to exist or otherwise. Justice is the macro-level control of things that balances a scientist's equations and prevents plagues of one species and the extinction of another. The same things apply to a government system. Justice is the ethical establishment and application of laws. We often perceive the term as seeking justice for ourselves personally. However, justice is also the quality of ethics applied to a polity. As mentioned, ethics define the quality of our actions. Therefore, it is reasonable to say that a law is an act or a set of rules.

Additionally, ethics must be applied to the law, both in establishing it, maintaining it, enforcing it, and judging others by it. Our ethics will be defined by the answer to the question, "What should we be?". Laws will ensure that established ethics are protected, and they shall determine what shall and shall not be part of the polity and government. Justice will ensure that all that is developed is adhered to without favor, corruption, or bias.

Even though these factors culminate in how a particular government is perceived, the underlying quality of the system can't be objectively measured. All the things that constitute a government, including ethics, laws, justice, enforcement, legislators, judiciary, and everything created and controlled by the government, can be summarised by the word Arete or virtue. "Arete" and "Virtue" are similar, but one is derived from Greek and the other from Latin. It is then worth noting that virtue implies some kind of superiority. In contrast, Arete refers to something more akin to an Alpha Class or an Elite in terms of human qualities, rather than wealth or worth. If ethics are themselves to be virtuous or arête, it must imply that the answer to "What we should be?" is righteous. If our ethics lack virtue, then the system based on them falls short of our ideals. The complexity of the matter is that some cultures engage in horrendous acts compared to others. Yet, one is often equally flawed as the other. We can live with flaws, believe they are normal, and think of ourselves as perfect, but such thoughts would be lies. We know perfection is not possible. It is a qualitative, subjective matter influenced by many factors; even if a pattern is found, there will be some degree of variation. This variation is part of life in a polity, and it is why a government system can never be perfect. Also, a government's quality depends on how people perceive it.

When we see a system that causes atrocities in any facet, it is not considered a system worth keeping. In contrast, if there is virtue in our ethics and all things that stem from them, we will be happier and more content with the outcome. Theoretically, a Monarch could be virtuous, like an Aristocracy or a Democracy. They are perceived as righteous by the quality of their work or through observation. However, as we know, this quality is also proportional to the time people have to invest in political matters. Irrespective of the type of government system, it will not be of high quality if proper time and effort are not invested. In ancient Athens, farmers and all citizens were paid to attend the assemblies where democratic voting took place. That is because they wanted a high number of people to attend. They knew that the more people involved, the more productive hours spent, and the more time and effort put into the system, the greater the benefit. A more pressing question that warrants further consideration is how we can define the better ethics that the polity will be founded upon. If the leaders act for any other reason than to benefit the people in a government system, will it be a virtuous government? How does tax become possible if the money comes from the people and is not seen immediately as something to benefit them? Perhaps it depends on how the state or government spends the money in return, how it is collected, and who is authorized to spend the collection. We cannot assess all these things from a quantitative philosophical point of view. However, to define democracy properly, all these matters must be questioned and philosophically developed.

In all fairness, a nation of people who fall short of their values, ethics, and virtues probably deserves a Monarch. The term Monarch implies a virtuous autocrat. If the monarch or even an aristocracy were truly ethical and virtuous, they would seem better suited to lead. But the reality is that this is not often the case. Ethics, virtues, and values are never truly defined by a minority but by the majority. Even when there is systematic pressure to define these aspects, the impact of the few – rarely in historical terms – has overwhelmed the majority. So even though we can foresee that an Ochlocracy will not benefit everyone, those people define the state—the kratos—and the power of the polity. When the people have higher morals, values, and virtues but are governed by a Monarch who embodies the opposite, then the Monarch and the system are not virtuous by any reckoning. Again, the definition of virtue is not a matter of the individual or the few, but a culturally based view of what is virtuous and what is not.

2.3.11 A virtuous system of governing

So, then, how do we measure the degree of virtue? These things are often developed within a society and reflect its culture, religion, and moral values. In a Democracy, therefore, a Democratic system would fail our test of quality if, at any time, there were proof that the function of government has worked against the interests of the people and the government. Yet it must be clear that robbing the rich by the poor is not Democratic but the symptom of an Ochlocracy. In a democracy, the people and government are the same. Since each individual represents the values of their polity in a democracy, it is the only system that simultaneously expresses the virtues and vices of the people and government. For all others, the assessment is ambiguous and speculative, as it can't be proven conclusively. The Monarch's decisions and arguments are their own; in an Oligarchy, the decisions and arguments are isolated to the few. However, if we examine it from a statistical or probabilistic perspective, we can identify certain aspects. Given a fixed number of people in a society who are prone to corruption, as determined by a sample survey, we find that a certain percentage are prone to corruption. If we then apply that number to an Autocracy, we have one chance in as many corrupted or corruptible people as possible. In an Oligarchy, the same applies, but because there are slightly more governors, we end up with a higher probability of having many corrupted or corruptible leaders.

Let us create a hypothetical example: Assume that 10% of the population is corrupt. In an Autocracy, the chance that the leader is one of these people is 10%, meaning that one in every ten monarchs will be corrupted. In an oligarchy, the chance is 10% multiplied by the number of people in the Oligarchy. So, if 10 oligarchs exist and the probability of corruption is 10%, then at least one of them will be corrupt. In a Democracy, let us assume that 100,000 people form a government; 10% of the government is composed of 10,000 people who are either corrupt or corruptible. This implies that as more people are involved in governance, the number of corrupt participants and the level of corruption increase. Of course, this eliminates the other ideas that are tangent and integral to the argument. For instance, we know that absolute power can corrupt a person. However, let us not think along that path, as we are objectively applying quantitative analysis to the degree of corruption. Let us recognize that, while there is a lower chance of a corrupt autocrat, the outcome is that everyone is affected by that individual during their reign. In an Oligarchy, the intent of one or a few corrupt people is countered by a larger number of uncorrupted people. In a Democracy, the number of uncorrupted and transparent people vastly outweighs the number of corrupted or corruptible people. In the previous example, ninety thousand would far outweigh the ten thousand corrupted. In an autocracy, the likelihood of being led by a corrupt person may be low, but the authority and influence invested in that person can corrupt the entire system. While an Oligarchy alleviates this to some degree, as power is shared and only a few are corrupted in proportion to the majority within the Oligarchy, it is only slightly better than an Autocracy. This qualitative argument can appeal to some in an autocracy and an oligarchy. However, as previously stated, we have made an assumption and created a hypothetical scenario.

What if we assume now that every person is corruptible? Suppose we replace the 10% example with a 100% example. In that case, we quickly see that the Autocrat is guaranteed to be corrupt, as is the Oligarchy, and even the Democracy. But if this is the case, everyone should vote or take lots as appropriate for their corrupt views and interests. Therefore, in an Autocracy, one person would create a system for their own benefit. In an oligarchy, a group of people operates the government for their benefit. Yet in a corrupted Democracy, everyone will represent their own interests or biases, and inevitably, the majority of similar views will count. Tyranny through corruption can manifest within all systems, whether it be the tyranny of one, a few, or the people.

Let us review that statement made regarding power and its relation to corruption. In Plato's work, known as The Republic (originally entitled Politeia), he describes a Socratic dialogue that aims to investigate who would be in the best possible position to steal gold that is locked away. The discussion leads to the assumption that the person holding the key and guarding the gold is the one most easily able to steal it. Socrates, through Plato, suggests that power, authority, and any elevation in status beyond that of others may lead to the use of those powers for self-interest. In many instances, it is a minor, almost trivial misuse of power. At other times, it can be obvious or blatantly vivid. Some things that may seem minor or not apparent are not adhering to a particular rule or code of conduct. Others may include theft of wealth and worse through opportunities that arise from within the individual's position. Indeed, besides the things we define by quantitative methods, there is also the matter of human tendencies to use opportunities to gratify their self-interests. Ethics that serve self-interest are why certain personal virtues and the virtuosity of governments require greater analysis. However, the next step would be to examine other quantitative indicators of government systems.

Two methods for estimating the virtue of a government system are the time devoted to it and the harmony within the polity. Harmony itself extends beyond contentment to the satisfaction of everything humans consider valuable to their well-being. These are spiritual and physical components of human life, but not essentially the material and wealth that appear within society. In other words, it is the things that affect the mind, body, and soul. It is, in theory, a virtuous and committed government that distinguishes itself between an Autocracy and Tyranny, Aristocracy and Oligarchy, and a Democracy and Pleistocracy. Where one person governs and holds the source of power, the ideal system is a Monarchy, and the leader is referred to as a Monarch rather than a Tyrant. Where a few people lead the majority, the Aristocracy is a better form of an Oligarchy. Where the majority are leading or have the power, the better system is democracy rather than a pleistocracy or an Ochlocracy. To achieve a virtuous system, time and effort must be invested in ensuring that those in power uphold ethical principles. In various government systems, this is highlighted by a constitution. The constitution limits the system and government through ideas on how it should operate. In a system with a virtuous constitution that establishes these ethics and ideals, the next step to ensure their enforcement is dedicating time and effort to their realization.

Since our three categories are based on the number leading, we can easily count those leading and determine the type of system in place. We can then look at the number of people participating, as this will indicate whether the Democratic institution has whittled away and is led by a few who choose to participate. We can also count the days, weeks, or months spent operating the government system. A good indicator is the frequency of meetings and their duration multiplied to produce the total hours or time devoted to the decision-making process involving people. It would be pointless to try to work out the total hours or time spent by every empowered group or government department.

Although we may have reasonably good indicators that can be quantified, none of them alone indicates the system's quality. I mentioned earlier that the time invested in the decision-making process is a good indicator. The reason is that the decision-making process assesses the Assembly, the people, and their level of leadership involvement. Time is an indicator of participation. However, these measures do not indicate how well they lead. However, by assumption, we presume that the more time invested, the greater the decision quality.

Also, we need to be clear about how we define leadership in a government structure. Determining where the leadership is invested would be difficult within a bureaucracy. A bureaucracy is a misnomer; the suffix –cracy indicates a form of kratos, state, or government erroneously. It can be any government system laden with procedures. Bureaucracy is a system of administration used to run a government. Many systems may be combined to form hybrids of our three fundamental forms of government. These hybrids often confuse people who are not entirely familiar with what governments and government systems are. Therefore, defining and accurately knowing the source of leadership is essential. In a bureaucracy, the leadership is delegated, and a Monarch can have many departments and government entities administering their rule. Likewise, the same can be said of an Oligarchy or Democracy operating in a departmentalized system of bureaus.

Leadership comes in various forms, but underlying the creation of a leader and followers are two significant matters: a willingness on the part of followers to follow and a willingness on the part of a leader to lead. These two factors are prerequisites for any situation in which a leader and their followers exist. If we take the example of passive leadership through idolization, we end up with scenarios in which certain people are willing to follow a particular person or group. The relationship between leaders and followers is important because our topic of bureaucracy involves many intermediate leaders who take charge and guide individuals.

Personality cults may even evolve from such situations. In the case of a personality cult, people are often not compelled to follow if an imposition is placed on them for doing so. For example, if it were declared that every follower should pay tax to the personality, then most people would not. Yet in many cases, people invest, donate, or purchase services or products from the Personalities they follow. Yet authority and a legal avenue for collecting such a tax are required for something like a tax to exist. The personality alone does not imply any authority, and this is why tax, unless a peculiar circumstance arises, requires authority to impose it. A strange contradiction is the following of religious personalities. In these cases, Authority exists in a religious context and, as such, serves purposes beyond the material or worldly definition of authority. However, because it exists, people of a particular faith may be obligated to perform certain actions to comply with the rules or leadership laid out by a given religion. In all other types of personality following, people usually follow for pleasure, enjoyment, relaxation, or anything they perceive as benefiting themselves and the moments they live. Musicians often have such followings; actors and other public figures who essentially entertain can have them as well. The other extreme is aggressive leadership, which typically involves high authority being imposed on people. It is often done with great force and promotes fear, anger, and a range of other intense emotions.

Authority, as noted before, therefore has some impact on how people lead and follow. The higher the level of authority, the greater the obedience followers will show. Authority is not a simple concept, as perceptions of it vary significantly. Some leaders often impose strict rules and punishments on their followers to ensure obedience. In many cases, this approach may be effective, but in others, it can lead to rebellion, ultimately undermining the leader's authority. Force, strict laws, and heavy-handed treatment of citizens will not always create a perception of Authority. Even if authority is achieved through this method, history provides ample examples to demonstrate that such leadership is often short-lived. It may create obedience out of fear, but relationships between followers and leaders typically do not last.

In some cases, the level of extremity in leadership has led to rebellion. In other cases, it has led to their assassination, resignation, and, other times, the people allied with a conquering army. A peculiar moment in Byzantine history reveals that the city was taken without a fight against a band of Crusader armies. The rightful king of Byzantium was on a march against another foe. It is said that the pretenders claimed the throne and began issuing new laws in their favor. Before the return of the rightful king, the citizens blockaded all roads, shut the inner-city gates, and sealed the pretender's armies within Constantinople, now known to many as Istanbul. The citizens themselves crushed the entire army and its leader. The traditional idea of Authority was not enough to satisfy the populace, despite the armed soldiers and the man posing as King.

There must also be an element of acceptance, love, or liking of the leadership for the relationship to last. The love of those in leadership is, in part, a prerequisite for creating social harmony. Therefore, authority and acceptance of authority work together to establish a lasting scenario of leadership and followers. Acceptance usually stems from a complex set of issues. We accept leaders when a person is in love with the leader, has mutual interests, and when the leader or the system can be used for self-gain. Love or liking of a leader can be personal or based on their ideology. It can also take the form of a Personality following. Mutual interests can arise from ideologies and actions that align with the views of individual followers. More important are the things done in favor of those perceived as necessary. Mutual interests can manifest as ideological and political beliefs. Self-gain for a leader can arise from opening new opportunities, such as employment, business ventures, or other material products or services. Self-gain is a powerful motivator, promoting a stronger relationship between citizens and leaders or the government. Often, people are sedated by copious amounts of material wealth and can live contentedly for considerable periods.

In some cases, where wealth is taken from the majority, it may lead to rebellion. But if people feel content through material gains, they often become sedated and do not act. They would rather enjoy their luxuries in the moment than risk losing them. I will cover this in more detail when we address the issues of modern government systems. It is enough to say that, of all three forms of relationships between leaders and followers, the most commonly implemented is through the provision of gain, ensuring the populace is content and sedated by viewing themselves as lucky or privileged. Therefore, the leadership of a system must then include authority and acceptance.

Let us apply these ideas to the definition of the three types of government. In a monarchy, the monarch will often be surrounded by numerous individuals who extend the monarch's authority. They may hold varying titles, such as advisors, councilors, lords, aristocratic councils, knights, royal guards, and governors. These people work closely with the monarch to perform a specific duty or task. The Monarch typically invests authority in such individuals to perform that particular duty. If it is impossible for any of the people forming the Oligarchy under the monarch to remove the monarch from power legally, then the system is a true Monarchy. If, however, a figurehead exists —i.e., a monarch —then it exists only because an Oligarchy has given it the power to exist. Then, the authority did not rest with the monarch but with the oligarchy. Often, dictatorships may appear Monarchical but are actually decided by a council of military generals or similar small minority groups, or by Oligarchies. In some rare cases, foreign Oligarchies install domestic puppet regimes or Dictatorships.

A valid Monarch or Autocrat is, therefore, a person who is the only source of authority and can delegate that authority to others. They also lead as an individual despite the formation of a large administrative body beneath them. At times, their role may even seem insignificant. All that matters is the question of where the authority resides and begins. If a Monarch is perpetually in power and is unable to be removed by the laws of a nation, then they represent a true Monarchy or Autocracy. I say Monarchy or Autocracy because, in either case, the question of leadership quality is not in any way affected by the source of authority. A poorly-led people will be led by an autocrat, and a monarch will lead a well-led people. This is different from our current concern about investigating and qualifying the invested Authority and its source.

The same arguments can be used to determine where true power lies in other government systems, such as oligarchies or aristocracies. If an Oligarchy is to be considered a true Oligarchy or Aristocracy, then that group must retain the ability to empower or authorize. In a system where the Aristocrats can be removed by the people or the monarch, legally within the government framework, then it is not a true form of Aristocracy or Oligarchy. The term 'removing' is not intended to mean changing the structure or organization itself, but rather the individuals within the Oligarchy, so that the people or monarch may replace the few who lead.

Typically, bloodlines and inherited titles are found in an Aristocracy (and Monarchy). Oligarchies typically involve wealth and military power, which give them authority. Many people assume that an aristocracy is bound to its position by methods other than the people's vote or the order of any other entity, but this is incorrect. An Aristocracy or Oligarchy can manifest equally through the same or similar criteria. Many government systems worldwide use a restricted form of government that preserves, by constitution or law, the seats or positions of an Oligarchy, Aristocracy, Monarchy, or Autocracy. These systems are referred to by various names—Republics, Democracies, Constitutional Monarchies, and Monarchies—and are often described by others as Oligarchies, Dictatorships, Autocracies, and so forth. The point is that all forms of government seek to preserve their type and power. Typically, this responsibility falls to those protected or whose positions and seats are preserved.

But what difference does it make, regarding Authority, if the Monarch is replaced by an Heir instead of an elected King? What difference will there be between an Elected Oligarchy or Aristocracy over a perpetual one? In terms of authority, there is no difference. An old story about Aesop describes him walking into a town where they were electing a leader. He remarked, "Why would you replace the fat and content cat with a skinny, hungry one?"

In some cases, elections can be beneficial, but not always. It can help prevent the rise of Autocrats and Oligarchs to power. The alternative of a hereditary claim, or bloodlines, is probably the poorest of the available options. The best would probably be a philosopher-king elected on the merit of their philosophy and ideas. As Plato, Socrates, and others pointed out, a person with vast wisdom and broad knowledge who is not corrupted but seeks the truth is also the best leader. But the ironic twist is that the philosopher, as gentle and wise as he may be, won't be able to lie or cheat or wage wars as well as an army general. A government system may benefit from Philosophy, but a philosopher generally doesn't have the skills to perform well as a King. There is a saying that stipulates that times of war require philosophy the most, yet there is no time for philosophy during times of war. Likewise, the contribution of a good and wise leader is beneficial. However, when the opponent or aggressors are waging war, the best man to lead is no longer gentle and wise but youthful, intelligent, cunning, and spirited. It is worth noting that various complex systems can often be confusing to some people. It can be challenging to determine the source of power in a system, especially when the system has gone to great lengths to conceal it.

In more elaborate circumstances, a bicameral government may be formed under the auspices of another foreign government, such as a monarchy. In such a system, it is common for various parties and members to occupy the same seats of power through elections. These government systems have tiers, such as lower and upper tiers, or representatives and senators. Similar systems exist in numerous systems called republics. In bi-cameral systems, although many parties may have seats in government or parliament, the party with the majority of seats is considered the ruling party or government. Because the seats they occupy will always exist, irrespective of who sits in them, such systems preserve an Oligarchy. Systems such as these use the demos to vote for a few or a small number of people into government. Yet, the people do not have the power or authority to prevent a candidate from entering the parliament or government in the first place. Nor do they have much more right or privileges to vote on any matter until the next similar election. If such systems claim to be democratic, democracy ends with a single vote. People are allowed to do so every certain number of years.

Looking at an Oligarchy or Aristocracy at an individual voter's level, the voting process may appear to have some effect. It may even seem that each person's vote counts. But these are illusions that contain the people. Typically, the media marks the party that changes its position, and people follow. The issues seem real and relevant to their lives, but most aren't. Finding anything to use against one party is a tactic to make people believe it is their choice, like false pretexts for war. To remove one party from their position, they must be blamed for something. The people believe the things said against the party and vote them out. Who then has the true power? Could it be that the groups capable of changing the minds of millions of people are the true source of power? The answer would be no. Yes, they can influence and manipulate people, even steering them toward anything they want. The authority and power will still be with the Oligarchy. Why? The Oligarchy remains perpetually in place because the people are changing the staff, not the Oligarchy.

In complex arrangements such as Constitutional Monarchies and elaborate Republics, the hidden nature of the government can make it difficult to categorize, as these systems blend various systems. The size of these governments grows so large that, in effect, they are very bureaucratic. So much so that the system is preserved by the law and by the many people who serve it. Often, the term "public servants" is used to describe people working in government, but in reality, it is merely a title fantasized. The public servant is nothing more than a servant to authority and power; that authority and power are not the people or the public but the oligarchy and aristocracies that have been formed.

Employees of these large governments act almost as bastions to the system they serve and protect, willingly or otherwise.

In circumstances where power and authority stem from the Oligarchy and Aristocracy, we can be certain that it will be a true Oligarchy or Aristocracy. In Constitutional Monarchies, the Monarch often empowers an Oligarchy or an Aristocracy to govern. The same Monarchy usually gives the people a choice of who will fill the seats of the Oligarchy or the Aristocracy. Of course, checks and balances are in place to ensure the Monarch retains the final say. In republics led by the few, authority often derives from their oligarchic or aristocratic nature. That is to say, they are proper forms of an oligarchy or aristocracy. Some may argue that republics are democratic institutions. Some may even suggest that the vote symbolizes a democratic system. The votes people have, although seemingly democratic, play a limited role in a nation's military power and in its authority through the courts and the formation of legislation, as a selected or elected minority operates them. The authority in these cases rests with the few. Of all the systems, the Oligarchy or Aristocracy, when combined with others, can be the most troublesome to define or realize. It can appear democratic, yet its very nature is deceptive. We have many "great" Western thinkers who attached several labels to democracy, such as liberal democracy, representative democracy, exclusive democracy, and delegative democracy. In all situations, they do not define democracy.

In most cases, these labels are misplaced and are often used to refer to oligarchies or aristocracies. Returning to the initial comment regarding the Constitutional Monarchy, we must appreciate that the source or spring of power is the Monarch. A Constitutional Monarchy usually implies an Oligarchy empowered by a Monarch. Ultimately, everything is empowered by the monarchy and not by the oligarchy. Where the oligarchy appears very powerful and almost independent of the monarchy, the reality can be – and usually is – strikingly different from public perception.

Democracy holds that authority resides with the people and that the system empowers them to exercise and express that authority legally. An Ochlocracy or Pleistocracy, just like a democracy, may derive its authority from the people. Without the majority, the system can't empower or authorize any action. In an Ochlocracy, authority may be unjustified, dishonorable, or lacking in virtue; in a Pleistocracy, authority may be perpetual under a misguided majority; however, in a Democracy, authority is expected to be exercised fairly and justly by the people. Suppose a monarch authorizes or empowers the people; similarly, an oligarchy or aristocracy does the same. In that case, the authority is no longer with the people but with those who empower them. In that case, a true democracy, ochlocracy or pleistocracy does not exist. If the people went through all the motions of Democracy and yet various decisions they made required the approval of another entity, then the system cannot be called a Democracy. Therefore, authority and its source must be the people for democracy to exist. In a democracy, one would expect a system that allows a fair expression of ideas and grants power to each citizen, stemming from the citizens to form a government. People working together in a sensible, fair, just, and reliable manner are among the things that define a Democracy.

It is perhaps worth noting that we can measure the authority's origin either through a legal declaration, such as a constitution, or through the functions of the legislative, judicial, and enforcement bodies. It can also be seen as the ultimate authority over the issues that govern the five classes of society. In particular, the military is the source of its power and its sense of empowerment. If an army takes orders from or is empowered by a monarch, it does not obey the people. Likewise, if they attain their order or empowerment from a group, as in an Aristocracy or Oligarchy, any other position within the system is powerless. In a

Democracy, the people decide who leads their army and by which laws they are bound.

Cascading authority can make source identification difficult. Many people can be confused by complex systems and live their entire lives without knowing. Cascading authority usually arises when a Monarch or Emperor empowers an Oligarchy, which in turn empowers the People. It also works in the opposite direction in the case of a Democracy. It can often be difficult to pinpoint which system a society uses when Authority is delegated in small doses to many recipients. What is clear, though, is that the three branches of government – legislative, judicial, and executive – along with control of the armies, must have a source of authority. That source can be hidden under multiple laws, courtrooms, enforcement agencies, and even in mixed local and foreign military recruitment and leadership. The mixed modes of operation aim to create stability through diversity within the system. It is often found in Empires where not everyone is of the same ethnicity or citizenry. More often than not, these mixed systems have an emperor or monarch as the source of authority. However, due to the scale of geographical sprawl, a delegation of that authority can almost make some places feel as if they are independent of any imperial rule. Until, of course, the Emperor or Monarch decides to impose or retract authority. I was raised in a system similar to what I have described.

Many people believed they lived in an independent country. The fact was that every facet of Authority was delegated along a cascading format throughout the nation. The people had the privilege to vote, but not the right to vote for who would occupy the seats of an Oligarchy, and in turn, the Oligarchy would rule with the interests of the Monarch and State, and at very few times with the interests of the people. On some occasions, the elected government leader was removed from office by a representative of the Monarch known as a Governor General. Instead of blaming the source, they blamed the Axeman or executioner. Then again, in my lifetime, I saw several governments come to power that were not elected by the people but appointed by the monarch's powers. This system is often highlighted by its actions, such as the voting system being there to appease and bluff the people rather than give them a choice or, even better, the power to lead. On other occasions, it felt fine to vote so long as it was the same person the Monarch's representatives wanted in power. Again, I could provide you with names of persons removed in such a manner, and elections would be based on these factors, but it would become politicized. It is enough to say that people can be blinded by systems in which authority is so widespread and delegated that the source becomes hidden or even invisible to the average person or citizen. There is no exact rule for identifying the source; however, as I mentioned earlier, we do know that the source of Authority is either delegated by a Monarch, an Aristocracy, or a Democracy. Therefore, despite various complications in identifying the source of Authority, it is indeed possible and can be both quantified and qualified.

Since we have discussed the quality and the spring of authority of various systems, the dynamics of acceptance of such quality and authority are also worth mentioning. For a system to function effectively, people must believe it is reliable, credible, robust, and durable. It also needs to be just, fair, and to allow certain freedoms, rights, or privileges in the absence of rights. All government systems can become accepted and tolerated, provided they do not overexert themselves on the people. Throughout history, we have noted that revolutions occur when people can no longer tolerate their circumstances or living conditions. Sadly, some places have learned that only a third of the people need to believe they are being treated fairly, and the other two-thirds will aspire to what the first third has, while the impoverished third will be the only ones seeking change. Whether statistically accurate or not, it is acknowledged that no system can cater to everyone, but a system can work for everyone. The type of government that aims to appease by giving does not have to satisfy everyone, but it must satisfy enough people to stabilize the population and keep them content. The type of government that does not provide for people but works for them may not entirely please everyone, but it would have benefited everyone. By working for the people, we imply that the system is meeting their needs. Typically, this style of government is founded on a democratic platform because all others work for their respective Authority or source of power.

We generally discussed many topics related to democracy. We must highlight how history has treated the term 'Democracy' and how the world's views have changed over time. It was essential to highlight how Democracies differ by contrasting a Democracy with Autocracies and Oligarchies. I also highlighted how religion, ethics, politics, justice, and all matters of government are entwined. While the definition of Democracy may not be clear from what has already been said, it is certainly intended to broaden the scope and understanding of Democracy.

Having discussed the definition of Democracy, considering its qualities, authority, and acceptance, we can further expand our understanding.

Monarchy: A virtuous form of government in which one person leads the majority. All authority within the system they establish derives from the Monarch. Their authority can be delegated as they see fit. The authority to legislate, judge, and enforce the Monarchy's laws may be delegated from the Monarch or retained.

Aristocracy: A virtuous form of government in which a few people lead the majority. The Aristocracy is the source of all authority within the system and can be delegated as it sees fit. They can also retain all forms of authority.

Democracy: A virtuous form of government in which the people lead. All authority is sourced from the people and delegated to those who serve the government. All legislation, judicial proceedings, and law enforcement are empowered and authorized by the people. The people can retain all authority or delegate it as needed.

Although we have provided a brief evaluation of virtue's value in defining a system, we cannot do so thoroughly without discussing ethics specifically. A discussion of ethics will be held later, as there is a preference to narrow the scope of this philosophy by focusing less on monarchies and aristocracies and more on Democracy. Additionally, it was briefly mentioned that organisation and order are required for any government to form. Yet, we have not discussed many prerequisites necessary for a Democracy specifically to exist. It is this latter point that should be addressed next.

3. Prerequisites

"The prerequisites to a democracy begin with a want or need to establish one."

The most important prerequisite for Democracy is that the people must be willing to participate. It is all well and good to set up a system that requires most people to attend regular meetings to make and enforce the laws, but how many people will be genuinely interested in the matter? How many will attend? How many could attend even if they wanted to? The success of a Democracy requires people who are passionate about the system and who are willing to make it work. This willingness is often tied to what people know about a Democracy. What benefits do people gain from it? What sacrifices do they need to make to attain those benefits? Education, to some extent, encompasses these aspects, and I will provide a brief overview of the education one may expect and the challenges encountered in education.

As mentioned earlier, achieving democracy requires an educated populace. If people don't know what a real democracy is, how can they form one? Additionally, individuals require specific qualities to achieve their goals. But to what extent are people in any place on earth prepared from childhood to lead their nation? I have yet to see such a place on Earth. For the most part, education has drifted far from the purpose the Greeks initially conceived of it. In those days, young men were trained to defend their homes, play musical instruments, and solve problems in mathematics, physics, and other fields. But one thing that stood out the most was their education on leading and participating in Democracy. We can't have a group of unethical people voting for unfair or oppressive rules and laws. We can't have people trying to manipulate the system or others in their favor surreptitiously. We can't let a democracy crumble away due to ignorance. We can't let idle people sit without a means to lead themselves. We need good people with a sense of fairness and justice. However, in modern countries, the art of leadership is often kept a secret among the elite, typically the extremely wealthy and powerful. They may share information with the people, but they will not part with the knowledge needed to rule. Who in a world of selfishness would dilute their power and fortune, forsake teaching someone else's child the secrets to governing?

These secrets are not encapsulated in a single phrase or paragraph of all-encompassing philosophy. These secrets encompass the tricks, skills, knowledge, and traits that define leadership. They are dynamic and change, yet some can be handed down by word of mouth from one generation to the next. They have undergone extensive training and education over many years. They encompass the arts of war, diplomacy, science, mathematics, philosophy, religion, politics, and many more subjects. No subject is more important than another, but understanding many creates the general knowledge needed to lead effectively. Plato, Aristotle, and many others mentioned that if a philosopher were to be a King, it would be the most favorable of all autocratic systems. That is because effective government leadership requires well-educated people. There is a far greater chance of finding a well-educated individual than an entire population. That is the weakness of a Democracy.

We are not expressing a conspiracy detailing like-minded people working together to enslave the world, but rather each of them acting independently and doing things for their benefit. They act by doing what they do best and, in turn, damaging the rest of society, turning polities into communities, profiteering through war, pillaging the defenseless, and manipulating the poor for the gain of the wealthy and elite.

If people are divided by pro and con arguments, they can, in turn, be used against them through the divide-and-conquer tactic. People's passion for their ideology or religion is often used to pit one group against another. These things can escalate into war if either party shows intent to fight for what it believes. Expressing an intention to fight for any ideology —pro-feminism vs. anti-feminism, one religion vs. another, or one political system vs. another —can lead to a divided society that, in turn, can be manipulated for the benefit of a few. The key principle of divide and conquer is that if one opponent openly shows aggression toward another, you can incite them to attack each other. People with power can devise things that boggle the innocent mind. In my youth, I could not believe the things that have been done in the name of so-called "Democracy" or in the name of God or the lack of God. It is fair to assume that some people will always seek more than others. The extent to which these people take such greed and ambition will vary. But do not underestimate the ability of some to raise armies, subvert entire nations into chaos, or spread lies to establish precursors for a profitable war. Understanding the palette of waging war is why many writers of war tactics begin by understanding the opponent. Understanding the opponent is not limited to their military strength. It also includes their religion, demography, and all things that can effectively ruin them through division. In our case, and as far as this argument is concerned, it is essential to understand human nature. After all, our worst enemy is ourselves. Therefore, we must first understand humanity before we aim to understand our opponent, as many Generals have asked us to.

Some individuals possess the wealth and power to influence the world in their own interests. Such wealth and power are often beyond the understanding of most people. The Cargo cult in Melanesia is an example of our simplistic minds. Melanesia refers to the westernmost Pacific islands bordering the seas of Indonesia. The Cargo cult began when supplies were dropped over some islands in Melanesia. The island's people began to worship the airplane as some sky God and the supplies they thought were a divine gift. In one instance, a pilot named John Frum was elevated to divine status. Although it may seem comical to some, every society is blinded to certain key truths and perceives the world in a distorted manner.

It would be difficult to tell someone within a particular society that an alternative and better way of life exists. For a pet, for instance, the master feeds it. Not very differently, human loyalty and effort are closely associated with how individuals earn or receive money. We have many sayings, such as "Don't bite the hand that feeds you." Or "Dance with the one who brought you." Humanity, in general, has a strong sense of self-interest. Many of us care for others, but the majority of societies or polities around the world do not establish their cities on a foundation of caring and love. The majority of cities are founded to serve someone else's interests. Every employed job or occupation serves another person's interests. However, people often assimilate into becoming employees because it benefits them to some extent. Yet all this describes why a Democracy cannot exist if the source of order, authority, and power does not stem from the people. There needs to be a standard scope for people, free of self-interest and benefits, to achieve the desired democracy. If we vote and decide on what benefits our wealth, it would be as foolish as making decisions based purely on our ethics. A compromise, caring thoughts, and all these things we know intrinsically to be part of our ethical framework become important in mitigating the vices of self-glorification, self-interest, and concerns.

In continuation of the previous, some methods force people into self-enslavement. Debt slavery is when people willingly loan large amounts of money and are forced to work for their entire lives. The loans are not there to help but to enslave the people.

People willingly enslave themselves because their target is usually something significant to their existence, like a shelter or home. To have the luxury of living in a house, people will willingly take loans from the rich and, in the process, enslave themselves to them. Had the amount they loaned been of a reasonable proportion, something that could be paid in a year or two, the system would no longer tend to enslave that person. But when people, and sometimes couples and entire families, work for a whole lifetime or twenty years to repay their debt, then this is self-enslavement. These are just small examples of the kinds of things done to control a population. If enough people find it effortless to repay their debt, the rest will voluntarily become slaves of varying occupations. For the most part, as you can see, these tricks are about how to dominate others. Some of these things are evil by nature, and if a good person were to pass them on to their children, they should do so in a negative manner. Otherwise, they may try or attempt to do the same. These methods should not be praised, but they should be identified so that they may never happen in the polity in which they live. To return the argument to track, these factors lead us back to more important topics for discussion: what people need before they can lead in a democracy, and what they must avoid or prevent from manifesting.

Suppose education is to apply to all members of the polity. In that case, the people must be aware of what others can use to subvert, sabotage, and dismantle a Democracy. I mentioned only some of these things previously. The system and its operation must be clearly explained. At the same time, education must be truthful, honest, and good. It is easy for people living in oppressive situations to believe they live in a fair and democratic society. It happens often around the world, where even dictators who have ruled for countless decades offer the people a chance to vote on who will lead, and the same person always wins. The people in such places are educated to believe they live in a democracy. In some situations, people believe it so convincingly that they would argue with anyone who doubted their government. Patriots and Nationalists often defend their polity blindly, unaware of its flaws. The same can happen when a few groups, usually two major political parties, contest for power. People are always given the same choices between the two parties. Perpetually, they lead together but pass the official leadership titles from one party to the next. So, education must include defining what is acceptable in a democratic system and what should not be allowed.

Therefore, to overcome the many obstacles to establishing democracy, the people must be taught to make informed decisions and think critically. A specific framework is needed so people can evade the tricks and manipulations that can pervert their chosen system. For example, money has long been regarded as the root of all evil. That corruption, and most of the worst crimes, stem from greed for wealth or money. But that is not always the case. Power, authority, and wealth work together to corrupt people. If we replace currency with any other method of credit or incentive for people, then that hand controls the incentive and has the power and authority.

Regarding education, it is difficult to distinguish what is true from what is not in a monarchy or an oligarchy. Those who control the incentive also affect what is considered true within a polity. However, if careful measures are taken through a democratic process, the truth can become a widely accepted thought. One such truth is that the people will need to know the three types of government so they can easily discern which of the many possible combinations they have established. They may also be able to assess the impact of certain decisions on their democratic system. Then, after this, the people would need to know how to operate a Democracy, and finally, they should know how to prevent the Democracy from being destroyed, distorted, or compromised. These aspects will be covered in a little more detail now.

3.1 Thinking logically

From the very onset of a person's education, they should be trained to make decisions. Those decisions should be based on both quantitative and qualitative deductions. That is important because if people are to take their choices and decisions seriously, there needs to be a respected method for achieving them. While some deductions can be based on quantitative data or analysis, most issues rely on qualitative assessment. In addition to using quantitative data, people will need a structured qualitative analysis method. Both systems complement each other, and both can be logical. These concepts are taught in risk management, loss control, and engineering disciplines, among others.

Qualitative analysis was often given less value in previous years because it was open to bias and speculative processes. However, qualitative analysis is very similar to a philosophical approach. We name the subject, define it, and consider as many of its relationships and peripheral aspects as possible. There are three qualitative approaches: the narrative study, the case study, and scientific observation. The narrative focuses on individual stories and their significance, much like an interview. Case studies usually involve multiple narratives alongside survey data. Scientific observation can be used to identify phenomena and explain cultural aspects, among other things.

Creating the serious type of thinking needed to make proper decisions requires considering the consequences of those decisions. For example, if selling a substance known to make devastating weapons is allowed, will there be a consequence when the opponent or enemy buys it from us? Is the risk elevated by performing certain actions or making certain decisions? Additionally, risks, accidents, and hazards are among the effects stemming from these types of deductions and decisions, for which we must reasonably foresee a particular outcome. A student's decisions may be influenced by familiar subjects such as mathematics, science, physics, and religion, among other topics, to facilitate learning, consider consequences, and assess the likelihood of outcomes. However, the implications or effects must also be made clear. The development of logic is crucial, and the ability to employ deductive and inductive reasoning is essential for effective leadership.

Sometimes, deductions or inductions do not necessarily require accurate truths but can be based on approximations. For example, suppose we know a certain pond can only water a certain number of crops. In that case, we do not necessarily need to know precisely how many crops there are, as we can assess them approximately. The same example applies to a bottle filled with water and ten guests waiting for a drink. We do not need to measure the contents exactly to determine whether the bottle has enough to fill all the cups. This form of special and observational reasoning may not be entirely accurate, but it does help develop the confidence needed to lead.

Additionally, as people can foresee certain outcomes without experiencing them and understand the consequences of specific actions, their minds steadily develop logical and strategic processes. It should be noted that we do not infer any prejudices against others from this statement. It simply means that some things are foreseeable, such as lighting a naked flame in a room filled with flammable vapor. Even if something can be quantified, such as the examples of the bottle and guests, making an educated guess or estimation is far more rapid and equally acceptable. This type of thinking is what we use when we avoid certain hazards in the natural world. Specific hazards, risks, and accidents can be foreseeable by monitoring and understanding a particular environment. That is important when considering the losses and gains that might be achieved through laws, judgment, and enforcement. However, this does not imply that using estimations will always be the best way to determine profit, gain, or loss achieved. Nor does it imply that justice will benefit the majority or what has often been termed the "greater good".

Logic is not an absolute measure, and therefore, two people will not necessarily share the same logic. People who have studied disciplines such as science and math tend to have many uniform skills and logical processes. That does not mean that all scientists and mathematicians draw the same conclusions. They follow standards and procedures that allow them to reason and deduce solutions. People do not change how they think. We have been the same for countless generations. How we use that process to figure things out or reach conclusions is significant. So, too, in a democracy, the deductions we draw require a balance of all that the polity in question considers most important. These could be freedom, liberty, order, control, education, justice, or anything that seems virtuous or important to a polity.

To complement the previous is the field of quantitative assessments. Quantitative approaches typically use numerical data and scientific data. Quantitative data can be classified into four significant types: stenographic, polygraphic, numerical, and categorical. Stenography usually refers to the qualitative decryption of information from images or other forms. However, it can also be used to study one subject in this context. Polygraphy also has different meanings, but in this context, it refers to the decryption of information present in multiple subjects or groups. Numeric data refers to information that has a numerical value. Categorical data is numeric data representing a category. Usually, numeric data is used for small groups and takes the form of traditional quantitative and statistical information. Categorical data is generally used for large groups, and although it uses numeric data, it can have qualitative, quantitative, or semi-quantitative labels.

Almost all formulas written in math or science can be solved when one variable in an equation is unknown. In math or science, the solution often determines the value of the unknown variable. This process is a fundamental part of logic. However, it is often not expanded to cases where a presumption can be made based on political decisions. People are not educated to understand that a particular political action can lead to war or disturbance. These things are often not discussed, and many people, although adept at solving equations, are not entirely competent at deriving the formulas in the first place. Developing formulas based on the relationship between variables is crucial for establishing logical reasoning. These variables may be economic, political, or military and, in turn, may affect the economy, politics, or military.

At this point, we are merely pointing out that deduction is the central axis upon which all other aspects of logic derive. To deduce anything, the logical process of gathering, analyzing, and assessing information applies. If we are to make any deduction or decision, it is entirely based on what we know. What we know is made of information, the analysis of that information, and the final assessment of it.

Aristotle wrote a remarkable philosophy regarding human logic. We will not elaborate on the subject further since Aristotle's works are almost complete. Very little could be added or amended, and his work's depth far surpasses the casual approach I am applying here. Human logic is a complex and detailed subject that many philosophers have covered. An in-depth analysis and the development of a philosophy of human logic are beyond the purpose of this philosophy.

Additionally, an often-overlooked aspect is the impact of ethics on the decision-making process. How we think is very complex. Here, it is enough to say that for deductions to be just, accurate, and righteous, a person must be able to deduce through critical thinking. The mind must be sharp enough to foresee consequences, and decision-makers will need to carefully estimate the long-term impact of their decisions on people.

Logic, therefore, is a skill or ability that would require training in a democratic society. But it should also be complemented with knowledge. Logic alone is merely the process of making deductions and consequential decisions. It does not account for the other factors that enable leaders to make swift decisions. As I noted earlier, rapid decision-making is often used to estimate and determine emergency criteria. However, creating what most would consider good decisions requires knowledge. In scientific circles, the decision process begins with data or information. That is analyzed, and then, following this, it is assessed in terms of the broader scope to which it belongs. For instance, the information and analysis may suggest that a particular pond could host an infinite number of frogs. Yet, we intuitively know that there are natural limits on such matters. The same principle can be applied to building a wall. If one worker places one brick, in theory, many workers will place many bricks. But in reality, the leading line of bricklaying is limited. A thousand people can't build the same small wall. Therefore, if a population used logic in a Democratic system, it would also infer that the data or information for many things was already known to them through intuition. The more knowledgeable a leader is, the better they perform their leadership and decision-making roles. A juvenile, for instance, would request that information be collected so that they can analyze the data. Still, a mature and knowledgeable person may not necessarily need to do so.

3.2 Knowledge and wisdom

Knowledge is a crucial aspect of both decision-making and logical reasoning. Knowledge can be compared to Wisdom. The more truths a person knows, the wiser they are. Knowledge is the long-term retention of information, analysis, and assessments. Knowledge in truth is all that counts towards wisdom. False propaganda and other facts that fall short of the truth can make up our knowledge, but they do not make us wiser. For a democracy to function correctly, the knowledge must be true. Not skewed or biased towards the interests of one or several individuals. If a minority spreads lies to the people, their knowledge and decisions are corrupted. Hence, unwise actions can arise from false information and may lead to undesired outcomes.

Therefore, credibility must be present in the exercise of acquiring and disseminating knowledge. To avoid many such situations in which information is skewed, people must approach any medium capable of transmitting information with great caution, including schools, universities, public media, and other avenues through which information can be relayed. All these things are essential to the well-being of a democracy. Of course, there is the issue of free speech. A democracy that censors information has, in effect, created a restriction upon its citizens. People should always be free to express their views, even those that are opposed to democracy. However, people should control the means and methods used to handle such information. At an Assembly, there would be little tolerance for recommendations to vote towards non-democratic changes. For instance, asking people to turn a Democracy into an Autocracy or Oligarchy would have little tolerance. Yet, the freedom to do so should be respected to some degree. The ancient Athenian Democracy treated detrimental speeches that favored the downfall or compromise of the Democracy as a serious crime.

In places where credibility is expected, such as schools and universities, and through public media, the truth should be allowed to prevail. These places should not become political arenas, and the information shared in such areas and through media outlets should be considered carefully. Ultimately, it is a subtle and delicate balance between the freedom to express ideas and the freedom to corrupt the democratic institution through propaganda and lies. There will always be some overlap between what is true and what is not. Yet, I hope you can see that guarding the credibility of information circulating within a democratic society is most important.

At the same time, those wishing to indulge in private affairs that consist of non-truths should be free to do so. Historically, we have been shown to have a higher tolerance for such skewed illusions and poor behavior, especially when paid for. The Roman Arenas were filled with paying customers to see human beings brutally die. Illusionists and magicians, and all matters of trickery are founded on lies, yet people, by the majority, laugh and are entertained. But what of our ideologies and ideas? For instance, if a particular person wants to sell a book on the benefits of Monarchies within a democratic society, should they be allowed to sell it? While ancient Athenian society tolerated lies, falsehoods, and illusions for entertainment, it punished those who attempted to subvert the democratic institution. However, in modern times, what was once called a 'Democratic institution' and what now operates as a government administrative system can be debated.

Private transactions and instances of consent, whether through contract or purchase, appear to regulate the dissemination of corruptive information. That has proven itself over the years, with a few people controlling the information that people are aware of. Great caution should be exercised to prevent the commercial sector or the media from becoming the primary source of information for citizens. The best source for such things is from the people themselves. If they wish to know the impact of certain chemicals, they will not rely on commercial media but issue an authoritative report that all citizens can read. The reports that the people require should stem from the government they control. But if the government is not democratic, the few who control the flow of information will write the reports.

If a businessperson owns a media outlet and uses it for their own benefit, this will not benefit society in any way. Any business owner of a media outlet aims to make money and profit. In contrast, a public media outlet in a democratic society relays the truth to citizens. Public media aims to convey the outcomes of local and foreign decisions, inform the public about actions taken by others, and stimulate discussion. Restating the previous point, public media must inform the people about the critical issues affecting their society. That is why facts should be included in people's education, and only facts should be disseminated to the populace through public media. There is a difference between censorship and the regulation of information. Of course, these differences are so subtle that in the hands of an Oligarchy or Autocracy, the regulated information can quickly become censored and misinformed.

While we may enjoy fantasy and other non-truths or illusions for entertainment, there is a fine line between an information source and such entertainment. There are times when our entertainment becomes a source of information for many. In the early years of humanity, history and religion were shared by poets, musicians, and entertainers. Lies had been mixed with truths for a very long time before the literary Golden Age, dating back to ancient Greece, where fiction, fables, and mythology were often separated from the facts and truths. In years gone by, people believed in Minotaurs and Hydras. Today, they believe in Dinosaurs of varying types and Aliens. In the past, the Greeks flew to the Sun and brought back Greek fire. Today, they have landed on the Moon and traveled to other planets. Yesterday, they believed in many Gods. Today, some believe aliens will save humanity. So, you see, fantasy has fused with reality for many people. Yesterday, they gave speeches and orations before Arena Sports began, and now they advertise similar events using other media. At some point, people lose touch with tangible reality and replace it with what is convenient, entertaining, or fun. It takes intelligent people to discern reality from falsehood and fiction from nonfiction. Very often, even when knowing the truth, many retain the lies of the majority rather than the truth. The saying "When in Rome, do as the Romans do" does not need promotion in the days of writing this book. Now, people require an urge to do what is just and right, true and sane. So far, humanity has followed a path of illusions, corrupted information, lies, and deceit, and as a result, people can no longer reach a consensus on what is true or not.

In conclusion, regarding knowledge and wisdom, it is wisdom that we need to preserve most. While having broad general knowledge is helpful, knowing the truth is most important. It should be stated that what we believe is fact, and we accept it as fact. In other words, how many people would measure and replicate the experiments to ascertain if they are true when we read a book of facts? At some point, we accept certain things to be true, and we do so based on our judgment. If that judgment is trained in critical thinking, it will differ from one that is not. Either way, faith and belief drive us as human beings. Also, variations in what we believe are based on what we have filtered as true. In the end, believing that one divided by two is half is a fact-based belief. Calculating in this way is the way mathematicians use numbers at the time of writing. However, Plato noted that one divided by two is two halves, thereby preserving the original object. So you see, what you believe as fact will vary from what another believes as fact, and when we combine all our factual beliefs, one person will be strikingly different in thought from another.

3.3 Educating a Democracy

We have discussed the importance of certain prerequisites for democracy to exist. These include a willingness to participate in the democratic system. It can only work if people are willing to invest the time and effort required to operate the system. The next prerequisite is that of education. People need to understand how a democracy works and how to guard against it. The key to this is having people with keen logic and a wealth of knowledge. People with these skills should be able to govern themselves fairly.

The problem most people worldwide have is that they do not fully understand what a democracy is in the first place. There are so many lies spoken about the subject that many people have attained, in most cases, a false knowledge of what a democracy is. Highlighting what democracy should be and how to prevent its collapse are essential prerequisites. We have already highlighted some areas of education, especially how the truth can be compromised. We have also described how people's knowledge and logic can be used against them if they are not diligent enough to control the flow of information. The next step is to explain some peripheral issues in education.

Other philosophers write more eloquently about topics similar to those discussed here, such as critical thinking and problem-solving. All seem to consider the education an individual requires a top priority. Some take a socialist view, arguing that social justice and literacy have become key prerequisites. However, it is worth noting that when we impose literacy on people, we eliminate dialects and nuances from the languages they use. It is good to have a common language, but not the only one. Then, there are the works of Aristotle, in which the development of a virtuous citizen is of utmost importance. Plato writes that education should never be left to a single person, but rather to many teachers. All these aspects have been incorporated into systems worldwide in various ways. However, suppose Democracy is not highlighted within a person's knowledge base. In that case, people will often possess the skills but lack the knowledge and wisdom to apply them towards forming, operating, and preserving a Democratic state.

3.4 What should a democracy be?

Having explained the key prerequisites for establishing a democracy, the next matter to address is what a democracy is or should be. Already, we know what it is, in part, the majority ruling the majority. But we do not want it to turn into an Ochlocracy. Also, we do not want people to lack good leadership skills and make poor judgments and decisions. Essentially, a democracy can degrade into a lynch mob. So, let us examine what a Democracy should be. A democracy is not merely the chance to vote. It is when the people are involved with every decision that affects their lives. Democracy puts the power to create and abolish laws in the hands of the people. That is the most fundamental aspect of a true Democracy. When people offer to proxy-vote on behalf of others, this is seen as a corruption of the system. No person can express another person's idea in complete truth. Governments, such as Republics, are not Democracies. Republics are a form of Aristocracy. If you refer back to the definitions of government, you will notice that when a few people rule over the majority, we have an Aristocratic or Oligarchic system; that is, exactly what a Republic is.

A Republic aims to invest the power of the people in a handful of people who will govern on their behalf and represent their interests. Because all Republics involve a few people ruling over the majority rather than the majority ruling over the majority, they are, at best, an Aristocracy and, at worst, an Oligarchy. The rise of the Republics came about through proxy voting. Others would vote on behalf of someone unable to attend a meeting. Later, the proxy vote was no longer one person handing their vote to another; instead, many people handed their votes to a single person. That person became known as the representative. As already stated, the level of representation is questionable. In fact, in some systems, the representatives do not even incline to represent; instead, they serve a higher-level oligarchy or monarchy.

Democracy is a pure system, so fragile and constantly under attack by those with interests to control it. It is pure because any compromise is almost always detrimental and must remain a pure democracy; otherwise, it can shift to an Oligarchy. For any people to have a democratic system, they must be strong, intelligent, and cautious. The people must pass everything that concerns the state and government. Otherwise, it is no longer a Democracy. A democracy is a transparent system. None of the state's work is aimed solely at benefiting a few people. This aspect poses difficulties for a Democracy when discussing matters of war. Because of its transparency, the people are aware of such discussions, and so is anyone who may visit the Democracy.

Matters of war are often thought of as things needing secrecy. The Athenians resolved this issue by discussing it openly in their forums without detailing their plans. Discussions in the democratic meetings were limited to what should be done. Should there be a war or no war? If war were decided, the generals would appoint the right people to deliver a plan on behalf of the people. The people would give a military general orders to prepare for battle. Thus, the planning and administration of wars were often left to the military arm. There was no outside influence in the matter, and the army consisted of the citizens themselves. They did not have a small group of mercenaries or formal soldiers; all the citizens were soldiers. Military service by the citizens was an essential attribute of the early Athenian Democracy.

Suppose we have a separate group of people to control the military. What can stop such a group from following a primitive leader and taking control of Democracy? Therefore, everyone needed to serve as a soldier so that there were no us and them, no niche group to seize control. Generals were appointed based on their previous experience and were elected to serve the people by being voted into office yearly. The people, in turn, allowed themselves to take command from the Generals on the battlefield or while in military service. It was a loop: the people gave the military the job of discussing war, and the military would further discuss their plans in private under military secrecy. Then the generals assume command and order the citizens to perform specific actions. Then the loop would begin again, and the people would discuss their required actions and so on. It was a symbiotic relationship sustained by the people's will.

Compulsory military service in a democracy has its benefits, helping to stabilize the democracy and maintain its freedom. That is on the condition that the people are in charge and armed, to be feared. They—the people—create a closed loop among all the arms of government they control. They make the laws, judge others based on them, enforce them, and protect the institution.

Many people in our modern age fear the liberal use of weapons in society. There is a worldwide trend: people without weapons experience the least crime involving such weapons. When weapons are introduced into a society, they can cause problems. Careful control of these weapons becomes an important political issue. While every citizen may be a soldier, that does not necessarily mean every citizen should possess a weapon in their home. Of course, people are free to decide for themselves; however, the idea of arming citizens can lead to many rebellious groups aiming to subvert or sabotage the Democratic nature of the state. Yet those same fears may be necessary in some places to establish a Democratic institution. It is a cautious matter that requires people to decide clearly and concisely how weapons are distributed to the public. It may be a case of having a public armory accessible to the public only under circumstances preordained by the people and the law. Restricting, by democratic vote, the circumstances under which people are allowed to use weapons and armor is better than banning their use altogether. People who can form an army within minutes of a declaration are far more prepared for the worst.

A Democracy requires the people to decide all matters of state legislation. Legislation or laws are the foundation of the life they will lead. When educating people about democracy, the idea that they can control their own affairs is paramount. If the passing, creating, and enacting of laws is left to anyone other than the people, then the people have lost all power over the government. As part of educating people, this aspect must resonate with everyone involved. This should never be compromised in any way. If so, the system is no longer a Democratic state.

Once a law is made, there is the matter of law enforcement. In a democratic system, all persons are empowered to enforce the law. If a citizen witnesses another person committing a theft, they can detain or arrest the person and bring them to justice. Because of the risks involved and to ensure professional enforcement, a democratic system can appoint a police force. The Athenians used their military to guard and patrol the streets; the police and army were the same, and their mission was to protect Democracy and its citizens. People requiring assistance in detaining or arresting a person could do so through the military guard. Because the military guards were exempt from prosecution as long as they were performing their duties, they provided an effective means for ordinary citizens to enforce the law. Usually, the guards were young men who were earning citizenship and were physically capable.

Where a law has been enacted and is being enforced, a system to judge those who break it is also essential. In a democratic system, the people are the judges. They form large juries and hear cases assigned to them. Again, attention should be given to preventing jury corruption and bribery. Therefore, the process requires carefully written procedures and laws to ensure a fair trial for all individuals.

We have mentioned the word 'state' many times, and it is worth defining, as it often has variable meanings across different countries. A state is all the cities and people considered part of the same government. The State can be a Province or Region, a Nation, an Empire, or a City-State. The term “State” has been used in the context of city-states unless otherwise specified.

"For states also are composed not of one but of several parts, as has been said often. One of these parts, therefore, is the mass of persons concerned with food who are called farmers, and the second is what is called the mechanic class (and this is the group engaged in the arts without which a city can't be inhabited, and some of these arts are indispensably necessary, while others contribute to luxury or noble living), and a third a commercial class (by which I mean the class that is engaged in selling and buying and in wholesale and retail trade), and fourth is the class of manual labourers, and the fifth class is the one to defend the state in war, which is no less indispensable than the others if the people are not to become the slaves of those who come against them; for surely it is quite out of the question that it should be proper to give the name of State to a community that is by nature a slave, for a state is self-sufficient, but that which is a slave is not self-sufficient" (Aristotle, 1944b, pp. 1290b - 1291a).

This translated reference to Aristotle is included because of its importance for understanding how Democracy functions in other nations. If a state relies on other states to function, it has suffered a blow to its democratic nature. In a world of international businesses and financial institutions, this single phrase, written over two thousand years ago, still carries as much significance today as it did then. If a state borrows money, then it is a slave. If a state buys continually from others, it is a slave. If the state is not self-sufficient and relies on foreigners outside of the state for the product or service of any of those five occupational classes of people that Aristotle mentions, then the state is a slave. It is no longer free. If we are to buy food from foreign countries, then the state and its people become slaves to the nation or state that offers the food. If all the engineering, architectural, medical, technical, and mechanical work were imported or done by foreign companies, then again, the nation or democracy has become a slave. Imagine if all the factory or production work were imported, then that nation would no longer be free. It would be in debt and reliant on others. So, even though the idea of democracy is applied to the domestic issues of the polity it governs, there is a broader statecraft that determines if the people within a state are free. Therefore, it is essential to keep the state and people free.

When writing this, the preceding was deemed to be true. To elaborate further, the extent to which some states or entities went to preserve independence consumed the entire world's resources under one Oligarchical umbrella. That is to say that some Oligarchies exported all their production and manufacturing, intentionally creating a consumer society within their boundaries. That is, we would assume outwardly that these entities were slave nations. Furthermore, they served a purpose to appease a minority. Therefore, they were permitted to exist, and the slave state was intentionally created. The status of the slave state affected the people, not the Oligarchy that manipulated the situation. That was apparent in most of the former European colonies of the autocratic period.

We must stress that the "Wealth of Nations" was a purely economic view of a polity. The entire philosophy, if it can be called that, was flawed; yet, it found its way into the teaching of capitalism. Capitalism failed, as much as communism did, but during the 19th century, authorities and power centers sought to justify their actions through academic literature. The urge to come up with a new philosophy or idea often gets in the way of solid, proven philosophies that have been established for thousands of years. So, Capitalism became a common term throughout the industrialized world. One of the recommendations or observations made by the original author was to export labor to nations with factories that produce goods at a lower cost. He did not describe the reality of the consequences. For a long time, the imperial nations of the world attempted to compel nations into agreements to produce goods for them. It worked for a while, primarily benefiting those who invested in such a business. It continues today in various industries, such as precious metals, oil, and a range of other commodities. The act of using another nation's resources, be they material or otherwise, is called plundering. The so-called industrial powers were great plunderers of wealth and resources abroad. Unlike the days when they could plunder without compensation, societies had changed and had become more difficult to manipulate by the sword and the military. They soon realized that taking resources could be done by establishing pyramidal authority structures in the places they sought to plunder. Wherever a pyramidal structure was found, it could be paid, coerced, extorted, or subjected to any manner of acts applied to it to enforce the agenda of the perpetrators. That was the model of Capitalism. That is what became of the world during and since the Industrial Revolution, and only after a few hundred years of Germanic rule in Europe.

Let's consider Aristotle's classes of people. That is to say that a polity is made of essential parts with no higher value than another, and then all must work together and complement each other. Historically, we see that making the merchant and business classes grossly overpowered skews power across all the other classes in society. Capitalism favors extremely rich individuals but does nothing for the state or people other than impoverish them and create unemployment in the other classes. The skew or bias in capitalism is toward the merchant class, or the class most involved in trade and profit. Some say that as long as imports are less than exports, then the nation is not reliant on others. But if a nation relies on imports or exports, it is no longer self-reliant. It is not a matter of how much in terms of currency or volume; reliance on the product or service is the most important. Aristotle rightly believed that a nation needs to be self-sufficient; if it imports or exports, it must do so with caution and moderation. The classes of people are important to the function of the city and state, and shrinking any of them in terms of productivity and prosperity, even though monopolization, will cause the whole state and its people to suffer. There is a balance between imports and exports, as well as between debts and credits. This is why self-sufficiency is important for maintaining a nation's freedom.

Based on the last two points above, Communism was also flawed for the same reasons as Capitalism. Where capitalism gave favor and liberty to the merchant classes to construct micro-oligarchies, the largest of them having millions of servants or employees, Communism sought to diminish the merchant class almost entirely through regulation. Because they tampered with the layers of society, both systems created problems regarding the freedom of their states and their people. Ironically, Capitalism led to Socialism in capitalist societies because of the highlighted issues. Specifically, when a merchant class takes away work, the state supports workers through small contributions or welfare payments. Communism sought to distribute the national wealth equally among all. The ideology of Communism was not as flawed as that of Capitalism, in that it implied equality rather than greed. In practice, however, when a central oligarchy holds ultimate power to control every known resource in the country, the slightest abuses send consequential waves through that society. For every theft of a million grains of wheat, each of a million people received one grain less – hardly noticeable to begin with – and ultimately, only some had, while others did not. Communism failed, and in the process of failing, it established that a government can't effectively provide for everyone. It also highlighted that any government system can serve only those in authority and power. Meaning that neither Capitalism nor Communism could work because they benefited the authority and powers they served. A nation relying on an ideology that gives free rein to the Merchants, as in Capitalism, will not benefit anyone other than those the ideology serves. By the same reasoning, Communism, while stipulating equality, was operated by an Oligarchy. In times of crisis, Communism ensured that wealth was equally distributed amongst the rulers, and what could be spared was distributed amongst the rest.

Maintaining balance among all individuals, such as workers, merchants, technicians, and others, is the most crucial aspect of governance. The compulsion to do so is for the sake of stability and order. Capitalism and Communism offered somewhat different views, but both were radical or skewed in their application and benefited a minority.

Some companies from foreign countries also bring their workers to work in those companies. What may appear as a business that hires many people may simply import foreign workers or colonizers. In my place, it was frequent that the colonizers would take over up to 80% of the new jobs in any given year. Therefore, while we are accustomed to hearing many positive things about business in capitalist systems and are often praised for the ruling party in Communist societies, the reality is that both systems have benefits and costs for the state and its people.

It is fair at this point and for the sake of balance to also criticize Communism, which aims to control every aspect of human existence and diminish the merchant class. It quickly realized that it was impossible to administer every possible form of merchant trade and industry. Ultimately, individuals with limited skills were assigned tasks that exceeded their capabilities or knowledge. If a family has been making a product for generations, then their business and product are best known by them. It is almost impossible to find someone who knows their business better than they do. Yet Communism created a state in which only businesses given government money would prosper, and they set about placing administrators in specific businesses who knew very little about making them commercially feasible.

Most places in the world recognize that both systems are flawed, and both have merged to some degree to compensate for each system's deficits. Socialism is probably a combination of Capitalism and Communism. It attempts to remedy the wounds but not the cause. It appears to perpetuate the flaws of both systems, yet it attempts to mitigate the impact across all facets of the system through welfare programs of varying natures. Socialism compensates through schemes for the poor and the middle socio-economic class, buybacks, and corporate and business interests, such as hospitals, medicine, resources, and infrastructure, as well as naval yards. Yet, it should be noted that in a democratic State, there may or may not be a welfare system, but under Pericles, there was an income paid for participating in the democratic system.

Also, it is important to note that ideologies such as Capitalism, Communism, Religion, and many others will arise from time to time. Those ideas may be suitable for that particular period, but they can never be applied in the long term. That is because ideologies and ideas change as we learn more, until the truth is established. Once the truth is established, things like religion seem to perpetuate.

The problem with a large group of people is that ideologies may seem like a good idea to the majority for a considerable length of time —perhaps more than a lifetime or even a few generations. Eventually, however, the truth about those ideologies surfaces, and often that truth changes people's minds. The things that remain perpetually true appear to be true at the time and for all time. Therefore, given enough time to operate a democracy, it can apply the truth and gain from it by its very scope of things. A true democracy founded on truths and perpetuating truths will be true to the people. That is why, although Democracy has its flaws, it is the best system that any group of people can operate. In more eloquent words, Democracy may not be perfect, but it is our best system. Yet the key to a Democracy is the people and their willingness to operate the Democratic state. Not only this, but their ideas, manners, culture, and all other aspects must complement unity and cooperation. Without the things that lead to unity and collaboration, a Democracy can't function.

It would now be appropriate to examine how the Athenians operated their democracy and to bring forward, as stated previously, the words of the ancients and the platform upon which any philosophy of Democracy should be founded.

4. Athenian democracy

"The premise of the ancient Greek Democracy is that all citizens make up the government."

So far, we have mentioned several key factors necessary for democracy to function effectively. Although we have defined it in a philosophical context, there is also the historical aspect of Athenian Democracy, which existed in Athens, Greece, from approximately 500 BC to 400 BC. Of all the government systems to date, it is the most credible. As we unravel the story of Athenian Democracy, we will also discuss and emphasize key issues, including what it was, how it operated, and how it survived. That will help clarify certain questions that may arise from the previous description of what a Democracy is and its prerequisites, and it will also elaborate on how a Democracy could operate.

The premise of ancient Greek Democracy is that all citizens comprise the government. A person had to prove their loyalty to the city by being born there and having parents who were also born there. At the age of 18, they were registered as candidates for citizenship, and they then served for one year as candidates and two years in the military. At the minimum age of 21, they were allowed to become citizens through a vote from the people. The Athenian Democracy attempted to preserve who could vote and participate in decision-making within their state. Citizenship was a qualification of allegiance to the people and the democratic state. A large number of people were excluded from citizenship, including those from other Greek cities. If we examine any nation today that is striving to become a democracy, whether multicultural or otherwise, the concept of citizenship should be taken very seriously. Often, we see passive invasions by groups of people from other cultural and social backgrounds entering a society. These individuals do not always arrive as legal migrants whom the state has accepted. They came illegally into the city from several lifestyles, including nomadic and semi-sedentary. Others invaded the city and conflicted at times with weapons. So citizenship should be a serious issue, and the people's loyalty to the place where Democracy operates should be given the highest importance.

"The present form of the constitution is as follows. Citizenship belongs to persons of citizen parentage on both sides, and they are registered on the rolls of their demes at the age of eighteen. At the time of their registration, the members of the deme decide between them by vote on oath, first whether they are shown to have reached the lawful age, and if they are held not to be of age they go back again to the boys, and secondly, whether the candidate is a freeman and of legitimate birth; after this, if the vote as to free status goes against him, he appeals to the jury-court, and the demesmen elect five men from among themselves to plead against him, and if it is decided that he has no claim to be registered, the state sells him, but if he wins, it is compulsory for the demesmen to register him"(Aristotle, 1944a, 42.1).

Note that the Athenian Constitution is not considered part of the Aristotelian texts. It appeared on two papyrus leaves, and a more thorough example was also found. Most respectable universities consider the text genuine, valuable, and accurate, irrespective of whether it was Aristotle who wrote it or not. Also, if you read further into the text of Aristotle's Politics, many things seem to match up well. Some think that, of the many constitutions Aristotle wrote, most were in preparation for his work, Politics. From the above quote, we know that citizenship is essential. It was not a light matter or conducted in secret, but rather a public matter carried out openly. As such, a person seeking citizenship could be scrutinized by those who knew them. Anyone could be barred from becoming a citizen, even if born in the same city as their parents. Their neighbors, friends, and even enemies voted for their acceptance.

Because the Athenian Democracy is described by the ancients far better than I ever could, it is better to read their works and then come back to what I have to say on the matter. But I do not expect everyone to do that, so I will try to elaborate, as clearly and concisely as possible, on how the Athenian Democracy operated. We should, therefore, begin with the issue of citizenship.

4.1 Citizenship

People will need to defend Democracy against all forms of intrusion. Citizenship is one of several safeguards.

"… And when the cadets have been passed by this revision, their fathers hold meetings by tribes and after taking oath elect three members of the tribe of more than forty years of age, whom they think to be the best and most suitable to supervise the cadets, and from them the people elects by show of hands one of each tribe as disciplinary officer, and elects from the other citizens a marshal over them all" (Aristotle, 1944a, 42.2).

"And the people also elects two athletic trainers and instructors for them, to teach them their drill as heavy-armed soldiers, and the use of the bow, the javelin and the sling. It also grants the disciplinary officers one drachma a head for rations, and the cadets four obols a head; and each disciplinary officer takes the pay of those of his own tribe and buys provisions for all in common (for they mess together by tribes), and looks after everything else" (Aristotle, 1944a, 42.3).

"They go on with this mode of life for the first year; in the following year an assembly is held in the theater, and the cadets give a display of drill before the people, and receive a shield and spear from the state; and they then serve on patrols in the country and are quartered at the guard-posts"(Aristotle, 1944a, 42.4).

"Their service on patrol goes on for two years; the uniform is a mantle; they are exempt from all taxes; and they are not allowed to be sued nor to sue at law, so that they may have no pretext for absenting themselves, except in cases concerning the estate, marriage of an heiress, and any priesthood that one of them may have inherited. When the two years are up, they now are members of the general body of citizens"(Aristotle, 1944a, 42.5).

Therefore, from these quoted texts, we notice that the candidates for citizenship are trained for one year by a local person of the tribe to which the candidate belongs. They then serve as military patrols around the city for a further two years. Also, you will notice that while serving in the military, a person foregoes many civil rights, including the right to sue others or be sued. They are also relieved from any public duties, except for military service, to ensure they do not leave their posts.

It is clear that, before all else, who is part of the system and who is not should be decided. The matter of citizenship and the process of earning it plays an important role. The military teaches the citizens the core necessity for security and peace. It also teaches the person discipline and the exercise of heroic defense for their beliefs. How long could a nation exist if not everyone knew the actual cost of freedom? Freedom is not given to any people; it is taken by those who are prepared to fight for it. Many people can be quoted on the matter:

"...you must yourselves realize the power of Athens, and feed your eyes upon her from day to day, till the love of her fills your hearts; and then when all her greatness shall break upon you, you must

reflect that it was by courage, sense of duty, and a keen feeling of honour in action that men were enabled to win all this and that no personal failure in an enterprise could make them consent to deprive their country of their valour, but they laid it at her feet as the most glorious contribution that they could offer" (Thucydides, 1906, 2.6).

Often, this is shortened to *"The secret to happiness is freedom, and freedom requires courage."* But as you may notice, for a city to be powerful enough to repel aggressors and to be prosperous, the people within the city must feel a duty to the city. So that there is an element of pride in what they do, and not merely live one day after another without thinking about what may benefit their city as a whole.

Therefore, this is perhaps the first and foremost aspect that would need to be considered in a Democracy. People will need to defend it against all forms of intrusion. From domestic to foreign assailants, the danger of existing as a nation requires that its citizens prepare for such possibilities. People should not be blinded by their love or good nature to the fact that aggressors have been a constant in human history. The people themselves must be willing to fight and defend their city-state, its inhabitants, and the freedom of the survivors. If such a consensus exists, people will be able and willing to defend everything they establish under their democratic system.

4.2 Organization of government.

The next matter to discuss is the organization of a Democratic government. We have already mentioned the issue of citizenship and the entry path for cadets seeking citizenship. It is now time to reflect on the issues we raised in the Prerequisites of a Democracy and its definition. For instance, we have now introduced the idea that Democracy is for those who are loyal to one another and united by the things we mentioned earlier. The method the ancient Athenians used was called citizenship. With all that in mind, it is important to elaborate on what such citizens did once admitted and allowed to function as citizens.

The government's core in Athens consisted of an Assembly, Council, and Court system. The Council was a formal government body that prepared the Assembly's agenda and performed administrative duties. The Assembly was known as the Ecclesia, or what is translated as "Church." The Assembly would be composed of any citizen who wants to participate. Because the people made it, it can also be called the Assembly of the Demos. The full power of the state rested with the Assembly. Aeschin, an ancient writer and philosopher, wrote:

"...He does not exclude from the platform the man whose ancestors have not held a general's office, nor even the man who earns his daily bread by working at a trade; nay, these men he most heartily welcomes, and for this reason, he repeats, again and again, the invitation, Who wishes to address the assembly?..."(Aeschin, 1919, 1.27).

The Council was composed of 500 elected citizens. These people were derived from the ten tribes of Athens, and each contributed 50 people to serve as Councilors. Also, a citizen was allowed to serve on the council no more than twice in his lifetime. These people were selected by random lot to avoid corruption and bias in the method the council was expected to use. Since they were important in setting the Assembly's agenda, such positions also lent themselves to omitting certain issues from being passed on to the Assembly. A block of information or a set of cases could occur. Councilors were not viewed as politicians, but rather as servants of the system. They had a service to perform on behalf of the people. In Plato's Apology of Socrates, although honored to have served on the council, Socrates did not consider himself a politician. It was expected that between a quarter and a half of the citizens would serve on the council between the ages of 30 and 60 during their lifetime. This was due to the high turnover and large number of council members. During the year, they kept the president of the Council unknown until the president was selected each month by lot. Each tribe was required to have at least one month of presidency in the Council during the whole year of service. You could liken this to ten districts that divided the city; each district had a chance to lead the Council. In conjunction, there were ten months in the old Greek calendar; as such, one month would be enough to allow every tribe to lead the Council once a month. To minimize corruption, no one would know who the council president would be before the lots were taken at the end of each month. Also, to further randomize who would serve as the Council's chairman, daily lots were drawn from the members of the tribe holding the presidency. So, even if the last month of the year could be guessed at as to which tribe would hold the presidency, no one knew who the actual president was until the lots were drawn the night before the next day. In other words, the presidency rotated randomly among ten tribes, and the council chairman was selected at the end of each day from the tribe holding the presidency.

The relationship between the Council and the Assembly was that the Council presidents of that month would appoint nine people from the other Council members who were not serving as Presidents. Those nine people formed a bench of chairmen to handle the Assembly's business, preside over the Assembly's proceedings, and address all related matters. Among their duties was deciding when to vote on a subject. Sometimes they can call for a vote or dismiss the call to vote. But the Assembly's people could counter them by making their voices heard. In other words, the people would yell out and demand a vote if they wanted one, or overrule the bench of chairmen if they felt so inclined, usually by vocally harassing them.

"Furthermore, when some of the Prytanes refused to put the question to the vote in violation of the law, Callixeinus again mounted the platform and urged the same charge against them; and the crowd cried out to summon to court those who refused" (Xenophon, 1921, 1.7.14). Note that Prytannes was the word used for the Presidents of the Council, and they also used to hold the chair of the Assembly before Aristotle's time. Later, the Prytanes appointed the nine chairpersons or Proedroi (Presidents) of the Assembly, as described earlier.

Other essential positions were elected by the people, aside from the Council members, who could be viewed as temporary officeholders. Some additional offices included the office of ten Generals, nine Archons, market inspectors, tax collectors, and a variety of other essential state duties. The ten tribes individually elected their Generals to serve as one of the ten Generals of the state. The service was to last for only one year. The Nine Archons were elected directly by the Assembly. Usually, they were people of stature and knowledgeable of the laws. There was no point in giving such a position to a poor man who couldn't attend meetings or perform his required duties. Archons tended to have a tone of elite status. But status is all it was. The powers of the Archons were usually restricted to overseeing the fair collection of evidence for and against an accused person. Their duties were to chair the courts but not pass any judgment, a role that was a cross between a lawyer who doesn't speak but collects all the facts and a judge who doesn't judge but ensures each side has a fair opportunity to present their case. Remember that Athens also had many rough periods, and a small group once seized power, forming an oligarchy. But a hundred years later, they were ousted, and the Democracy returned to its golden form. The roles of the Archons were dismantled from an elitist band of leaders to a democratic position of high honor and status. The three principal Archons were the Eponymous Archon (Chief Magistrate of the entire government), the Polemarch (General Commander of All Military Forces), and the Archon Basileus (Religious Leader). Now, the titles and what they did were not so aligned. For instance, the Eponymous Archon, although the year would be named after him, was essentially an overseer of the Assembly and the Council. He had no direct input other than to act as a figurehead who could, for example, scrutinize or investigate any claims made against any individual or group in government. Amongst the most peculiar duties was to look after the city's Orphans.

The Archon Polemarch was reduced to ensuring military funeral services and a range of other non-combat military functions. He was also responsible for organizing the trials of foreigners or non-citizens. Archon Basileus was usually a coordinator of religious festivals and affairs, but also served in a judicial role, chairing cases involving the most serious crimes in the city, such as homicide. The actual title, Basileus, can mean King in translation or the “vessel of the people”. The Archon Basileus was far from a King. His role was initially to handle the matters the former Monarchs of Attica would have handled. The other six Archons were part of the judicial or court system leadership, ensuring everyone received a fair trial, just as the other archons did. The only difference is that they were usually assigned to lesser courts, which handled minor issues that did not typically carry the possibility of capital punishment. These six archons were also known as the Thesmotetai.

4.3 The courts

The Court was usually a place where a jury panel heard various legal issues and passed their decision on other citizens. Admission into a jury court had some prerequisites. People had to be citizens aged 30 or over, be free of any debts to the state, and not have lost their citizenship. The selection of jury members was randomized, and checks were placed to prevent anyone from predicting who the members would be. Many measures were taken to prevent jury bribery. The jury was also made up of judges, and the number of them was very high. Estimates indicate that some trials may have had as few as 501 jurors and as many as 1501. The process by which the number of jurors was determined is not entirely clear. However, the term "Demos" or "people's court" was not used for jury courts because of the restrictions required to serve on the jury, namely, being 30 years or older and being debt-free to the state.

There were several significant courts in the Athenian system. The most important Supreme Court was the Heliaea. The jury's duty in this court was to hear cases against the Archons or Council members. However, their role steadily increased, involving criminal, public civil, and international cases. The only cases they would not sit for were extremely sinister crimes such as murder. Serving on the Heliaea was not compulsory, but payment was arranged for anyone who wished to serve, given its essential role. The entire body of jurors numbered up to 6000. Each tribe or district of citizens is offered a group of 600 members to serve. Typically, 501 standard jurors were assigned to each room for the year, and additional members were often added from the pool of 6,000.

"The Jury-courts are elected by lot by the Nine Archons by tribes, and the Clerk of the Lawgivers from the tenth tribe.

The courts have ten entrances, one for each tribe, twenty rooms, two for each tribe, in which courts are allotted to jurors, a hundred small boxes, ten for each tribe, and other boxes into which the tickets of the jurymen drawn by lot are thrown, and two urns. Staves are placed at each entrance, as many as there are jurymen and acorns to the same number as the staves are thrown into the urn, and on the acorns are written the letters of the alphabet, starting with the eleventh, lambda, as many as the courts that are going to be filled.

Right to sit on juries belongs to all those over thirty years old who are not in debt to the Treasury or disfranchised. If any unqualified person sits on a jury, information is laid against him and he is brought before the jury-court, and if convicted the jurymen assess against him whatever punishment or fine he is thought to deserve; and if given a money fine, he has to go to prison until he has paid both the former debt, for which the information was laid, and whatever additional sum has been imposed on him as a fine by the court.

Each juryman has one box-wood ticket, with his own name and that of his father and deme written on it, and one letter of the alphabet as far as kappa; for the jurymen of each tribe are divided into ten sections, approximately an equal number under each letter.

As soon as the Lawgiver has drawn by lot the letters to be assigned to the courts, the attendant immediately takes them and affixes to each court its allotted letter.

The ten boxes lie in front of the entrance for each tribe. They have inscribed on them the letters as far as kappa. When the jurymen have thrown their tickets into the box on which is inscribed the same letter of the alphabet as is on the ticket itself, the attendant shakes them thoroughly and the Law-giver draws one ticket from each box.

This attendant is called the Affixer, and he affixes the tickets taken from the box to the ledged frame on which is the same letter that is on the box. This attendant is chosen by lot, in order that the same person may not always affix the tickets and cheat. There are five ledged frames in each of the balloting-rooms.

When he has thrown in the dice, the Archon casts lots for the tribe for each balloting-room; they are dice of copper, black and white. As many white ones are thrown in as jurymen are required to be selected, one white die for each five tickets, and the black dice correspondingly. As he draws out the dice the herald calls those on whom the lot has fallen. Also, the Affixer is there corresponding to the number.

The man called obeys and draws an acorn from the urn and, holding it out with the inscription upward, shows it first to the superintending Archon; when the Archon has seen it, he throws the man's ticket into the box that has the same letter written on it as the one on the acorn, in order that he may go into whatever court he is allotted to and not into whatever court he chooses and in order that it may not be possible to collect into a court whatever jurymen a person wishes.

The Archon has by him as many boxes as courts are going to be filled, each lettered with whichever is the letter assigned by lot to each court.

And the man himself having again shown it to the attendant then goes inside the barrier, and the attendant gives him a staff of the same colour as the court bearing the same letter as the one on the acorn, in order that it may be necessary for him to go into the court to which he has been assigned by lot; for if he goes into another, he is detected by the colour of his staff for each of the courts has a colour painted on the lintel of its entrance. He takes the staff and goes to the court of the same colour as his staff and having the same letter as is on the acorn. And when he has come into it he receives a token publicly from the person appointed by lot to this office.

Then with the acorn and the staff they take their seats in the court, when they have thus entered. And to those to whom the lot does not fall the Affixers give back their tickets " (Aristotle, 1944a, 63.1-65.4).

As you can see, an elaborate system was put in place to ensure no one knew which jury would sit for a particular case. Each jury was randomly selected, which protected the system from bribery, intimidation, and other tactics that could influence the trial's outcome.

Another court worth mentioning is the Areopagus. This court was designed to hear the cases of murder and other horrendous crimes. Usually, the Archon Basileus would be responsible for all the trials entered into the Areopagus court. Normally, there would not be many cases, and this court's system was a little different. Due to the seriousness of the crimes and the importance of fair judgment, only skilled and honorable individuals were permitted to serve on the council that oversaw the trials.

The Areopagus consisted of former Archons. All members of the Areopagus had been thoroughly investigated by democratic officials, as described during the process of selecting Archons. But it also meant that the people entering the Areopagus had gained significant experience presiding over numerous cases in the People's Court.

The candidates for the Areopagus underwent further investigation into their qualifications, skills, and fitness to serve before they assumed office. At the end of their year of service as Archons, the People's Court (Heliaia) would appraise the archons for their suitability to serve in the Areopagus. If an archon violated any of the laws governing his conduct in office, he could fail the audit. Membership in the Areopagus was lifelong, and as such, the entry process was strictly and carefully conducted. However, this did not deter any Athenian from bringing charges against a member of the Areopagus, and the same scrutiny would be applied, with a thorough investigation to determine whether the matter was punishable by trial or could lead to expulsion. The status of an Areopagus member was great, but the power of the people was uniform; no one was above the law.

Additionally, the actual court of the Areopagus did not have a people's jury; instead, the jury and judges were members of the Areopagus. Over the years, their numbers would have grown significantly, and the jury size they formed would have been large enough to ensure a fair trial.

To allow all people to participate in all the functions of the state, including the Assembly, Council, and Courts, the Athenians would pay a sum of money to everyone who participated. Upon completing their duty, they were given a token to redeem their payment. So, regardless of the service requested, everyone was compensated to ensure that the poor or those without the means to attend could participate. In the later years of Democracy, the amount paid was significantly higher and was comparable to a wage or viable income. This concept was identified in Aristotle's work, Politics, where he describes how a state can function properly without biasing the system toward the rich. To achieve this, a respectable sum of money should be paid for temporary offices or duties that people perform.

5. Other issues and a critique

"The people who lived further away from the city found it very difficult to travel to the Assembly meetings."

There were several notable issues with early Athenian democracy. People living farther from the city found it difficult to travel to Assembly meetings. Usually, the pay they received for attending was less than most would earn from their trades, farming, or other occupations. Additionally, many rural people could not always leave their flocks or crops unattended, regardless of the pay or monetary compensation. There was a high level of absenteeism in the early Assembly meetings. The people who generally had free time did not need to work. After the reforms of Solon and Pericles, pay increased dramatically to a fair wage or income. That was an excellent initiative for the people to attend the meetings. A pay increase was also an incentive to live closer to the city.

5.1 Male and Female Roles

Another issue related to excluding some people from citizenship is the distinction between males and females. While the exclusion of foreigners may be a valid thought, the exclusion of females and children from the Assembly and other political duties may be seen as problematic. There is no definitive way to describe the lives of people in those days, in my era, or in future generations. We will never truly know why they made the specific decisions they did, aside from those clearly stated in their writings. From such writings, we derive that any male citizen's immediate family had certain privileges available to citizens. The females, for instance, were not called by their own names but by their husbands'. Females were entitled to inherit their husband's wealth and undergo any legal proceedings necessary. The wife was also allowed to take legal action against anyone else in the polity, regardless of whether the other party was a citizen. Yet women led different lives and did not necessarily participate in the democratic assemblies. It was a peculiar arrangement. Given the sensitivity of this point today, it would be beneficial to discuss it a bit more thoroughly.

Some people believe that the exclusion of women from the Assembly was because the duties of the citizen were seen to be uniform, and women were not seen as equally capable as men in certain functions. Socrates said that duties and jobs are trainable, and a woman could be trained to do a man's job. However, there is also the issue of roles, which are defined by custom and, in part, biologically. Like any other place on the planet, women had specific roles in life, while men had others. Only recently, in modern culture, have women become involved in traditional male duties, including politics, military service, and manual labor. In the past, women were considered necessary, but only in the roles defined by their culture. Females were often tied to more delicate forms of work, such as art or music, at symposiums. The word music derives from the word muse. Muses would entertain through poetry and song. Females, in general, would also weave. Some would help on farms, and so forth. The muses could put their lyrics into the ears of the most powerful men. Young women in rural areas and villages shared heavy labor with their husbands or other men. But the idea of a woman marching into battle with heavy armor and weaponry was never considered viable. Nor was it considered culturally acceptable for women to be present at male gatherings. Some gatherings, such as those at church or for religious purposes, seem appropriate for females, males, and children to walk together side by side. Yet some gatherings seem inappropriate for females and children to attend. It is entirely cultural, with nothing to do with ability, rank, etc. Exclusions generally are borne out of a protective agenda. They were and still are often excluded from certain gatherings to protect one party. The elderly rarely gathered with the youth, nor did the males gather with the females.

Many early civilizations protected females through exclusion because males in the streets and at particular gatherings were often looking for sexual encounters. We know from the writings of Sophocles and others that women had a tough time in Ancient Greece, but no more—and perhaps much less—than others at the time. The play Antigone by Sophocles shows how Antigone rebels against authority, forsaking her civic duties and her role as a daughter to bury her brother properly. The play shows that women, like men, had to appeal to authority, but unlike men, women feared the consequences of speaking out. The fear was justified because the males were hardened. Men of the time were not liable for injuries they caused to each other, women, or children. That is why, although civilized, the Greek society was tough. They did not differ significantly in their views of females from those of most other civilizations at the time. Yet, compared to other cultures, Ancient Greek culture offered enormous luxury and freedom. It is similar to the story of the serpent and the fruit of knowledge; women were free to enjoy everything except for a few areas of society and government. Yet, even though there were rules, even those had exceptions.

There was also the idea that the decision to go to War should be made by those expected to fight that War. Like in our age, we often see rich and powerful men wage wars using the children of the middle class and the poor. Had the middle socio-economic class and the poor been asked, most modern wars would have never occurred. Similarly, the males, who were also soldiers, preferred to address such issues rather than leave them to their wives and female companions. It was a violent age, and Athens was, for some time, one of the few places offering tranquility.

Other reasons that could have led to the selection of the Assembly concerned the uniformity of legislative application. Uniformity in law was important, and having exceptions was hard to monitor and enforce. People did not have computational devices or free access to writing materials. These were expensive new inventions of that time. Records were usually costly, and making laws with various exceptions also required a system to monitor such exceptions. For instance, it could not be said by law that every citizen must attend assembly meetings if breastfeeding, giving birth, or other intrinsic female duties seemed of higher priority. How would they monitor such activity to provide an exemption? Even a male farmer would stop his work to assist in delivering a baby from his wife or stock. I mean that people can have many valid reasons for not attending an assembly. Therefore, although women were generally excluded from the Assembly, they may still consider it beneficial. A wife at home or attending to the male's or husband's chores freed the male to participate in the Assembly. Laws that did not make assembly attendance compulsory also helped, as they gave citizens the freedom to pursue their own gender-based and profession-specific roles.

Women were given much more flexibility in how they prioritized their lives. They could do almost anything without being obligated to the government or the system. The only drawback was their limited influence in political and military spheres. It was considered fair since the system did not obligate the female to bear arms, attend military drills, or perform any other military or political duty for the state. They were given the freedom to bear only obligations to their family. While that was their only requirement or obligation, they were free to participate peripherally in the citizens' obligation or duty. Such as not partaking in military drills but assisting in feeding the soldiers or helping the organizers. We are not entirely sure of the particulars of their peripheral occupations. Yet, Sappho was the head of an Oligarchy on her island, and Antigone was a princess of sorts with two brothers fighting each other in a civil war.

Many other interesting stories and references exist regarding women in ancient Greece, but, like the males, the women also had their own stories. Little in the literature explains why females were not allowed to participate in government through assemblies or other venues. It is an anomaly because we are aware of several females who have assumed the role of monarchs or the head of an oligarchy. Yet, in Athens specifically, the literature is somewhat absent because the histories of Herodotus, Thucydides, and others describe the men at war. The Iliad of Homer was a poem dedicated to the men of war. Little was written about women, but at least we know they had little to do with government and the military. Homer wrote about the ideal female in the stories of Odysseus and the Odyssey. He describes Penelope, Odysseus's wife, as a loyal, stern, trusted keeper of the home. Who, in the absence of a male figure in the house, had tried to defend her virtue in a female fashion and upheld respect and honor for her home, family, and husband. She remained celibate during the 20-year absence of her husband after the aftermath of the Trojan War. Turning to archaeological evidence, including vases and artifacts from that era, we know that women had a hugely diverse role.

We could argue that the first proxy vote occurred when a wife instructed her husband on what to say in those assemblies. The amount of frustration women would have had in steering their husbands is probably well known worldwide now, under the numerous systems that entail representative government.

Physical strength is often used as a reason to exclude females from battle. At the time, it was perhaps the more feasible option, given the heavy metal armor, hand-held shields, and swords soldiers were expected to wear. Recently, several reports of reproductive system damage or sterility have occurred due to the extreme endurance required by soldiers. Excluding women from war was a worldwide standard. From the most primitive cultures to the most sophisticated, men defended their families and friends. There were many exclusions. In several tribes, the women were the leaders. There is even the legend of the Amazons, where women led and fought alongside each other. Yet this cultural attribute of male exclusiveness in the military remained a part of most of the world's customs until the advent of the Jihad. Some villages in Persia during the Roman-Persian war sent their entire populations to fight against the Eastern Roman army. Therefore, the reasons for excluding females from the military are the same as those for excluding them from politics. They were not entirely philosophical reasons; at best, we would describe them as customary. Under Oligarchic rule, jihads were declared in the East, and later, in the West, women were allowed to serve after a long period during which they were not allowed to serve in the military.

Even by elaborating all the possible reasons why women may have been excluded from the Assembly, there is no definitive reason for it. As Socrates mentions, it was a cultural issue. But rest assured, the women did complain. Women's status in society was almost entirely dependent on their husbands' success. Female status caused some anxiety and conflict between women. In some traditions, daughters were used as bargaining chips.

Irrespective of our modern interpretation, most Athenian laws were simple and easily enforced. The laws did not have exceptions, any more than the philosophical categories did. Monitoring every person and fairly assessing them were beyond the police's ability. It would have been difficult to include women of those ages as full citizens and participants in government and the army because they would have had specific requirements that the city could not provide. However, in a modern context, those amenities can certainly be provided for women.

Additionally, females can draw logical conclusions and participate in discussions and decision-making processes. However, we also need to consider the family unit, the home, the way people want to live, and the customs, culture, and way of life they desire. There is no definitive answer on whether women should be equal in political and military roles. Circumstances and the will of the people determine these things.

In conclusion, in a matriarchy, females possess specific intrinsic qualities that place them in a position similar to that of the Queen Ant or Queen Bee, where their role is central to the male's life, who works, defends, and provides for them. In other societies, the male is central, and he takes many wives who work for him. They protect him by standing in front of him. Both societies also exhibit significant discontent, characterized by an extreme Patriarchy or Matriarchy.

In the systems that undervalue women, women will not feel love and companionship with their husbands, especially if they share with other wives. Often, they think that they are treated like stock. The males in such societies believe that the natural order of things places the male in a position of authority, and the female's biological role places her closer to the nest. In contrast, matriarchy can also create significant discontent among males. The most critical problem is that the males lose their ability to perform the roles they consider manly or essential to them. Both systems I have described are extreme Matriarchy and Patriarchy.

Even though, admittedly, a male can impregnate many wives at the same time. A female can only be pregnant at a time. Like the breeding stock, the male is in a biological role to be promiscuous. The female biological role, on the other hand, is not to be promiscuous. This centers purely on her role during pregnancy. That is why, in many cultures, men are given little thought as to their virginity, but females are often sought after as virgins. It also contributes to the arguments often used to justify a Patriarchy or Matriarchy. That is often used to justify the male's right to take many wives, and indeed, many ancient and tribal people still do. But in almost all circumstances, polygamous relationships develop jealousy and other forms of antagonistic dynamics. There is constant competition to be the favored wife. Husbands almost always have a favorite because it is natural to like or love someone more than another. That is where Monogamous societies tend to also lean towards matriarchal structures. They tend to place the woman or female in a central role, and the male who takes such a wife becomes bound to her. In either case, the male is given the freedom to act outside the home, while the female is often expected to be domestic in her duties. The females guide and steer the males by other means, making the man a proxy or representative of the will of the female or females. As we have highlighted, women and men, wives and husbands, social structure, and all things relating to how people live their lives are still cultural matters, even with some biological or scientific reasoning.

The participation of females in government and the military is entirely a cultural choice. There are many reasons that people can give for both sides of such an argument. But none qualify as being philosophically true. It also depends on religion, culture, and circumstances. Because even societies that typically prevent women from serving in the military often have women serving in their own accord. During the siege of Constantinople, also known as Istanbul (Eis-tin-poli, to the city, Gr..), the women and children were kept in churches for their safety. But at night, those women led their children to the battered walls and began repairing them by placing mortar and stones back in place. Very few women have led military initiatives, but several have. Therefore, even in places where we presume local culture prevents women from serving in the military, some circumstances force women and even children to act.

The issue of female and male participation in government and, ultimately, the military has been reasonably dealt with. It should be considered fair for a democracy to exist with or without female direct participation in government and the military. Depending on the society, way of life, and what people consider important, there should be room for people to incorporate their cultural views into how their democracy operates. No philosophical reasons exist to conclude that females and children should not participate. A lean and tough Democratic institution would probably prefer male citizenship with the exclusion of females. Additionally, national decisions and actions initiated by males may be perceived by other males as more impactful than those made by females and children.

5.2 Other limitations on citizenship

Citizens were considered to be thirty or over. Young men are prone to aggressive actions without wise temperament. We can say many things about the youth, most of which they will refute until they reflect on their own lives as they age. We can most certainly appreciate that mature males form different opinions from young males. Similarly, mothers differ in their minds and priorities from younger females. Having said that much about the roles of males and females and the issues affecting youth, it is sufficient to acknowledge these aspects of society. There are nine parts of cultural life: the culture of the young, married, and single; the culture of the middle-aged, married, and single; and the culture of the elderly, married, and single. These parts of society are based on age and marital status because age and marital status seem to have the greatest impact on how we prioritize. Having, as the new colonies do, adults and active citizens at the age of eighteen who are made citizens at birth or by spending less than a handful of years in the city appears as foolish as building their cities on the riverfronts, as they have done. Now, they complain that the youth have no understanding and waste their votes while their properties flood along the rivers. Had the colonial cities been free, perhaps discussion would have avoided such unwise choices.

Another limitation on citizen participation is that some events and positions require a person to be debt-free to the State. This means that the bias of using a powerful seat to help pay off a loan is avoided immediately. Having a powerful seat enabled this corruption for debts one owed to the State and directly to the people. However, it can cause problems, as seen in the modern era following World War II, when people took on debt to buy homes and shelters. If debts are organized and structured to affect many people, those people can become debt slaves. That means that they are obliged to work and enslave themselves to work. Debt slavery is an age-old system used as part of tyrannical slavery. Aristotle, in the Athenian constitution, remarks,

"Solon having become master of affairs made the people free both at the time and for the future by prohibiting loans secured on the person, and he laid down laws, and enacted cancellations of debts both private and public,…" (Aristotle, 1944a, 6.1).

5.3 Systemic slavery

Some people presume that the Athenian Democracy allowed citizens to have servants or slaves. I am not sure which historians to believe on the matter, as there are many revisionists and anti-Hellenic and anti-academic establishments around the world. Father Romanides alerted us to the various distortions of historical fact. As such, it becomes difficult to reference modern historical works because any serious historian would first examine the sources before making interpretations. The actual word for 'slave' is not used in the majority of ancient texts. Words like "doulos" implied a servant. The word is often used in Biblical texts as a non-derogatory term for workers. The phrase "O doulos tou Theou" means "The worker of God". Other meanings of "doulos" in Hesiod's day included "prisoner of war." Words for home servants, craftsmen, and various other duties were often used in ancient texts, making it difficult to determine whether these individuals were slaves in the modern sense. Non-citizens were, for example, allowed to function within the city in any capacity except politics and office-holders in the government. Yet no ancient text addresses the issue of slavery to clarify the exact circumstances that may have existed. As a result, it is furthermore difficult to determine the conditions of such employment. The lack of evidence to support the use of slaves does not automatically disprove the theory, but it does strongly support the presumption that the non-citizens were not slaves.

Even women who did not have full citizenship could not be regarded as slaves, although their lack of rights on particular issues could be seen as a form of oppression. If slaves existed, then the majority would probably have been captured prisoners taken after war campaigns. The prisoners were thought to be used for heavy labor in the city. We do know from the ancient texts that a servant or non-citizen could ask a citizen for a recommendation to become a citizen. Although the citizen was not empowered to say yes or no directly, his recommendation would go a long way. In fact, the more people support a non-Athenian or non-citizen becoming a citizen, the stronger their case becomes.

There were several other anomalies with the democracy that revolved around ancient customs and ideologies. If we look back, some things may seem peculiar, like taking oaths on the entrails of sacrificed beasts. But be cautious of saying un-Democratic. To use a very sensitive subject of slavery, if the people of a Democracy choose to enslave other people, then that is, even though evil by our standards, still democratic. Remember, the definition of Democracy is not justice, freedom, or fairness. However, it is arguable, based on our ethical standards at the time, that such a decision was made. Democracy is a system of government in which the people control everything. People's investment in themselves is why a common ethical code goes a long way toward defining how a particular Democracy will function. Without such ethical restraints, we can quickly degenerate a Democracy into an Ochlocracy. Therefore, slavery and other ethically influenced components and ideologies of a government or democracy are something that deserves separate and detailed attention because they pertain to faith, religion, ethics, and culture. It is worth noting that, whether ancient Greeks had slaves or not, the extent to which such slaves were bound and enslaved seems almost trivial in the context we have come to know during the period of Autocratic colonization. On the issue of slavery, the preceding is not an apology or excuse but rather a realistic comparison.

The division of Ancient Greek society placed priority on those born and raised in the relevant city and its surrounding state. The least rights, in terms of priority, were afforded to foreigners and visitors. While they often resorted to using prisoners of war to perform various tasks, it is not clear how long such capture was retained, nor the conditions of such capture. Philip of Macedon, for instance, was such a prisoner, yet he was eventually released. We also know that a formal release could be purchased in many parts of Greece. Not everyone who was released from servitude was a viable candidate for citizenship. So, upon release, many left the city.

The Helots of Sparta, for instance, were Greeks who were subjected to serving as farmers and were often treated harshly by the ruling society. They were not entirely enslaved people, yet they were not freemen. In those days, having wealth was a sign of being a freeman. Since the Helots were Sparta's workers and farmers, they were often poorly educated, lacked material wealth, and were considered unrefined. They would be the last to represent the state of Sparta in any affair other than perhaps sports. The term "Helot" is often referred to in the same context as "servant" or "slave." But this is very far from the truth. There are classes in every society, which vary from society to society. The Spartans established a hierarchical system with three tiers of rule: the Spartiades, the Periokoi, and the Helots. The Spartiades were the ruling class. The Periokoi were non-citizens, a free class, and the last were the Helots, who were tied to the land or a specific job. The Helots comprised the bulk of the population and were also considered Spartans by other cities. Their place within the system was considered the lowest of all. We could liken the Helots to the working and unemployed populations found in modern cities. Despite being Spartans, they were also perceived as inferior in status to the Spartiades and even to the Periokoi, who may not have even been from Sparta. The ruling class of Sparta evolved into an overly militaristic society, placing the wealthy and those capable of administering an army at its head. Unfortunately, the Spartan customs dominated our modern cities more than the Athenian model.

Therefore, when we speak of slavery or enslavement, it is not a simple matter of visualizing chains and shackles. Numerous examples throughout human history establish that, given the opportunity, most oligarchies and monarchies will establish some form of control over the populace. Caste systems under a Monarchy or Oligarchy were very common in the past and are still in use throughout some parts of the world. The lower castes often struggle to survive, while the higher castes enjoy enormous luxuries. Well, this issue of disparity, oppression, and segregation is not entirely restricted to those forms of government. A republic, a democracy, and all forms of government can facilitate the creation or propagation of disparity and segregation within society. These were addressed at the start. Typically, five occupational classes are found in a city, and each seeks a fair life. It is sufficient to establish that layers of society will form, regardless of the type of government. The difference is that, in a fair and just democracy, the people create the strata or layers of society. They decide where to spend their time, and over a lifetime, they may be found in any of these classes or layers. Mobility through these classes is a good indicator of how liberal a government system is. If people are born into a class like the poor Helots, who had to save their money to buy freedom, then we do not have a proper Democratic institution. Similarly, modern society compels people to work long hours and forces many to borrow in order to continue working.

Typically, people borrow enormous amounts of money for homes and become obligated to repay those loans for many years. A large number of people have had home debts for twenty or thirty years. By the exact mechanisms, they are not too different from the Helots. The Helots paid for their freedom, but the so-called free in modern society repay enormous loans, like the Helots' lump-sum payment, to gain independence. We will certainly address these matters in more detail later. It is clear that when we look at the Athenian system, we may interpret certain things as bad; some may make us flinch, but sometimes, in many instances, we are blinded to our faults and shortcomings. We should not be too quick to judge the Ancients and their choices; instead, we should analyze them, as we have here, and ascertain whether we could do better.

5.4 A list of rights

The Athenian model had rights written into their constitutional laws, but did not have a list of rights. At the time of writing, the system lacked state rights for people almost worldwide. The Athenians lacked a moderate bill of rights. Therefore, to protect the ethos of a constitution and the will of the people, to ensure the system preserves ethical rights, the following could be established:

1. The Right to believe in God.

2. The Right to freedom of thought and speech.

3. The Right to congregate, meet, and protest freely and peacefully.

4. The Right to the operation of the press and other media.

5. The Right to ask and be provided with temporary shelter by the government during times of extreme need;

    a. For an extended family, the parents, children, and those they care for, such as grandparents, shall be placed in such a way as to keep them together,

    b. for a family, including the parents and their children, shall be kept together,

    c. for couples, so that they remain together,

6. The Right to ask and be provided with access to water and food for consumption in times of extreme need.

7. The parental Right to raise, educate and shelter their own children.

8. The Right to deny any medical or other treatment or procedure affecting the self.

9. The Right of the mother to protect and preserve the life in her womb.

10. The Right to demand the enforcement of these rights.

11. The Right against discrimination or other adverse effects, for demanding the enforcement of these rights.

12. The Right to petition the government, including the right to petition for

    a. the creation, alteration or abolition of laws,

    b. the enforcement of laws

    c. the establishment of fair juries.

13. The right to defend our nation or state with arms and firearms.

14. The Right to elect the government

15. The Right to elect the judiciary

16. The Right to elect principal commanders for the military, including the

    a. Army

    b. Navy and

    c. Air Force.

17. The Right to elect principal commanders for the Police

18. The Right to own land and property and refuse entry and the use of that land and/or property, including military and police.

19. The Right to protect against unreasonable search and seizure.

20. The Right to protect against warrants issued without probable cause.

21. The Right to protect against
    a. Trial without indictment
    b. Double jeopardy
    c. Self-incrimination, and
    d. Property seizure
22. The Right to a fair and speedy trial
23. The Right to informed charges, and this shall be
    a. established before making a formal statement, and
    b. done in a fit mental and or physical state to understand the charges and their potential consequences,
    c. done knowing that they are making a formal statement, and they shall be
    d. informed of their right to Legal counsel
24. The Right to remain silent.
25. The Right to be confronted by witnesses.
26. The Right to call witnesses.
27. The Right to legal counsel.
28. The Right to trial by jury.
29. The Right to protect against,
    a. Excessive bail,
    b. Excessive fines,
    c. Cruel and unusual punishment.

30. The Right to persist eternally - No law, judgment or constitutional change shall ever infringe, diminish or alter these rights.

31. The Right of the States to determine the Federal government's powers.

32. The States must act on every petition received by the People.

33. Where a government can't decide by a convincing majority, they may call for a referendum to include the people's direct vote.

34. The Right to fair discussion – On any matters that require the people's vote or decision, they may;

a. require a majority to attend a discussion on the raised matters,

b. establish a case-by-case comparison debate,

c. gives fair time allocated so that each case has had equal time,

d. request discussion on the consequences of their decision,

e. amend the question put forward to the people.

35. The Right to Public Space and Forum - The State shall provide for every political division, such as a suburb, within it, a free space that the People may use at their peaceful discretion. It must be of a size and accessibility that do not hinder the use of such a forum or space.

36. The right to enter parliament and submit matters for discussion may include, without limitation, a petition, confidential matters, or military matters, verbally or written.

37. The Right to travel without restriction.

38. The Right to hold specific political views

a. Without being discriminated against,

b. punished,

c. hindered and

d. incarcerated.

6. Ethics

> *"…we could say that every system has its merits and faults just like every human has merits and faults."*

Plato's Republic concludes that there is no perfect system. Jesus Christ tells us the same thing about each of us: none of us is without sin or flaws. After evaluating numerous systems and their inherent flaws, as well as the countless atrocious behaviors that humans are capable of, it becomes clear that there is no such thing as a perfect system. Such a system does not exist because we are all intrinsically flawed in some way or another. During wars, the brave fight for the weak, but what good is an older man or a coward at such a time? Alternatively, when coming together in a democratic assembly, the intelligent and wise will put forward the most truthful and useful speeches. Still, these same people would possibly make weak warriors. We can view certain qualities as faults or imperfections. However, the situation demands certain qualities over others.

Equally, we could say that every system has its merits and faults, just like every human has merits and faults. Recognizing that no system or individual is perfect, we must establish the ethics of both the system and its people. Can a system have ethics? Some aspects of people's ethics are vivid and pragmatically interpreted through systemic frameworks, such as the rule of law and its composition. In both cases, the system and the individuals who make it up will have ethics influenced by environmental or external factors. A polity and its system under attack during a war will want to defend and have the qualities of a solid defense. When droughts strain a system, solutions will be required, and scientific and practical knowledge will be needed to address the crisis. Therefore, the ethics or valued qualities of the system will vary.

If we know that imperfections and strengths exist for each system as they do for each person, then it must at least be clearly stated which of these merits are worthy and which of these faults are disposable or not tolerated. In this way, if the people or the system act, they will produce ethical effects and results.

Ethics should be considered very important because they will be reflected in people's laws and actions. As mentioned, a government system can only be as good as those who constitute and administer it. If we immediately establish which ethics are needed to develop, maintain, and propagate a Democracy, we are presented with three distinct functions, each with its own requirements. These requirements are not typically a part of the same person. One person may be outwardly strong and youthful in their actions, and such individuals are best suited for establishing change, as these characteristics are often associated with warriors. Where a Democracy needs to be maintained, it will still require warriors, but it will also need a large number of administrators. The maintainers of a system are typically quiet individuals who are willing to be patient and work methodically towards their goals. Maintainers include technicians, professionals, merchants, and agrarians. Therefore, as you can see, when we highlight one ethic over another, we need to exercise caution, because we are all different and valuable. The perceived value of a person is influenced by circumstance. It was wise to say that there is no time for philosophy in times of war, and yet the single thing needed most in times of war is philosophy. The preceding explains the third function, which concerns ideas, philosophy, and religion. While religion is seen as a source of ethics, it has not always been the case.

Socrates considered knowledge and understanding as a source of virtues. Ignorance causes people to develop fewer virtues than those who develop wisdom and knowledge. However, Plato was influenced by cults of pleasure, which held that pleasure was the source of happiness, and thus, by extension, the source of virtue. Aristotle, as described, thought of a median value that is displayed the most, and on the periphery, those things that are displayed sometimes—for instance, cowardice, courage, and rashness. Where courage is in the middle and cowardice and rashness are on the periphery. Other systems of categorizing virtues include social contract theories, which equate what is good with what is legal. Natural law sees good in anything that is of natural law. We can gain a broad understanding of what ethics is. Some of these approaches to ethics are valid at times. However, religion remains the most consistent and widespread source of expected and anticipated ethics.

6.1 Religion and the State

To ensure that everyone understands what is ethical and that the government system reflects these ethics, the people must establish a legal system that also reflects them. Education on the required ethics is important in youth, but so is the allowance for people to choose what will form the framework of their laws. The ethics that we consider good and valuable must be common amongst the people attempting to operate a democracy. Otherwise, democratically, the minority would decide the common ethics for the majority and, in turn, define the laws.

Through observation, some secular systems attempt to separate government and society from religion. The problem with this concept is that there is a grey area. At some point, a distinction is made between the law and the people's will. That is to say that if the law is the will of the people, then the law would reflect what the majority thought was important. The law in a Democratic system is an extension of the people and their rules and ethics. By no means could anyone divide religion from democratic systems completely. It is expected that the people's religion will be reflected in the legislation. However, the rule of law as an independent system is possible and is used in secular societies.

Most secular nations that have clearly defined boundaries between religion and government are mostly not secular but atheist in nature. Some people go further and call them Satanic. These systems, instead of simply keeping religion out of politics, have evolved and continue to evolve into atheism-promoting institutions. It is clear that through many years of so-called secular government, atheism has increased exponentially. There is also a large stream of people who merely reject mainstream religion and find some obscure faith or religion instead. To some, atheism becomes a religion. It has the dogma—the philosophical body of knowledge—and a devout following. Disheartened by institutional churches, some people have created their own faiths and churches. Religion, indeed, should be kept out of politics. However, the impact of the government on the people and the people on the government is a two-way equilibrium. Each affects the other, and people constantly react to and act on the effects and changes of government.

At the same time, we must acknowledge that if the majority holds a set of ethics derived from their faith, those ethics will eventually become law. In turn, the ethics entrenched in the law affect the people. If people become secular, there can be a tendency to create a subculture of atheism or other alternatives. Furthermore, suppose the majority think women should cover their heads because of a passage in holy scripture. In that case, the majority will eventually pass a law mandating the wearing of such a garment. At this point, people must be cautious about including their religion in their statutes. While wearing a garment to cover the head may seem trivial at first, it becomes a problem when the freedom of a woman to wear or remove it is taken into consideration. In many East Asian countries, it is forbidden to separate religion from the state because the state establishes the religion, and the religion establishes the state. A democracy, as I or others would imagine it, could not exist in such a place, not because of the relationship of state and religion alone, but because of its mandate and inability to flex to the political environment around it.

Mythologies were once part of a religion. Imagine, from mythology, that Zeus, who banished Prometheus for giving humans fire, also confiscated humanity's fire. It could be considered wise to do so, as no bullets, bombs, or rockets would fly. But neither would warmth and shelter from the cold, nor energy to cook our food. Imagine then that a polity refused to use fire indefinitely because of such a religious belief. Bans and restrictions on any technology or invention by religious texts should be carefully considered. If people give priority to religion or even mythology over affairs of the state, then we have a serious problem. That prioritizes the interests of an external group over those of the state's people. We gain a Theocratic system if it were to happen.

We can see from previous examples that religion, directly involved in a nation, may not be the best option. We know this to be historically true, as many religions were spread by conquest, while others were spread through colonization. Those religions created spheres of trade that could be seen as beneficial. However, the colonization process also created political segregation or, at the very least, antagonism. Alternatively, many instances of new religions were created to serve political agendas. Here, in a philosophical context, a religion can only serve the God or Deity to which that religion is established. Religion cannot serve two masters: the state and God. While many will try to argue that religion and state are one, especially in the East, the reality is that it can never truly be so. A polity and its interests are not always going to be beneficial to the religion of that polity.

While Christians may be told it is better to turn the other cheek, this way of thinking does not include a military pre-emptive strike. History has proven that to survive as a polity, there will be times when the polity must strike before the opponent attacks. However, most polities highly regard the caseus beli. Caseus beli is used to refer to the precursor of war. Given a good enough reason, such as two strikes upon the cheek, seeking an eye for an eye is common. An example of pre-emptive strikes and retaliation was the Trojan War. The Trojan War's casus belli was the abduction of Helen. Helen was known in different cultures as Beautiful Hellen, Helen of Troy, and Helen of Sparta.

In times of diplomacy, we may turn the other cheek many times, but when others resort to conflict or war, we must defend and counter with force. It becomes apparent that some religions will not always be compatible with the system of government. Certainly, the religion of the people will influence the law and the system, but not every law or action taken as a Polity will serve their religion. As an example, other religions ask people to be warriors of God and to conquer so that the whole world will be under the boot of that religion and a combined state. The conquest of all humanity is a disturbing thought for Democratic thinkers. If a polity truly believes that its mission is a blood-letting war against all who do not believe like them, then Democracy is not going to operate within such a system. Religion and the State have different masters, each serving a different purpose. Ironically, working with such opposing ideologies would require a democratic approach. For one group of faith to listen to and work with another group of a different faith, they would need to find a democratic resolution that gives each group a mutual voice.

Additionally, from the example of Prometheus's fire, we must acknowledge that there are suitable applications for technologies that are otherwise deemed dangerous or undesirable. There will be times when religion and the state complement each other on matters such as these. While most religions advise against certain scientific uses, they also support others. That will certainly happen when the things we consider dangerous become accepted, like electricity used to light the interior of Churches.

We are also aware of numerous instances where technologies that were initially considered detrimental have become indispensable. One of the most controversial technologies in human history is that of imagery. While some thought it was good art, others considered it evil. Imagery has shifted from physical to electronic and digital forms over thousands of years, and along the way, it has been blamed for many poor applications. Within specific denominations, some accept certain forms of imagery, while others avoid it. Some don't accept imagery in their places of worship. Accessing imagery, such as that found in entertainment, would become a significant political topic if there were intentions to eliminate the art form.

Yet even when a partnership may arise where the religious belief and the State have a common interest, the relationship between the two comes under question. Religion should not influence all facets of government. We know that State and Religion are independent variables, but the administrative system or government is where either of these can be affected. The people's government becomes the dependent variable. Also, what the people decide is best for the State will not always comply with their Religion. Similarly, a religious action or belief may not benefit the State. The way religion should be reflected in a government system is through the government's laws. The most significant contribution that a Religion can make is to offer its set of ethics to be included in the laws of the State. Therefore, if people believe in the Ten Commandments, they should be allowed to formulate laws that support this belief. However, we cannot equate religion and law to be equal or the same.

Even when the very same religious people have acted in favor of the State, not because they are less faithful, but because they believe a particular action serves their State better, and the people place the Polity and State before their Religion, then such a thing is a hard thing to do by any pious person or group. But if the system openly accepts religion as a source of ethics and creates an ethical drive and stimulus for the state, then surely there is no greater asset. Similarly, the State must respect those who have faith. Furthermore, a government should not put the pious in the way of harm, discrimination, or in any way detrimentally act against the pious. The pious should have the same rights as any other citizen. They should not be barred from participating in the Polity and State. We must accept that there will be religious institutions. Some will deem fire as a valuable technology. Others will think that imagery can be a beautiful art form. Some will resist following traditions, etc. Similarly, pious people should not be judged when they put state and polity before all else. Because if any religion is of any worth, it will uphold that love is the priority among humanity. Therefore, what better way to love than to put the welfare and ethical benefits of the people before all else?

We have supported religion in this philosophy because love, passiveness, and harmony are the most important things to achieve. The scope here is purely with the perspective of uniting religious ethics with the ethics that existed during Aristotle's time and the original Democracy. Some may consider Aristotle's ethics as Pagan derived just as much as the Democratic philosophy. After all, it was the Pagan Greeks who created Democracy. But I think some sympathy should be expressed in their favor by not thinking of them as Pagans but as pious people. Their ethics were not too different from ours, but since the coming of Christ, the ethical standards in society have increased. So once again, we should confirm that our interests are biased towards visualizing an open, transparent, loving, passive, and harmonious polity.

Jesus, in particular, and the New Testament provide us with ample examples of a faith heavily biased towards passivity, love, and harmony. Ghandi of India himself confessed that he followed Christ as an example. He firmly believed that with peace and numbers, anything can be established. If people work, protest, and support the critical things that lead to their freedom, they can achieve it. However, such coordination and common cause cannot exist independently. In the case of Christ and Gandhi, both were seen as leaders, even though they were not seen as fighters or generals. That implies that people do not necessarily follow military or aggressive movements. Most people follow passive and non-aggressive movements. That is why the Christian faith seemed very popular at its inception: it was characterized by a passive and loving nature. At a time when the world was engulfed in bloody war, a faith that spoke of love, kindness, sharing, peace, and solidarity was welcomed with open arms. The initial spread of Christianity was not spread on the back of the Roman legions. The initial spread was achieved by the Apostles and their followers, who hid and often fled the legions and many who persecuted them. Many families secretly began to believe in Christianity. It was against all odds that a faith founded on the martyrdom of its founders, aside from the Apostle John, would gain popularity.

Usually, misinterpreted signs of favorable winds, health restoration, and other false miracles kept people believing in Pagan Gods. However, the martyrdom of Christianity paved the way for a faith so moving and powerful that its followers endured centuries of persecution. It was during this period of persecution that Christianity reached its height. However, as Christianity became synonymous with the Germanic Romans, the East began to stir against them and, as a consequence, against Christianity. That mainly happened once the Latins and Germanics began to enter the Middle East as Romans. Gone was the simplicity of early Christian life, and now (500AD onwards) the Church entered a period of autocratic reign. Bishops began wearing crowns, mimicking the King and his court.

The original Turks were viewed as foreigners in the Near East, as were the Germanics and Latin peoples. The arrival of these ethnicities in the region caused immense hostility and contributed to multiple wars. The most severe fighting occurred during the Middle Ages. For example, the Germanic expansion into the East during the Crusades demonstrated how religion could be used to form a part of a national or state identity. It also showed how humanity has fought countless battles by using religion as a tool to recruit innocent people into armies serving alternative Oligarchic and Monarchical agendas. None of these wars, or any others, brought freedom to the people, East or West.

A nation, if it were to exist as a Democratic nation, must acknowledge that while religion can be a source of ethics, it can't be a source of absolute law. Tolerance must always exist for other people, their religions, and their religious laws. That tolerance is usually not turned into respect unless people have valid reasons to respect another faith. The faith that an individual may have usually places the person within a social sphere predominated by that faith. So the majority of friends for a Christian will be Christians, and the majority of friends for a Muslim will be Muslims, and the majority of friends for a Hindu will be Hindus, and so forth. However, this is truer in a homogenous state than in places such as colonies or where multiple ethnicities and tribes exist under a common culture. In a Democracy, such groups can be seen as threatening to the majority. Conflict may arise when the majority adheres to one faith and a sizable minority holds different beliefs. This conflict will eventually manifest in the assemblies and nearly all aspects of meetings. Therefore, tolerance is insufficient, but love for one another is required.

At the individual or larger polity level, it is easy to see how conflicts may arise when people gather into groups with political, religious, or other interests. Parties or political parties may form informally or formally. Therefore, while several tribes may unite within an Assembly and have equal rights, they must show love for one another to work together. That would mean religion should be external to the operation, but integrate certain aspects within the government system. In some places, all the tribes may unite under a single faith; in others, they may join multiple faiths. There is often no safe middle ground with religion. You either believe, or you don't. Everything in between is a realm for the lost. That is true for any religion, Eastern or Western. To avoid clashes and arguments, it is advisable to separate state and religion. This separation will create a grey region where the interface between the religious institutions and the state will be fluctuating.

Additionally, a common ethical approach is likely to be encouraged by the pious or religious population in government. As stated, careful attention should be given not to turn the government system into an Atheistic religious entity that promotes Atheism. Such was happening in many places worldwide at the time of writing this.

6.2 Democratic Ethics

We begin to see how religious ethics shape government operations. There is no quantifiable method to determine what is and isn't ethical. It is entirely a process of qualitative preference. While reasoning and logic may be applied, the terms are almost entirely non-quantifiable. Added to this are the diverse backgrounds and attributes of the people, their various religions, and all matters that influence what they consider ethical. Ethics and their importance change over time, and the popularization of certain behaviors over others can easily sway them. In this respect, very few philosophers have completely qualified all human ethics. However, we can develop an estimate of those ethics—a guide or a general path towards ethics, life, polity, and governance.

In his work The Eudemian Ethics, Aristotle presents an underlying ethical concept that leads to happiness or satisfaction. That should be considered different from cults that promote personal indulgence and over-saturating the senses. There are many cults of excess in human history, but what Aristotle means by happiness is also our health, well-being, and satisfaction. In the first part of his works, he debates the issue of freedom with other aspects of life. Each person values courage, honor, wisdom, and goodness differently. So, this leads to different perceptions of which ethic is higher or more important. Because people want to live the life they choose, they generally also choose which ethics are more important. Some may succumb to greed and pursue a merchant's lifestyle. Others may deem knowledge and science more important and adopt a lifestyle akin to that of a philosopher or scientist.

Each person should have the freedom to do as they please, but not the freedom to harm others. While we tolerate, or even openly accept, the benefits of cheaper products a merchant offers, we do not like being in debt for such products, land, or homes. Likewise, we enjoy the benefit of scientific progress, such as new pharmaceuticals, but may not like the side effects of new medications or the processes used to test or make them. There is a degree of restriction placed on what merchants are allowed to do, as there is on what scientists are allowed to do. Laws typically impose these restrictions, but they also stem from our ethical principles. So, even though the merchant would only be completely satisfied if they could fulfill their appetite for wealth, would they be satisfied with the restrictions of not causing anyone else harm or loss? Can one truly be satisfied with what they like most if any restrictions are placed on what they enjoy? If a part of the business is to exploit, find cheap wares or products, and sell them more expensively, then how do we decide how much such exploitation is permissible?

In the past few centuries, a period of immense industrialization led to the exploitation of young children in the most hazardous circumstances. For instance, narrow coal-mining shafts were dug, and small children would enter them to mine coal. At the time of writing, children are used to large food companies. According to most laws in most countries, they are entitled to considerably less than an adult. If we require a balance in society and a tier of exploitation for merchants to prosper, then it becomes clear that a system of such nature can only produce discontent. If we wish to keep the merchant class content, then it would be at the expense of the people they exploit. Suppose we wish to ensure that the exploited are only minimally exploited. In that case, we have done so at the expense of the merchant's fulfillment and possibly others affected by their service.

Aristotle's other works on ethics take the view of creating an ethical platform based on what is considered ideal in society and by each individual within it. The problem with such a relative system is that each family or group of people deemed to be living a perfect life will inspire others to do the same. Often, this leads to corruption and decadence, since the ideal in a materialistic world is an overabundance of wealth and material goods. Since not everyone can have the same resources and wealth, there is a high level of discontent in such societies. However, if people focus on what is truly valuable in maintaining and perpetuating a Democratic system free of corruption and flaws, then ethics take on a different form.

Additionally, consider the ethics derived from a religious context, which become part of the democratic institution. For instance, the passiveness of Christ's words has merit in such a

Democratic system. We do not want laws that kill people for punishment. We do not want people treated unfairly. We do not want people to be overly excluded from participating in a Democratic assembly or from becoming citizens.

6.2.1 The Atheists

Religions around the world share many common elements and differences. Many secularists or atheists may have a problem with the term religion, but we use the term here also to include the faiths and beliefs we have. For an atheist, those beliefs can be different from those of people who are pious and worship God. The same can be said of some religions as compared to others.

Before proceeding, it is necessary to clarify a common argument made by atheists about the ethics we expect in a democracy. Many believe that ethics can be achieved without the need for biblical scripture. They also believe that atheism is capable of establishing ethical behavior comparable to that of Christians or other religious people. For the most part, those people making such claims have been raised within a system that has established laws and ethics heavily based on religious scripture and philosophy. What many atheists seem to think is that the ethics they were taught were separate from the passage of religion within their polity. The preceding point is not the case. Christian nations have similar laws among themselves, as do Muslim nations, Buddhist nations, Hindu nations, and other nations in which the majority of the polity adheres to a particular religion. The laws reflect the people's faith, but they also reflect their ethics. In a truly atheist nation, as opposed to a secular nation, the laws tend to be emphasized as the pinnacle source of justice. Therefore, that creates an Authoritarian government. Liberty becomes less critical than conformity, and the methods of ruling tend towards the drastic or draconian under Authoritarian leadership.

So then, while atheists may believe their ethics are attainable without scripture, the reality is that if we follow human history far back enough, we realize that almost all instances of atheistic states led to severe conditions of rule over the populace. In contrast, almost all pious and faithful nations have modeled their laws and ethics on those derived from scripture. Also, faith can curb the powers of the Oligarchs and Monarchs.

6.2.2 The Pious

To begin with, the Septuagint gives us ample definitions of ethics based on the Ten Commandments. It forbids murder, theft, adultery, jealousy, and bearing false witness, to name a few. Most of these form the foundations of ethics found in the laws of any society worldwide. Jesus went a little further than the Old Testament. He summed up ethics with the phrase "Love thy neighbor." In other words, if we are to be good people, we must accept that we should always place love and show love before all else. That matter, as it relates to a government system, is that for the system to create the environment needed for love, the people must also be the driving force to show that love. With love, there should not be a single person starving or thirsty, nor a single person who is ill without care. These things are important for a polity to achieve if that polity is to be remembered as a good entity. Love is our first and foremost ethic. Without love, everything good that a polity achieves will be a mishap or by-product rather than derived from intent. Similarly, achieving the pinnacle of the good can only be achieved with intent if it is the target. It is a pinnacle good that is achieved through striving. Therefore, the pinnacle of good can only be achieved by chance or consequence without striving for it.

To be more specific regarding religious-derived ethics, we should also mention the following:

Be Merciful. "Be merciful just as your father is merciful." (New Testament, 2023, Luke 6:31). "Happy are those who are merciful to others; God will be merciful to them" (New Testament, 2023, Matthew 5:7). When the people form juries, they must be merciful and not draconian and heavy-handed with their judgments. They should make decisions without judgment.

Forgiveness. " Do not judge others, and God will not judge you; do not condemn others, and God will not condemn you; forgive others, and God will forgive you" (New Testament, 2023, Luke 6:37). When we form juries, we should avoid bringing people to judgment. If that is not possible, then it is better to be forgiving. Finally, if that is not possible, then judge without condemnation.

Seek Goodness. "A good person brings good out of the treasure of good things in his heart; a bad person brings bad out of his treasure of bad things. For the mouth speaks what the heart is full of" (New Testament, 2023, Luke 6:45). Goodness is related to the ethic of love. It forms a pinnacle good that we must aspire to.

Respect Others. "For everyone who makes himself great will be humbled, and everyone who humbles himself will be great" (New Testament, 2023, Luke 14:11). When we form juries, then remember to respect others because, ultimately, wealthy or poor, sane or not, humble or not, we are all united.

Be Kind. "Do for others just what you want them to do for you" (New Testament, 2023, Luke 6:31). When the juries form, let them do for others just what we would expect done to us had we been on trial.

Jesus showed love and tolerance toward people of other faiths, religions, cultures, and social levels. But he insisted through kindness, respect, mercy, goodness, and forgiveness that only one religion was true. That is important because some people attempt to create a universal faith, believing that we all worship the same God. However, it is not merely the belief in God but what we think and how we serve and worship God that makes a difference. I mention this, not in a polemic way, but to be truthful about the reason why so many religions and denominations exist. While many may wish we were all uniform in our perceptions of God, the reality is the opposite. Every group of people, whether they are religious or not, varies in what they think or believe is true. Therefore, bringing forward that love in the form of mercy, forgiveness, respect, kindness, and goodness is important. These ethics should be in the hearts of those who wish to establish a Democratic nation. If they instead hold zeal, contempt, hatred, wrath, and an assortment of lesser ethical attributes, their institution will be a bane to all those around them and even upon themselves. Most of us have a common understanding of what is Good and what we perceive as good. However, this is where ethics need to be clearly defined, because what one person deems good may not be the same as what others consider good.

The same can be said of the term common sense. If it were common, then everyone would share the same sense. We know this isn't true. As described earlier, many variables shape what we consider the truth, and the same applies to what we perceive as sensible. The term common sense may apply to most people, but not everyone. We know this to be true from the number of incidents, both in and out of work, that have resulted in injury and harm. Therefore, we can equally conclude that unless a clearly defined target exists, any work towards that target would otherwise be random.

In his ethical philosophy, Aristotle emphasizes that good, as much as the term' ethics' implies, is qualitative. Additionally, something that we may consider beneficial can actually cause harm. He emphasizes that while we consider courage to be a good quality, it has also led to the loss of many courageous lives. The ethics we present here are based on a democratic system. The ethics of interest are the principles a system would require to operate in its most ethical manner. I would recommend reading

Aristotle's works for a more detailed analysis of ethics. Keep in mind also that Jesus Christ established everything that needs to be said about the subject, so both the Bible and other sources provide a solid foundation for understanding ethics. Here, we will focus on a few important ethical principles of democracy.

6.2.3 The Ethics

Getting people to vote and participate is based on the energy they have to do so. If a democratic system forces everyone to work until they are exhausted, no one will have the energy for meetings. Likewise, if a democratic system encourages recreation and relaxation, the people may become too apathetic or lazy to participate. The most important ethics people have in a democracy encompass interest, social concern, and participation. Therefore, the ethics needed by the people would be the opposite of laziness, such as liveliness. However, liveliness without regard for the system differs from liveliness and diligence. Such ethics can also harm us, taking both passive and active forms. Also, Diligence ensures that democracy does not rapidly devolve into control by only those who attend meetings. If a system experiences the same minority attending assembly meetings, it would promote oligarchic rather than democratic interests. So, participation by being lively and diligent in the happenings of an assembly is probably the most important of all the ethics a polity can have. A population that establishes a Democracy and then stops participating in a Democracy has demonstrated a weakness that others will exploit. The power of a democracy depends entirely on those who attend and their numbers and proportions. From the very outset, a Democratic people are required to participate fully in Democracy.

When people in a democratic polity are gathered by their interests, liveliness, and diligence, they will also need to be able to make decisions and pass laws. Because the ability to make, judge, and enforce laws covers a wide range of ethical interests, the ethics needed will be more than one. In this situation, people need to be fair. Fairness entails the ability to love. If a person loves, he can also have compassion and understanding for another person or their circumstances. It is this that dictates the ability to be fair when making laws. Fairness, in the sense of Justice, is to provide the object of interest with the thing it most deserves. Aristotle's idea of justice can be represented by a rhetorical question: "To whom do we give the best-crafted flute?"

Many people think it is fair to give it to those without a flute or to children to learn the flute, or many other variations. Although most answers derive from love, compassion, and understanding, Aristotle argues that the best flute should be given to the best flute player. Because in the hands of those who can use it, it will be justice to the player and the object of interest, namely, the flute. In many cases, viewing things this way can be effective, but in others, it isn't. Where Aristotle's method works best is in distribution. But changing the object to currency becomes a little more complicated. If there is a surplus of wealth in the government treasury, the people wish for it to be distributed. Many would argue that it should be given to the poor, as they would likely use it for their own needs. However, giving it to a merchant has numerous benefits for both the merchant and those they serve. In both cases, the object of currency is put to use equally by either the merchant or the impoverished. Depending on the situation, the merchant may even put it to better use by hiring a worker, treating the money as income for others, and simultaneously producing his products. But if it is given to the wealthy who do not need currency and merely store it rather than spend it, then it is neither fair nor just. Fairness, in the sense of material distribution, requires careful attention by a polity. In a democratic polity, financial distribution is usually best handled by the democracy's administrators. So, if a project were agreed upon, the people would provide financial support. Ensuring all citizens are treated fairly is a priority for democratic people. A well-balanced system would offer a particular standard of living:

nothing was given for free, but everything essential to that standard was accessible. There should not be, as in many other systems, an expectation to earn a certain amount of money, but rather an expectation of how much an individual can generate within a society. Rather than relying on how much people earn from employers, there should be a gauge of how much an unemployed person can earn from their own endeavors.

In some cases, philosophers of the past have argued that justice is what best serves the majority. This application of justice, although seemingly in favor of the majority interest, is similar in nature to declaring courage as an ethic. Both can lead to horrendous outcomes. This line of thinking was prevalent when Capitalism and Communism were introduced. It is somewhat part of a line of thought known as Utilitarianism and the Common Good. To put this matter into perspective, if a democratic polity were given the choice of mistreating a minority, then what would justify such an action? Would it be easy for someone to assume that such an action would benefit the majority? We saw this during the colonization period, when the native peoples of the Americas, Australia, Canada, and South Africa were treated in this manner. We saw the outcomes of such thought when Nazi Germany declared the Jewish people as the reasons behind economic and other national failures. We saw this form of thought manifest in the slaughter of countless Greeks, Armenians, and Christians during the period of ethnic cleansing in Asia. It is clear that while such an idea may have a benign sense of doing the best for the majority, it often manifests as "the greater good at the cost of others". It is more often neither greater nor good, but a horrific treatment of any given minority. Therefore, it is essential to note that the term justice, which is used in many languages, often strays far from its roots. That root is the word dikaiosi. Dikaeosi means that the individual's worth is recognized. Perhaps the closest equivalent is the term "rights". So, an ethic of being just and righteous must be reflected in a population that sharės a common ethic of dikaeosi. People all have value. Every occupation, every race, and every human has equal value. Within a democratic system, Axia's worth or value may be limited to the functionality of the democratic polity. This may lead to a person not being a citizen, finding themselves in a minority without any Axia (worth or value). This highlights how any number of approaches to ethics always lead to some area of discussion. There is no perfect system, but the least dangerous to apply first is the one based on the human rights people have beyond the system. Most of Jesus's ethics apply to this area. Love and don't harm others were the foundations of almost everything he taught. When that method fails for any reason, a discussion of democratic rights should follow. These methods derive from the Aristotelian approach to ethics. So, we should treat each citizen as we would want to be treated. Fairness and justice, or dikaeosi, must be applied in the process of judgment. Also, and only in rare cases, should there be a need to evaluate the degree of worth an individual or group has to the majority. Sacrificing or committing a crime or unethical action and justifying it as serving the majority should never be allowed. However, when people are starving and one individual or group has enough food to feed them, that individual or group has an ethical obligation to offer help in such desperate circumstances. Finally, the costs and benefits of a particular ethical situation could be used. This final method is the least important to us. How can the death of a person be summed up in a numismatic figure and presented as a cost? By this reasoning, as long as the deaths in a factory cost less than the profits, the business is doing well. How can we compare two things where the profits are almost always expressed in dollars? Yet when we lose a human life for the sake of commerce, how can a cost be placed on that person's life? I am sure many families who lose a family member would rather burn the world's money than place a figure or value on their loved ones. Cost-benefit analysis can also have a sinister motive when applied to humanity and ethics. However, it has some value in determining minor issues, such as whether certain public works or projects should be considered. If, in any instance, costs are placed on living things, then these should not be in terms of currency. For example, the habitat of certain animals may be disrupted, while others may relocate. In other instances, they may not. The value of that animal becomes an ethical question. A world without bees, for instance, would be a world without food. They do the majority of cross-pollination. Perhaps the animal is on the brink of extinction; in such cases, these issues become ethical questions, and to some degree, the cost-benefit approach offers the least value, alongside the utilitarian approach. Animals have worth and rights. These issues are within the sphere that Jesus and scripture taught. Specifically, we are guardians of a garden, not its destroyers.

Therefore, judgment should be viewed as a technique that requires a broad set of skills. The process of judgment and the judging itself must respect the value of the citizen, his dikaiosi. The judgment must be respected without bias or prejudice for each party or individual on trial. The methods of determining justice must also be given a hierarchy when justice is sought for the object or individual. There is a difference between judging a person to seek to punish the bad and judging them to do everything possible to ensure their rights and dikaiosi. But if true judgment is to be made, the expression of rights and dikaiosi count the most. For instance, if an individual had committed a crime and was found guilty of it, the purpose of the judgment was not to punish them but to ensure the individual's rights were complemented and augmented by the process. The law states that the punishment for such a crime is not the judgment itself. The judgment is to determine the truth of a particular matter fairly, with respect and honor. It is based on the truth that the individual's rights are being respected. Because if a case against them is built upon lies, then that individual is not being treated with respect. Respecting the subject or person is the purpose of judgment. It acts to seek the truth for both those who consider themselves victims and those who consider themselves perpetrators. Sometimes, even the good and wise will break unfair laws. The issue of judgment is why we raised the idea that the ethics of love and loving even strangers are essential. Otherwise, judgments would be made no differently than that of a mob seeking to lynch a man without a trial or jury.

Our ability to judge as individuals is not perfect. There will not be a single citizen without their own sins to judge. If that sinner is a judge, then the chance of injustice is far greater. Judging contradicts the very essence of Christian law. However, under Christian law, we can give our opinion, and a jury can decide the judgment. As in the ancient Athenian model, no single person should judge anyone or any case. An extensive jury would be needed to ensure that all opinions, concerns, and possible ideas are expressed and that the majority cast a decisive vote. However, the majority opinion can only be justified if people honor the ethics we have described regarding judgment.

The next ethical concern is the handling of corruption. With love and tolerance, how can people cope with instances in which society's ethics are compromised? If their laws reflect, to some degree, righteousness and justice – or dikaiosi –then how do they deal with corruption? One way is blatant censorship, which leaves little trust in the skeptical. We have seen in several nations that bans and censorship achieve the opposite. The other is regulation. By imposing a degree of regulation, a polity can benefit from tolerating certain corrupt behaviors while simultaneously curbing them when they affect the innocent. Corruption is any act that violates the ethical values a democratic society considers valuable. If, in democratic meetings, citizens place great value on honesty, truth, and the credibility of information, then corruption is dishonesty, lies, and unreliable information. Corruption can include the taking of bribes, the exchange of wealth and money for services that undermine productivity and the course of a democratic meeting, the formation of laws, and the course of judgment or enforcement. So then, it is up to the people to protect their system against corruption at all levels. To do this requires an intelligent and wise person. This brings us to the ethic of honesty. Honesty is a difficult ethic to maintain. People generally find it far easier to tell lies and engage in deceit than to tell the truth. Truth and honesty seem almost impossible for humanity to grasp. Why? Look at our history of those who spoke the truth. Humanity can be evil, nasty, and far from any of the ethics I mention. Humanity crucified the Son of God for speaking the truth to cover over the flaws of those who conspired against him. Humanity poisoned Socrates for speaking the truth, under the charge of corruption, to cover their own flaws as authoritarian Oligarchs whom he contradicted. Humanity has slaughtered millions of martyrs of faith, and many have died trying to write and tell others the truth. The war of the meek, honest, and truthful people has always been lost to those in power. In a democracy, we must wonder, will there be anything to stop such an action against an accused individual or group? However, the answer to such a question lies in another question: Why do people lie? There are many reasons, but one that seems particularly prevalent is to cover up a flaw or to protect a secret. People lie about their own abilities and those of others; they lie to gain attention and to put others down for their own benefit. Lies, false testimonies, and all matters of unjust punishment are all related to this flaw of dishonesty in humanity.

In contrast, honesty has often led to the punishment of the honest, as already illustrated by well-known examples. Therefore, people often tend to be dishonest before being honest, as self-satisfaction is at the core of dishonesty. Whenever it is in their best interest to be honest, people will be honest. Whenever it is to their benefit to be dishonest, they are dishonest. That is how simple-minded the majority of humanity is. It is much like children being unable to admit their wrongdoing.

Tolerance for those who fail a particular expectation, duty, or law is often very low. Ironically, people often dislike dishonesty in positions of power or oligarchical structures, yet they are equally guilty of it themselves. The way humans act creates the motivation to be dishonest. If humanity were to tolerate dishonesty but simultaneously grant tenfold benefits to the honest, the world would be entirely different. To understand this peculiar aspect of human character, I wish to draw on a situation in prison. A prisoner who is always doing the wrong thing wishes to continue doing so, but he thinks that a witness to his misbehavior will lead to his punishment. Therefore, the misbehaving prisoner falsely reports that the other prisoner is to blame for his own misbehavior. The person who reports the incident is given a particular favor over the person who tries to prove their innocence. If the witness cannot prove they are innocent or that the other is guilty, then they are the ones punished. This prisoner ethic is found in many societies, organizations, and institutions.

There is no perfect human being, but if we strive to establish an ethical way of life, this will lay the foundation for a better polity in the future. We must consider that, since we are not perfect and many people lie to cover their imperfections, we should also acknowledge that the systems we develop should show mercy and understanding for this flaw in humanity. Honesty is necessary so that innocent people are not wrongly accused. Honesty is needed so that the laws, judgment, and the system do not fail. Honesty is needed to ensure that honesty is not always punished, even in cases of failure to meet duty or expectations. As we said before, humanity is as imperfect as any system that is created. So this is why we should work with our flaws rather than always punishing them. Instead, our flaws should be identified and regulated. If a person has the duty to watch over the treasury but often falls asleep while doing so, is it better for that person to lie about his or her ability to stay awake or to tell the truth? Even though the duty is of great importance, it is surely better for the guard's authority to know and replace him with another guard or change the times he guards. But if the consequence of telling the truth amounts to a loss of income, job, punishment, imprisonment or worse, then how can the sleepy guard be honest?

Tolerance has now become a crucial aspect to identify. Since the ethic of tolerance is a notch down from love. It implies that while certain behavior may not be appropriate, we would rather tolerate it than punish it. High tolerance should be given to honest people, and lower tolerance should be given to those who willfully abuse and conspire against the ethics and framework of the democratic polity. With this approach, a polity can continue to operate despite its flaws, provided that regulations, preventive measures, and several checks and balances are in place. Tolerance should also be given to those who wish to question the system and the people. Speaking and discussing should be highly tolerated and given exceptional freedom within a democratic polity. Even if the speaker wishes to discuss the benefits of monarchical rule over a democratic people, they should not be punished. However, in the place of public meetings, law-making, judgment, and enforcement, little tolerance should be afforded to those who damage the system's processes.

While I have mentioned a few key ethical principles in a democratic system, many more could be considered. People approach such ethics in different ways, and while mine stems from a religious conviction, others may argue that ethics is a secular topic. The problem with this separation is that if we presume we can logically analyze a purely qualitative issue without a benchmark, we have failed the very concept of philosophy. I would rather shift the scale in temperament so that the scale of measurement is religious and spiritual in part and secular and logical in part. The Septuagint and the New Testament comprise the bulk of the ethical principles with which most people would agree. Many of the ethical principles have been tested over millennia and, as such, have proven true. I feel no need to list or derive these ethics into a secular list. Where they rest, within scripture, is entirely acceptable to me. Yet, thinking that scripture is the only form of ethics is also a lie. The scriptures merely provide a framework for us to build on. The free thought and choice we have as human beings, be it seen as a divine gift or not, places an onus on all of us to try and work out the good thing to do. Some worry that granting credit or merit to scripture may lead to a clerical rule forming within a Democracy.

Provided that no oligarchy exists in any form, clerical or otherwise, then a Democracy can function properly. It may even be a case where the churches return to their roots in democracy. I will elaborate on this last point more thoroughly, as it deserves special mention.

Jesus and the Apostles were raised within a region of the world that had just finished a phase of Hellenisation. Greek literature and the Greek language were considered Koine, or the common language. This Koine form of Greek, a layman's version, became the language of the New and Old Testaments. What I am trying to establish is that Greek culture had spread throughout the region of Judea and Israel. Oligarchs and monarchs primarily influenced Greek culture. Towards the end of his reign, Alexander the Great thought he should be respected like a living God through proskynesis or bowing on one's knees. But during this period, the literature people craved to read was entirely centered on a Democratic world. The armies of kings and generals did not transmit a passion for what they were, but for the literature of the Golden Age of Athens. Knowledge of the Democratic system flourished, inspiring many people in the early days leading up to Christ's arrival.

Many people argue that the structure of the modern church has always been the same. Others argue that the church has undergone gradual changes while retaining its core principles. I refute those ideas entirely. I am somewhat disheartened by all of the primary European denominations of Christianity: Protestants, Catholics, and Orthodox. Here is why:

When Judas betrayed Christ and died soon after, the Apostles numbered eleven and sought another to make up the number of twelve.

"21. *Wherefore of these men which have companied with us all the time that the Lord Jesus went in and out among us,*

22. *Beginning from the baptism of John, unto that same day that he was taken up from us, must one be ordained to be a witness with us of his resurrection.*

23. *And they appointed two, Joseph called Barsabas, who was surnamed Justus, and Matthias.*

24. *And they prayed, and said, Thou, Lord, which knowest the hearts of all men, shew whether of these two thou hast chosen,*

25. *That he may take part of this ministry and apostleship, from which Judas by transgression fell, that he might go to his own place.*

26. *And they gave forth their lots, and the lot fell upon Matthias, and he was numbered with the eleven apostles."*

(New Testament, 2023, Acts 1:21-1:26).

From the immediately preceding biblical quote, we see that the two candidates for the bishopric, as Apostles (citizenship), were Joseph and Barsabas. Modern Bishops are supposed to be representatives of the Apostles or their replacements. They are at the pinnacle of the church and offer guidance. The Pope of Rome is also the Bishop of Rome. The Patriarch of Constantinople is the Bishop of Constantinople, and each country has a leading figure, much like when the Apostles moved out into different countries. Each was working independently of the other Apostles in their respective regions. There were visits, traveling together, and sometimes they prayed together, but they mostly worked alone, evangelizing in their respective areas. Going back to the biblical texts, Joseph and Barsabas were given the eponymous, or surnames, Justus and Matthias. After they prayed consistently and drew lots, Matthias drew a lot—a winning token—and joined the rest of the Apostles. Does the church still choose its Bishops in this manner?

Some will argue that this was during the Roman period, when the Romans, who followed Hellenism, spread the faith while preserving many of its traditions. I argue that Greek traditions claim to have been the origin of the Roman polity before Latin speakers and Germanic tribes overran it. So, it is expected that, at a time when the Greeks ruled, the methods people used to decide would be Greek and democratic. But it is not so:

> *"1. Now these are the divisions of the sons of Aaron. The sons of Aaron; Nadab, and Abihu, Eleazar, and Ithamar.*

2. *But Nadab and Abihu died before their father, and had no children: therefore Elezar and Ithamar executed the priest's office.*

3. *And David distributed them, both Zadok of the sons of Eleazar, and Ahimelech of the sons of Ithamar, according to their offices in their service.*

4. *And there were more chief men found of the sons of Eleazar than of the sons of Ithamar; and thus were they divided. Among the sons of Eleazar, there were sixteen chief men of the house of their fathers, and eight among the sons of Ithamar according to the house of their fathers.*

5. *Thus were they divided by lot, one sort with another; for the governors of the sanctuary, and governors of the house of God, were of the sons of Eleazar, and of the sons of Ithamar"*

(Septuagint, 2023, Chronicles 1:24).

In the Old Testament, which preceded the Greeks and their reign, King David used lots to determine the jobs of all his brethren and immediate family. This story is important because, as already discussed, the Athenian Democracy's constitution selected people for various positions or jobs by drawing lots.

If we examine other stories in the Bible, we find numerous examples that support the idea that Democracy was evolving from the very onset of biblical times. The claim that the Septuagint was written around 300 BC and the Athenian democracy existed

500-400BC is not a mere coincidence of dates. During the collapse of the Hellenistic world and the decay of Democracy in Athens, the writings of those associated with Democracy became very few. Surviving texts suggest that many more writings on the subject existed, but those that followed democratic principles must have been persecuted. Socrates comes to mind as the most significant and detailed example of how he was blamed for corrupting the youth and sentenced to death. This is said to have happened around 399 BC. Plato and Aristotle wrote their works in ways that avoided detection and trial, resulting in the emergence of cryptic forms of philosophy.

After their exile to Persia, the Israelites and the Hebrews returned as the Elites who would build the temples and fashion the faith of the majority. However, most Hebrews were not Jewish in their faith. At the time of Samuel, they worshipped similar Gods and practiced religions similar to those around them, believing in many different deities. A significant proportion of the Old Testament is dedicated to the story of Samuel. The Old Testament bible is also known as the Septuagint. Samuel was a highly qualified Judge and was considered amongst the elite of his time. He was a Levite.

In contrast, the Monarchy of the Israelites was given as a token because the people wanted a King on earth instead of a Kingdom in Heaven. The story of David demonstrates that God was angered when the people of Israel, who were given a choice between a Kingdom on Earth and one in Heaven, chose a kingdom on Earth. Yet he asked for the final decision to install a King to be made according to the people's voice. The first book of Samuel offers valuable insight into the topics we have discussed regarding Democracy, Monarchies, and Oligarchies. It also marks God's democratic nature, as he commands that the will of the people be done.

> *" … 1. When Samuel became old, he made his sons judges over Israel.*
>
> *2. The name of his firstborn son was Joel, and the name of his second, Abijah; they were judges in Beer-sheba.*
>
> *3. Yet his sons did not follow in his ways, but turned aside after gain; they took bribes and perverted justice.*
>
> *4. Then all the elders of Israel gathered together and came to Samuel at Ramah,*
>
> *5. and said to him, "You are old and your sons do not follow in your ways; appoint for us, then, a king to govern us, like other nations."*
>
> *6. But the thing displeased Samuel when they said, "Give us a king to govern us." Samuel prayed to the LORD,*
>
> *7. and the LORD said to Samuel, "Listen to the voice of the people in all that they say to you; for they have not rejected you, but they have rejected me from being king over them …"*

(Septuagint, 2023, 1 Samuel 8:1-7).

This highlights that a system that relies on the good and honor of men is fragile. While Samuel was a good leader without any systematic powers to rule over people, but rather to give opinion and guidance, he was a form of Monarch. Samuel could be considered a Monarch and Aristocrat with considerable sway and influence.

In continuation with the above quote:

> *"… 8. Just as they have done to me, from the day I brought them up out of Egypt to this day, forsaking me and serving other gods, so also they are doing to you.*

9. Now then, listen to their voice; only-- you shall solemnly warn them, and show them the ways of the king who shall reign over them."

10. So Samuel reported all the words of the LORD to the people who were asking him for a king.

11. He said, "These will be the ways of the king who will reign over you: he will take your sons and appoint them to his chariots and to be his horsemen, and to run before his chariots;

12. and he will appoint for himself commanders of thousands and commanders of fifties, and some to plow his ground and to reap his harvest, and to make his implements of war and the equipment of his chariots.

13. He will take your daughters to be perfumers and cooks and bakers.

14. He will take the best of your fields and vineyards and olive orchards and give them to his courtiers.

15. He will take one-tenth of your grain and of your vineyards and give it to his officers and his courtiers.

16. He will take your male and female slaves, and the best of your cattle and donkeys, and put them to his work.

17. He will take one-tenth of your flocks, and you shall be his slaves.

18. And in that day you will cry out because of your king, whom you have chosen for yourselves; but the LORD will not answer you in that day."

19. But the people refused to listen to the voice of Samuel; they said, "No! but we are determined to have a king over us,

> 20. *so that we also may be like other nations, and that our king may govern us and go out before us and fight our battles."*
>
> 21. *When Samuel had heard all the words of the people, he repeated them in the ears of the LORD.*
>
> 22. *The LORD said to Samuel, "Listen to their voice and set a king over them." Samuel then said to the people of Israel, "Each of you return home" ..."*

(Septuagint, 2023, 1 Samuel 8:8-22).

Regardless of your religion, the historical value of the biblical text reveals that the concept of Democracy was not a sudden invention, but a development that occurred from the early Bible through to the first actual democratic government in Athens. Since then, the pyramidal forms of government prevailed over the very same people that the Bible was intent on giving absolute power to. Even the church that sprouted after Christ deviated from a libertarian, passive, and headless Democratic gathering to one of a more restrictive, autocratic, and pyramidal structure. The latter was the influence of the Germanic invasion of Southern Europe and its impact on politics and religion. In the Bible, the entity we call God replaces an earthly king and, as such, liberates people and gives them clarity that they do not need a King on earth. Yet Samuel's life also shows how a person of the faith can become so influential that it makes no difference whether they are kings or not, because they wield similar influence and power. It shows that when a person is in a position to appoint Kings, it is a dangerous scenario, since that same person has far too much power than a true Democracy would allow. However, for the time when the Bible was written, the system they developed was not altogether flawed, but rather flimsy and weak. The ideas that had existed since these early years of human socialization or civilization did not reach their pinnacle until the rise of the Athenian Democratic model. These biblical examples illustrate humanity's ongoing quest to establish governance systems that meet its needs. It may seem unusual for modern literature or philosophy to contain quotes from religious texts, but if you do not believe in the spiritual value of the texts, please consider them as a narrative to demonstrate examples of how we think and what we consider ethical.

Regarding the ethics required within a democracy, it is essential to acknowledge that humanity is flawed. Jesus highlighted this when he called for the first man without sin to cast the first stone. In other words, no one is without flaws, faults, behavioral errors, or reproaches. Knowing this, a democratic people should not be interested in punishing those flaws but in inspiring each other to be what we all should be. Self-improvement comes in many forms, but I am not discussing assertive or aggressive individualism. Self-improvement in how well we live with others is the highest concern. Unlike those commercial self-improvement programs, I am referring to becoming functional social beings who genuinely desire the company of others. Self-improvement can initially be related to the purpose of goodness we attain from the scriptures. Not the violence, trickery, wrath, or other parts of such religious texts, but the aspects that show us how to live in peace and love of one another in the same city. This ethical framework makes it easier for a Democracy to exist. Consider that the Greek word for a villager is a pun for the same word used to describe a separatist. Horikos (villager), the prefix Hor – or Χωρ, means to separate or be apart. As such, villagers are seen as isolationists or separatists from the main population because they live apart from the rest of the population. These people cannot, intrinsically, commune, trust, or live with others. They prefer solitude or small groups to large groups. Some argue that as we age, we increasingly prefer isolation to socialization because we also become more vulnerable. There are certain risks we take when we walk in crowds and engage in public matters. The Bible is one of many religious texts that serve multiple purposes, not just spiritual or mystical ones. A substantial number of the populace have ethical values that can help develop a Democratic society by fostering trust among people and enabling them to live together in harmony.

From the philosophical appraisal of ethics, we obtain a filter to exclude religious and spiritual content, focusing on the value of a secular, analytical evaluation of each ethic. Wise, intelligent, honest, and good people can achieve democracy. But unintelligent, dishonest, suspicious, and evil people are unlikely ever to achieve a true Democracy. Yet, from what I know of the world's religions and of the philosophies at hand, I think that wise, intelligent, good, and spiritual people could achieve an even better democracy. Spirituality, in the sense of passivity, can elevate a person's work ethic. Some children, for instance, do chores at home for money, and some are told that God sees their good and will give them a bigger and better reward when it is time. We can view the world in many different ways, and some of the things we do as parents to train our children have lasting effects that extend beyond their initial purpose. The parent may, for instance, be training their child to enter a capitalist or communist world, but the ethical impact on the child can also be affected. So then, when we try to establish a philosophical truth, we must take into consideration as many views as possible. For instance, I remarked earlier that a spiritual person could benefit a democracy. But I was then compelled by the interest of the truth to clarify because if I did not, then spirituality can mean many different things, and many of them would be detrimental to a Democratic society. For instance, some people have a spiritual connection with demons, others follow Satan, while others have brutal Pagan rituals. Which of all these spiritual people do we require in a Democracy? Some argue that no spirituality or religion is inherently better, but doing so undermines the way people comfort themselves. Religion has been a part of humanity for as long as humanity has existed; therefore, it can never truly be omitted from society. Even in Atheist places, people attach the types of behavior of religious people to other things. Some Atheist societies still recognize ghosts and spirits and other metaphysical things, but are not specifically followers of any religion. So, while I used a general term like Spirituality, my definition was far narrower than most would use it. So, for philosophical truth, we should restate that people who have essential spiritual qualities to a Democracy would benefit that system more so than people without such spiritual qualities. If wisdom and intelligence are not applied daily, democracy can slowly become a Pleistocracy and, from there, an Ochlocracy. We know that intelligent and wise people are at the core of operating a Democracy. But what if we completely omit wisdom and intelligence from the equation and put ethics alone in place? In that sense, if everyone had the same ethical qualities, they would, in turn, produce the most ethical system, irrespective of its type. But to what extent would such people be able to identify corruption or those masquerading? Like the phrase wolves in sheep's clothing. How would a flock of sheep be able to identify such wolves if they are innocent, good, loving, trusting, and so forth? As you can see, they would most likely not be as good at identifying a criminal as a criminal is. So then, even a criminal can have value in a Democracy, but only when he works in the interests of that Democracy alone. Can that be the case? It is unlikely, but some criminals have done that. One that came to mind was a bank robber who would burn the bank records that contained people's debts to the Bank. It was a time when the Demos opposed the progress of the banking system. People, by and large, were against the pyramidal structures that had dominated the world since the fall of the Athenian Democracy. The Banks, in particular, were seen as an elite encroachment on the Demos. Their service was valuable since they created that value, but the trade-off was that people lost their financial freedom. The elite no longer needed tax collectors. The people's money was already in their coffers through the Banks they owned. However, to maintain the illusion of financial freedom and the impression that people had their own money, they taxed what they already controlled and had in their bank accounts. The tax process evolved from a person collecting money to deposit into the government treasury to a system in which people deposited their money into the government treasury through a bank and then paid a tax on the money they considered their own. Of course, they could access the money whenever they wanted, take it, spend it, and do anything they wanted with it. But, by the majority, there was a need to save that money because no one could afford anything of significant value – like land and homes, ships, or business properties – without a period of saving and filling the elite's treasuries through the banks they owned. Dissecting reality is a laborious task, but as philosophers, we need the ability to see through the veils of deception without appearing excessively suspicious or mentally unstable. You see, a person who talks about things other people disagree with is often called mad. Another popular way to discredit some truths is to use the word 'conspiracy'. Conspiracy groups do exist, and they are found in all parts of society. They create lies and have a large group of followers who believe them, allowing them to exert various forms of political influence. Yet sometimes, as in the case of real philosophers, the things we say are trodden over and called lies. Sometimes they say what we write is a conspiracy to discredit what is written in our philosophies. One politician wrote a book about cooking, for example, and the media claimed that her book was about indigenous cannibalism in an effort to slander the politician's name. Jesus called his own to eat and drink, bread his flesh and wine his blood, and many considered it, at the time of writing, as a derogatory thing to prevent anyone from believing him. Even during his time, some discredited what he had to say by slandering and accusing him (New Testament, 2023, John 10:19-20). I have taken a risk in highlighting what I perceive to be the truth, and an even greater one by mentioning things that many would otherwise argue against. So, in such a world, Democracy is a fragile thing that requires a lot of attention, and its worth and quality entirely depend on the quality of the people. This is true of any human-operated system.

The Ethical foundation of a democracy is often difficult to articulate. We know that some ethics, as described previously, ensure that Democracy operates effectively. Yet, we have not thoroughly discussed the foundational ethics on which a Democracy should be founded. That is to say, which of those many ethics should form a society's core beliefs? The very nature of ethics is that they shift in importance from one generation to the next. They even have situational value; for instance, who has time for wisdom at a time of war? Yet war is entirely dependent on wisdom. It is, therefore, important for all of us to establish a particular form of ethics that will not change over the years or fluctuate in value but remain seemingly consistent and true to the benefit of a Democracy.

Democracy should be founded on love. Some say we are all brothers and sisters, so we strive for this in our lives. Love is not a mysterious word. Love is simply giving and receiving without considering how much was given or received unnoticed. Love is an accumulation of good things that can be enacted upon others so that they will benefit from such action. Love is to sacrifice and not think twice about such a sacrifice to help others. I do not mean life or blood sacrifices, but choices that cost us yet befit others. Love forms an essential part of a Democratic institution. Suppose the foundation has Love at its core. In that case, it becomes apparent that all the laws, judgments, punishments, and actions of individuals and the state in which they operate will perpetually personify that love. Some will argue against it as many people are authoritarian and want authority and domination over them. The vast majority want their freedom, yet many are content to live with the illusion of it, often as a compromise to maintain a particular lifestyle. When people are accustomed to a specific way of life, they become too institutionalized to consider or adopt alternative lifestyles. There is nothing truly stopping anyone from living a free life, but those people are so few that we often label them as eccentrics, hermits, monks, cave dwellers, and, in some cases, insane. These people live a free life, but they are often mocked because they are exceptions to the majority. This is why often such people try to convince others to join them; they are not essentially isolationists or horikoi (villagers or separatists); they want their freedom above all else.

But in most cases, these people wished others would have the courage to join them. Of course, this does not describe everyone who has left society. Some went to the extent of establishing families and tribes, only to have them rounded up by those with an army. That is to say that some people have left society to create new societies, and in the process, they have been defamed. Yet, when they were seen as a threat, they were considered enemies to the interests of those who rule. The point is that love may benefit a system, but it will also require those prepared to defend it and fight for it. A minority dwelling on the outskirts of a larger society has little chance of survival, which explains why such groups emerge and often disappear quickly.

If we accept love as a defining foundation upon which a Democracy is built, it will have many exceptions. For instance, what is the meaning of passiveness and aggression? Is love an act of showing passiveness without anger and aggression? A passive ideology founded on love makes it easy for those to manipulate and use others. At some stage, the people may well be good amongst themselves, like a large family that argues and feuds, but at the same time defends each other against those not part of their system. Being passive when needed and aggressive when needed are situational qualities. Therefore, a society must decide when to be passive and when to be aggressive. It is worth noting that Jesus and all his Apostles, aside from one, were murdered under the guise of law, and all of them were pacifists. Alexander the Great was an aggressor who conquered by force, but his legacy ultimately failed because his generals continued to fight for generations after his death. The medieval wars ultimately contributed very little to the advancement of civilization. It is interesting to compare the generalized outcome of historical figures and events. If anything, the story of Alexander and Jesus offers examples of opposing ideas that seek to unite people in different ways. Both failed to achieve their agenda, but they remain historically crucial due to the ongoing impact they have had on humanity. If civilization is built upon the principle of war, such as military generals, then the system is bound to fail, as did Alexander's empire with his generals. So, too, if we try to maintain a passive-loving system like Christ proposed, we would be beaten by aggressors willing to harm and brutally take what they want.

Good people are often said to come last because they lack the intent to harm others and, in fact, seek to do good for all. An external influence may exploit good people in a city or state. We know from history that many raiders and plunderers existed. Additionally, a system founded on love is challenging to establish and maintain with credibility due to the numerous exceptions that will inevitably arise. For instance, we say murder is wrong, and killing is bad, yet how many wars will be fought, and how many will die? I have difficulty rejecting love as a principal foundation of any society based on the history of humanity. Given a chance, society and those around them can establish and embellish the principle of love. It may seem hypocritical or an antithesis of the system to claim it is founded on love, but with enough people striving towards such an ideal, it can have a substantial impact. Far better, we know that absolute love will fail us, and yet we strive for it, than the opposite.

Equality has become a serious issue for many nations in the last few decades. As commercial globalization seeks to create a common global trade market, it also drives a dynamic shift in wealth in favor of those pushing for such a market. To understand terms like globalization, we need to reflect on where such an ideology derives from. The term "globalization" is no different from "world domination" as used in a military context. In the same way, many nations and empires have tried to rule the entire world; similarly, many businesspeople believe they can achieve this through business. Attempts to create a fictitious global market led to many wars. While we have seen some overlap and some markets have engaged in a common market, it is far from truly global. For instance, a very small amount of trade occurs between all nations, but it is far from being a free global market. The push for so-called globalized and unified markets works against the philosophies and ideologies that founded Democracy. In many ways, globalization is a barbaric concept, similar to the early Roman idea of achieving domination and peace through bloodshed. Democracy is about independent, individual cities, whether in a league or not, working together. In other words, the Democratic system is about the preservation of identity and individuality, while people who prefer Globalization and uniformity, or empires, are antagonists of the Democratic state. Where one sees equality as being equally subservient, democracy deems people to be equally free. It is important to realize that for a Democracy to exist, it requires consistent liberty expressed throughout its institutions. A democratic people cannot become imperial overlords, meaning they control other cities or leagues. Doing so demolishes the concept of Democracy. We can not have a perfect Democratic city and state being the oppressor of some other foreign city and state. Such actions are limited to the notion or ideology of empires and the domination of others. Democracy is about enjoying the freedoms and the fruits of such freedoms for all people.

Equality of the individual within a system has particular limits. In a democratic system, equality is limited to the polity or citizens qualified to be citizens and participate in politics. Individual freedoms are limited by two main factors: compulsory duties and restrictions on who can participate and become a citizen. To clarify, I do not mean people need to be qualified by examination of knowledge or other such matters, but by a sincere interest in the city or state and its well-being. This is why the Athenians made it mandatory for citizens to perform voluntary duties for two years, then pass a character questionnaire, and ensure they were born to city citizens. In other words, letting anyone become a citizen is not a good idea. Many dispute this because it can lead to exclusions and often create an Oligarchy. However, let us examine the matter closely; we can begin to say that all humans are equal and deserve equal rights to participate in a democratic institution, just like any other citizen. Indeed, this is an attribute a Democracy should abide by. How else can a democracy survive if it does not mandate that the majority are always the people and that the citizenry is not a small, exclusive club? However, a balance must also be struck to prevent foreigners, strangers, and others from exploiting such an open system to infiltrate and subvert it. To ensure the system remains fair, citizens should be treated equally; however, the term "citizens" should be carefully defined to ensure the city's best interests are in their hands. Otherwise, we would see what happens in small organizations where one party brings in friends who have little to no connection to the organization and encourages them to canvass and vote in favor of the party leaders.

Similarly, people travel from city to city to influence votes. Initially, we can see that for citizens to have political power, they need to be local or have an interest in their city. That "interest" in many modern cities is land ownership, which, in my view, is not valid because this only allows men of wealth to vote in any city they wish. Qualification for citizenship or the ability to attend and participate in politics should be limited to those who reside in and are a part of the city and its surrounding state. Other measures, as the Athenians proposed, are not trivial, and although they may seem unequal, they are intrinsic and fair measures of self-preservation.

The composition of cultural roles also restricts the equality of citizens in a Democracy. In Athens, males and females were segregated in their roles, which were clearly defined. In modern society, males and females are given ambiguous roles. At the extremes are two conflicting ideas: one aligns with the view that women should do what men do, and the other holds that women and men have different roles. To me, the logical situation is that women and men are both capable of similar activities. In most situations, a female can do what a male can if she is trained to do so. But, regarding political issues, I would not want my daughters or females close to me to conflict in arguments with males. Even with laws to protect them, we know that many males react with violence against people, male or female, during heated debates.

While political life may appear, at first, to be a soft and accessible endeavor that most people can engage in, the actual task can be very vocal and aggressive during an Assembly. This is one reason women were initially excluded from the Athenian Assembly, despite being full citizens. In terms of gender, it should not essentially matter on an ethical basis whether women were allowed or not. However, I will discuss this further and in more detail later due to its sensitivity and complexity.

There should not be any discrimination concerning equality and the color of skin, height, or any other form of morphology that distinguishes people. I live in a place kept together by Imperial rule, and within a single city live many ethnicities. Seeing that some form of unity can arise, it may be better to persevere with such a mixed city than to create a homogenous society. Each city, each ethnicity, and each combination of people will be different, and as such, no rule will suit all humanity.

Equality is a diverse term that can refer to equality in wealth, property, job, status, and many other aspects. These ideological approaches were mainly shaped by modern attempts to move beyond the Communist-Capitalist conflict over the last two centuries. Libertarians and Socialists, among many other ideologues, hold rather conflicting ideals. Is it truly freedom to restrict people and what they do? The short answer is no. Is it Democratic to take from the rich and give to the poor? The short answer is No! Respect and love are critical things that need to be applied. As much as a starving family deserves sympathy and help, the wealthy also deserve to continue doing what makes them happy. A statement like this during my lifetime would be met with a majority who felt the opposite regarding the wealthy, in particular, the Capitalists who have, to some degree, run away from any truly legitimate control. But it is a core principle of democracy that the government not intervene in how people live their lives, so long as the manner in which they choose to live does not harm their fellow citizens.

Laws need to protect everyone, including the polity and the Democratic system. But laws should never favor or enhance the rights or abilities of one class of people over another. To do so would mean that the favored class would rule over the others. Also, as I mentioned in the Prerequisites, citizenship equality should not be considered a de facto process granted to people simply because a certain number of years have passed since they lived in a city. In countries such as those recently colonized, where populations are continually increasing due to migration, the consensus is to grant most entrants citizenship without qualification. This is because those countries require growth and promote migration to their country. Most immigrants, regardless of ethnicity, consider themselves equal to others in the colonies; the majority who migrate to these countries have come only to make money and get out. They arrive, make money, and build a family, but eventually stay for their family. So, when evaluating the financial equality of citizens, we must consider that not everyone living in a country supports its political or military agenda. This is important to understand because places like those mentioned would face an internal conflict if citizenship entailed military service or qualifications. As stated earlier, we do not use the term 'qualification' in the same way academic institutions do; rather, we use it to describe a process of demonstrating intent rather than capacity. Therefore, equality among citizens is important, but in some instances, attempting to compel all citizens to serve the agenda of a dominant ethnic group within a polity often creates conflict.

Since the task merely highlighted some ethics a polity should consider valuable, we can assume we have covered enough to proceed. However, many other matters have not been raised. The key is that the policy should be composed of ethical people with a relatively homogeneous set of beliefs. Those ethics can be many and varied, but a polity must be smart enough to understand that courage should never be taken over logic. Because many people will try to attain more than they should, be it in power or wealth. Courage will only lead to violence, and often, blows go astray or hit the wrong targets. Logic, in contrast, helps identify threats and problems and addresses them effectively. In the same way, the ethics important to a polity will unfold and become established naturally through their own workings.

Understandably, many will think this is not clear enough a direction or that we cannot end our topic so loosely. Still, ultimately, it is not for me or any individual to decide what is ethical and what is not. All we can do is highlight some of the issues that must be considered. However, as we strive to be thorough in everything we have written, we will list some attributes that may be considered valuable in a Democratic system.

The next most important thing will be the intent behind our gatherings and their purpose. This can be seen as a reflection of our genuine intent. The honest and sincere will to make a democratic system work is a prerequisite. It requires enough honest and sincere people for such a system to come into existence in the first place.

Secondly, there is the ability to communicate and talk with others. This ability or virtue could be called articulation. In particular, the ethic of encouraging articulation of the truth is important for a Democratic system. The ability to convey information coherently, talk, and debate is also important. Of course, there will always be some people more skilled than others, but a basic level of language skills is enough to be considered articulate and to form a Democratic system.

Thirdly, once people have gathered, they must organize themselves and form an administrative system. The ethics that would be of interest are the qualities of dauntlessness, determination, and persistence. At times of failure, we will require people to be loyal to the democratic cause and sustain their involvement. With one or a few mishaps, people often walk away from their problems. What is needed is for people to want the system to work so much that they will not flounder, desert their posts, or simply betray everyone for their profit. Loyalty is hard to achieve amongst people, especially when they feel that their loyalty to a system strengthens others by usurping power and command.

Fourthly, we would require people with empathy and understanding of the topics and issues that will be raised. Without understanding, people will be unable to make just decisions. Making laws, judging, and policing require honor, transparency, and candor. Understanding contributes to the processing of information, enabling the establishment of decisions of the highest quality and ensuring fairness and justice.

Lastly, wisdom among the people helps them determine what is true. Wisdom lets them see what is not always visible. Wisdom provides the basis for a philosophical system that considers all things, not a narrow view. Wisdom will ultimately prevent wars and determine their success.

Now, these things may all seem like ethical values to a polity. There will be a need for courage, daring, heroism, and all the other things that make us human. However, "when to be heroic?" is what is of concern. In times of battle, when a window of opportunity arises that can turn the course of a battle, it is the hero who takes that opportunity in the hope of success and against all odds. We cannot say we do not want such people. Our situation often determines whether our actions are ethical. A thief in a market is considered a criminal, but a thief of enemy plans is often regarded as a hero. We have merely outlined some ethical values that, to some degree, determine the quality of a democratic system. But there will be times when we will need even the most unethical at some point. The important matter is to promote that which is good and generally acceptable. The unethical will always exist, as teaching everyone how to be ethical is never possible.

We have established that Ethics affect the entire polity, and hoping to have everyone with high ethics attend assemblies is unrealistic. The best thing to happen is that the vast majority are ethical people. At worst, the Democracy will turn into an Ochlocracy as it will lack the virtues or ethics needed to create, maintain, and propagate a Democratic system.

7. Government peripheral issues

"The purpose of government is to govern, but what it should govern is for the people to decide."

So far, we have defined democracy and examined some of its prerequisites. We have also taken snippets of historical evidence to see how the Athenians operated their democracy. We have also discussed the peculiarities of the ancient democracy and provided a platform for assessing it. Lastly, we have addressed the quality of government by inferring that, for the most part, the quality of a Democratic system entirely relies on the Ethics of the people. Ethical individuals can contribute to the creation of an ethical, democratic state, but just as one is not without flaws, so too is the other.

Now is the time to take a broader view of Government. Other types of governments also face many of the problems and issues that a democratic government does. Investigating how each system addresses the same problems is an interesting endeavor. Given that there is no such thing as a perfect system, we should try to determine which system we have at our disposal is the better one.

Many people have debated the role of government. Many views and opinions exist on what constitutes a perfect government. Generally, the consensus is that a government should make most people content with their government and the way it manifests in their lives. Suppose you think a government should only make us happy. In that case, we should reflect on the serious issues of immorality, substance abuse, and the security bubble that a society can be placed within. Happiness is often tied to ignorance, and generally, people who are content and happy are also ignorant of others' actions. They live in a bubble centered on narcissistic tendencies. Yet contentment and happiness can also come from wanting the least in life. That is, a few who are wise, intelligent, aware, and understanding can also be content. Yet such people are rare, and they are genuinely content with the least. That is one of those things that distinguishes a good man from a bad one. Typically, those with bad intentions seek to benefit themselves without considering the consequences. Good people are capable of turning the other cheek. They can let things they know to be wrong and against their best interests occur. Because most of us are good people and will not consistently take advantage of others for our own gain, we are also vulnerable to exploitation of our goodness and kindness.

If you think that the government should only be there to protect and shelter people from the outside world, then we would only need two occupations: police officers and soldiers. Women are said to be particularly predisposed to ideas of security, safety, and well-being. Also, Men who effectively do not command their homes are often led by women towards the needs of security and safety. We can see that many males would rather live under a tree, in a cave, or someplace attached to nature. To fish and hunt and to essentially enjoy the earth around them. Women typically want the opposite: the least exposure to environmental risks. As mentioned, the more they evade or eliminate risks, the more comfortable and secure they feel. That is why they are usually the driving force behind home purchases. Of course, not everyone is like that; some would say these are stereotypes, but they are generalizations based on the observation of many thousands of people, couples, and relationships. If the idea that the government should secure and shelter people is common among the majority, then certain considerations are warranted. Firstly, which of the two lifestyles is to be catered for, the one that utilizes nature or the one that shelters from the elements of nature?

In any case, such thoughts are not uncommon and are mentioned not to reinforce their validity but to highlight the two ways of thinking. One side wants to take certain risks to feel alive. The other wants to evade or eliminate risks to feel safe and secure. Despite what has been said, it is not entirely bound by gender, as mentioned. The governing systems also play a role in defining the importance of security. In many nations that have become military or police states, the methods used to establish security are not based on differences between men and women. The government justifies itself by creating a real or imaginary need to "secure" society. In this way, they are supported by both men and women, making it easier for them to control the nation directly through the army or the police.

That is why diversity, with a degree of homogeneity and culture, a little unpredictability, and yet stability, and all the other things that keep us interested and content with our world, needs to be experienced when living within a system. These unpredictabilities and uncertainties can be used to present imaginary threats and exaggerated security concerns. The oligarchs use to legitimize more and more military and police control. A stagnant, monotonous system that operates like a machine will not make people, or the majority, content. A system that suppresses people and controls their lives will eventually collapse. Yet, the duration of these rising and collapsing tides is substantial enough to scar the people within such systems for many generations. A dictator, an autocrat, an oligarchy, and even an ochlocracy can create a monotonous military state with long-lasting ramifications. Similarly, as a militarized society, ancient Sparta ultimately had a profoundly adverse impact on its people for many generations, not only while in power but also for generations after that.

To understand what we expect from the Government, we should first consider what most humans deem necessary. Humans feel that several essential needs are most important, including economic, health, educational, and security needs. These four primary needs are complemented by religion or spirituality, making up five essential aspects of human life. For those without a religion or what is alternatively considered spirituality, the term can be substituted by the concept of the psyche. Because a substantial audience already understands the term "Religion", we would rather use it than directly address the Psyche. As Plato once mentioned, the Psyche is a part of our existence that makes us live and gives us breath. If what defined us were purely physical and chemical, there would be nothing to explain life and its existence. While we may know some of the reasons, there is ultimately nothing we can prove to be absolutely true.

The Psyche is a part of us that we wish to satisfy, but it is neither somatic nor cognitive. For instance, we may be physically perfect, and our minds free of worries or thoughts that obsess us. We could be enjoying ourselves thoroughly at any given moment. But within that moment, many feel that something is not entirely fulfilled unless we address spiritual, religious, or other issues that affect the psyche. For this reason, some people believe that our behaviors measure the psyche. A person at peace and calm will display different behaviors to a person who is anxious and polemic. The things we do, say, and think about are affected not by our emotions alone but by what we consider a part of our being and the psyche. These three things – somatic, mind, and psyche – have been the traditional triad of well-being; satisfying all of them has been considered the correct way to approach contentment and happiness. But these things all concern the self and our social or environmental interfaces. Over the years, we have come to realize that many of us derive joy from social interactions and other aspects of our surroundings. Sharing a view of a sunset or a gathering of friends can give a person more than just satisfaction. Then there are the sacrifices spoken of earlier, as well as the sharing and charity work people do to satisfy their psyche.

7.1 Health

Most essential needs are typically detached from our bodily and social needs. Yet, the physical and social needs seem more critical to most people. Also, our environment shapes what we consider a need rather than a want. Spirituality and Health are mostly personal, though social elements include church assemblies, banquets, and festivals. Our mental health and self-esteem needs can be established through good friends and companions. If we were to classify all our needs, it would begin with our personal needs, but we should also consider the social needs that humans require later. Our personal needs are often considered the most important of the two. Yet exceptions exist, such as the sacrifices parents make for their children. We can say that our powerful instinct to preserve ourselves equates to our personal and other essential needs. However, some social needs, as demonstrated by mothers and children, and fathers and children, depict selfless acts and sacrifices to preserve themselves and their offspring. Such acts place social and personal needs on a par as priorities. However, since these acts, like those of the brave in battle, give us examples of people putting others before themselves, we must generalize to what the majority do most of the time.

The reality is that most people care more for themselves most of the time. It is that centric view of ourselves that often creates a seemingly narcissistic lifestyle. It is further encouraged, at the time of writing, through self-improvement programs that focus on the ego rather than the psyche. Furthermore, people often buy homes and lock themselves inside when writing this. They rarely communicate with their neighbors and often do not even know them well. Of course, this does not happen everywhere; it occurs only in some larger cities and in some cultures. Yet many people who live such lifestyles may not be content and seek more through social interactions. Most people enjoy socialization, which suggests, based on practical evidence, that there is more to life than our mind and body; it also includes our interaction with our environment and social existence. There is also another facet – our psyche – that adds another layer of needs to be fulfilled.

Selfless acts almost always revolve around health, safety, and security. While a person may buy clothes for a less fortunate individual, donating them to goodwill, that act is not considered selfless, brave, or heroic. Instead, it is considered charitable and takes a lesser position than acts that put a person's safety, security, and health at risk for others. Safety and Security are both contributing factors to our Health. For the most part, health can be seen as a pinnacle long-term somatic need. Our safety and security are merely a part of ensuring we remain well. Parents can sometimes put their own safety and security at risk for their children. That type of sacrifice is given the same weight as that of heroes and people who have truly risked their health, safety, and security for the benefit of others. More prestige and admiration are given to those who sacrifice their health, safety, and security for strangers. As already stated, we see some sacrifices in Economics, Education, Health, Security, and Spirituality. Yet most people seem to value these things differently. For instance, sacrificing our education, spending our money, or devoting our lives to a religion does not weigh equally with the majority of people at the time of writing this. There is, however, a high degree of respect for these economic, educational, or spiritual sacrifices.

We esteem people who have placed others before themselves; this seems to be true perpetually. The degree of esteem varies; for the religious, there is greater esteem for the Monk who devotes their entire life to God and forgoes a place in our modern world. For instance, the Monks of Mount Athos would consider themselves dead to the world and wear black to mark their death to our world. Such people are often misunderstood, and many ridicule them. However, by understanding what they have done, we cannot sit back and scorn or mock them. They live simply every day, seeking spiritual fulfillment and redemption on their path to eternal life in the age to come (the afterlife). They do not seek to convert but to save people. They offer medicine for the psyche; many come to them seeking healing and cleansing. Therefore, these people are not testing the waters or putting on an act. They are not here today and gone tomorrow; they are not following a trend but are entirely committed to what they believe. Yet, while many of us hold immense respect for those who apply a passive theology, many do not.

The rate at which selfless acts occur in terms of security, safety, and health is daily. The amount of selflessness or the quality of our actions is judged by others, and it isn't easy to measure what we all consider selfless. Explaining an order or hierarchy is difficult. Yet we know from the outset that the acts that sacrifice our health, security, and safety are viewed as significant and of higher quality and ethics. That is perhaps because these things impact our biological well-being, and, due to their direct somatic effects, take precedence over economics, education, and spirituality. The things that appear most vivid and somatic are understandable without description. A person leaping a crevice to save a child or hurling themselves into flames to save others does not require words to describe their bravery. However, when a strategist succeeds in a plan that affects everyone, only those who understand will appreciate that person.

Arguably, spiritual and somatic health can be the same thing, much as nutrition and wellbeing are represented by the wellbeing of all three soma, mind, and psyche. From a human behavior perspective, we know that people respond to physical and somatic stimuli more rapidly than to any other type of stimulus. People can see that a person is disabled if they have a physical impairment, but they can't see if that person has an internal problem. On this point, modern medicine, in my time, has almost eliminated the psyche from its practice. While the term remains in an archaic form, it has undergone significant reinterpretations and definitions. Today's psychology is divided into two parts: the spiritual psyche, often associated with religion, and the secular psyche, which scientists consider. Secular views of the Psyche have been condensed down to a form of behavioral analysis that stems back to cognitive therapy of some sort. An angry person, for example, is often considered mad or is thought to be in an unhealthy state of mind or psyche. People who are displeased with something often voice their opinions. Still, if they are a minority, they are often labeled with derogatory terms such as conspirators and many other labels in an attempt to defame or slander.

In any case, the point is that the study of the psyche has become so condensed that it is associated with the state of the mind. However, this is a defeat for science and a victory for those who control society. You see, the majority of people with so-called mental issues have serious issues with the psyche. These issues are so potent, yet they are hardly ever addressed. For instance, some people suffer long-term unemployment, so long that they have never been able to afford shoes or what would be considered a proper meal. Others have, for whatever reason, become entwined in narcotics and drugs to escape reality, and yet when they are sober, the pain of life is too much for them to continue, and they seek ways to escape again. Others have been financially successful and have lost all their possessions, and live in perpetual poverty. If precautionary psychological therapy existed, it would provide people with what they want, what they desire, and what they truly need in life. You see, the mental illnesses and the somatic illnesses all stem from a psyche that was not tended to. Yes, people develop mental illness, but many develop somatic illness because of a poor psyche.

So poor are the living conditions in some countries that they perpetually counter this state with positive thinking as a way to remedy the unhealthy psyche that develops. Positive thinking involves disregarding negative thoughts and addressing and resolving past emotions and problems. Positive thinking is like dealing with people who have a profound inability to grasp reality without feeling emotional or in some way affected. Let us highlight some things that positive thinkers think: "Elevate yourself", "Keep away from people and information that makes you jealous, envious, or makes you feel lesser about yourself", "surround yourself with smiles, pictures, photos, and people that make you smile", "Remind yourself of your strengths every day". Now, superficially, most of this seems harmless advice, but ultimately, it addresses people's problems when they realize that their expectations of life are significantly different from reality.

Many people cannot understand why their lives are the way they are or how they ended up where they are. Their so-called friends may have abandoned them years ago while they pursued their plans for success. Many people, even those in wealthy and successful occupations, envy those ahead of them and fall into the same problems that envy and jealousy can bring. Expectation and reality are two different things. This philosophy may not be what many people want to read, especially those struggling to find a foothold for their psyche or well-being. A person's health requires particular attention to the specific matter that ails them. Actions to support good health require more than one treatment; at least three are needed for the mind, body, and psyche.

Additionally, to summarize these points, the psyche comes clearly before our cognition, which in turn precedes our behavior and somatic needs. That is to say, if we were to put things in hierarchical order and in the order of their flow, we would place the psyche first, then the mind, and then the soma. The soma is where our behaviors are exhibited, and our mind is where those behaviors are formulated or initiated. But the Psyche, in the first instance, affects what we think and act. Poor treatment of the Psyche leads to symptoms found in the mind and soma. The medical field has generally accepted that stress can cause real and visible somatic changes in a person. Therefore, it is important to attend to the psyche.

It is plausible to suggest that our surroundings influence our behavior. As mentioned earlier, the social or things detached from our body but related to it impact us as much as the psyche, mind, and soma. We consider health to be an essential part of our lives, both as individuals and as a group. Without health to enjoy life and to function properly, all other facets of life will be adversely affected. What contributes to Health is often debated. Here, we have established that the somatic, mental, and psyche all require nutrition and attention. A balance between these is far better than placing one over the other. But if we are to start somewhere, then the order will vary depending on the circumstances.

Similarly, our social surroundings significantly contribute to the state of our psyche. There is little purpose in living in a place or with people who adversely affect our lives. People have very little say in most government systems, such as autocracies or oligarchies. In such systems, people tend to suffer more from issues of the psyche. The Psyche is the interface between the universe, our mind, and our body. It is not just the life force but also the interface between ourselves and our surroundings. It connects all of us to the universe, just as our heat can be felt but not seen. If we sit with others in a dark, cold room, many of us will huddle together in-discriminatorily to survive. We are living things that affect other living things not merely by our thoughts (mind) and actions (soma) but also by our very existence (psyche). That is why, in a democratic system, the people and their psyche elevate them —not in a meaningless, comforting stroke to our ego or self-image, but to the very scope of our existence. A democratic system empowers the people and their psyches, making them believe they can achieve anything they want. How do we know? Hundreds of geniuses were born during the Athenian Democratic age. Nowadays, you can count them on one hand. That is an extraordinary thing!

Health, from a somatic perspective, is significantly influenced by what we eat and drink. Too much of anything is considered unhealthy because the body parts required to process that particular food or beverage will become overworked when it is repeatedly consumed. Variety, therefore, is essential to the diet. In addition, white meats are seen as easier to process than red meats, but they are lighter, and those with enormous appetites will find it difficult to curb their hunger with white meat alone. Some Athletes have been known to eat several chickens or roosters in one sitting.

In some cases, such as the example, it may be beneficial to condense the meal by choosing red meats. Also, if the question were raised, how many meals should consist of meat in a week? In a seven-day week, one would aim for two strictly vegan days and one vegetarian day, with the rest being a mix of vegan and non-vegan days, as preferred, with or without meat. For those who abstain from meat, the solution is to eat vegetarian meals most of the week and preserve two days for vegan meals. These diets were established as modifications of the diets used by the monks of Mt. Athos and were influenced by the readings of Plato and other philosophers. It is a diet considered the correct Christian diet. Diet is critical to good health and is one of the few things we can do as a preventative measure. Our genetic composition is influenced by what we eat. Therefore, we can pass these genetic modifications on to our offspring. Thus, food and beverages should not be considered trivial but essential to sustained health.

While mobility varies with people exercising, it remains important. All body parts depend on the well-being provided by regular, light, and consistent activity. Attempts to condense activity into high-intensity exercise bursts are not as healthy as sustained, light activity. That is because the muscles, blood, and other bodily systems are interrelated. If you constantly move your legs, you can facilitate blood flow. Therefore, sustaining light movements throughout the day is far better than performing high-intensity exercises. The impact on fat deposits may seem beneficial, but the overall benefit gained is minimal and even detrimental compared to sustained regular activity. There are specialized fields dedicated to the study of regular exercise. What has been said so far is merely a synoptic view.

The current system, at the time of writing, has contaminated our food and water. The level of contaminants is considerably high. These contaminants include residual antibiotics, preservatives, and chemicals used to increase the profits of those raising livestock or crops. Water contamination is often touted for its health benefits, but these are questionable, and some argue that they are detrimental. In addition, the governments of the world at the time of writing had declared an arguable global pandemic that coerced people into receiving detrimental vaccinations. Therefore, there is the overbearing question of whether the government should regulate or become involved with people's health. The answer is that, for a government to function, it must perform the most basic functions: legislate, judge, and enforce the state's laws. Anything beyond this is not a sign of a lean Democratic state or of any other system. It is akin to assuming a business partnership between the Oligarchs and the industries they control, such as the healthcare industry, which is often silently or otherwise partnered with the governing Oligarchs or persons in power. Although it may be part of a state's laws, the extent to which those laws apply should follow specific guidelines.

The Nuremberg Code, established in the aftermath of World War II, aimed to end experimentation on humans. The condensed ten points are:

1. Patient Voluntary consent

2. Beneficial outcomes for the patient

3. The procedure should have a non-malicious purpose

4. The procedure should avoid risks of harm

5. No experiment or procedure should be conducted where death is a possibility

6. The risks should be treated

7. Adequate resources and facilities for the procedure

8. Only qualified persons should conduct the procedure

9. The patient's right to cease the treatment

10. The scientist must be prepared to stop at any given time.

Therefore, it is important to recognize that people's health should not be governed; rather, regulations such as the Nuremberg Code should be established. It prevents forced procedures and the potential catastrophes that could befall humanity through medical and genetic manipulation. Some people in my time, such as Yuval Noah Harari and Klaus Schwab, are working with the elites and guiding them down a road that will be described. They were people who sculpted a world in their minds that would somehow change the status quo. They believed there would be a world where we were like cyborgs, linked to a common system —a matrix of humans. We will be genetically modified and electronically enhanced like machines to perform specific functions. We will become a device. Such ideas gained popular support among the elites for the first time in human history. Therefore, we require prompt, decisive, and attentive action to counter this possibility and ensure our autonomy remains intact. The idea that anyone has the authority to undertake any procedure on our own body without our consent, through coercion and force, has already happened during the coronavirus 2019 (COVID-19) years. It remains, at the time of writing, a warning of what may happen if people do not take control of their destiny.

7.2 Security

Security ensures our physical health, safety, and ease of mind. Security is not merely a physical form of protection but also one that helps people relax, which, in turn, affects their mental and physical health. People are stressed about their security due to a lack of trust, and those who feel threatened or for any other reason will not have a healthy psyche. This leads to poor cognition or mental processes and eventually leads to unhealthy behaviors. A lack of security also implies the direct ability to defend and aggress as needed to ensure the health and well-being of the individual and polity. The security provided by an individual for themselves and perhaps those around them is different from the Security that others provide. They affect the psyche in different ways. Security forged by oneself or family members, such as siblings and father, is direct and immediate. Because of its immediate access, family members within reach will feel most secure, and their psyche will be comforted to know that those around them will offer the same protection they themselves provide. This is one of the benefits of a Democratic people who take on the role of securing their polity. While Athenian citizens were politicians, soldiers, policemen, judges, and lawmakers, the

Security they enjoyed was formed through their participation as soldiers and policemen.

Additionally, the concept of security often differs between males and females. Not so much biologically, but through their cultural roles. At the time of writing, females often strive to create nests and secure places to raise their children. Males often view a hill as a safe and secure place. Hills naturally protect against flooding and wind-carried debris. They also have military functions. Everyone highly regards security; it manifests differently among people and is not gender-specific. It is therefore essential for people to feel secure, and not only that, but it also has a direct and immediate impact on security when applied practically. In a Democratic state, the people feel most secure when they not only participate in their own security but also decide what will be part of establishing it. However, despite these differences, most people feel less safe and secure when some undisclosed entity, such as a mercenary army, offers the security they enjoy.

As mentioned earlier, people require a certain level of safety in their lives. Safety and security are similar in nature but differ in that safety concerns typically involve matters that are not directly related to the threat or risk of detrimental behavior by others. However, modern definitions also include those things. In other words, when we are worried about others' actions and their impact on us, it typically becomes a security issue. When the matter concerns the environment and does not immediately relate to the actions of others, but may include that, it is usually considered a safety issue. Also, safety concerns any harm that may result from unintended incidents. Security concerns intentional incidents, typically involving interactions between individuals. Safety, security, and health are related, overlapping, and mutually reinforcing. Retrospectively, safety is one of those matters that can also be like Security, an issue affected by those around us as much as our actions. Therefore, safety focuses more on accidental actions, and security focuses on deliberate actions.

In addition, security can infer the military strength required to defend and maintain the autonomy of a state, territory, or objective. It is also often used to describe the need for shelter and a place to abide. It is also used as a descriptor for certain finances, such as a deposit of funds or currency to secure ownership. The term security also has several other common uses. It can have beneficial or detrimental consequences, depending on how it is established. A sense of safety and stability for individuals and minority groups, as well as reductions in violence, crimes, and other threats, can be achieved. People's rights can be protected by ensuring they are educated and have access to guidelines on health, political participation, and other essential matters, which laws, the judiciary, and enforcement can secure.

However, many detrimental consequences may arise. The most significant is the umbrella term Freedom. The manner in which security is attained, especially within an Oligarchy or Autocracy, impacts the people's Freedom. It is more impactful for oligarchies and autocracies because the efficiency in taking away the rights and privileges of their subjects and citizens is fearfully expedient. The tyranny of the few is often disguised as a means of helping the people. Therefore, security may take the form of enforcers, surveillance, and control by oligarchic authorities, thereby significantly impacting people's privacy, freedom, and liberty. Security concerns have been used in the past to place alternative thinkers, activists, and other people opposing an idea into prisons or facing torture and death.

Freedom, as noted elsewhere in this philosophical text, is a catalyst for creativity, productivity, and genuine participation in any field of interest. It allows people to turn their hobbies into something more than that. It lets them excel at what they do best. This is why freedom promotes democratic ideas. It indirectly empowers people to pursue their interests and participate freely in matters that affect their state. Freedom and democracy give people ultimate control and power to define their destiny by enabling them to maneuver their polity. If handled with accountability and a fair scope towards other minority groups, freedom and democracy can foster pluralistic or tribal acceptance and, in this way, become inclusive rather than exclusive. Therefore, freedom is an essential part of a democratic state and must be preserved by limiting the reach of security measures and holding everyone accountable, from decision-making to enforcement.

Government involvement in Security affects several areas of political life. These include the liberty to establish one's abode. It can have a financial, military, and political impact. Financial security was demonstrated by various systems and was described by Aristotle. It was one of the precursors to a Democratic state, where debt slavery was abolished, marking the beginning of freedom. In the military, the draft or compulsory service often forced owners to abandon their properties and farms to serve. Therefore, they of ten lost their ability to secure a political existence until their return.

Politically, the liberty to secure against perpetrators diminishes with age, while dependence on others begins to develop. It is, therefore, at that point in life that enforcers and other systematic government aid exist. However, caution must be taken regarding the factor of fear, as noted elsewhere. Often, a need is artificially created, especially under a coercive and manipulative Oligarchy or Autocracy. Fear is often created when people react and act in particular ways that demonstrate a fear of others and their impact on them. This type of system forces people to adopt reclusive and withdrawn lifestyles. Therefore, the cost of security is liberty in that, in all aspects of its applications, the liberty of people will be compromised to some extent. Considering security in relation to a shelter, we lose mobility.

Security, as it relates to a military objective, we lose the freedom to attend to other things. Security relates to financial issues; we gain security but also incur liability and lose some or a significant portion of current assets. Therefore, it is foreseeable matter that security impacts all matters of society and requires attention and monitoring. Accountability and democratic processes are essential to maintain the freedom necessary for a democratic state to operate effectively.

7.3 Spirituality

Thirdly, our priority, especially for those of a spiritual nature, is our religious and spiritual fulfillment. For those without a pious nature, this is often filled by another aspect of our lives, creating a belief that consoles our minds and comforts our bodies. The Psyche is what elevates us, both somatically and mentally. It is what makes us alive. Some, especially Plato, would place the soul or psyche above all else, but because of the nature of the times that I am writing in, I can only say that whatever gives us life is surely the most important thing to maintain. While it is not visible or tangible, many prematurely conclude that it does not exist.

But in the same way, there are small organisms we cannot see and things even smaller than them that we cannot see; they are as real as the things that give life. That thing, in a spiritual context, is an existent entity that is not seen but gives us life. Some people have a closer connection with their psyche than others, and this disparity usually results in spiritual and non-spiritual differences. Yet the effect is visible: a person can attend to their soma and mind, but never feel content or fulfilled until they start to address the issues of their psyche.

The Psyche and the things we attribute to it vary considerably, but what a government system should be able to achieve is to ensure that it respects our spiritual needs. We do not need governments that dictate which faiths are allowed or not, but we do need to ensure that those faiths do not become immoral or unethical in their values. The best way is to understand how religion, faith, and beliefs fit into our lives. You see, a lot of science is based on belief because not everyone has checked the results they read. Call it laziness, perhaps a lack of knowledge, but the majority of people do not have time to test every fact they read or discover from others. They end up believing, without investigation, the facts they have received. Ironically, the same weakness in character is what prevents a democracy from existing. If a Democracy were established by people who believed and trusted others, then it would be those they trusted who would eventually betray that trust. If you can trust a person to vote and decide on your behalf, then you have lost the fight for freedom and have allowed your strength and power to be wielded by another. There is, of course, merit in the fact that if action is needed, the few in an aristocracy or oligarchy can initiate it faster and perhaps more efficiently. If we place faith in the wrong things, then our very freedom can be compromised.

The faiths of the world share many similarities. While their content and stories vary, the underlying concept of the faiths remains the same. It defines the core characteristics of the society that adopts that faith. In a matriarchy, women are empowered and men are diminished. In a matriarchy, a woman chooses a husband, or a husband asks a woman to marry. However, they are limited to one wife, thereby empowering that woman. In the patriarchal system, men often have the freedom to choose their brides and are permitted to have as many as they can support and treat fairly. It is worth noting that in the days of Socrates, Plato, and Aristotle, people were polygamous and lived under a form of patriarchy. It was a Patriarchy that was diminishing and showing signs of an emerging matriarchy.

Perhaps both systems exist perpetually and flux in characteristics from one to the other. However, when religions stipulate characteristics that define a Patriarchy or Matriarchy, then we must accept that these religions were formed through one of these systems. Christianity, for example, was a faith that many women supported and encouraged men to follow. Its content empowers females but is neither Matriarchy nor Patriarchy. There are a few instances where the Matriarchy of the Roman Empire enters and affects the content of the Bible, such as it relates to the marriage of one wife (New Testament, 2023, 1 Corinthians 7:2). These things are not of significance to the core of our interest in the recognition of our needs for a healthy psyche. However, they help us understand that religions all serve similar purposes and are powerful ways of uniting people in a shared way of thinking.

We must understand their place in any system. We must also understand that, in some instances, religions can be effective only under specific forms of government. In those cases, caution must be taken to ensure that the government system is not modified or altered over time by various faiths and beliefs. For example, when a system has a set of rules, people must know why those rules exist. By understanding why they exist, we know what they protect against, and if our faith or beliefs contradict those reasons and rules, we must ensure that the system and government are not undermined by votes, drawing lots, or other mechanisms that would compromise the system. Some countries have restricted constitutions, meaning that within a certain framework, they can be changed, but they cannot, for example, change from a Monarchy to a Democracy or an Aristocracy to a Monarchy. The constitutions protect against various changes, so it is important that a Democracy also consider restricting what can and can't be changed. At the same time, we should be fair to people of all faiths and religions, because most people who have faith do not see it as strictly religious; they practice it for the benefit of a healthy psyche and spirit.

As mentioned in the section on Religion and the State, spirituality or institutional religion must be kept out of the political arena on all matters except those related to spirituality or religion. This is true for any group, whether Masonic or another secret organization. The formation of parties, cults, and all manner of unity must never override the principal system established by the people. If it does, then it has become infiltrated by an Autocratic or Oligarchic influence. This emphatic commentary is required because the religious institutions have, for a long time, lost the directional model established by their founders. I speak of all religions at the time of writing. This is because the same Oligarchs have influenced all elite organizations, including religious institutions worldwide.

7.4 Economics

The mindset of many people typically prioritizes economics as a high-priority issue. However, this is not because of the importance most people attribute to it, but rather because of the significance that economics has in modern life. Usually, that importance is imposed on people; as a result, economic issues become serious problems for many.

Social activity relies on economics, and in turn, that activity forms businesses that cascade their impact through society. While domestic or home economics may be important to most parents and households, others consider economics for entirely different reasons. For the poor, the importance lies more in the indirect relationship between a service, such as medical attention, and the availability of money. Or money is seen as essential for their survival. For the wealthy, the importance lies more in maintaining and accumulating wealth. The middle class or those with a slight surplus of money are typically the most prolific spenders and, at the time of writing, do so in a most narcissistic fashion. However, the poor, middle class, and wealthy spend currency to obtain goods and services, and in return, they receive currency. The interaction of making and spending money creates a social activity.

So, economics, like other essential needs, may have the greatest extent of social context. Yet, each individual is affected by economics, both in their personal finances and in those of those around them. Equally, both are important. Some may argue that Economics are superficial or fabricated concepts, but humanity, with or without currency, has had various economic systems. Not all those systems relied on currency, as some were exchanges for services, assistance, and produce. The use of representative currency, as coins and similar tokens of value, suffers the same corruptible usage as found in other places where so-called representation occurs. Currency has such a bad reputation that the Greek word for it has been adopted in many languages to mean 'evil,' 'bad,' or 'unlawful.' The term Χρήμα (Chrema) means money in Greek. The etymology appears to be closely related to the Latin term for Crime (crimen). It would not seem surprising that when imperial currencies were first circulated, there would have been resistance to them. If someone took your Ox or your chickens and placed a piece of cheap copper in your hands, I am fairly certain the first impression would have been that of thievery on the part of those who took your possessions. Also, the accusation of crime would further be exacerbated when, in the future, you could not buy what you sold with the same piece of copper. Representatives or representative or abstract representation, no matter where they exist, be they in government, currency, or any other manner, are intrinsically flawed in concept. Even the abstract alphabets we use around the world are slightly flawed, as they require many characters to represent the languages they convey. Additionally, the characters and words change their meaning, so the grammar used changes accordingly.

Alternatively, Νόμισμα (Nomisma) means legal or lawful tender. Therefore, in the hands of the Democratic people of Athens, the currency was called lawful tender. However, in the hands of the Roman state, the word came to mean criminal tender. It is a double-edged sword with benefits and consequences. If it is in the power of the people, it is considered legal and formal. In the hands of an Oligarchy or an Autocracy, it is seen as a method of criminal control.

The economic model used in a democratic system is significantly different from that employed under an Oligarchy or Autocracy. Initially, oligarchs or Autocrats supply the currency, and their faces are often imprinted or featured on physical currency. In contrast, a Democracy places the supply of currency in the hands of the people. They control the treasury. Then, currency under an Oligarchy or Autocracy is initially distributed to the ruling elite and then to the next tier of operatives.

In contrast, Democracy distributes funds according to the will of the people. If what has been said here is considered, then they would be wise to distribute it according to merit and fairness among the five classes. Therefore, farmers secure contracts comparable to those in the military or professional industries, such as medicine. The circulation of currency is then limited by oligarchies and autocracies, so that, by the time it has been spent several times, it has all been returned as taxes, fees, tariffs, and other means of recouping the funds. When writing this, it was anticipated that it would all have returned to the source by the time money had been exchanged approximately five times. Therefore, it limited the trickle effect and starved and impoverished the lower socioeconomic classes. Within a Democratic model, there is a tendency to circulate the currency more times, without excessive taxes or tariffs, as a means of returning the funds. That is said to be guided by the Biblical notion that 10% should be considered a fair tax. That allows currency to circulate approximately 10 times before most of it is returned, thus trickling to more people. It is therefore clear why the ancient demos called one lawful tender and the other a crime.

7.5 Education

With the previous point regarding representation in mind, let us consider our essential need for Education. Education, typically for the youth or adults, involves specialized teachers. For adults, education involves seeking knowledge from others. Aristotle tells us that education is too important to be taught by a single person. It became a custom in Ancient Greece that knowledge came from many people, not just one. The youth were sent to different teachers to learn a variety of things. The importance of having as much input and opinion as possible is also part of the dynamics relating to our essential needs: Economic, Health, Education, Security, and Religious issues.

However, interestingly, many people seem content with the concept of specialization, and in the process, create a set of dynamics that are quite peculiar. People tend to visit specialists to gain input or opinions. However, this idea of specialization intrinsically encourages the niche development of groups or professions with particular powers and authority. Through apathy, we create representatives in almost all facets of society. We leave our health in the hands of others, much as we do with our education, and we consider all these things essential. Even the currencies we use represent the hours we work, and in many cases, this representation is unfair.

Many aspects of our lives are often left to the fittest and most able to conduct or perform the duty. In a family, it may be the strongest male member. Other philosophers have highlighted why Security and certain professions are usually left to specialists. Everyone can learn economics, but achieving a favorable outcome requires specialized knowledge. From a governing perspective, a particular favorable outcome is not the same as a personal gain or profit. Health, security, spirituality, economics, and education all become more complex when applied to a polity, government system, or business. The interface between the system used and the needs of the people requires a balance. While the economic model in a democracy is not meant to be equally distributed or to ensure everyone makes a profit, the conditions, mobility within the system, fairness, and circulation levels ensure that everyone has a fairer chance of starting from the bottom and gaining momentum wherever they intend to go. In some cases, rather than personal investments, public funds can be used to finance large projects authorized by the people.

Regarding freedom and the right to live as one chooses, legislating for health, security, spirituality, economics, education, and other aspects is a sensitive and perplexing matter. These things are important to a democracy, and it is important to note that social, political, or economic factors should never impose on freedom. However, freedom without duty is a poor basis for discipline. As we noted earlier regarding borders and anarchy, freedom also requires ethical moderation and restraint. Usually, that restraint should be done through ethics before anything else. A complex system is created under a Democratic institution, a blend of formal laws and duties, and informal cultural and religious expectations and behaviors. Therefore, sometimes important matters can be addressed culturally rather than through legislation. That applies to all areas where our needs are protected or secured, including education.

Within an Oligarchy or Autocracy, the pederasty is delivered by a formal, legislated education system that teaches everyone a uniform version of what is intended for them to know. In contrast, Democracies allow people to gravitate toward teachers or masters in schools that are culturally established to teach in systems similar to apprenticeships. The main difference is that a Democracy allows a person to go to a mechanic to learn about mechanical skills. Then, if they choose another related skill set, they can find a teacher for that subject, much as they would go to a specialist in medicine rather than a general practitioner. While both serve a purpose, if a person wants to learn a specific skill, they can learn from a specialist. The number of people who offer their skills to teach others varies by culture. It is not necessarily a legislated requirement. However, some aspects may require legislation, such as the accessibility of schools that the people approve.

One person cannot teach us anything more than what they know. As with Socrates, I know very little about the truth, so aside from this statement, I know only a handful of true things. None in absoluteness. This is why getting a teacher is important, but who should that teacher be? There are individuals with extensive knowledge of specific subjects, making them highly specialized. Those individuals have a passion for a specific area of knowledge, so it would be best to teach it. However, what incentive is there if it is not culturally ingrained that we must pass on our knowledge? It is how we have kept specific knowledge and truths in circulation for millennia by accurately passing them on. While teaching is a skill in itself, those with specialized knowledge must also learn how to effectively convey it to others. Therefore, in a Democratic system, Education is not left up to one person with excessive teaching skills but a lack of substance. Instead, it is given to numerous people who can effectively pass on the knowledge they have acquired.

8. Preserving the system

"All our needs require satisfaction with varying importance over time. Once we have satiated our hunger and thirst, we may look to satisfy other things."

In addition to all these matters, caution should be exercised to prevent niche authorities from emerging to control our Health, Security, Religion, Economics, or Education. These things may occasionally require specialists, but the control of those essential matters by specialists must remain with the people. Otherwise, just as money represents a physical object, such as livestock, grain, or fruit, we end up with specialists representing our health, security, spirituality, economics, and education. None of them represent what we expect or what is expected. At the time of writing, doctors under oligarchic rule and in some societies often act as sales representatives for pharmaceutical companies. They know what you need, and they sell you whatever suits your needs. The pharmacist is the warehouse holder and dispenses it for you. In this way, those who control these groups of Doctors also control how they operate. The knowledge of doctoring the ill is replaced by knowledge of a database containing four essential elements: symptoms, diseases, medicine, and treatment. Several specialist services are selected, which limit the treatment. Doctors in many countries are considered specialized and general practitioners; they refer patients to the appropriate products or services. When it comes to prescriptions for the purchase and dispensing of products, they are limited to what the oligarchs and pharmaceutical companies produce. That is why the freely grown medicinal herbs and foods are not sold to the patients. There is no profit in such a practice. However, times have changed, and some of the products and services produced by pharmaceutical companies and their Oligarch owners make effective and promising medicines. Yet many products were hastily introduced to make a profit at the expense of those who suffer the side effects. That is an example of how an Oligarchy can control a world organization, impact the medical choices available to doctors, and limit their functions.

In the context of economic issues, we entrust those with vaults or banks to hold our earnings or wealth. This occurs when we can't equally guard and protect our resources by ourselves. Treasuries of various sorts are usually entrusted to those who have honor, a sense of loyalty, and integrity, and are trusted. The field of economics has specialists who deal with its various aspects. As a polity becomes more complex and specialization occurs, niches of power arise. These niches, as Plato rightfully explained, are in the best position to steal or cheat. Any person granted some authority can use that authority, so a guard of a vault holding a key is also the best equipped to steal from the very thing they protect. Likewise, in government, any position given or granted will have some authority, and it is therefore important that the extent of that authority be monitored and kept to a minimum. Otherwise, those who guard us can act against us, just as the banker or keeper of money can steal from us, just as the food merchant may sell us watered milk. Just like the security that can arrest us if we speak out against the authority that they serve. In the same way, we are taught everything except how to be free. Similarly, when we give someone our vote to do as they wish with it, as in a republic or similar system, the person who has our vote or trust is also in the best position to use it for their own benefit.

The five essential needs are not all critical survival needs, but are essential to a polity. They elevate our lives. The needs mentioned become essential to maintaining a healthy life within a polity. They are the platform for a lifestyle within a polity or civilization. Health permeates all facets of a polity, including hygiene and sanitary public places. Security ensures the existence of the Polity. Education permeates all facets of a polity, providing the knowledge to maintain democratic institutions and to produce skilled people for the polity's benefit. Economics provides the mechanism of exchange and becomes a core component of the polity. Spirituality and the Psyche offer buoyancy to people's minds and spirits. While many will dance and drink, others will pray and abstain, yet both things affect our psyche.

Religion and ethics are the pathways to the pinnacle of spirituality. When people discover something they enjoy, they tend to repeat it; religion provides a regular cultural expression of ethics and spiritual exercise. In contrast, our most essential survival needs are merely access to food, water, shelter, and the well-being of our psyche. Yet, achieving these things within a large population requires accessible, systemic, and culturally relevant health, security, spirituality, economic, and educational services. That is why many civilizations worldwide leverage our fundamental and essential needs for survival. People work and borrow money for food, water, and shelter. In addition to working, people borrow money to achieve particular standards of health, security, education, and spirituality through the economic systems within their polity. Therefore, the greatest incentive to work and borrow comes from the intentional or systematic restriction of access to those needs mentioned, and potentially to all our needs. It is a system that creates a problem and then offers a solution.

All our needs require satisfaction, which has varying importance over time. Once we have satiated our hunger and thirst, we may look to satisfy other things. Our most essential needs seem to revolve around our Health and Security, our somatic needs. Our need to preserve ourselves is very powerful, which is why Health and Security, before all else, are the most important parts of human thinking. As stated, food, water, and shelter are our most basic and essential survival needs. These affect our somatic well-being, which is encapsulated by the term Health. Survival needs differ from life-sustaining needs but are closely related. Survival needs to exclude mention of air and light because, for the most part, they are taken for granted. Life-sustaining needs are water, air, food, and light. All of these factors have a direct impact on our health. On the other hand, Economics and Education also indirectly affect our health. Spirituality and religion also play a role in somatic, mental, and spiritual health; they become an essential part of life for people who are aware of their spirituality.

Now, some may argue that many need to drink or take substances to damage their health. That is true, but those same people would still need a place to sleep, food, and water. Everyone tries to meet at least these needs. While some people take certain risks and behave in a seemingly destructive manner, it is not normally done with the intent to risk life. What brings people to behave in certain ways beyond what I have described is a complex issue. While our commonality lies in maintaining our mind, body, and psyche, people's priorities diverge due to individual differences in thought and experience. As we stated at the beginning of this philosophy, variations in our wants stem from environmental changes and our individual uniqueness. They can be environmental, educational, or circumstantial choices, and influenced by experience. All these things make a difference in how people perceive particular living standards. Some will have high standards for their Health, while others will have lower ones. Some people will be content with only food, water, and shelter. Others will require access to doctors, hospitals, diets, exercises, medical equipment, and pharmaceuticals. There will always be variations in prioritization across needs, based on many variables.

While it was stated that health and related aspects, such as food, water, and shelter, should be prioritized in our thinking, the variations among humans in their wants must be understood and respected. In some government systems that rely heavily on economic or currency-driven lifestyles, financial issues determine how much a person can afford to meet their basic needs. Money will somewhat govern which products and services a person can afford. That means that, while people are busy working for an income in some systems, they may seem to have prioritized economic concerns over everything else. However, such systems force people to work so they can meet their most basic need: their Health. When money or anything derived from the government system prevents the fulfillment of basic human needs, then the system has failed. Be this shelter, food, security, education, spirituality, fulfillment of the psyche, etc. Additionally, this describes the Oligarchies at the time of writing.

Within every society, there has always been debate on who should provide the Economic infrastructure. How should it be developed, and what kind of system should be devised to ensure economic contentment? That contentment usually arises when a state's economic system allows a person to establish their standard in the areas that interest them. If people enjoy their time by purchasing beverages and drinking them, or by paying to listen to music or other forms of art, then all this can contribute to their psyche's well-being. But this is not true of all systems. This is only true for those who emphasize the importance of currency. It has been a serious and persistent issue for many generations, dating back to Ancient Greece. The only time after the advent of abstract currency to represent produce and services that they became almost cashless was during the Byzantine era of Rome, also known as Christian Rome. Many influences existed back then, including debasement of their coinage and a new Christian outlook. People actually gave others food, water, and shelter as a form of payment. This developed into a very prominent culture of hospitality, or as the Greeks call it, philoxenia (literally, "befriending strangers").

The issue of economics began when coins were being minted, possibly in Ancient Greece. The world had never used the system before, and it encountered problems when it was introduced. Initially, gold and silver were used because people considered the metals rare and precious enough to serve as a viable medium of trade for products and services. But before this system, numerous methods were used, including accounts marked in clay or stone. Poorer people usually bartered a product or service for another. People drew contracts and deals for larger payments in the form of traded products rather than services. For example, contracts could be a simple exchange of cargo, a ship's cargo of Oil for a ship's Cargo of Tin. Trading was an actual barter or fair exchange in those days. One problem with this system is that it can't be taxed. How can a king or government collect chickens, horses, and eggs as tax payments? Well, perhaps it could, but eventually, it would reach a point where they could not store such things. Joseph had told the pharaoh to stock wheat in Egypt because a famine was approaching. Until such time, we can presume that most of the wheat was exchanged and used in various ways. Although some long-lasting grains could and were used for taxation, they were still inconvenient. Rare metals and stones were often accepted as payment, but their value was determined entirely by negotiation, with no established quantifiable method. That is why coinage, as it started in Greece, was unique.

The coin was not sold by weight, as were rare metals and stones. Coins had a particular value to them, imprinted along with the eponymous or monarch's name. The true freedom people had in trading was eliminated. Everything soon began to cost coins. Thus, the coin and its significance began to create a system that enabled some individuals to facilitate large transactions. Coins in those days were extremely valuable, and lesser coins made of less precious metals eventually evolved. This system also began to create several tiers within society for the first time. In the past, government systems, such as those of the Pharaohs of Egypt and the Persian Emperors, typically had a circle of Clergy or priests who also served as doctors. At the same time, the rest of society was enslaved or forced to work. At most, we could distinguish two classes beneath the Monarch. The ability to move out of the working class or enter a higher class was extremely difficult. The differences in wealth and lifestyle were also enormous. However, with the advent of coinage, society began to form more obvious tiers. These were entirely related to the occupations people chose. However, where a farmer in Egypt had all his toil taken, farmers in Greece became considerably wealthier than workers. The five classes of a polity began to evolve, and as a result, the tiers within society began to take shape.

The poor were defined as those possessing the most common products or services. The more common a product or service was, the lower its price. On the other end of the scale, the rarer a product or service is, the more expensive it tends to be. The tiers of society, as seen in the Athenian Democracy, have not changed significantly worldwide. It was a system perhaps related to the Pharaohs of Egypt and the Monarchs of Persia. In Athens, a distinct movement emerged, characterized by the development of five occupational classes. Those who offered the most common product or service were Workers. They offered their bodies for work or used their bodies to provide a service.

The Farmers or Agriculturists formed a tier above the workers, encompassing essentially all forms of food production. Some were fishermen; others tended to farms; others had orchards, livestock, and so on. They may also have had refined products, such as olive oil, pine resin, and leather and wool, in stock. They had slightly rarer and more difficult things to attain, and many could hire workers. The next tier consisted of tradespeople who worked with wood, metal, and clay, offering art or skilled handicrafts such as ceramics, net-making, construction, and building. Because their hand-crafting skills required training and knowledge, their products and services were rarer than those of workers and agriculturists. Therefore, their services and products are more expensive than those of both agriculturists and workers. The next group was the Technical or professional class. The technical class included all those who required a certain extent of education, as opposed to the manual skills of the tradespeople.

The educated technical class produced scribes, teachers, doctors, and a variety of highly educated people. What they provided was rarer to find in society as a service or product, such as medicine. So, these individuals were paid the most out of all those mentioned. Then came the Merchants. Merchants were the type who usually aspired to make or earn coins. They included all forms of large businesses but did not necessarily engage in any form of direct work. Buying and selling were their priority over setting up production plants. However, out of necessity, they occasionally established production areas, set up trading posts, and hired large ships to transport their cargo. So, the Merchant class was not necessarily the same as the Agora salesmen. The Agora was a marketplace for a variety of goods and services. While mainly dominated by people selling food, tradespeople, technical individuals, and farmers were also present, along with the Merchants' stalls.

In his Politics, Aristotle also mentions a fifth class, the soldiers. In his time, soldiers were all male citizens during war, and only young candidates during peace, plus regulars. Regional armies contributed to the central army but were also composed of locals willing to defend their districts or regions. The military was not decentralized in its administration, but it had two tiers of function. One was for any area or district within the realm of the Athenian Democracy, and the other was to serve locally as a defender of local interests. The Soldier class was poorly compensated for their duties, as it was considered part of the discipline to abstain from various luxuries. One group of luxuries the Greeks seemed to accept for soldiers was music, wine, and women. But usually as ordered or permitted. Otherwise, the military was something that trained and disciplined men. It enabled them to function at their best with the least possible supplements and luxury. Endurance, disciplined formations, and other features made military service one of the most serious and goal-oriented experiences. It did not care for the individual but for the formation and the group.

By the end of their military service, most Ancient Greeks favored lives of the least decadence. Given the option to sit on cushions or a log, they would prefer the log. They would take the fur over a stone to sleep on rather than soft bedding. It was the psyche of the Greeks to live with the bare minimum, to be self-sufficient, and to seek or ask little of others. Marcus Aurelius, one of the better leaders of Rome, may have been such a man. In his memoirs, he writes of what we might call a Spartan life—a life without material luxuries—despite his contact with the Greeks of Macedon. But this did not describe everyone.

The soldiers were paid the least of all the classes within a polity. That is why many soldiers also took on varying occupations in Athens. In contrast, the Spartan system placed Soldiers above all other classes. In Sparta, soldiers earned considerable wealth but had a large class of servants. The degree of exploitation of that servant class was considerably high, allowing the elite soldiers to fund their war equipment.

8.1 Economics and a Plutocracy

In those ancient polities, economics, health, education, security, and spirituality had different levels of importance. Throughout our history as human beings, we have had various classes dominating others, forming different forms of government with monarchic, oligarchic, or democratic structures, and creating distinct elements that distinguish them. Economics, controlled by the few, may turn a Democracy towards a plutocratic system, where the wealthiest will influence all aspects of government. They may not be elected or appointed, and they are not part of government, so their leadership is different. Their leadership may exist outside the formal government structure.

The development of power within a class of wealthy individuals or groups can create a Plutocracy. A plutocracy is a form of government in which the rich hold significant power in the state. They have used their wealth to exert political influence over the government. It is not a type of government; it is a variation that can exist in a Democracy, Oligarchy, or Autocracy. The wealthy can use their powers to direct the legislature, judiciary, and enforcement. The consequences are systems aimed at preserving their wealth and prohibiting others from attaining a position in government without their approval or without themselves establishing a level of wealth and power.

Excessive control over a state's economy by the few can create a need for specialists who are given an influential voice in government. The more people listen to them, the more power they gain. It depends on many variables, such as the individuals or groups involved, the economic market conditions, and their ability to manipulate the market in their favor. The Plutocracy can manifest in any government system. Therefore, the only way to handle this scenario is to ensure citizenship and that the systematic operation remains within the power of the people. Losing the people's control to an Oligarchy that is formal or informal equates to the same effect. The system may remain a Democracy, yet an informal variant may emerge. That is why the Ancient Athenians used Ostraca to vote leaders of such Oligarchies into exile. Although this is a possible solution for all the variations mentioned, alternative methods exist to deal with the formation of Oligarchies.

8.2 Health and a Technocracy

Health, controlled by the few, can create a system of science, doctor, and or technology worship. It is a system in which individuals trained and educated in particular areas become the most influential. For instance, the combination of Medicine and Spirituality in some cultures leads to a particular type of cleric. But the cleric is both a doctor and a form of priest. It can also be that science is followed by faith rather than by facts established by the person learning. An Oligarchy can manipulate the need for health services and steer the population towards a technocracy.

Furthermore, an emphasis on science and health can lead to a form of government known as technocracy. That became apparent during the COVID-19 crisis, also termed the COVID-19 pandemic, which was not a pandemic but rather a deliberate manipulation of a virus to sell massive amounts of underdeveloped vaccines, among other reasons. Vaccination rates reached 80-90% in some cities. The manipulation of technocracy by numerous entities, including the World Health Organization, led to the adoption of technology as a means of saving lives. Universal World Health Organization guidelines prompted almost 195 nations to implement a similar-scope vaccination program for their populations. The vaccines were poorly tested and made available to the market prematurely.

While our health is considered one of the most critical needs, it can also be used to harm people. For example, fear of a virus led people to queue for vaccines that were, at best, described as being released prematurely. A technocratic Oligarchy led to the manipulation of governments worldwide. The most affected by the vaccination process were Europe and its colonies and former colonies. Poorer countries, although they were signed on to the same agenda led by the World Health Organization, had less access to vaccines. Disputes over the distribution mechanism led to the most affluent nations receiving the most vaccines. At the time of writing this, the vaccines are claimed to have severe adverse reactions, and the technocratic Oligarchy has yet to be dealt with by the people.

The only way to curb a religion based on technocracy is to establish a counter to it. Usually, this takes the form of a belief in God. It is not always the case; several religions have many Gods, and others have philosophers, kings, etc. It is these alternative Theological models that counter the belief in science alone. Atheists, or those without a philosophical background, tend to gravitate toward other faith systems. As described, Atheism can be a religion of its own, but it often manifests as faith in technology or science. Science, or the scientific method, tends to generate indisputable facts. However, unless a person tests the facts by following the same method, they are taking what has been said in faith. Therefore, faith in science emerges in this way. Eventually, faith in science becomes increasingly abstract. More can be stated in the name of unproven or incorrect science, yet people believe these scientific facts. Ultimately, the people faithfully follow science and the oligarchy that has formed within the science professions.

The only proper way to compensate for such a system is to present each item to the public and establish an expectation that the proof is credible. For example, demonstrating how a formula works is essential when presenting it. When discussing science, it is essential to demonstrate its validity. Similarly, this philosophy draws on observations and general knowledge to confirm that the points made are valid. Without people's critical thinking, technocracies may emerge.

8.3 Education and an Aristocracy

Those few who focus on controlling education may create an intellectual elite. The elite class is the Aristoi (Arete) as described by Aristotle. They can be philosophers, educators, scientists, or other occupations whose premises are based on good, justice, and, to a great extent, ethics. The Aristoi can include anyone from any other societal class, but typically, the glorification of Education creates this Elite group. It is perhaps the only one with the potential to improve everyone within society and, as such, form an Aristoi for a Democratic, Oligarchic, or Monarchic system. Aristoi are needed to establish an Aristocracy. However, unlike previous thought, the aristocrats do not necessarily need to be an oligarchy, a monarchy, or anything related to them. An Aristocratic Democracy is an oxymoron; it describes a system in which the people are all elite, or as close to it as possible. By elite, we mean that they are well-educated, seek and prefer truth over anything else, are fair, good, and have high levels of ethics. That is what we defined as Democracy in the first place: the Aristoi, or elite, being the best people possible operating a government. If it were simply an uneducated mob, it would be called an Ochlocracy. A simple majority vote, regardless of the quality of their decisions, would leave us with a pleistarchy.

As mentioned earlier, education can be manipulated by those given the authority to teach. The truth is not always the primary purpose of some educators who are working or being paid by others. Like any other service or product provider, a teacher or tutor shows more interest and dedication to pleasing the person or people who pay them. There is a bias in teaching, and some governments that pay teachers also give them a syllabus of learning materials that serve the government's purpose.

Oligarchical groups can develop from niche interests in education. As described, the Aristoi first form by attaining and propagating certain knowledge. Then, as the Aristoi develop, two things may happen: Firstly, the Aristoi may influence the current system type, whether it is a Democracy, an Oligarchy, or an Autocracy. Secondly, the Aristoi may gain such power that they hold the State's power. As such, it forms an oligarchy of aristocrats known as an aristocracy.

The Aristoi can provide positive influences to a Democracy through magistrates, Archons, and other notable positions within the system. However, monitoring the number of years served, the group's composition, the election process, and an audit of their functions and the structural authority chain are important. Otherwise, the detrimental influence is that their interests overbear those of others, thereby corrupting the system.

8.4 Spirituality and a Theocracy

Next, we have the issue of Spirituality being controlled by the few. With a system that over-glorifies Spirituality or Religion, we may attain a Theocracy. This system places the spiritual or religious leaders in close communication with those governing. Alternatively, the Spiritual leaders become the government. Religion and politics can become, to some extent, blurred. In human history, only a few instances of a truly Theocratic system exist: the pharaohs of ancient Egypt and the Vatican. Others existed around the world during the Medieval period. The Vatican is a truer Theocratic state than any others we have mentioned because, although it is a Monarchy or Autocracy, the entire government is composed of the Church's clergy.

Spiritual or religious establishments tend to be intolerant or unaccepting of other faiths. Some claim universal acceptance; however, in practice, the governors serve the institution and its preferred interests. There is also the claim that they serve religious or spiritual purposes better, but as mentioned, at the cost of minority groups. Other freedoms unrelated to faith are often directly imposed, such as limiting rights, pluralism, and tolerance.

Respecting spiritual or religious institutions and keeping them separate entities requires a substantial number of people who are either not in support of that faith or do not have the character to assess secular, spiritual, or religious issues fairly. The methods by which these are achieved have not been well documented in our histories. The current models have taken religion and spirituality out of the classrooms, educated people in science, and taken a view of promoting dialogue against such establishments. It has become a systematic war against the pious and their faith to the point where they have weakened the faith in the West so that another Plutocratic Oligarchy can overtake it. The principle learned is that the Theocratic state usually exists as a vassal to a higher Oligarchic structure. Rarely is the Theocratic ruler or oligarchy competent at waging conflicts directly with assailants and hence relies on protection. The ancient Egyptians, in contrast, were well-equipped to wage war and defend their domain. There is no set way to curb or resolve the emerging issue of Theocratic oligarchies. There are numerous variables related to religion, including pious beliefs, opposition, majority faith, minority faith, and environmental factors such as disputes and alliances. Therefore, it is best to avoid Theocratic Oligarchies by respecting each institution — religious and secular states alike — and keeping them culturally separate.

8.5 Security and a Stratocracy

Finally, there is the matter of excessive Security under the control of the few. An Excessive desire or obsession for security can turn into a Stratocracy. That happens when the Military or Police influence the government so much that the line between who governs blurs as other government influences are mentioned. In other words, a Military commander does not necessarily have to be elected or formally take control of the government to possess power over it. Similarly, businessmen, priests, health professionals, and the academic elite can be influential enough to create a system that promotes their ideals through the government they influence, and so can the military.

If people create a state that elevates some Military leaders into Gods or the status of the divinely gifted, then this is not a Theocracy. It is not so much a Theocracy as it is a Stratocracy. The path of perceiving divine nature in humanity can lead to glorifying those humans as Gods or instruments of God. The ultimate position in human understanding has always been God, or Gods to pagans and some others. Giving people glorification—what some call idolization and social status—can lead to placing them at the ultimate helm of Divinity. For example, if the ideal religious role model is a warrior, then this elevates the warrior to divine status. The system that forms this is not a religious system or a Theocracy. It has a Militant nature. Since the ideal is the bringer of death, so too is the ideal person, one who is willing to bring death upon others. This is not establishing a Theocracy, but a Stratocracy, similar to the Spartan way of life. However, unlike Sparta, they did not glorify themselves or anyone among them as Gods. Additionally, the Spartan stratocracy was a vivid example of the military's influence on every aspect of Spartan life.

One of the hardest Oligarchies to remove is a military dictatorship or stratocracy, a state held in the power of the army or military. Stratocracies have existed in almost every polity worldwide at various points in history. From Darius the Great through to Alexander the Great, the Roman Empire, and the Mongolian Empire of Genghis Khan. While other empires existed, the empires mentioned here mostly had a military leader. The functions and structural entities varied considerably from one. Darius was seen as the king of kings; Alexander the Great, the conqueror; Rome, the strategic empire; and Mongolia, the rapidly expanding power of the combined Asian tribes. Each had its own distinct customs and systems of government. However, they all formed an Autocracy and then an Oligarchy at similar points. On the rise, they were Autocratic, although not as applicable in Alexander's case. Then, upon the demise of their leaders, the empire was carried on by the generals who divided it, except for Rome, which retained, between emperors, the strategic unity of its domain. However, the Roman Empire split into East and West Rome. In an extremely brutal synopsis, the stratocracy offered limited rights in all these cases, and where rights existed, they were skewed in favor of the Stratocratic Oligarchs. The only way to prevent such an emergence is to monitor and review the checks and balances within the military. This is done as the Athenians did by rotating military commanders, using sortition where possible, and permitting the ostracising of specific commanders deemed too powerful.

8.6 Other Variations of the State

Plutocracy, aristocracy, technocracy, theocracy, and stratocracy are not all types of government. They are variations of Oligarchic systems. These terms help us identify who may be in charge or have the overall power. The types of government systems always remain the same as described earlier. In other words, all those variations of government can be created in a Democracy, an Oligarchy, and an Autocracy, except the Aristocracy, which is supposed to be the better form of an Oligarchy. These variations can influence all types of government. A democracy with an aristocratic group, such as the Archons, may become large enough to overpower the system, and at that point, the Democracy no longer exists.

In the same way that the issues that we consider important can, in turn, influence the core government, so too can the classes of people within the polity. Each class has a set of particular interests that varies between classes. Those interests can and do influence the Government. That is as much as can be said in general, without providing specific ideas that entirely depend on the type of government and the methods it chooses to govern. In the majority of the world, when writing this philosophy, workers typically felt equal to everyone else. In their view, equality is something they wish for. There are many more workers within any state, so the issue of Equality becomes very important to the workers and those they influence. There are also the Agrarians, who tend to share similar sentiments with the workers. The Agrarians do not want to be paid as little as workers; they want the same as the other classes. But the agriculturists, if they have enough land, can be wealthier than any individual providing a service. Unlike services, produce can yield considerable profits.

There is a blur at the time of writing between classes because underlying all of them is not the purpose of performing a duty, role, or service, but of essentially earning currency. Then, a person pursuing wealth, regardless of their social class or how they acquire it, is eventually a merchant, except for the worker. An economically driven country and a Plutocracy may result in a particular blurring of class structure. Farmers are no longer the same as they were a few generations ago or in many other countries today. Farmers can be employees of Merchants. Large merchants who buy all the farming produce can use all the farming lands. The farmers no longer have to worry about an Agora or a place to sell their produce. However, they are usually offered at much lower prices for larger volumes. Tradesmen, like the technical class, can also become part of a merchant enterprise, as doctors or pharmacists do. In some places, wealth can also buy personal armies and so forth.

So then, with these aspects in mind, it is worth mentioning something more personal to our nature and how we perceive contentment. Discussing these variations in government highlights how overemphasis and control by a few in one area of interest can create a subsystem or peripheral system that influences the government. There are three types of people: those who enjoy giving, those who enjoy receiving, and those who enjoy both. People who enjoy receiving gifts are often those who also appreciate free services and products. Most people like receiving, which raises the question of how much they are content with receiving. On the other side of the scale are those who like to give. They like to give for many reasons. Usually, they prefer to give and, as such, lead lives in a position to give or supply. Then, some feel comfortable with giving and receiving. It is rare to find people willing to do both in equal proportions.

Within a public context, receipt is seen as submissive. Socrates categorized women as those who like to receive, and men as those who like to give. One's mind could probably drift on such a statement. In a sexual context, then, usually, the males give seed to the females. But in a broader cosmopolitan context, both men and women prefer to receive, give, or both. Socrates mentioned this thing within the context of defining the roles of a female and a male. In many cultures, these definitions align with traditional male and female roles. However, determining who prefers to receive, give, or do both is ambiguous due to the diverse nature of different societies. It is safer to accept that, while females tend to prefer receiving and men tend to prefer giving, this is not entirely true. Outside the context of gender roles, the idea that some prefer to receive, give, or do both remains true. Jesus mentions that those who can give and receive are blessed. The context used in that statement is that those who can give as easily as they can take are generally better people for it. Sometimes, people will not receive a gift from a stranger or an enemy. But showing goodness allows a person to receive that gift. Another example may be a miser, someone who refuses to give even a small portion of what they have to those in need. Therefore, equally giving and receiving is more of a blessing than merely giving or receiving alone.

For some people, giving demonstrates a sense of power and domination. At the same time, receiving is often perceived as a sign of submission and weakness. These things occur naturally, and most people are not fully aware of their behavior or how others perceive it. Also, what is given and received varies in importance from person to person. For instance, a guardian of children, such as a mother, may prepare a meal and place it on a table for consumption. To that guardian, the action is one of giving and of high importance, and for those who eat the meal, it is one of receipt and gratitude. If the meal's ingredients were collected, hunted, or purchased by the other partner guardian, then giving them to the cook fulfills the requirement to provide. In this scenario, we see from our humble homes and lives that giving and receiving are done regularly. However, the importance of this giving and taking is not always appreciated. A cook who does not receive a compliment can feel their effort is wasted. A hunter bringing the catch home to see it unprepared or touched would feel that his effort had been wasted. There is a degree of satisfaction in giving and receiving, and both are important to our lives. As with all things, and in particular with humanity, the diversity of what makes us happy and content, recognized and made to feel of some worth, varies. Some people take many things for granted and only recognize diamonds, gold, and precious stones as worthy gifts to give or receive. It is no surprise, then, that humanity's expectations of the government can vary according to these giving or receiving tendencies. Those who prefer to receive would likely prefer a government that gives, and those who prefer to give would likely prefer a government that does not take what they have to give.

So, considering that some people prefer a government that gives, while others prefer one that does not take, very few feel content with a government that both gives and takes. This is especially true if the taxes cause a significant loss of lifestyle. But taxes are important to a state. It is a method for creating a large volume of resources that can be used to carry out projects or tasks that any individual or small group may not be able to accomplish. Tax, as much as people in general despise it, is a necessity. However, the importance and necessity of taxes are established only by the things and projects they are expected to support. If the project, venture, or thing receiving tax funding is of great importance, then ensuring taxes are paid is equally important. To some degree, people feel alienated from the economic models within Autocratic and Oligarchic systems. It is, therefore, difficult for people to determine if the actions justify the degree of taxation and work that depend on those taxes. In a Democracy, there will be a similar effect, especially if the system's economic model is left to a group of specialists to operate. Letting the state's financial matters be handled by professionals hired for the task can pose problems.

Where a state budget or economic plan is prepared in advance of the tax period, the people may vote on the budget or plan. However, if these plans are brought forward for a vote, those who design and budget them may be susceptible to corruption. In paraphrasing Socrates from Plato's Republic, is it not the person who guards the treasury, but also the one in a better position to steal from it? The abuse of power can stem from personal flaws in character and from external influences from individuals or groups. Many other factors can lead to corrupt thoughts and actions by those given not only powers but also unregulated, unmonitored powers. This is why an economic model within a government system also requires careful monitoring. Like all other areas of government, it requires diligence and perseverance on the part of the people who form government.

Inert citizenship can occur in a society where citizens are of little importance beyond being a source of tax revenue and welfare recipients. Active citizenship, in which citizens independently provide welfare infrastructure and through private organizations, represents the kind of people and society that would please the givers. In more oppressive states, the government can tax and collect far more wealth from its citizens, almost as if it were plundering its own people within its borders. Some ancient societies conducted this form of government. Draconian rule and heavy taxation or property confiscation do not leave citizens happy, except for those who get to spend and use the profits. As we described previously, Aristocracies and Oligarchies tend to create groups, committees, and sub-committees. But all these groups are sub-entities to either an oligarchy or an autocracy. So, even if we make one committee responsible for keeping the others free of corruption, there is nothing to ensure that all of them remain free of corruption. These systems have traditionally led to the most corrupt forms of economic handling when raising economic issues. We will elaborate further on the matter, but before we do, let us address the economic systems used in the past and, most importantly, those that have had the most significant influence on the twenty-first century.

9. Communism and Capitalism

"As with communism, capitalism did not offer a program to teach people how to operate and establish a Democratic state."

The two most significant economic ideologies of the 19th and 21st centuries have been Communism and Capitalism. It is, in some ways, ironic that, after almost two thousand years, humanity is still trying to define new ideologies, even as one serious catastrophe after another unfolds, especially when we have had the solution in our hands since approximately 450 BC. Nevertheless, the ideologies of Communism and Capitalism may date this philosophy as they are replaced by something else. However, the development of alternatives, such as Socialism, may combine the two systems, as they have. It is difficult to find a purely communist or capitalist state at the time of writing. However, the two philosophies are almost opposites; as such, everything between these two systems is related to them. Hence, have they been mentioned and will be briefly discussed?

Communism was established to ensure that all people received the same share of the state's wealth; it is a system that its beneficiaries would prefer (Marx & Engels, 1955). Those who wish to give cannot do so in such a system, since they have whatever anyone else has to give. Usually, those who give have substantially more than others. We are speaking of materials. The issue of giving and receiving our time and participation, as well as many other factors, is not typically discussed in the context of economics, but rather in other contexts elsewhere in this text.

Rarely do people give half of what they have. The type that prefers to give usually feels wealthy or in surplus in some way. A teacher may feel wealthy in knowledge, and a merchant may feel wealthy in currency and/or materials. They share or part with a portion of their abundance. In a system with little diversity or difference among people, the givers would be less content.

In Capitalism, the idea was to ensure businesses had broad freedoms. Capitalism could be defined as an economic ideology that favors the wealthy. Alternatively, it has been defined as the economic model that allows trades and industry to be invested in and operated by private undertakings. A myth emerged that capitalism would favor the wealthy, enabling them to spend their fortunes wisely for the benefit of society (Smith, 1976). They would refer to this as the trickle effect. Using a similar example based on our concern for justice, when considering how money should be distributed, Aristotle believed it should be based on merit. As stated earlier, if the wealthy are given money and use it to benefit the workers or society, then it is a valid ideology. It is as valid as giving that money directly to people experiencing poverty, who would most likely spend it and help smaller businesses. Suppose we adopt Aristotle's elitist ideology. In that case, the system is designed to be given to those best positioned to utilize it for the betterment of society. However, the best way to spend it is to give to those who need the most. If many people are hungry, wouldn't they be the ones to spend the currency immediately to get what they need? Indeed, the same Elitist ideology would define the merit of expenditure as going to those in most need. Therefore, serving our call to justice and preserving the old ideologies, it is better to give to people experiencing poverty so that they may satiate their needs than to give surplus to those without immediate need. This is, of course, based on the idea that people receive rather than give and that there are poor people to start with. In a Democratic system, neither of these things could exist. Capitalism is for those who give and receive because some will give their surplus and receive when needed.

Capitalism, as witnessed at the time of writing, has evolved to the point where private industries are taking leading roles in sectors that would normally or historically have been controlled by the government, such as mining and infrastructure. It tends to skew toward accommodating the Plutarchs formed between industry and government arrangements. The government gives its backing to those it wants to succeed. This model has also created a severe disparity between most of the population and the Plutarchs. The disparity, at the time, crippled many financially, rendering them unable to work or earn enough income to survive. In such a system, there is greater variation and a more systematic application of giving, receiving, and both.

In contrast to capitalism, the Communist system, as witnessed, sought to create a communal lifestyle, with the government's sole purpose being to distribute wealth, goods, and services evenly among all citizens. The idea was to take control of the businesses of the elite businesspeople and the very wealthy. By taking control of extensive mining, shipping, telecommunications, and other industries, it was envisioned that the wealth generated by these businesses could be distributed to everyone within the system. Essentially, the idea was not entirely bad. Monks in monasteries live lives similar to those that Communism promised. In fact, the Apostles attempted to establish a communal structure in the Acts of the Apostles. The system had some merit, and the idea was not altogether flawed. However, as noted in other books, such as Democracy and the Oligarchy, the Apostolic commune failed partly because the wealth they shared had an external, dependent source: autocratic rule. The people had whatever they were allowed to have as surplus to share. The limitations came from the Autocrats who ruled at the time. A similar limitation existed for those attempting to implement a communist state.

Regardless of the system used, a typical government department in the 20th century and at the beginning of the 21st century spends approximately 80% of its revenue on administrative costs, and only 20% or less reaches production and worker levels. Private industry can operate with as little as 10% of its budget allocated to administration, with the remaining funds dedicated to production and worker costs. These are general terms because the figures vary depending on the work and the amount of regulation and administrative tasks involved in a particular operation. Not all government departments can be compared with equivalent private operations. It remains consistent that the way they are administered under both economic systems is not altogether different.

9.1 A Critique of Communism

9.1.1 Health

Regarding health, the communist model lacks a policy. Historically, it is an area that receives funding based on the ideology of the Oligarchy that operated the communist state. However, during the 20th and early 21st centuries, it was criticized for receiving minimal expenditure and, as a result, inferior service compared to that found in polities that adopted capitalism.

9.1.2 Security

Security is another area that lacks a policy within a communist model. Historically, a Cold War emerged after World War II. By the Cold War, we mean a conflict characterized by direct military presence, without direct engagement with the opposing forces. The key players were the communist nations, led by the Union of Soviet Socialist Republics (USSR), also known today as Russia, and the capitalist nations, led by the United States of America (USA), abbreviated as America. Security often served to complement Cold War objectives. There was a polarisation of Capitalist and Communist states or nations. Also, there was an escalation of arms development and manufacture. During that time, the communist side competed and often out-produced the Capitalist side with military arms. The quality of the manufactured arms was affected on both sides.

Security under communism employed a military standard of service, and distinguishing between police and the regular army came down to the perks of the communist party. Special arrangements made between the 1960s and 1980s made the police force an attractive career option for young people. In some instances, housing and pay advantages were offered. A more humanized police force enhanced the population's security. Additionally, the Khrushchev Thaw was a period spanning the mid-1950s to the mid-1960s. It involved de-Stalinisation or relaxing military force security issues. It also involved distinguishing the roles of police officers from those of the regular military, among many other aspects.

9.1.3 Spirituality and Religion

Although, for the most part, the communist ideology is an economic model, it tried to replace God with atheism. According to Karl Marx, religion was, for some reason, a deterrent to change. It was seen as the tool that prevented people from accepting the stark reality that they faced. Among many other infamous quotes, he said: "Religion is the impotence of the human mind to deal with occurrences it cannot understand"(Marx & Engels, 1955). Although some people interpret the unknown causes as effects of God, there is little to substantiate the claim. A person who is entirely ignorant of the Christian faith would not be able to understand or see truly how erroneous this passage is. Because throughout the faith, Christ is the truth and the path to God. Religion, especially Christianity, teaches people how to be free and live a life of freedom. It liberates us; hence the term 'saves us'. The historical Christ walked among humans, not above them, not on the back of an army, not in command of them, but with them side by side. Suppose you can see that this itself is the Democratic principle, where Archons are inspired to walk with the people rather than rule over them. In that case, you can also see and understand that religion, particularly Christianity, rallies the people to work for God before all else. Therefore, the communists thought to eliminate faith as it acted against their task of entrapping the people within their system.

Historically, communist systems erroneously forbade the worship of God and instead forced people to worship authority invested in the government. Communist states all resorted to Draconian measures to create their Communist state because people did not want to live in a commune without God or to serve under the boot of some militants trying to change their culture and lives. As such, only Draconian or forceful measures could be used to convert and subdue the vast majority of people under the Communist system. Not all places embracing Communism underwent the same extreme measures, but Russia, where it first started, found the path to Communism a bloody event that stained its history for generations. The ideology of Communism sought to make government more than a superficial system. It attempted to integrate government into every aspect of life within society.

9.1.4 Economics

The integration caused a significant problem when applied to the Merchant class. The number of administrative employees required to operate every large and critical national business increased when government employees were used. In contrast, the same businesses under private administration required far fewer administrative staff. From the onset, it became apparent that the government had to relinquish some areas of industry to a controlled private sector. In addition, internally, an ongoing tradition had emerged of claiming that various KPIs, such as volume quotas, were being met, even when they were not.

Communism aimed to place all production into the hands of the community. The community owns all capital. However, the community had no mechanisms for decision-making or for implementing their ideas. Instead, the Communist Party and its leadership participated in the decision-making process. Additionally, the wealth generated by the state was distributed among the people based on their needs, rather than on their contributions to the work. However, this led to situations in which certain perks and incentives were given to encourage occupations considered necessary.

9.1.5 Administration Efficiency

Communism's fundamental flaw was that it tampered with the five basic classes found in any given society, the Merchants. The merchants include businesspeople, bank owners, and large industrial operators in various industries, such as mining, healthcare, communication systems, fuels, and refining, among others. According to the ideology of the Communist Manifesto, merchants were referred to as the bourgeoisie. Merchants during the Communist era could only become profitable when the government assisted their businesses through contracts, cash deposits, or government partnerships.

This form of ideology was not too different from the way autocratic rulers applied their economic model. In medieval Europe, only a few families had substantial wealth, while the vast majority lived in poverty. The most popular system in Western Europe was feudalism. Feudalism allowed some families to become excessively wealthy, almost as rich as the autocrats who ruled the state. Feudalism was usually achieved by getting favor from the autocrat in power. Be it by relation, honorable actions, or some other matter that could be rewarded with an estate. Estates were typically large areas of land granted to competent and loyal individuals who would assist in defending the greater state and its borders. Only a small portion of Estates were established through gifts. More often, Feudal wars pitted rival families against each other, and much time was spent plundering the competition. Over time, Western Europeans achieved order, a prerequisite for a polity.

These Feudal systems were a system of multiple Autocrats, each with their own army and population, who also served a single-state King or Autocrat who ruled over them. As long as the central King had more wealth, power, and money than the others, they would remain passive and cooperative. The system of communism, as well as autocracy and Oligarchy from that time onwards, tended to create a similar effect or system. We could even go back to the Diadochi of Alexander to revisit a similar symptom of Autocratic rule. But the Diadochi or Alexander's generals were Autocrats of their territory, almost constantly trying to defeat each other. In the case of feudalism, it was a unique situation in which many wealthy individuals, an army, a serf population, and often castles or fortresses defended their mini-states. Yet residing over all these mini kingdoms was a central king.

Concerning Communism in Russia, a similar effect occurred indirectly. The rich, wealthy, and powerful Allies of the Monarch and Church were disposed of. However, this did not significantly impact the wealthy and powerful enemies of the Church and the monarch. It was the Communist Party friends who prospered when Communism emerged.

Some say that the system of Communism failed because those in charge were Greedy. But that is not entirely true. It was not the Communist economic system that invited the Greed. It was the state constitution. I am not saying that the USSR's constitution was particularly flawed. It is almost identical to any other State that established a "representative" government.

As you know, a representative government is one in which a few people are elected to rule on behalf of the majority. It is, in all respects, a form of Oligarchy. Under a Communist Oligarchy, the government's relationship with the people and their new, powerful, wealthy allies created substantial problems. The interface with the people was draconic, heavy-handed, and often brutal to subdue and convert them to the Communist ideology. Trust couldn't be put into the hands of politicians to ensure Communism was brought to life. They needed military leadership with no intention of caving in to foreign or domestic pressure. Thus, Communism, as it manifested into reality, was not the idealistic commune where everyone lived in some utopian receivership of rewards without much merit.

The other interface was between the government and businesses, which the government wanted to utilize to fund its system. Direct redistribution of wealth was possibly beneficial to read on paper, but the men helping the generals and government wanted a particularly bigger slice than what the average person received. This disparity created, like elsewhere, an Oligarchy influenced by Merchants, the wealthiest people within the state.

9.1.6 Market model

The Communist system lacked incentives and motivation. Karl Marx's ideology urged workers to demand the same pay and working conditions as those in other higher-paid occupations. In practice, certain occupations need more incentives to attract people. This was particularly true for occupations that required extensive education and training. In some ways, during the Industrial Revolution, with countless work-related deaths occurring, often off the record, we could see how workers and the working class were not happy at all.

Additionally, the wealthy and the poor had a significant separation in their lifestyles. Just before Karl Marx's ideology, Russia had lost millions to starvation and disease. The Famine of 1891 marked the beginning of a series of famines and diseases that would afflict the Russian people. The poor considered the wealthy to be the cause of their plight and targeted them, as well as the monarchy. Communism can be seen as an attempt to address the problems and side effects of the Industrial Revolution and the runaway Merchant classes that had emerged in Europe for hundreds of years prior. Yet, the supply-and-demand model did not exist in the communist system as it is understood today. The oligarchy and the state always provided supply, and the demand was a constant need for essentials. The state proved it could not sustain all industries, provide a supply, or meet the growing demands in all areas of the state. Decentralization of business and industry began to emerge through politically aligned businesspeople and the Communist Party.

9.1.7 Employment

Within a Communist system, the workers expected commune wages to be on par with those of other workers. Under a Capitalist system, the least educated are deemed the best candidates to exploit the most, and the least educated are exploited the least. It would seem impossible for some Capitalists to comprehend that a lawyer would be theoretically paid the same as a cleaner. But that was the idea behind commune wages. The level of exploitation in Communist workplaces was theoretically eliminated because everyone was accommodated and given a basic wage. For some things, they were given stamps to collect and redeem for items based on their value. Yet, certain professions, such as doctors and lawyers, in reality require monetary incentives to attract top talent. From the onset, the system began creating ways to create an incentive without it being material, such as socioeconomic status. Some would join the Communist Party so that they, too, could attract promotions and clearer career paths. Housing location and subsidy were also other factors used as incentives.

Additionally, where families had held businesses with generations of experience, they eventually came under the control of individuals who knew little to nothing about the products they produced. The inefficiency within the administration of the government-controlled businesses increased. Also, the ability to operate those enterprises at a profitable level began to diminish. These failures led to numerous economic problems that cascaded throughout the communist system.

9.1.8 Education

The communist states did not directly address the education system. Ideologically, it was left to the leading Oligarchy. However, education was given considerable attention. This emphasis on education was especially pronounced during the Cold War era. As addressed elsewhere, it was challenging to provide incentives that motivated students to persevere through difficult subjects. There was little opportunity and incentive to give to the system and the people. Furthermore, in some places, a register showed the number of each occupation required for each subsequent year.

9.2 A Critique of Capitalism

To understand capitalism, you need to understand that everything is an illusion. Just like how the true Oligarchs created a communist pilot state and installed an Oligarchy to look after it like in Russia, the West had an Oligarchy installed to look after each nation considered a part of the West. In saying this, the allegory of the cave should be clear in your mind. People typically understand things only through the illusions they were taught.

9.2.1 Health

Capitalism, like Communism, lacked a direct policy on health. Health in the West was like a system that served the industry. The large pharmaceutical organizations were tied to larger investment bodies and corporations whose purpose was to conceal the identities of the Oligarchs who owned substantial stakes in various business entities. We became aware of it during the COVID-19 years. Where there was no government, only Oligarchs were installed to ensure the people conformed. The people were told that they had representatives, when in fact, they had people allied with the true Oligarchs who had installed them. Yet only a portion of the people could see it this way. The majority had an illusion that they were doing the right thing and that their government was there to help, so they offered their full compliance.

9.2.2 Security

Capitalism does not have a direct policy on security. However, it opened the door to many inventive private industries catering to the war effort. The primary issue with applying capitalism to security was that the so-called private companies relied heavily on government contracts. Since the Oligarchs controlled the wars, they also controlled the sales of technological materials, weapons, and ammunition. In doing so, governments, especially in the USA, controlled which companies would exist by granting contracts. It was decentralized, and mass production of any given item was limited. In communism, they adhered to a single model and mass-produced it effectively; in contrast, places like the USA diversified the models available and their applications. Military standards varied across capitalist countries, as one workshop couldn't produce the same item in large enough quantities without branching out into additional factories.

9.2.3 Spirituality and Religion

Capitalism does not have a direct policy on spirituality and religion. However, religion was given some flexibility in most capitalist nations. The problem, as in the military scenario, was that the religions the Oligarchs wanted were funded. Those without funding were left to recoup costs privately. Some denominations and religions were often more prosperous than others and could perform duties that they otherwise couldn't. However, as stated, all the denominations used 80% of their funds for administrative costs and only 20% for where it was most needed. As described, religions were freer under capitalism because there was no official stance. However, what ended up happening was that there was a massive growth of Atheism. Especially when the leading figureheads of the Catholic and Orthodox faiths, as well as some Imams from Islam, sided with the Oligarchy and their COVID-19 vaccination program. It left people unable to accept the truth; many are hiding from reality, running away, and distancing themselves. However, their Democratic strength relied on participation and on steering, or taking control, of the entities that betrayed them. Hence, a void was created by the Atheists and those who sought to remove themselves from institutional churches but maintain their faith.

9.2.4 Economics

Economically, the system of Capitalism decentralized the economy more so than the Communist states of the 20th and 21st Centuries. As a consequence, it led to substantial product diversity. Still, instead of direct control, the Oligarchs, who were in most cases foreign, would buy shares in public companies and maneuver them through that system.

9.2.5 Administration Efficiency

In communist states, the incentive was the crux of their problems. Defining a similar Achilles tendon for capitalism would be decentralization. Decentralization has enormous benefits, as discussed. However, regulating decentralized entities proved daunting. The government had set up departments to address legislative breaches, but could enforce the law only to a certain extent. The number of trials had reduced even if the number of successful trials had increased.

Additionally, numerous private companies were involved in ordering large quantities of products. This may appear reasonable. However, when identical products are required with the exact specifications of a standard-issue rifle or weapon, there is practical variation in quality from one producer to another.

On the surface, Capitalist states appeared to have a more efficient administration system. They used departmentalized and subdivided operations through delegated authority. Although not entirely different from communism, it merely had a greater number of decentralized operations. Capitalism's impact on the system's efficiency was significantly influenced by the currency circulating and in circulation. Often, this prevents long-term projects from arising because the currency was not a standard or continuously supplied luxury.

In some cases, people were fighting for and stealing bread and milk. While others had luxurious assets and lifestyles, the disparity was enormous. Yet, the ability to administer the system was always prioritized in terms of cost and currency. When choosing a product or service, it often comes down to cost over quality. However, from an optimistic perspective, efficiency was maximized in each private business because it aimed to increase profits.

9.2.6 Market model

The market model within a capitalist system is a complex entity. However, prices are primarily driven by supply and demand rather than government mandates and regulations. The market under a capitalist system placed far too much emphasis on the merchant class and created an Oligarchy of plutocrats across the capitalist world. There were, of course, merchants from communist countries who were equally empowered by their state. Combined, they formed a part of the Oligarchy that influenced and impacted the world.

9.2.7 Employment

Private industry also has a high level of exploitation. The term exploitation can be subjective in use since some people have a low tolerance for being used, while others do not care much. Often, poor individuals become institutionalized by the very system of government to which they belong. The degree of this institutionalism greatly affects how they perceive things. It affects the degree to which others can use a person. However, businesses thrive on hiring individuals with high tolerance. Some people are not as desperate or in absolute need, but are simply willing to follow the commands of their leaders or employers. These people are so institutionalized that they do not for a moment consider an alternative life, let alone attempt to forge one. Businesses can thrive on the backs of the meek, subordinate, and institutionalized. If a business were composed of pioneers, heroes, and individuals who considered themselves equals of the employer, it could not function. This is why many businesses in the past relied on caste systems and slavery to operate. It is in the very nature of business to manipulate and exploit to make a profit. While we have talked about individuals being exploited for profit, the number of things that can be exploited is immeasurable. Additionally, there was no mechanism to regulate or determine what constituted a fair exchange of work for income. The Oligarchs set laws and regulations, but Capitalism isn't a fair system. Therefore, those limits often became archaic before they could be used. Such as the setting of the minimum wage, which, due to inflation, quickly became outdated after its implementation.

Incentives to become employed were encouraged by minimal state debt, low fees and taxes, and other factors that people considered the cost of everyday life. To maintain their lifestyles, they sought work to cover their expenses. However, after World War II, life was more abundant in capitalist states than in the early 21st Century. By the 21st century, employment had declined, positions in the private sector had become scarcer, and only large corporate (oligarchy-owned) enterprises were hiring in significant numbers. All this created a pool of people who were compelled to work but couldn't find work without assistance from a specialized employment agency. The employment agency boom led people to look for work through an agent, because the days when workers would line up outside the place of hire and the first number needed was instantly hired were gone. Gone were the days when they drew lots to determine who would take a position. Instead, the Oligarchy selected the employees through agencies. In the private sector – businesses whose income did not include government funds or contracts – hiring was traditionally done through interviews. The incentive to work was high, but the gratification and satisfaction for the work done were arguable.

9.2.8 Education

Education is not a direct policy in capitalist ideology. However, education was also affected by the capitalist system. Capitalism created a system whereby education was skewed in favor of the wealthy. While public schools operated alongside private schools, the private schools usually offered higher salaries to their teachers and thus attracted better-quality teachers. This led to a situation in which the wealthy could afford a reasonably good education. The elites could hire personal tutors for each subject and, as such, had an even better education. However, the problem with education in public schools was that the students responded to the general apathy of the teachers and the caste they knew they couldn't break free from. Mobility in the 1950s was barely possible for the poor, but by the 21st century, mobility and the ability to move out of poverty were highly restricted. Education worsened over time since World War II. In some parts of the 21st century and around the world, governments have used public funds to subsidize private schools. This enabled children who could not normally afford to attend private schools to do so. Therefore, education has endured declining profit margins, reduced teacher quality, and the implementation of government syllabuses or programs in public and private schools.

As with communism, capitalism did not offer a program to teach people how to operate and establish a Democratic state. In some classes or units, they talked about a version of Democracy that suited the Oligarchs. But none spoke about the truth. The system of Democracy has balances and checks that are integral to the use of sortition over voting. Voting on some matters, such as laws, was important to other parts of the system. However, if done correctly, sortition solves the problem of predictability and its consequences, such as bribery and coercion. Therefore, it was a system that was not taught in schools anywhere in the world. Who would teach an enslaved person how to take off their chains?

9.3 The Left and Right

What we consider right- and left-wing politics at the time of writing this philosophy differs from those used before the 18th century. Right-wing referred to the supporters of the Church, the Monarch, and the Merchants. There was only one type of government in Western Europe and most of the world at that time, an autocracy. The Left-wing philosophy was traditionally opposed to the Church, the Monarchy, Merchants, and the extremely wealthy.

The system of left and right eventually led to pluralism in government, resulting in an outward-facing portrayal of opposing right- and left-wing politics. However, the actual function of the political seats was determined by those who employed the politicians. In communist states, it was those who controlled the communist party. In capitalist states, it was controlled by independent parties. All use the same model to influence, coerce, and force the parties to comply with the Oligarchs' demands. It may seem unlikely to most people that such a system exists or could exist. However, at the time of writing, we are aware that globalist ideas are attempting to unify the world under a global government. Historically, this concept was referred to as the New World Order.

Figure 1.

The New World Order Hierarchy

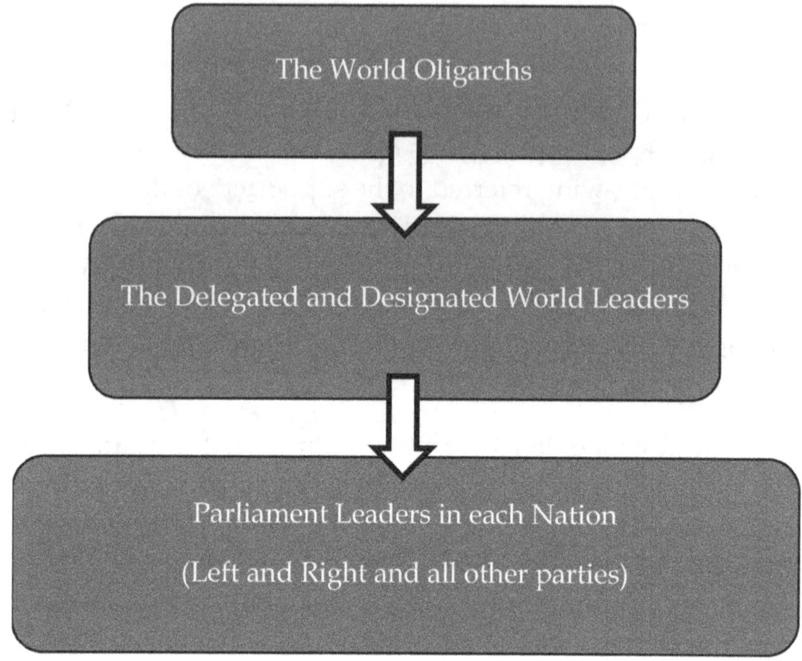

Of course, the illusion of having an opposition and the illusion that there are different parties successfully work to keep people believing that their vote counts. The reality was proven by the COVID years, during which every nation implemented the same agenda in almost the same manner. It is the first time that politics has intruded on our genetic composition and attempted to alter it through the injection of genetic material into our bodies. The method is discussed in other books. Both left- and right-wing parties collaborated to advance a global agenda and subsequently maintained their pluralistic relationship.

9.4 The West and the Classes of Society

We will weave through various histories to highlight the significance of favoring one class of people over another. By class, we mean the five Aristotelian classes of a polity to which the merchants belong. We will define them later, as it is essential to recognize that Merchants, or those involved in business and trade, are often among the wealthiest citizens.

Let us revisit Medieval European estate owners and Barons. The upper class in feudalism held hereditary ownership of estates, as did the central autocrats and their heirs. It took several hundred years of Feudal wars to stabilize Western Europe. In such a vicious cycle of war, the surviving Estate Owners had become extremely wealthy from the booty and plunder. By 1099 AD, most of Europe had become militarised for the Crusades. By 1209 AD, rebellions broke out against King John in England. The most prominent landowners organized these rebellions within their kingdom. Unlike previous rebellions, none of the organizers wanted the King's throne. Nor did any of the rebel Barons have anyone to nominate for the seat of King John. Instead, they feuded with the King not very differently from when they feuded with other Kingdoms and estates. Eventually, the Magna Carta was formed to resolve their ongoing disputes. The Magna Carta, signed in England around 1215 AD, was an attempt by numerous wealthy families and the merchant class to reduce the powers of the autocrat. The Magna Carta reduced the power of monarchs and autocrats, initiating a process that would ultimately lead to the emergence of a merchant revolution. The steps towards a Plutocracy were being laid. Initially, the Magna Carta sought to grant certain liberties, freedoms, and rights to the Barons, their heirs, and those who served them. It also created an Oligarchy of Barons who worked with or manipulated the King. This history of England would not have been at all significant to most of the world had it not been that the periods that followed were, in many ways, reflecting the meaning of this single treaty between the Autocrat and the Barons. The Wealthy could influence the government, but they did not prepare for King John to renege on the agreement's terms.

With the freedom to accumulate assets and wealth and with restrictions on the Autocrat's powers, the Barons initiated a process that led to the development of mercantile trade. Since the Barons and King were essentially now part of a single Oligarchical relationship, there was little gain achieved by plundering or competing with each other. Eyes turned to lands abroad to achieve greater wealth for their families. It is often speculated that metal for coinage was the key driving factor for the initial wave of the Mercantile trade. Due to the successes achieved, many Western European countries were encouraged to adopt this form of decentralized rule and, to an extent, Mercantilist trade policies. Britain, Spain, Germany, and France were the most significant competitors, along with Portugal and the Netherlands. The period of Autocratic Colonization began in the late 1500s and was driven by the mercantilist trade system. Many claim that the search for metals to use in coinage was the incentive for trade, but it soon expanded to include all kinds of metals, gems, and produce.

Mercantilism was an economic system of trade that spanned Europe from the 16th century to the 18th century. The scope in that era was to minimize imports and maximize the national exports, thereby creating a favorable balance between the two. Otherwise, imports from other nations had to be paid for in gold or coins. As stated, these purchases soon included rare gems and objects, too. However, such arrangements were not fundamentally beneficial to monarchs. If we see it from their perspective, they owned the printers that made money or currency. They could order as much of it as they needed. Money was a play toy for an absolute Monarch. However, to an Oligarchy with members without such liberty, the accumulation of currency and wealth was the main ambition of the majority. While some powers were seemingly reduced for the Monarch, they retained the incentive and power to motivate the Oligarchy as they saw fit until much later in history, when they no longer controlled the currency printer.

By the year 1600 AD, the heirs of the original Oligarchy established by the Magna Carta in England and other places with similar arrangements began to call themselves Aristocrats. These "Aristocratic" merchants had set up numerous trade networks backed by government military power. As mentioned earlier, the terms "Aristos" and "Aristocrat" in a philosophical context differ from those used in certain cultures. These so-called "Aristocrats" were far from being Aristocrats as the philosophers defined the term. They were wealthy Merchants and inheritors of their Baron ancestors' wealth. They had various liberties that could be passed on through inheritance and were protected by certain rights to inherit wealth. The Magna Carta ensured inheritance could be passed on to female family members and children. It was not merely their wealth or liberties, but their close relationship with the government, that created vast amounts of disproportionate wealth. While the absolute monarchy reduced its powers, the oligarchy that emerged alongside it became more powerful.

The issue of hereditary wealth became a problem as many families rivaled the state's wealth. It is estimated that three-quarters of the United Kingdom's national wealth is owned by less than 1 per cent of the population. The term "the one per cent" refers to those who comprise the Aristocracy. The Aristocracy found ways to infiltrate positions of power within the parliamentary system, where the Monarch would hold sway. Hence, the House of Lords was established, an Aristocratic judicial chamber that often prioritized self-interest over what was best for the polity. The Aristocracy also influenced the legislature by controlling the funding to various parliamentary parties.

Because these "Aristocratic" systems typically forced a caste or class system on people, those born into a lower status often resented their positions in life. With some freedom, as evident in the Americas, many lower classes found it easy to revolt against the Lords and so-called "Aristocrats". Subordination and the idea of a lower caste did not sit well with many American colonies. The Americans, especially those born into serfdom, did not particularly respect the concept of one man's blood being inferior or superior to another's. Although many revolutions occurred in South America, it wasn't until the French and the American revolutions that the Merchant class became even more privileged. While the old system of hereditary rule was abolished during the Communist and American revolutions, the divide between the extremely wealthy and the poor persisted.

As before, the most prosperous were the wealthiest families who worked closely with the Government to advance what appeared to be common interests. The hereditary roles and titles may have been eliminated, but inherited wealth almost always ensured greater respect and cooperation from the government. Therefore, history shows that the Merchant class and their somewhat skewed significance to the polity began during the Feudal ages. The Merchant class, known to Communists as the Bourgeoisie and to capitalists as businessmen, gradually altered how they maintained power and wealth. With hereditary wealth and status established under the Magna Carta, businesspeople inherited enough wealth to influence those around them, including Autocrats and Oligarchies. Eventually, they secured seats of power within the government system and effectively stood as a union of approximately 600 families alongside the Monarch.

The fact that the government helped the Merchant class through military and naval support to create markets and facilitate trade defined the period between the 16th and 18th centuries. Moving forward, the early 20th century, 1917 saw some additional changes worldwide. When the revolution ousted the Monarchy in Russia, enemies of the Monarch who were also very wealthy began to influence the Government. What happened was that the removal of the monarchy didn't prevent an oligarchy of aristocrats from taking the seats of power and effectively controlling the entire state as a union of aristocrats. The same thing that happened under the Magna Carta. While key figures during and after the 1917 revolution, like Leon Trotsky (exiled in the USA), Vladimir Lenin (exiled in Switzerland), Peter Kropotkin (exiled in Britain), and Joseph Stalin, worked independently, they all had significant blind spots regarding the foreign interests to create an Oligarchy in Russia. The Mensheviks were a socialist faction aiming to achieve a system compatible with international capitalist systems. The Bolsheviks were more concerned with an absolute, almost totalitarian Communist state. It was the first phase of the Menshevik-led revolution in February 1917, which disposed of the monarchy. Later, in October 1917, a second revolution occurred to exile the Menshevik oligarchs from government and to return Lenin and others from exile.

The same thing happened during the French and American revolutions. The Americans may have eliminated King John's direct influence, but they didn't eliminate King John's oligarchy. French businesspeople invested significantly in the USA during its infancy as an independent nation. The French also supplied the revolutionary army with weapons and ammunition. However, even in France, the government was now influenced by businesspeople, merchants, or, as Karl Marx referred to them, the bourgeoisie. To paraphrase, we are referring to places like Greece, where they fought numerous historical wars and battles to achieve freedom. Yet, they never achieved true freedom, aside from a brief period when they established a democratic state. The same can be said of the Americas. While Spanish, Portuguese, French, British, and other colonies rebelled, they did not shake off the yoke that bound them to the Oligarchs who owned their systems.

Through a series of historical events, Western Europe and the countries most influenced by them saw the Merchants become extremely liberated, free, and influential. The only other thing that could be done to benefit the wealthy elite was to devise a way to be above the law. They needed a system that protected them and their assets, while only exposing those that belonged to their business. Achieving that goal required them to form a corporation. In most countries, this form of business, during my time, was protected by corporate legislation. The legislation ensured that the corporation's owners, shareholders, and directors had immunity from any damages or losses they may have caused. They became immune to the laws that otherwise would have applied.

Plutocracies have existed since the days when currency circulated. But it wasn't until Western Europe became a significant entity in the broader world that Plutocracies flourished. They flourished and, in many instances, became more persuasive and powerful than the governments they aimed to control.

If a person or group controls the currency, they also control the incentive to influence people's actions. Through a gradual and systematic process of altering the laws to favor the wealthy, they became the controllers of the government and all within it. Could it have been prevented? Well, Aristotle raised this issue in less detail. But he did highlight that if a state is to be free, it also needs to be self-sufficient. So if the state treasury is empty or has less than what its citizens need, it becomes powerless to employ and operate. In a currency-based system, the state's self-sufficiency is guaranteed by its status as the wealthiest entity within it. Plutocracy began to emerge as merchants gained influence over autocrats and oligarchs. It has taken almost a thousand years to develop this system into what it is in the 21st century.

Capitalism sought to liberate the merchant classes further. It tried to suggest that the whole world is for the spoiling. It was the kind of thinking that had been common in Western Europe under various names, such as 'plunder' and 'booty'. It was that very same ideology that destroyed Athens and Hellenistic Rome. However, it underwent a fresh ideological revival. Merchants were encouraged to enter defenseless countries, establish markets, and initiate trade. Where difficulties arose, the government would assist with the army and navy if necessary. The colonies that the Autocrats established served many purposes for both the Autocrats and the Merchants. Between them, they formed a circle of Oligarchs. Together, the merchants, autocrats, and the state's military could essentially generate significantly greater wealth than ever before.

In places where production and work were being done, it benefited society because workers had jobs. However, in places where production was relocated to other areas, large numbers of people suffered. It is worth noting that England's prisons were filled by the end of the 1700s and remained under such conditions until the mid-1800s. The prisoners were mainly bread thieves or thieves of things vital to sustenance and survival. Many were also war captives, revolutionists, or political prisoners. Financially, during the same period, the autocrat's treasuries and his merchant allies' bank accounts flourished beyond anything Western Europe had seen before. The Wealth of Nations seemed to gain great favor among the wealthy and the class of people who thought themselves superior to others.

Since universities during this period also admitted this type of person, it was no surprise that The Wealth Of Nations became "academically" important to Western European intellectuals. Capitalism became popular because the education system in Western Europe promoted Capitalism. The education system promoted capitalism because academic institutions were primarily filled with children from the elite merchant class. It was inevitable that the education system would promote an ideology that served its interests. Later, when the universities were attended by those they considered the lower caste, the children were still taught Capitalism and, despite being against their benefit, were made to believe that it was better than Communism. For those raised towards the end of the Cold War era, many were conditioned in the West to demonize Communism. But rest assured, the Communists demonized Capitalism with equal passion.

As mentioned earlier, the ideology of Capitalism simply promoted and gave rise to a more powerful merchant class. The most significant blow to the polity was the establishment of Corporations. As mentioned, the pinnacle of Merchant power became a reality only under Capitalism and the development of Corporations. Corporations, as they are referred to in writing, are more than partnerships. They are legal entities established under various laws in capitalist societies. These Corporations, being legal entities, can be fined, closed, or punished, as well as rewarded and traded with. However, the people who operate them and those who own them through a system of shareholdings are immune to the law. It is a very peculiar institution in which a group of Merchants can invest in a corporation's shares. These shares in a corporate company ensure that profits are divided among the highest shareholders, according to the agreement and the number of shares held. This aspect of the corporation is entirely understandable, as shares enable many people to co-own a remarkably successful business. However, the peculiarity arises when the people who own these corporations cannot be taken to court or held accountable by the law for the actions of their companies. If, for example, the company illegally disposes of hazardous waste at the command of the directors and owners, this hazardous waste kills innocent people or children. There was no law to hold those individuals accountable for their actions. This, at the time of writing, has changed slightly; the operatives of companies may be liable, but the passive owners wash their hands of sin.

Instead, the company could be fined a specified amount or be required to undertake specific duties. The development of the corporate business was the pinnacle of capitalist thought. It was also the result of a Merchant class that was given too much freedom, wealth, and power. It was a slow process that began as far back as the Feudal age of Europe. People entered revolutions to try to displace the Merchant class from positions of excessive influence, but they ultimately failed. People tend to direct their revolution and attacks against the ruling party but fail to identify those who influence it. During these revolutions, the merchants simply took different paths behind the scenes.

Therefore, in a democratic society, ensuring that the wealthiest entity is the State is crucial. To ensure that people are content with their government, it must be ensured that no favors or preferential treatment are given to any class within a polity. We have described this scenario in detail elsewhere. It is enough to say that just as we wouldn't want the military to control the government, the workers, the technicians, or the professionals like doctors or priests, then by the same reasoning, neither should the merchants.

9.5 Ownership and the State

During the time of Eastern Rome (Byzantium) and within its borders, feudalism did not exist until it became overrun by the West in 1210 AD. Until that point, the Byzantine monarchs applied Ancient Greek or Roman law and culture. The ancient Greek aspects of the Byzantine Autocracy were present in the form of extended functions of the people. For instance, it was up to each individual to defend their home, city, or village. This was the equivalent of the City Patrol of candidates in the Athenian Democracy. Specifically, it was called the Thematic Army. Unlike Western Europe, Roman rule was more centralized, yet still retained elements of decentralization. A large bureaucracy and administration existed, and the system operated primarily with the support of one state or the imperial military. The same central authority controlled the thematic army. This was different, but not altogether different, from having many people with castles and private armies, as in Western Europe. However, while the people appeared to have some freedom to defend themselves, the extent to which they did so for their own benefit was arguable. The same could be said of any other community obligation under Roman rule.

Even without considering the community obligations, in every other circumstance, some might argue that they shouldn't risk their lives for something they didn’t own. This sentiment may have arisen from the fact that several Eastern Roman emperors, Alexios I Komnenos, Leo III, and his son Constantine V, held that no individual can own land or property, as all land and property belong to the State. It was a pretext for confiscating church assets and diminishing its power. Believe it or not, this was the same idea the Ancient Greeks had. While they may purchase and sell properties and live on them for as long as they like, the land itself cannot be owned by anyone but the state. In other words, the state comprised all the people, and the people had the power to evict, take, or give land.

There are a few instances in history where this principle has been applied to state law or to such rights. In Western European Feudalism, Eastern Rome (Byzantium), Asia, the Islamic Caliphates, and African Aristocrats, aristocrats generally could take land whenever they wanted. The Magna Carta did not essentially stop this. It simply made it impossible for the Autocrat to take the land from the mini-kingdoms, Feudal estates, and the Church. The Magna Carta was a dynamic document, as many versions existed, and its impact on other places and cultures is subject to debate. In the Athenian Democracy and during the period of Hellenistic rule, the story of Pericles being ousted from Athens best illustrates the concept of land ownership and the control of merchants, or the elite and wealthy. Pericles spent a considerable personal fortune to save Athens from the Persians. His success in his military campaigns earned him a reputation throughout Athens and Greece. But when he tried to be re-elected, because he was a wealthy and powerful hero, the people feared he would use his growing personality cult, achievements, power, and wealth to restore the system to an Oligarchy. So they ousted him from Athens and seized a considerable portion of his wealth for the Benefit of the People and the State. The people probably did so with solemn regret since they adored him. That was evident when they later reinstated him during the Peloponnesian Wars, until his natural death due to plague (Thucydides, 1906). The Byzantine emperors, such as Leo III, used the actions against the iconoclasts as an opportunity to seize their wealth and property for the realm, thereby replenishing their coffers and army. In one instance, we see the same basic idea that wealth, property, and assets can be stable and transferable. Under certain circumstances, authority and power are invested in state leaders to manage land, property, and wealth. In part, the state leaders have the authority to take, sell, purchase, or manage land in any other way. They can also freeze, take, or trade a person's or group's wealth.

This aspect of land ownership within a Democracy is a sensitive subject. If an Autocrat has the right to take a person's land and home, as does an Oligarchy, then the reasons for doing so and the laws for doing so are without any influence from the citizens. In the case of a Democracy, the conditions that allow assets to be seized and properties to be managed by the government, by the people, are rights they have a particular right to exercise. However, the conditions for such interventions need to be clear, fair, and just. Crimes of a severe nature that warrant the loss of citizenship are those that the seizure or sale of assets could otherwise punish. However, a home should not be included in establishing a debt settlement. It would be unfair for a family to be forced to be homeless to settle a debt. But if the debt has caused another family to be homeless, then this is where careful judgment and flexible laws would be needed. Losing the contents of a home and all other assets is not the same as losing the shelter over the heads of infants and children.

In some cases, punishing the father or mother should also consider the children and the innocent. Punishing one person and yet affecting many by that punishment is not the purpose of justice. Whether a home is to be broken or not, taken or sold, the law must always stand to unify and support its members.

Also, just as we are guardians of the garden we call Earth, the democratic state has the same duty with all the land within its borders. A Democratic people with an understanding of this will respect that land. While it is in use by another, we can't take it, use it, buy it or sell it. We are not the owners of the land, but its guardians. Suppose a person who once was able to till large amounts of land in his youth is not fit to do so in his elder years. Then, we must question why those lands were being toiled in the first place. The farmer may have believed it was to sell the harvest for profit. But in reality, within a Democracy, the land was not being tilled to fill his pockets with money but to ensure the self-sufficiency of his state and himself through his produce. It is like the issue of Justice raised earlier and the distribution method. Aristotle, in paraphrasing, remarked that the most perfectly crafted flute is best given to the most perfect flute player.

In the same way, land of agricultural importance or other commercial use should not be wasted but used by those most capable of using it. This does not imply gifting land, confiscating it or in any way interfering with the occupant of the land. What is implied is that every person within a Democracy needs to have a common ethic entrenched in law, whereby their work is not for profit or self-gain, but a mutually beneficial action to guarantee the citizens' freedom and the state. A person who can no longer utilize land to produce crops or other products has an onus to sell or transfer the occupancy to another who can. In ancient times, inheritance ensured that the land remained within a family and was passed on to offspring to continue working it.

To some extent, this ensured cumulative wealth, which can corrupt a system by creating tiers of extremely wealthy landowning families. Inheritance, especially excessive wealth, is a regressive ideology that can lead a government system back to feudalism or feudalistic ideologies. However, the poor who pass on their homes and farms to their offspring ensure some level of autonomy for their offspring. Then, inheritance is entirely acceptable in a democratic system. We may be guardians of a property, but while we occupy it, we can pass it on to others as we see fit. Land, homes, and any place that offers shelter are tradeable and can be sold by occupants and those who inherit them. Yet what often happens is that the land is inherited and can no longer be used for its intended purpose. So what good is it for a lawyer or doctor to inherit farmland that slowly reverts to becoming wild land again? What good thing for the state is it for the wealthy to monopolize farming? Yet, most people will only sell land if they feel it can help them financially. If they do not need to sell it, they retain it, and by doing so, they place it out of use. This is why strict laws should govern land and home ownership. In some cities, the extremely wealthy own most of the housing, and the poor can't afford accommodation or purchase homes. That is entirely preventable if the people within a Democratic society respect the guardians or owners of homes up to a certain level. For instance, a family man who owns as many houses as he has children should not be perceived as greedy or someone who has harmed society. Such people have paved the way for their children to have a home to call their own. But suppose upon maturing and becoming a citizen, the offspring or children are not given their homes or prevented from living in them. In that case, the ownership of their parent and its value depreciates ethically.

On occasions within my lifetime, the state has demonstrated its authority and power to remove or purchase a particular business, company, or operation. It can also remove citizens from their homes. That most frequently happens when roads are to be built and are blocked by housing. The citizens may have their homes compensated and paid fairly or otherwise. In some places, governments have simply confiscated land and farms, as in various former colonies. The state's authority or right to own all land appears to be almost universally accepted in principle. This principle or right of the state seems evident in almost all forms of government. It can be a problem when the process is unfair. In some instances, housing or property on valuable land, such as a beachfront or a scenic landscape, may be considered non-tradable. Remember that some states sell their islands, unique mountain or hill landscapes, natural monumental features, and the like. Yet, some extremely influential or wealthy individuals find a way to acquire valuable community land legally. This type of corruption usually occurs in Autocracies and Oligarchies, where the authority to issue titles is not in the hands of the people. Therefore, it allows those who control titles to misuse their power. If a highly wealthy individual were willing to pay authorities a considerable sum, the amount they offered would be divided among the Authority's members. In an Autocracy, the purchase of favor from the Autocrat is much cheaper since only one sum is received by the Autocrat. In an Oligarchy, it can be more expensive or less impactful, since if the amount is to remain the same as that given to the Autocrat, it must then be divided by the number of Oligarchs, or at least by the majority of Oligarchs. Alternatively, if the amount offered to the Autocrat is also provided to the Oligarchs, the cost of such a bribe increases substantially by multiplication. But in a Democracy, it is much more difficult to bribe. When an assembly has 10,000 or more individuals, bribing them, or even the majority of them, is no longer an option. Even if the individual or group offering the bribe had the money, they could not stop the news of such a transaction from being communicated. It would become public quickly, and whatever action was taken could be undone.

Land ownership within a democracy can be far more stable and useful if it is deemed as occupancy. Land occupancy, especially held by the poor or those of reasonable means, requires protection. Homes and family agricultural lands have always been hereditary within most human polities. However, doing so requires caution because hereditary land occupancy does not essentially serve the state if the individuals who inherit the land do not produce from it. It is also concerning how much is inherited from the previous examples detailing the plutocratic and/or feudalistic influences on government.

Some argue that all land should be communal and owned by all the people. This type of society won’t be as productive because communal land means everyone has equal authority to do as they wish on it. Conflicts would arise over how the land was used, what was on the land, and how it was shared. It also has no incentive to work. For example, if people aspire to purchase homes, working towards that goal is important. If people want farmland, the same should apply. But if people own the same farmland, there is a tendency for one to do more work than the other.

In some cases, people will not bother doing any work, thinking someone else is doing their share for them. Communal land ownership is inherently problematic. However, land that is transferable in occupancy is owned by the occupant for the duration of their occupancy, and their ownership is transferable to other occupants. This promotes all the necessary ethics to act as incentives for people. The occupant has security in knowing that their land and investment exist, or are nonexistent, based on the whim of the majority or government. Their tradeable land allows them to sell to those seeking such property and, therefore, satisfy our need to keep agricultural and prime farmland in the possession of those who intend to use it.

At this point, many individuals preach that under a democracy, the poor will strip the rich of their possessions. However, this is not necessarily the case if the people and their laws are fair and just. As noted earlier, with historical justification, land use should not be simply handed down from generation to generation, especially for commercial purposes. Land use for its intended purpose is more important than ownership and the business of land sales. An area rich in essential metals or minerals can't be restricted from use because a particular individual is using that land for recreation or some other peripheral purpose. If the state needs minerals and people are willing to sell or lease the land, then such land should be acquired with compensation to the previous occupant. So, in such cases, the people should have the authority to take or be compensated for the taking of land.

However, this does not imply that such people would strip everyone of certain wealth. However, they may indeed restrict the number of empty residential homes and land they own, since this affects families' housing, a fundamental need for all humans.

9.6 Systemic Economic Classes

Democracy encourages and needs to encourage a difference between the wealthy and the poor because it creates a long-term incentive for individuals to lead productive lives. But remember how the Plutocracies developed on the backs of Aristocrats and Oligarchs. The wealth variation needs to be visible in a polity, but not so much that the difference is unattainable by a substantial number who try to achieve it. By this, I mean that if a person is born into a particular class, such as a worker or a farmer, then nothing should prevent them from transcending into any other class. The vertical mobility within a tiered society based on wealth and capital should be as fluid as possible. Otherwise, we end up with a system where people are born into poverty and remain there, or are born into a particular caste or some form of suppressive system. One of the best ways to limit wealth is not so much through taxes as by limiting corporate structures, making them more like partnerships. In this way, no person or class is above the law. Another approach is to regulate wealth to some degree. For instance, a person who owns many houses within a city also causes problems for those seeking their first home. Such things as housing require regulation. Also, their taxes or obligation portion should increase when people earn a certain amount. In the past, many Autocrats limited competition for their thrones by imposing wealth taxes. Irrespective of how much a person earned as profit, the simple matter of owning a specified amount of assets incurred an unforgiving tax. Many methods like these can be used to ensure that those with the most wealth do not become so wealthy as to subvert the very cause of government or Democracy. However, regulation contradicts the underlying ethos of freedom and liberty. It also conflicts with our moral and ethical obligations to our fellow citizens. Why take another person's opportunity to live in a shelter when that resource is limited? This then becomes a dilemma that the polity must somehow resolve.

Another way of looking at the situation is to allow those who wish to express their greed or sincere needs for more housing. But a Greed that causes harm needs to be tempered. While Autocrats were quick to seize the assets and wealth of their rivals in an attempt to cripple their ability to raise an army, there were instances where they did so for the "Greater Good". The subduing of a particular violent minority often led to the seizure of property and wealth, as seen in the eventual defeat of the Iconoclasts in Constantinople and their subsequent punishment. These seizures and confiscations were often given as gifts to those who benefited the Autocrat and his treasury the most. While most of us acknowledge that greed is not a wanted ethic, we would not want every greedy person punished.

In the same way, we cannot punish every Gluten that has a greed for food. We cannot go and punish the promiscuous who have a greed for bodily pleasures either. Well, not until that greed causes harm that requires careful judgment.

In a fair society, variation of wealth is tolerable, but certain levels of Greed and the actions that can proceed from the greedy may not be fair. Immense disparity has often led to the poor despising the wealthy, and the wealthy despising the poor. However, logical and fair people would not judge an individual's value, ethics, or character by their wealth or lack thereof. It is fair to say that a logical person would not harbor hatred towards the wealthy. They may, however, despise the methods that some use to become wealthy. A logically wealthy individual would not hate all the poor, but may despise the methods some use to try to become wealthy. It is the process of acquiring wealth and utilizing that wealth that has a far greater impact on society. Suppose wealth is used purely to create more wealth. In that case, it can be as catastrophic to society as if the money were being used decadently or purely for the recreation and satisfaction of one individual or group.

We highlighted previously that Communism may have seemed like a reasonably fair system. However, it did not grant freedom to the merchant class or to the greedy and affluent. Historically, the result was that the vast majority of citizens became impoverished. The impact of poverty was a direct repercussion of restricting trade, merchants, and industry. It was an extreme ideology, and in the process of trying to make it work, it led to considerable damage, cost, and loss of lives.

Capitalism, often seen as its opposing ideology, did not offer any solution to the problems faced by Communism. It was the source of many of its problems. Under capitalism, the merchant class, which encompassed all businesses other than tradespeople and technical services, was given too much freedom. The business or merchant class influenced the media, schooling, knowledge, and all facets of life. They could afford to advertise and change people's ideas, and to invest in authors, actors, filmmakers, politicians, and the government. The wealthy merchant class could also take extreme actions with little risk of punishment, as international law recognized corporations as legal entities. The only thing they could not do was govern or control the state directly by law. However, if a system uses a numismatic (currency-based) incentive, the person or group that controls the incentive also controls the system. That incentive within capitalism was money or nomisma (currency). Currency control is why the merchant class persuaded governments to mine foreign nations' resources by invading them using the state's Army. Capitalism is far more seductive and gentler than Communism. For instance, the worst of evil, according to the Christian Bible, known as Satan, tried to tempt Christ in the desert. He offered him wealth and great things, but Christ told him to be gone — metaphorically, to stand behind him. Capitalism exploits the temptations that many people are weak. There is a product to suit your weakness in a Capitalist society. There are even some weaknesses shared by the vast majority, and a product or service is available for those as well. While Adam Smith possibly thought he was onto something with his Wealth of Nations, he was as flawed in his reasoning as Karl Marx. Both tamper with the merchant class and have the exact opposite problems. Communism results in problems related to a restricted merchant class, while capitalism gives rise to problems related to granting too much freedom, influence, and power to the Merchant class.

In every society, the tradesmen, soldiers, workers, merchants, and farmers need to be balanced. No power or authority should be given to any class over another. This brings to mind the idea of corporations that take people's money in the form of shares and use it to generate profits for those in power. At the time I am writing this philosophy, many countries allow a group of people to invest together in a merchant business. The number of shares that each member has determines their profits. However, in reality, small shareholders often receive little or no profit; instead, the profits are divided among those holding the majority of shares. These economic entities, known as Corporations or Shareholder-Owned businesses, are given a status equal to, or perhaps higher than, that of a citizen. This means that a group of businessmen or merchants can have their business referred to by a legitimate name, and all responsibilities and onuses otherwise placed on an individual or individuals are now placed on the company or business. You judge or find the directors or those who operate such a business liable for their decisions. Instead, the company is liable only for a select number of matters. If the decisions of the Directors have a wider impact on society, their assets and wealth are safely hidden from the courts, whereas the business's assets and wealth are exposed to the court's ruling. When the merchant class reaches this level of freedom and power, they may even knowingly sell poison to infants, and yet their personal assets remain intact. A case similar to this one, which I described earlier, involved children affected by illegally disposed materials, and the company attempted to conceal its involvement. Nothing happened to the people who organized the events, yet children died because of their decisions. Obviously, a fundamental flaw in the philosophy drives such nations and governments. Another example is one known to many; tobacco has for many generations been sold to people knowing very well its addictive properties. Over the years, governments using a capitalist system have been making numerous laws to try to stop the exploitation of people. Yet the companies continue to sell the products, and the deaths and illnesses that arise do not impose any threat to those involved with such a business. Perhaps this is a historical note about the early part of the twenty-first century, and that things will change in human systems in the future. The time of legislators in a capitalist society is often overburdened by the need to cover, legitimize, punish, control, and ban the conduct of the merchant class. Unions of workers and socialist ideologists try perpetually to counter the Capitalist approach. Ironically, within Communist Russia, it was not so much protests but a conscious decision to accept the failure of the state and move on to a compromised Socialist ideology instead. The socialist systems that exist today are a combination of welfare states and market freedoms. The extremely wealthy often receive welfare in the form of negotiations, contracts, and other deals with the governing body. The upper middle classes, who possess considerable wealth and property, are often able to afford investing in government projects, such as "alternative energy" schemes, which are popular worldwide at this time. These buy-ins offer them a cash flow from the government treasury to their bank accounts. These schemes can manifest in many ways. Schemes of this nature may include promoting the growth of certain plants, vegetables, or fruits. Each farmer may be given welfare payments or the plants themselves. In the case of the "alternative energy scheme," many people are given cash to put their energy produced into a shared community grid. Then, the poor receive the least within a socialist state. They usually receive payments while unemployed, as well as being single mothers, widows, etc. When most people think of welfare payments, they often imagine the poor receiving a pension. However, in reality, a Socialist system distributes cash in various ways. The entire educational and medical professions within these societies are entirely dependent on massive volumes of currency being invested in them. They are among the most significant recipients of welfare. What we consider as welfare or socialist payments should be restricted to any payments to anyone except those who render a service to the public through employment by the state. In other words, government workers are not receiving welfare payments. However, a grey area exists in how the state implements certain schemes and contracted services. In any case, aside from the potential corruption of favoring one person, group, or business over another, there is the underlying issue of whether the government should distribute any funds to non-employees at all. Unlike the hiring of workers, soldiers, or technicians, the money injected into merchant and trade industries/or various profiteering projects raises the issue that the decision to fund such operations is often considered illegitimate by the populace.

A compromise between Capitalism and Communism has led to the rise of Socialist States, also known as Welfare States. When such ideologies exist within a Democratic institution, they result in the investment the people thought worthy. If the majority felt a new hospital or more doctors were needed, they would vote to achieve it. In ancient Athens, we know that the people wanted more people to attend the church (democratic assembly), so Pericles paid everyone a sum from the State treasury for attending. The amount was almost equal to a basic wage. While the extremely rich would find attending beneficial since they had the time and could only benefit if their proposals were voted for, the poor often worked hard and had little incentive to attend. A payment considered an incentive was paid as a wage to people during the time they attended the assembly and any other duty, including jury duty. It could be seen from a distance as some form of Welfare State. However, the welfare state differs from the payments for services rendered as part of the democratic system. Even if the Jury and those at the assembly were not direct employees, they served a purpose directly related to the perpetuation of the Democratic system. Pericles and the assembly deemed paying for rendered services honorable. That was perhaps the only significant form of payment received by citizens. It was perhaps seen as a payment to do their job of operating their government.

In Autocratic and Oligarchic systems, the main problems arise from how and why payments are made. Paying a person to be an Autocrat or Oligarch member could probably be argued in the same way we did for Democracy, that the payment could ensure the continuation or perpetuation of the system. In a Democratic system, any random person attending is given payment for their attendance. However, in autocratic and oligarchic systems, individuals are not typically randomly selected. Although they could be, the vast majority of human history tells otherwise. The Autocratic and Oligarchic systems can also benefit more from a Socialist system than from a Democratic one. In a democratic system, people will want to allocate their collective resources to things they deem important. That is not the case with other systems, since autocratic or oligarchic systems, even in a hybrid form such as a Constitutional Monarchy, will inevitably spend money according to the decisions of a minority or an individual.

Additionally, Socialist systems can create a degree of complacency among the impoverished. By providing them with a certain degree of financial support that the government can recoup through taxes, rent, accommodation costs, food, or other means, the poor will perceive themselves as being able to survive. People experiencing poverty or those typically happy with little are the easiest to convince and keep complacent. But without such social payments, chaos or anarchy may often arise. Very rarely do the poor successfully revolt against a regime or an unfavorable government. They would also need the support of the median financial earners, who, again, are complacent with their incomes. This means that, between the poor and median earners, the substantial majority can be pacified by welfare payments, family or tax-class bonuses, and similar welfare-based incentives.

Where is the compromise regarding Socialism, Communism, and Capitalism? It is possible that a Spiritual or God-fearing Democracy could solve a substantial portion of the problems that those ideas create. An Autocracy and Oligarchy would not be able to provide a solution since those are the systems that established the Socialist, Communist, and Capitalist systems. In contrast, Democracy ensures that justice is done in how State money is spent. In all other government-type instances, a minority or an individual decides where the money is spent and how. I also mentioned that Spiritual or God-fearing people would be better, because traditionally, the role of welfare and looking after each other fell within the realm of our personal beliefs and ethics. These ethics were often organized through the formal church. Without a church of common belief, it is very difficult to have a functioning democracy. In the hands of atheists or secularists, a democracy can become dysfunctional very quickly. This is not an effort to blame the secularist or atheist, but to highlight that the absence of a common belief unbinds such people from common ethics to each other. Additionally, the belief is that nothing can be replaced by something if it is to be functional and have a purpose; otherwise, issues of nihilism arise. Therefore, without a common belief, the details of what each person believes are entirely random in nature. I am not saying that an atheist or secularist cannot be of an ethical nature. I am saying that the term 'ethic' will be defined differently, depending on the ability of such people. Variations of this nature can render a democracy dysfunctional. This is why the populations of many nations or states are usually vastly dominated by a particular faith. In some countries, a growing number of atheists creates dysfunctional systems. I refer to the simple fact that if we all define our ethics and what we consider important individually, they will vary drastically. Each person will base their deductions, judgment, and all things on an entirely different set of principles than their neighbors. This problem had arisen in a few of the autocratic colonies. Initially, their ethnic diversity was mixed. Superficially, the various groups had their own language and customs. But the majority would speak a common language. They also had a common faith. The years that followed saw an increase in the diversity of the colonies as immigrants from diverse cultures arrived. Along with an increase in language diversity came a diversity of religions. Some of them were, in fact, polemic. This caused problems between the colonists and immigrants on several occasions. Because the majority of these colonies operated under an Oligarchy, the people of the city or polity were forced to accept the individuals of the new faith. Soon after their arrival, merchants were required to adhere to the new religion's dietary mandates and prepare food in specific ways. At the same time, the new arrivals attempted to form political parties to assume control of the government. Being a minority, the Oligarchy seemed an easy target since only a few people needed replacing. These events, or similar occurrences, take place in many places for various reasons. But religion is one of them. While the majority might accept other religions and allow them to practice, it is a different matter entirely whether the majority should accept the religion and customs of the minority. In an Autocratic or Oligarchic system, the minority may even be the leaders, not the populace. In a Democracy, it could be any minor group of people with common beliefs. It is important to consider that while we can accept that even Atheists can have ethics, even differing faiths can lead to the same problems as having an atheist faith. It is the diversity of faith that is the problem within a Democracy. Within an Autocracy or Oligarchy, provided the military power to protect those positions is maintained, the autocracy and oligarchy can stipulate which faith people will believe in. Many Secular nations have done this by introducing various laws to protect Secular ideals. But these Secular ideals have translated into an Atheist society. It is a well-known characteristic of people to follow what is bigger and better than themselves. People often follow authority without questioning it. The same happened when Constantine declared Christianity the official faith of the Byzantine (Roman) Empire. The same can be said of Mohammed's creation of the Islamic Empire. People growing up in those government systems were essentially forced into a particular custom or culture. They were expected to follow a set of ethics and rules based on their respective religions. However, if the government lacks a common ethical framework and presents itself as an Atheist or Secular entity, the effect trickles down through society. Eventually, the society becomes Atheist or Secular. The movement away from religion is why even in places where the government is considered Secular, the same governments invest heavily in church building. The Russians, to the north of the Balkans and Greece, have started to restore pre-Communist Russia. The government spends heavily to restore the common faith among people. Further back in history, we know that many national leaders have defended or tried to defend their faith against change. Even the pagans did so. All this talk of religion is simply to identify that having a common faith also establishes a common platform in which all citizens can participate with equal value. Yet all these approaches do not address the mitigation of the pious when a secular state is in operation. Among the systems available, Democracy is the most susceptible to issues of diversity, since everyone needs to vote together. What those people believe will also impact their vote. The least affected by diversity is an Autocracy and Oligarchy since the vote or opinion of any minority or even the majority does not necessarily become implemented.

The issue of Socialism, Capitalism, and Communism is redundant within a Democracy, as these systems ideologically construct a purpose for the Merchant class that contradicts the Democratic principle that all classes are equal. These economic models can only exist within the context of an autocratic or oligarchic system. Elements of socialism may arise within a Democracy when the people choose to implement them, but this does not imply that the system has a socialist ideology. The economic model of a Democracy differs from those of Socialism, Capitalism, and Communism. For a Democracy to be stable, all five classes of a polity need to balance. A particular class can't be hampered or favored because each is equally important as the other. We derive this importance from Aristotle's account of the Athenian constitution. If merchants prosper, they can only do so without compromising the State and the other classes. There is an obligation on merchants and all classes to abide by the same rules as the other classes. These rules, according to the Ancient Athenian democracy, ensured the self-sufficiency of the state and its people. Self-sufficiency implies that when merchants import more than they export or when production is taken away locally and implemented elsewhere, this will affect the worker population. If imported foods and beverages flood the local market, this compromises the state's self-sufficiency again. The idea of self-sufficiency should never be taken to an extreme. Some people perceive this as an iron curtain that isolates the polity from others. But this is not the purpose of being self-sufficient. The purpose of establishing a high degree of self-sufficiency is to ensure the freedom of the people and the state. Suppose a State becomes reliant on imports or allows foreign merchants to exploit it; that State is no longer free. It is similar in context to the individual who must work instead of having a choice to work. When a person works, and the option to work or not to work no longer exists, then the individual is enslaved.

In the 20th and 21st centuries, self-enslavement has replaced the previous race and caste method of slavery. During the Industrial Revolution and the Mercantile system, people were born into a specific working class and remained there for their entire lives. Self-enslavement has developed over time, but focuses on taking away the ability for people to live, and yet offering it to them by enslaving them. For example, raising the price of a home to a level where it becomes unaffordable, and then loaning the money for it. Usually, the more people earn as a wage or income, the less they feel enslaved. If I were to tell people in my time that they were slaves, most would ridicule me. The idea of slavery has always brought images of chains and whips. But the modern version of it is far more subtle because, by nature, Capitalism is like that. Business people don't want a fight; they don't want direct conflict. They want money. The cost of the Greed of the few translates into the cost of the people's freedom. Many people think they are free while they have an income. Only the elderly and the youth can truly see the impact of a moneyless life within a capitalistic society. The pensioners or those impoverished may have worked all their lives but have nothing to show for it by the time they enter their final years. The world around them starts to change as the money they took for granted and the freedom they thought they had are suddenly restricted, leaving them unable to even walk out the door. I say this because when the standard of living is designed for people to commute by expensive means of transport, the design of cities means people need to walk kilometers to find a place to buy essential items. In previous generations, commercial areas were designated so that citizens could walk around them. Their proximity was very close so that even the elderly could reach these commercial zones.

By design, every aspect of a capitalist society keeps people alive solely for the sake of taxes and money, nothing more. People can't be free if they have a home loan, a mortgage or pay rent for shelter. People who have such high debts will work without much choice since they have been deprived intentionally of their own right to be sheltered. Despite the abundance of land and inexpensive materials, restrictions, laws, and every facet of the system ensure that housing remains unaffordable without incurring serious debt. This is the nature of capitalism, which works with autocracies and oligarchies. To offset the significant cost to human freedom, Socialist governments have simply set up a similar arrangement with the merchants and the people. The distinguishing difference is that the proportional benefit of the relationship is significantly less and not always in favor of the citizens. People are essentially appeased, pacified, and kept sedated through a partnership with the Government.

People must realize that setting up such a complex system requires autocrats and oligarchs to give merchants the freedom to devise mechanisms for entrapment. That freedom we described in historical context was a long process of events, many of which I have omitted, that culminated in the emergence of Capitalist systems. However, Socialism, which aimed to pacify the growing resentment of the ongoing Capitalist ideology and the runaway Merchant class, has begun to fail. Socialism, as an evolution from Communism, is not very different from that evolved from Capitalism. Business and government work together in a manner that facilitates each other. In these societies, a small minority has time for recreation or other activities. Most people entrapped in this manner work for many years and enjoy little of their lives.

Those with money may feel for a moment free or free enough to turn a blind eye to others. A system that requires everyone to work only needs to employ half the eligible population to ensure that at least half feel content; therefore, this is enough to stabilize the state. If only a small portion of the populace had money in a system that made it mandatory or impossible to live without it, the populace would become unstable. Approximately two-thirds of a given population are unable to work, namely the elderly, the youth, and the impaired. Of the approximately one-third who can work, only half need to earn money through work. If that is achieved, the rest of the people considered unemployed would see a chance of employment. As employment rises above 50%, the state's stability also increases because the number of people feeling content rises. Overall, people volunteered to be slaves, much like many volunteered in ancient Roman times to fight as gladiators to pay off debts or for status or other reasons. Few people in the world follow a dream or aspire to be the best at what they do. Instead, they try their best to make money. That in itself is an ethical corruption found in almost every place where currency is used.

As mentioned earlier, a democratic system does not function in that manner at all. A Democratic system ensures the opportunity for each person's freedom. Also, the people may have duties to the state, but the state also serves them. While currency and the economy are important, certain requirements, such as accommodation and lifestyle, are not compromised, since the people operate the government. A wise and ethically good person would not be able to implement previous economic models. They would need to adopt a system of self-sufficiency to ensure that each citizen's freedom is protected as much as the state's. There will be times when certain facilities, services, and products will need to be shared, but it will be the people who decide how to do so and on what terms. Freedom cannot be compromised in a Democracy without corrupting it, and once corruption starts, it infests like rot and consumes the entire system. This is why freedom is the key not only to how merchants operate but also to how workers, technicians, tradespeople, farmers, and soldiers live their lives.

The issues of economic modeling have received sufficient time and attention. The next step is to consider the various reasons why many people around the world dislike their governments. To prepare for this component, I have read numerous news articles and constitutions. Also, I talked with many people from around the world. The purpose of this component is to highlight common issues that people often attribute to the government. I have already addressed the economic models, so arguments regarding the type of economy won't be mentioned. But in other areas, such as asking why I should pay taxes or why they have the power to conscript, Many other similar questions will be addressed.

Before we proceed with these issues, we should address one more thing that has been left entirely unmentioned until now. You may have noticed the avoidance of words like 'nation,' 'empire,' and similar terms that refer to a country, state, or polity. Instead, we have used the term State. State implies a polity. A Polity can be a city-state, but it can also refer to an empire and a nation. For the most part, polity in this philosophy refers to a city-state, unless otherwise specified. It is important to raise awareness because many problems arise as government size and geographic space increase. Those issues are considered, but not specifically of interest beyond the city-state model.

Some would argue that the size of government does not necessarily imply any greater issues than those of a small one. Within a very large government, the ability to be maneuverable diminishes. It becomes bureaucratic, weighing down processes and procedures. It also becomes increasingly impossible to sustain without great cost. A lean government, as is often idealized by contemporary right-wing individuals, consists of a military, a tax office, and basic community services such as roads. This is all that such people hope the government will become involved with. These individuals are often extremely unhappy when the government becomes involved in areas such as health, education, and security. The extreme left wants the government to provide every conceivable service. The leftists like the government becoming involved with hospitals, health, education, police, military, taxation, park and recreation establishments, etc. Without prepaid or free services, the leftists believe the government is not doing well. Now, I use the terms' right wing' and 'left wing' loosely. These terms may be used today and have been used in the past, but they mean very different things between generations. It is probably better to say that there are two types of ideologies, both with large numbers of supporters. One type is those who feel safe and secure when the government becomes involved with their lives. Some want the government to have absolutely minimal impact on their lives. The degree of Government involvement in everyday life increases as government power grows. Departments within a large government also tend to seek ways to ensure, attain, or perpetuate revenues. Revenue secures workers and their jobs within the department. The methods used to attain those revenues have often left people displeased with the government. Within a democratic polity, the government's involvement in people's lives is minimal, aside from upholding the laws of the people. It is a lightweight government with only one tier. It does not have a bureaucratic hierarchy by design. Also, a Democracy, if operated manually—which is the preferred method—cannot be conducted when the population is spread over large areas. The number of diverse ideas, ethics, religions, and languages increases as the number of people or cities increases. As the population increases, the size of the democratic assembly also increases. So, democracy is typically limited to a single city. Some people think an Assembly needs to be a singular entity that all citizens are expected to attend. However, a network of assemblies could be used to debate and take votes. In ancient Greece, torches on towers were used to pass on information. The system used a common numbered agenda or set of commands. The towers would use torches to identify the item on the agenda and give it a value or vote. Other systems used water and flags or torches, in which a valve was released upon lifting a particular flag or torch, and shut when another torch or flag was raised. The water level was measured, and this was the item on the agenda. Using a system like this in modern times could link an entire city and pass the vote from each suburb to the next until all votes were collected. In other words, the myth that Democracy cannot be practiced in a large city is just that— a myth. The reality is that Democracy can count votes using any number of manual methods. The key to that process is decentralizing the Assembly. But despite this aspect of Democracy, the increase in government size works against the Democratic quality. When I mention 'government,' we must consider that it refers to the professional people performing the clerical and other duties necessary for the government to function. This body of people in a Democracy is not individuals in power or who control the State in any way. But in Autocracies and Oligarchies, the government usually refers to those who govern and their respective departments. The Democracy, however, can no longer be called a Democracy if its body of professional servants exceeds it in power. This is why Democracies tend to favor lean government agencies with minimal services and little influence on people's lives. At the same time, the system requires citizens to demonstrate full participation. Large government agencies, such as those implemented by Autocrats and Oligarchies, are mainly used to retain order. Empires usually resort to this form of large government to control the people. The multiple tiers of a Constitutional Monarchy were developed to facilitate the ruling of other nations and are an empirical form of Government. As the government grows, individual rights diminish considerably. This is evident in the historical record of Athens when it formed the Delian League and demanded tribute from other cities. As the number of cities increased, the nature of Athenian Democracy quickly reverted to an Oligarchic form. While the people in Athens may have felt little had changed, the circumstances abroad defined the situation. The Athenians began to use League equipment and Ships for their own interests, and they received tributes from other cities. This essentially made the Athenians masters of other cities. Inadvertently, they became an Oligarchy over other cities. One city or population controlling others was in itself an Oligarchy. By 404 BC, the league was abolished, and the Democracy was restored. But to do this, a raging war with Sparta erupted. Many would argue that the Persians influenced the war to diminish Athenian influence in Anatolia. Another example is that of the rise of the Roman Empire. The city of Rome was formed by an Oligarchy of Latins who conspired to conquer the neighboring Greek cities in Italia (modern-day Italy). The same oligarchy evolved into a dictatorship and then an autocracy, assuming various titles, such as Caesar, Basileus, and Monarch. The ironic thing about Rome as an empire is that while it conquered the Greeks, it was the Greeks who had won. It seems that, since the common language of the Roman Empire became Greek, so did its culture. Despite these aspects, Rome became a place with little to offer in terms of democracy. For the most part, the Roman polity became a sprawl of subjugated cities. As sprawl spread across Italy, the government swiftly shifted to an Autocracy. These examples demonstrate that as the population increases and the number of cities expands, or the area governed by a Democratic government increases, so does the likelihood of Oligarchic rule emerging.

In addition to what has already been mentioned, if a particular autocrat or oligarchy controls a government, then the size of their government determines the difficulty of replacing them through revolt or legal means. Many people, with respect to this, feel that a reasonably sized government is on the smaller end of the scale rather than the larger one because controlling a smaller oligarchic government through the people's voice is easier to achieve. Concerning a Democracy, the size of government is desirably small, as we mentioned earlier, because the governors are the people, and the government is the servants that administer the system. Having a large government or bureaucracy (phonetically, "boule" or "voulis") in a Democracy can be problematic, as it may give rise to Oligarchic operations.

So far, I have mentioned most of the issues that affect my society and those of the recent past. However, it is perhaps important to highlight some philosophical issues, such as whether people need a government.

People do not need a government in the formal sense if there is another mechanism to establish, maintain, and perpetuate order. If people develop a system that can maintain order without establishing a formal government, it would be a system of anarchy. As I mentioned, Anarchy does not necessarily invite chaos, but it almost always does. Within that chaos—or at least disorganization—there is a certain degree of weakness. People without organization can't compete with those who are organized. This can apply to all the classes within a polity. Organized workers will perform better than disorganized workers; organized farmers will perform better than disorganized farmers; organized merchants will perform better than disorganized merchants; and Tradesmen, Soldiers, and Technical classes will all achieve better and more favorable results when organized. The answer to the question of whether humanity needs government or not is yes. Does humanity need an Autocratic or Oligarchic government? It is a question that can be debated in many ways. If the Autocrat is a Monarch, then perhaps yes; if the Oligarchy is composed of Aristoi or is an Aristocracy, then perhaps yes. However, inviting such a system, even with the best leaders and individuals involved, does not guarantee that the same quality will persist for generations. Therefore, the Autocratic and Oligarchic systems are the least needed. Instead, Democracy is a better option, since its quality depends entirely on the majority. There are, however, times when Autocratic or Oligarchic rule, such as in families and tribes, can achieve more and better results. Each system has a place, time, and particular value. When the population is ethically lazy, lacks knowledge, and is unwilling to stand up for itself, it is probably best suited to Autocratic and Oligarchic rule. If the people have higher ethics, aspire to freedom, and seek happiness through self-governance, then Democracy will suit them better.

Monarchs or autocrats are also typically needed in expansionistic and military states. Throughout human history, all significant acts of aggression worldwide have been carried out under the leadership of Monarchs and Autocrats. By this, I mean every empire, almost every expansionistic state, was led into such a condition by a Monarch or Autocrat. There are a few exceptions, but alongside these exceptions are subtle differences in the degree of aggression. The most violent times in human history were times when most nations or states had Autocratic leadership. There is a sense of prestige, favor, and glorification given to conquerors. If an autocrat loses land or cities, they are seen as weak and earn little prestige, favor, and glorification from the people. This is one of many reasons why the peculiar nature of autocracies tends towards violence and expansionism. Numerous clashes between kingdoms mark our medieval history. Even in ancient Greece, Egypt, Persia, Assyria, Babylon, China, Yamato, and many other kingdoms, continuous warfare was a constant feature.

Oligarchies tend to prefer less profile or status. They operate in shadows rather than in the light. While the type of Oligarchy that allows the election of politicians into office may seem high profile, and the elections may even be great public events and festivals, the leadership is benign. The greatest fear of Oligarchs is to lose their circle of power through conflict with other similar groups. They pursue diplomatic solutions and seek to resolve issues through the legal system to enforce their demands. To what degree the laws are fair or just is up to them to decide. They will happily use unfair laws until the public highlights the unfairness. They may do so if they can change the laws with minimal impact on their power and wealth. Otherwise, they often lead long, drawn-out campaigns to turn the public's otherwise logical stance in their favor. Since the oligarchy controls the methods of informing the public, such as the media, there is little dialogue. Instead, it becomes a lecture or monologue from the Oligarchy. It can utilize various media, such as speeches, advertisements, and other forms of communication, to convey its intended message.

A popular children's company insisted on replacing the words' God' and 'Divine Intervention' with the term 'Magic' so that its programs could be more universal. They produced countless children's movies that portrayed magic in a positive light. The generations growing up during this company's existence seemed to have had a childhood that believed in magic as a positive thing. By coincidence, at the early start of the 21st century, the company and other similar companies promoting magic increased the promotion of pagan Wicca or magic worship. All the statistics and official records deny any correlation. Yet, the occurrence of related incidents and crime increased after three generations were exposed to the same and similar media, which remains more than a coincidental matter.

Although this may have little bearing on the issue of government and democracy, it highlights that Oligarchs, not only those found in government, can persuade and change the ethics and even the identity of people.

Democracy, compared to other systems, is vocal, exposed, transparent, and works in the open. There is little chance for personal or group interests to persuade the majority unless they form an Oligarchy within or without the government and work towards changing the attitudes and ethics of the people through propaganda, false information, and essentially lies. In other words, people can vote against their own interests when they have been persuaded to do so by individuals and groups outside the role of government. The ancient Democracy of Athens often had orators to speak publicly on various issues before an assembly was held. Many of the Orators were skilled public speakers. Many of them were part of some group with particular interests, and they often espoused propaganda and emotional monologues in public areas.

10. The classes

"Aristotle's five classes are Professionals (Clergy), Military, Agrarians, Merchants and Technicians."

According to Aristotle, the Athenian polity was divided into different classes. These classes were centered on the primary occupation of the people. He drafted a system with five classes: Clergy, Military, Agrarians, Merchants, and Technical people. His classes did not specifically mention artists, musicians, and other service providers. However, the technical class consisted mainly of employable people. The clergy were typically educated individuals who provided professional services related to spiritual matters. The military included most people in their polity for most of their lives. However, the standing army or regular army was usually a career. This allowed those interested in military matters to maintain the military's administrative and operational functions when citizens joined its ranks. It is worth noting that the military's role underwent significant changes, as citizens were often inclined to act on their own initiative rather than follow orders. Agrarians were responsible for providing food and water to a polity. Merchants created the forum for exchanging produce and materials.

If we were to modify these categories, we could merge Clergy with the professional class, resulting in the following categories: Professionals, Military, Agrarians, Merchants, and Technicians. The distinction between a professional and a technician can be confusing because the term professional implies an occupation in exchange for services. A technician is more technical, whether in an artistic sense – such as knowing how to play an instrument – or in fields like building, construction, or engineering. Yet a professional may be technical, and most are highly skilled. There are professionals in the military, Agriculture, Commerce, Technology, and the Clergy.

Additionally, the term 'professional' should ideally not be used, as amateurs can possess equal or better ability. However, because we are focusing on occupational socio-economic classes, there must be some form of exchange for products or services. We may confuse the classification if we place the clergy alongside other occupations that require specialized knowledge. However, the exchange of service exists despite being somewhat different from that of other professionals. Therefore, the Clergy are professionals, as are other highly educated occupations.

Additionally, we may use the terms "tradesman" and "technician" interchangeably to mean the same thing, in the sense that a person who trades a basic skill is usually a technician, but not as specialized as a professional. Some overlap exists, but the fundamental qualifier is higher education for professionals, practical experience, and other learning avenues for tradespeople. Therefore, we are justified in slightly modifying the Aristotelian classes. The term "Professionals", as used throughout this philosophy, does not imply only exchange for services but also higher-educated and scholarly occupations other than those in the Military, Agriculture, Trade, and Technology.

Figure 2.

The balanced Democratic societal classes based on occupation *

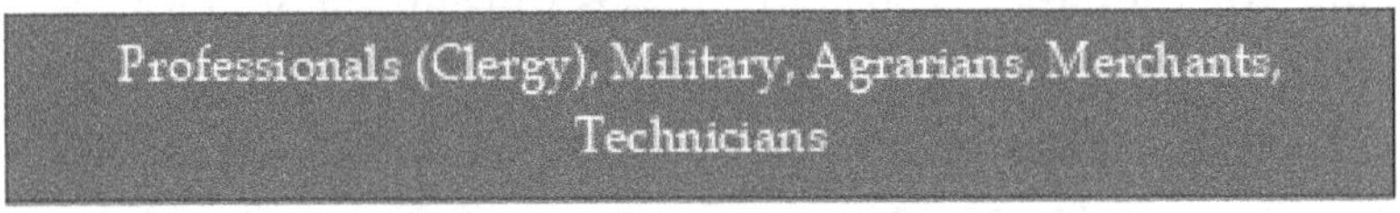

Professionals (Clergy), Military, Agrarians, Merchants, Technicians

* Note: At different times, one class would be held with more esteem, power, and economic strength than others. However, in the context of Democracy, it did not matter how much a person earned. It was how valued their peers found their ideas.

Figure 3.

The unbalanced societal classes based on socioeconomic status

Top Class
Middle Class
Lower Class

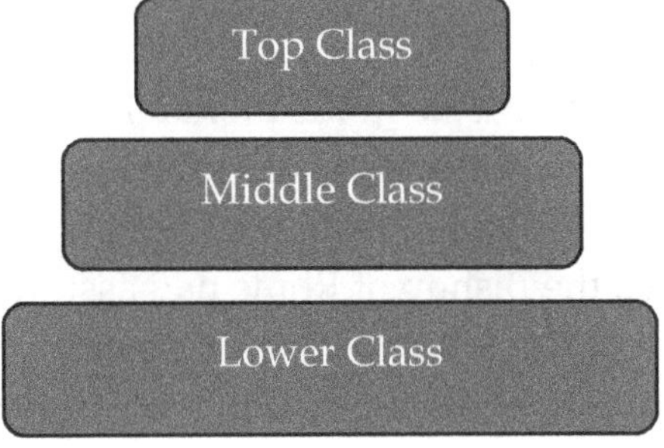

In addition to Aristotle's ideology, there is the Feudalistic view that a polity is divided into hereditary socio-economic tiers. Those tiers are composed of the Peasants and Serfs; above them are the Skilled workers, the Knights and Vassals, the Nobles, and finally, the Monarch. The sixth class is the church or clergy serving varying functions and roles within the Feudal structure. The Peasants or Serfs form the base of a feudal society, while those above them can earn an income, such as merchants, farmers, craftsmen, or technicians. Then, those who offer merchandise, agrarian produce, or crafts are of slightly higher status. Then, above these people are the Knights and Vassals, who act as police and mediators between the lower parts of the system and the Nobles and the Elite, or the Monarch. The elite, or monarchs, were typically army commanders, representing both the military and the family and friends who held power. In some places, like the West, the Nobles also had a decentralized Army that often engaged with other nobles and their armies. The Peasants and Serfs usually fought the battles. However, highly trained professionals such as knights were in charge.

Feudal systems varied based on the monarch's role. By 1417 AD (around the time of the second church schism), in the West, the Monarch was also the head of the Church or controlled the local church. In Rome, the Bishop of Rome had assumed the role of monarch and head of the Roman Catholic church. In the East, the Patriarch of Constantinople assumed the role of head of the Ecumenical Catholic Church, later renamed the Orthodox Church, and remained separate from the state, which became Islamic. Therefore, the church was a pyramidal structure, with a monarch at times controlling it. Constantine laid this precedent around 313 AD and introduced a formal Christian state religion. He placed himself in charge of the church's affairs through ecumenical councils. Thereafter, it impacted the structure and function of the church as an institution. Many nuances of monarchical rule had become part of the institutional church's operations. These included the dress and attire of the clergy, the services within the church, the development of a creed, and many more actions established through the ecumenical councils.

Figure 4.

The Feudal Classes

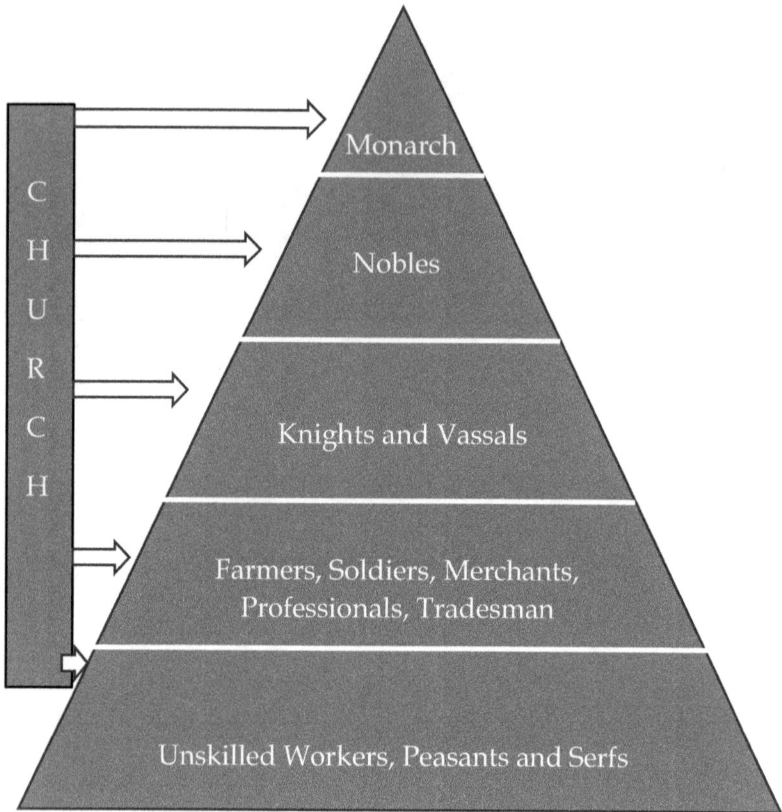

Other models derived from Feudal systems include the high class, middle class, lower class, and serfs or enslaved people. This model describes four tiers: the first three are part of the system, but the bottom layer of the pyramidal structure comprises serfs and enslaved people. This model describes socio-economic tiers with emphasis on the economic model. The more you earn, the higher up the ladder you go. However, the problem with these systems worldwide is that the top tier is hereditary or by invitation only. Mobility is rarely possible between classes. Historically, the chances of entering the higher class were minimal, despite the lower and middle classes often interchanging and exhibiting mobility.

As highlighted, different systems tier people based on their income and survival ability. They also take into account the power of the people within the classes. The feudal model is not very different from the generic rule of an oligarchy. The Monarch and Nobles form the Oligarchy, but the control over the currency is in the hands of the Monarch. A snippet of the Magna Carta in 1215 AD, which was removed in later versions, tried to suggest that people of a particular minority had a specific place within the economic system: the Jews.

"In like manner let it be with debts owing to others than Jews"(King John & Nobility, 1215).

If debts are to be handled in this manner in every other situation, why mention the minority? Scapegoating was a typical strategy. Let us be clear that no minority has special or otherwise powers unless they are systematically provided. By 1215 AD, a long-standing alliance had existed between Jews and Christians under the umbrella of the Judaeo-Christian alliance. A little after the establishment of the Magna Carta, the Barons, along with the King, formed the Oligarchs and embarked on several crusades known as the Baron Crusades, which included a journey to Israel, among other destinations. Also, during that time, the Jewish people were given special places or positions within the system of the West. Some would think they somehow managed it alone, but in reality, the alliance between the two gave them special treatment. The Koran had warned the Islamists of the alliance, wherever else it was kept secret. It was such a relationship that they could blame financial issues on the Jewish people. Still, in reality, it was the Monarch and Nobles who had control over the entire system, including the Jewish employees.

This is where we need to accept that each system and each populace will define these tiers and classes. They are not fixed things. However, some things remain constant, and Aristotle's model of a flat-tier, composed of equally important classes, is considered the most accurate. It is more precise in that these classes of people are primarily found in most models, even under the feudal system. Unlike the pyramid structure of an Oligarchy or Monarchy, the flat, layered system of a Democracy will have periods when the power of these classes varies. Thus creating a pyramidal structure with one class above the others. The upside of the model is that the soldiers are part of the system, so they do not face the same problem as mercenaries, knights, or other professional soldiers, who can impact their freedom. Philosophically speaking, a nation or polity requires an army to protect against aggressors. But all too often, when we leave an army to be administered by others, the army is no longer borne by the people but is installed over the people. Having a military can both reduce people's civil liberties and protect them. As for the other classes, there needs to be a balance among them, and unlike the feudal classes, the classes in a democratic society do not fix a person to a particular class. There is fluid mobility between classes in a democratic system. Whenever such mobility is lacking, we must question if the tiers are linear and flat or pyramidal, such as in a feudal or monarchical system.

10.1 Harmony between the classes

As mentioned, it is time to refer to the balance needed within a polity to function syncarpously. Balance and harmony within a polity can be seen as a process that involves neutralizing or restoring equilibrium. But in this sense, balance refers to the proportional distribution of authority and power within a system. Harmony refers to a balance of power and authority, ensuring everyone is content. Powers and authority may shift within a polity as one or more groups or individuals gain certain authority. This happens naturally because the polity is a dynamic entity, not a static one. Even with five classes to define the constituent groups of a polity, the size and, therefore, power of each of those groups will vary. The military class refers to a group or class with a history of domination. We rarely find doctors, carpenters, or technicians usurping power. Additionally, power changes can come from the passive majority, even without the intention to usurp.

Due to the dynamics of a polity, we sometimes find that administrators who may not have power or authority invested or delegated to them by law are, in fact, holders of power and authority. Additionally, this phenomenon occurs in societies that develop peculiar forms of personality or socio-economic status worship. The Clergy of most faiths are respected for their religious value, but not more than that. Yet, among all the classes, the Military and the Clerics have the most power and authority, historically grounded in two strikingly different and opposing sources. The soldiers attain power and authority through their numbers and the use of their weapons. The clerics establish a level of respect for others by delegating the authority and power of God. I am not trying to isolate the Clergy and Military based on historical accounts. Still, we need to acknowledge that the classes within a society can shift. While clergy or religious figures historically seem to attain power through methods other than the law, so do other constituent groups within a Polity. While we have mentioned a recurring instance of the Clergy and Military attaining various powers and authority, it may be worth noting that in other systems worldwide, such as in communism, the clergy are rendered almost entirely powerless.

Additionally, in various systems, merchants or the extremely wealthy are granted such liberties and freedoms that they often use them against those who empowered them. None of these fluctuations in balance and harmony is explicitly derived from the law or government system. All these things are peripheral to a government.

Balance of power concerns how a polity perceives and values various classes and individuals. Yet even while these factors may be peripheral to the government's function, they nevertheless affect the government and others within the system of government. We can't blame one group or another. We can't blame merchants, priests, soldiers, or others within a polity. This is not democratic at all. We should strive to acknowledge that there will be instances when one group may appear more powerful than another, and that specific issues of fairness will need to be addressed. How we deal with them requires careful consideration.

An extension of this idea is that, within a state or polity, the classes that compose it must have a balance of power. Then, at the next level, the state or polity must maintain a balance with its neighboring states and polities so that none dominates the others and none becomes a vassal or dependent state. Then, at the national level, where a league of states or polities exists, the constituent states must balance their power outwardly with other nations and empires. There will always be a problem balancing power among all these entities, especially when the models under which each polity is established differ. Some ideologies anticipate an Oligarchy as the ultimate rule. In others, they favor or anticipate Democratic rule.

To appreciate the powers of these classes and the balance required, we should first examine the powers of the individual. That way, we can understand which factors will affect individuals and groups, regardless of the formal definition of their class. The reason the solution rests with the powers of the individual is that matters that pertain to individuals are also reflected in the systematic application of those powers to the state and the state to the people. It also affects how one polity influences another through its core constituent—the people.

10.2 Powers of the individual

The power of the individual within a system should enable an individual's aspirations to come to fruition within it. So, if the son of a farmer wishes to become a doctor, or if a person wishes to be a soldier at any point in their life, then that individual should retain the freedom to transcend their class. No matter what people choose to do in life, their occupation should always be something they can change. If we define a system as composed of occupational classes, then this implies that people in a democratic system should be able to transcend and traverse classes as they change jobs. But keep in mind that I do not use the term class to refer to financial earnings, wealth, or other separations that result from such things. Others have decided that society is divided into financial classes: the wealthy, the middle class, and the poor or low-income earners. This can be true of any society if our interest is in an individual's economic value, but in the context of a political state or philosophy, it has little use. Our primary concern in evaluating a government is not the distribution of wealth alone, but also the balance of power and authority, as well as freedom and balance within a system. This balance, or isoaxioprepia, is a state in which the worth of individuals is equal. It should be equivalent in all matters and bound by only one condition: that they are citizens of the state.

Therefore, in that context, the classes, modeled on Aristotle's philosophy, reflect the proportions of people within a particular occupation. They are not classes by which to judge each other, but classes or categories to help define the society or polity and maintain a particular order. Suppose a state does not know how many farmers, soldiers, doctors, carpenters, or workers will be available: It will certainly have a very difficult time coordinating large-scale efforts. The five classes of Aristotle have been a perpetual part of any given society. Unlike the economic views of governments, the political views established remain consistent throughout our history. While three economic classes may exist in some states, they do not in all. In the past, there were poor and wealthy rulers. However, all this is merely a reflection of the economic conditions at that moment. In that very same society, a middle class or even a pirate class could occur, in which wealth remains undetermined. Let us not confuse the classes used here with some form of societal division, but rather as a means to categorize people into groups, revealing their strengths and weaknesses. This is not the intent of this philosophy. Instead, we create the classes so there is understanding of why certain decisions will be made and why others will not, within a balanced system that ensures the five classes remain balanced and in harmony.

Concerning the individual's ability to transcend classes, occupations, and so forth, this is vital in ensuring that a niche group is not created. The mobility of individuals ensures that the size of each class changes in proportion to the state's needs. Incentives to enter a particular class will be driven by demand from the public. It is a natural economic and social condition that supply and demand flux, and as such, there will be times when one class is more profitable or has more incentive to join than others. Mobility across the various parts of a polity's informal structure, such as those based on socioeconomic or occupation-based criteria, is important to people's well-being.

There should also be the power of equal participation in any Democratic polity. For example, there may be fewer agrarians than technicians, resulting in weighted outcomes in assemblies and other meetings. The question is: Does democracy ensure that minorities or smaller groups have an equal and fair say? Given the principle of equality and the assumption that a democratic state exists, it could also be anticipated that each class would have a voice. However, the issue of fairness is another matter unless people democratically preserve their rights within their system. For instance, knowing that one class has significantly fewer participants means the only way to ensure a fair outcome is to convince the other classes to side with them. This should not happen formally, but it should differ within each meeting; otherwise, there is a risk of creating parties. These parties are oligarchies and will eventually change the nature of the Democratic state.

The time allotted to individuals to participate in the democratic process is important to the system's quality. Ensuring that individuals have the freedom and time to participate enhances the quality of their democratic process. That then translates into the system's quality as it interfaces with the other states, leagues, nations, and empires mentioned.

Limiting the number of cases and the amount of information to manageable sessions within a given time frame. That means time is used well and outcomes are achieved. Also, cases heard by each side of an argument, i.e., from each class, should be equal in time. Therefore, spreading and maximizing the number of cases over the given period as much as possible allows the most to be done, and ensuring each class has its say in that time will balance the decision-making process. That also ensures the earlier-mentioned interfaces are addressed with equal time and in a manner that can lead to a decision.

The size, selection, and composition of the committees within each tribe or district must be guided by the principle of equal representation for each class of people. The smallest class should set the limits of the quorum. This approach means that although the assembly is open to any group and occupation, classes should be organized by occupation so that one class does not steer another from its course. This also ensures that the interfaces more fairly represent the classes within a polity.

As described earlier, the selection process, such as sortition in place of elections, should permeate the system. This ensures that the power of the people remains untainted by mechanisms that could corrupt the selection process. Again, this translates to better interfacing with other states, leagues, nations, and empires. The randomness of the sortition process serves as a check-and-balance mechanism. In general terms, randomization built into the system ensures that the original qualities remain authentic and unaltered. It has already been discussed that there may be times when it is necessary to select the fittest for the task, and that this process should be carried out through discussion and collective decision-making, rather than by a few individuals.

Experience gained in short-term, rotating, and changing positions also ensures that those within the systems are not affected by external corruption. The interfaces are better handled by having experienced people develop those skills in short-term, rotating, and alternating positions. Some would argue that long-term positions would give a better experience, but it is better to randomly select from a pool of experienced people than to appoint a life member to a position. Those short-term duties may be repeated to provide the necessary experience. Also, because the position would be randomly appointed, grooming a person to exploit it through heredity or other ongoing influences would be difficult.

An individual's ethics and values ultimately shape their ethical system. This, in turn, affects the interfaces with the state and all matters of dealings with the people. Over time, it builds their reputation, and their reputation would impact their potential judgment. Therefore, it is essential, from the outset, that individuals develop ethics at the personal level before they influence the groups to which they belong and the system within which they operate.

The other powers of the individuals will be centered on decision-making, and all the factors affecting it will play a significant role in all system matters. Their liberty would depend on the laws they create and the system within which they operate. Their organization and all forms of gathering would need to be considered so that the checks and balances exist and are functional.

10.3 The classes in more detail

Let us examine these classes of society in more detail and how they interact. Firstly, it must be clear that very few people are interested in acquiring employment for its own sake. I am not talking about the interest in finding work, but the intrinsic nature of humans to associate work or employment with anything other than a means to an end. Intrinsically, this is most evident when analyzing the cultures of older European, Asian, and African societies. A striking reality that few wish to acknowledge shines in many other places where they are considered underdeveloped. People without debts, pressure to earn money, and without zeal or motivation to earn money or do work for others will live a natural, simple, and relaxed life. These people work and perform;

they are not slothful, but there is little need to work beyond what they deem necessary. Often, life is free of employment but is filled with work, duties, and chores. We imply that the work they choose is not for an employer other than themselves. There may be some specialization in tasks, duties, jobs, and work, but not to the extent that a person will forever receive the same duty every day for the rest of their working days.

Compare, for instance, the agrarian lives of people who drifted from plain to plain with livestock. Or people who would build boats to catch fish. Most ancient jobs we know of were not permanent or long-lasting. That was especially true for those who relied on crops and livestock products. In winter, fishing became too dangerous, crops were not yet sown, and sheep produced their thickest wool coat and had not yet been sheared. That is the context of how ancient people approached their work. They were tied to a local or domestic view entirely influenced by nature and the external forces of weather, day, and night cycles. Their rest was used if there was a rest period in the year. Work was done if there was a period of heavy work in the same year.

Work as doctors, nurses, clergy, and other workers that emerged later in human history evolved from a sedentary lifestyle. It was that sedentary lifestyle that allowed people to focus on other things that could benefit others. Medicine and spiritual context were initially part of the same healing process, but specialization occurred: natural medicine evolved into commercial medicine, and spirituality became a distinct practice within a religion. As time progressed, we saw that large cities developed five basic social classes. The emerging classes were the military, merchants, professionals, tradespeople, and agrarians.

There is always a history that supports the way things are today. Within that history, we find only small parts of the full truth, but enough evidence exists to gain a comprehensive understanding of how things were and how they led to the present state. A government system will always have a history that supports its current state and operation. In some places, at approx. 1066 AD, people were expected to wake at sunrise, go to work, work all day, come home near sunset, and arrive home to eat and sleep before the next day. In Feudalistic Europe, this lifestyle began and would later influence the world. It was a system that enslaved a substantial majority of the classes and formed one class of poor under the knights, nobles, and monarchs. Higher life typically only consisted of the extremely wealthy and powerful. Needless to say, other places in the world were adopting the same or similar systems, and many ancient civilizations used slavery. Almost all ancient systems of government utilized some form of slavery for labor. Usually, they were captives of other states, sometimes prisoners of war. However, many were migrants and newcomers who were used to doing all the undesirable work. In context, systems that enslave others are nothing new. What is new is that the citizens are now enslaved instead of "others". In the past, citizens have always enjoyed some degree of freedom. That freedom was not always at the cost of other people's freedom, either.

There were processes for becoming an Athenian in Athens, but they were strictly controlled. Foreigners and non-Athenians were not in any way encouraged to partake in Athenian rule. Yet there was a pathway with a slim chance of becoming citizens themselves. That is because it was very dangerous to do any business or perform any tasks within a society that afforded you no rights or legal support. The system was skewed in favor of the well-being of the citizenry. Therefore, people living in Athens as non-citizens had considerable incentives to excel and earn a good reputation, which would ultimately lead to their freedom. Some argue that only the merchants and those who found a way to become wealthy were allowed to become citizens. It is another lesson to learn from history.

It, therefore, becomes an important part of our investigation that the classes that exist should, under democratic rule, not be of the type that tiers classes but treats them all the same. Each of the classes has dominated the others at different times and places: the farmers of India, the merchants of Babylon, the doctors of Egypt, the Spartan soldiers, and the Athenian traders, etc. Of the five, the tradesmen were usually the least powerful; however, in Athens, democracy gave them substantially more power than they had under any other system. Their pottery was distributed throughout the known world. We also need to examine how we live to understand how these classes influence the governing system and how the system, in turn, affects the classes. After all, history shapes us as a people and helps define our culture.

10.4 Our lifestyles

The vast majority of cases and examples in human history demonstrate that humanity is born with an unquenchable appetite for freedom. Yet, in some polities, we may view humanity as domesticated sheep or cattle; many societies in the world are like this. Even in Plato's time, many simply followed what everyone else did. Some, like today, place the system and government before their own family. In one of the Socratic dialogues, Plato wrote that Euthyphro's definition of piety included the persecution and judgment of one's father if they are thought to have murdered someone. Few people can bring themselves to convict a father or a family member. Even if they have committed the worst crimes, compassion and love can somewhat impair justice. Yet many people who put the laws of the state and the state itself before all else exist. Some will be obliged to take many unthinkable actions under the pressure of broader society and formal and informal authority. Youth have historically been the easiest targets across various authority systems. The youth of

NAZI Germany burned their schoolbooks and formed large groups that opposed the ideals taught by their parents.

Yet, with a few doses of freedom, a lifetime's domestication and influence can be undone. We are aware of this instinct, as many long-time workers who have taken extended holidays often struggle to re-enter the system upon their return. Every weekday, they may work, and on the weekends, they may rest, but on the first day they return from their rest, they like it least. To become domesticated has taken only a few centuries during and after the Industrial Age. It required constant pressure on a polity to turn it into a working population. It would be difficult in my time to explain to the majority that the world had never been like this before. Very few could believe that an overwhelming majority did not need to work every day to survive within a polity. Not because they were rich, but because the demands to attain a basic level of existence within a city were not at all hard to achieve. But it did have downfalls; otherwise, people would not have wanted to change. Single mothers and widows were the most affected since they relied on the Church or temple charity to survive. Certain luxuries we enjoy today were more expensive in the past. There were oppressive environments and even periods of slavery, involuntary military service, and many things that often caused unrest within a society. But none of these things sprouted from the will of a democratic system. The Democratic system acknowledges that we must dedicate some of our time as volunteers to the system. The democratic system also defines the duties and obligations that citizens are required to fulfill. Initially, we may conclude that although most people do not aspire to work their entire lives, humanity has worked in one way or another, as archaeological and historical evidence suggests. The only differences of importance are how and why we worked and for whom.

According to old census data from 1800 AD in the USA, many people worked for others. In contrast, most developed countries of today have proportionally fewer people engaged in work. Most people lived in a semi-rural or rural environment. This created a degree of self-sufficiency for most people in most places. In some instances, the use of slave labor or servant labor can enhance productivity and facilitate rapid expansion. Yet both these systems had far less impact on the proportion of workers to non-workers. It is challenging to navigate the state-by-state records of the 1800 USA Census. However, certain approximations were discovered. Archaeic USA census data show that 40% of the population was employed. This is significantly higher than that found in other parts of the world. The sole reason for this is that slave labor was used and alone contributed 17-30% of the entire workforce in the USA before the 1900s. Most other people in the USA were landowners, farmers, and small business owners. By small business, I mean that they offered their products and services as a trade, be it medicine, pharmaceuticals, welding, carpentry, or almost anything that could be traded. Small businesses were often operated like farms, with family members typically running them. Very rarely did businesses grow large enough in trade to hire others outside the family. This fact remains consistent with conditions in almost every other part of the world before the mid-1800s. Therefore, it is essential to clarify the terms' worker' and 'servant'. Worker and servant imply similar things, except that a worker may not necessarily render service but also produce a product, harvest crops, and essentially partake in the manual handling that can either be of service or produce in nature. A servant is usually someone who offers a service to another.

For example, a group of islanders is offered some coins to pick coconuts from a palm tree. The people who pick those coconuts think they have a business. The person paying them also thinks he has a business. The difference, though, is in how the trade is arranged. Since one is required to work and climb trees to retrieve the coconuts, they are workers. The person purchasing all their coconuts is the businessman or merchant.

In another scenario, a small retail operation selling coconuts pays for the coconuts to be sold. Therefore, a group of workers now has the exclusive right to produce and sell to retailers, the public, or others. That retailer may then be part of a group of retailers doing the same thing, purchasing all their produce from the initial retailer at a lower price. The concept of franchises is what I am describing. The difference between being in business and working is that although business can be time-consuming and hard work, the actual item for sale or the service being traded was not carried out by the businessman or merchant.

The businessman is a merchant who buys many products and pays for various services, but does not engage in any further activities. They may even pay to have products made, but they will not make them themselves. The workers, however, are those who have harvested fresh produce or crafted something that can be sold. The worker can sell his own produce or services, or allow a merchant to sell his produce or services. In other words, he can work for another. So, when we use the term "small business," it should, more correctly, imply self-employment. The individuals who operate small businesses are, in fact, the same as the workers who happen to provide a product or service. There is no difference unless the small business hires others to perform the work. In that case, the enterprise owner, who may have started working and selling their product or service, may become a business upon resigning from manual labor and hiring others to do the work. It is essential to clarify this because many people struggle to distinguish the tiers of enslavement. The self-employed are typically among the highest-income earners. Those who allow themselves to work for others are positioned in the middle of the hierarchy, and the lowest are the servants, who tend to perform the most menial tasks, such as cleaning and serving others. My father was a musician for most of his short life. If I were to ask him which profession he would consider the lowest of all, he would say musicians. When I asked him why? He would reply, "I once heard someone say that we play music for even the whores and politicians to dance to". Yet it is not always the case that a musician or artist serving in this capacity is also the lowest-paid. Some artists become very wealthy, and their status is often seen as higher than that of many other professions. Some artists attain a group of idolizers who like their music or art. But this hierarchy or degree of enslavement is pedantic. Our concern is not the degree of enslavement. Our concern is more to establish whether work and enslavement have a thin boundary to which people may slip from one to another. It matters not in a philosophical sense how much you are paid or how thick the chains that bind you may be. It only matters that there are chains that bind the people. For this reason, it is of no particular interest to us to determine the tiers within a society based on some economic model. That has little philosophical value, since what is held most precious from one generation to the next is subject to change. Most certainly, though, when we consider the terms employed, worker, servant, or slave, they can imply the same thing. Similarly, the term 'self-employed small business owners' or 'micro business' refers to a business with one individual or a family working together. All these professions can become enslaving when the choice to work or not to work affects the degree to which a person can exercise their freedoms within the polity. In all these cases, the people are workers as much as they are slaves or servants or any other term that may be implied. We may reserve the term servant for those who offer services, but to what real extent is that different from the worker who toils a field or creates furniture or anything else? Enslavement can emerge within a polity if the freedom to work or not is absent. If people resort to statements such as "We need to work to survive", then that indicates to some degree the enslavement in which they participate. This is not the same as a farmer who works to ensure he has milk, eggs, or crops to see his family and/or others through winter. What I am talking about are situations where slavery emerges in the form that choice and freedom are imposed on by doing work or not doing work.

Additionally, even when the choice is present, there are times when a polity and its structure compel people to work but offer no immediate penalty for not doing so. These systems, however, make it impossible for a worker to live or survive without working. They create an incentive to work, enabling individuals to access necessities such as food, water, and shelter.

Returning to the issue of employment, although people worked in the past, they tended to do so for their own business, trade, or service. In other words, in the type of employment where a person has decided to offer their product or service, the self-employed has attained a degree of self-sufficiency. That self-sufficiency allows them to choose who may purchase their product or service. It allows them to work up to whatever they consider fair. In this sense, the self-employed are free from the dependency that workers, servants, and slaves may have. It is with this in mind that we should assess the statistics mentioned earlier. The majority of working people in the world are not employees of others, but rather self-employed individuals. By the mid-1800s, though, the majority of the working population was not enslaved or servile. Even with forced slavery in the United States of America, which offered little or no reward, the forced slaves constituted 17-30% of the entire working population. If all of them were to be slaves, which was not entirely the case, but assuming as a maximum of values, then even with forced slavery, most societies did not alter from a steadfast tradition of organization. Workers in any society have never constituted a very large proportion of the population. As mentioned earlier, at one point in history, most people were self-employed on farms and in other enterprises. So, even with all the forced slavery available, the number of available workers in the USA was considerably smaller compared to the broader society. It was one of the reasons that slavery was considered a viable option. Since the majority of people minded their own affairs and did the work that brought them the most happiness, they had no immediate need to facilitate the growth of grand plans by the extremely wealthy and/or powerful. There was simply no incentive to work for others, and as such, the large plans of the government, as well as those of the oligarchies and monarchies, required many hands to be tied to the task. This story of the United States of America is no different from any other place where slavery was used. Often, in the Autocratic colonies that emerged between the late 1600s and the mid-1800s, prisoners were used as slaves. In many instances, people were imprisoned with the intent to send them off to work.

Bread thieves and those who committed minor offenses were dealt with intentionally harshly so that the poor constituted those who would be deemed criminals and sent abroad to colonize. Another sad incident and example in the place where I live, and while writing this, is that many orphans were sent as workers to the colony, and they were told a better life awaited them. Many were bound to work and struggled to survive since none were old enough to be considered citizens. None could claim a fair wage or earnings, and none possessed the necessary qualifications or trade to succeed. The orphaned children were sent to colonize, and so were the prisoners from a few generations before. However, in compensation, upon arrival, they were granted leniency by businesses owned by foreign oligarchies and monarchies. When such grand ideas exist in the minds of the few, the many will suffer.

Although I used some examples out of chronological order, the context was that most people in the past were not employees. The rise of the Industrial Revolution created a need for considerably more workers. Ironically, in the last twenty or so years, workers in those societies have feared being replaced by machinery. I say ironically because it became a common delusion amongst people that they needed to work. They even thought that working had been a necessity throughout all ages, or that their duty was to work. It could only be summarised as people believing that they needed to work. By need, I mean exactly that. It went beyond the idea that work was a means to an end; it became almost institutional, with humans on earth working for someone. They called this by many names, such as "the work ethic," a rather paradoxical term, considering that whether to work or not is not an ethic at all, but rather a disposition. The humans of my time were hard to persuade to believe the truth, mainly because it threatened the security and safety they felt while hiding from it.

By the mid-1900s, the majority of people in the developed world lived in cities, and most of them became employees. It is difficult to use the word 'city' to describe both ancient cities prior to the Roman Empire and the cities we call cities in my and your epoch. The cities of the ancient world were comprised of self-sufficient individuals who rarely required the services or products of others. They did not depend on much but had access to several luxuries and, most importantly, protection in numbers. In a modern sense, cities act as entrapments: once people are drawn to living within them, they steadily become devoted to one obligation —to work for others. As I described earlier, many methods promote this, such as debt self-enslavement and making basic needs difficult to attain, to encourage work. The methods used and the things done by those who govern vary by city and state. Many Greeks who have recently traveled abroad have commented on the challenges they face in navigating such ideologies. To them, freedom is still, at the time I write this, a powerful word. It defines every aspect of their life. People from other cultures have called them lazy and corrupt. Ironic words that, in turn, describe the very passage of human history since the fall of Civilization. If people had the motivation and enthusiasm to build and sustain a democracy, and if their system had been modeled on the Athenian democratic system, neither laziness nor corruption would have led to the demise of what was left of civilization. While the Greeks still hang onto the withering ideals that their forefathers forged with their blood and sweat, those around them and even those who govern them try to dismantle and destroy those ideals every day.

For a long time, Greece has been without sparrows or doves—the symbols of freedom—flying over the hills of Athens. Doves no longer fly high and free in the world around me. Without those doves, the world has lost the songs that tamed beasts. The flutter of many doves' feathers and wings caused gushes of wind that felled tyrants, like hurricanes sweeping the plains. When they gathered together upon the earth, their coos and voices were so loud that they could topple flimsy constructs, and you would be forgiven for thinking that their voice could cause quakes to topple the pillars of tyranny. Without the doves flying over the hills of Athens, the inspiration that the world had is also gone. Where once the mention of Athens, Hellas, and Greece brought a significant elation to the mind of the educated, the layman of these lands chose to mock them.

Athens and all the riches of Antiquity, from Egypt, Persia, and Greece, created an enlightenment far greater than any could consider reality or believable. After all, nationality and duty to serve seem far more important in many lands than in others. However, I do know for certain that the Hellenistic enlightenment gave me and countless others hope, endurance, and a cause to suffer for. If a purpose or cause is so great, then the greatest sacrifice a person can give is their life to those who take lives. Because such causes do not intrinsically allow a person to take lives but rather to sacrifice their own, this can be a lifestyle sacrifice, a well-being sacrifice, or any aspect of one's life given for a higher purpose. None greater to serve an example than Jesus, who was so convinced of the truth, so sure of his cause and path, that even with all his powers and chances to escape certain death, he was also convinced that his cause was worth dying for. We may say that the Hellenistic enlightenment gave sight to the blind, a metaphor for the divine light that truly brought sight to the blind. But alas, Hellenistic enlightenment comes from mortals and is passed on to mortals. All our grudges, pride, biases, and flaws are passed along with them. It also makes you wonder how an absolute truth could be passed on from one person to another if people are busily avoiding reality. Even to those who believe in God, is it not true that the truth is the word of God and that wisdom is a gift from God? That having knowledge alone is evil, but knowledge of the true and good gives rise to the gift we call Wisdom. So then, even in these times, where the developed world has undermined our liberty, freedom, and civilization, it is the onus of all those present to act. Not to hide and pretend it will get better. Not to think that if we leave it in the hands of those who hold weapons, wealth, and power, our lives will somehow become better. Indeed, at some point, people within a polity need to take a step back and determine what really matters in life. Based on their decision, they will also answer the question: What action should we take? At least become aware of the lies and truths that surround this subject of Democracy. At the very least, discuss it and share your ideas. Develop and enhance this philosophy. At least, that is a start. But do not let others develop a philosophy for you because, by the time you receive the news of this philosophy, you will most likely know more lies about it than what I inadvertently wrote myself.

10.5 Finding a balance

In many ways, the creation of nations from empires was a positive development. However, free-standing nations and those dependent on others are two distinct types of nations. Or should I say that the term "nation" is often misused to refer to the controlled states of bigger financial and military powers? Without that holding of power (kratos) by the people, they are simply like sheep in a pen kept in place, not by shepherds but by wolves.

In Medieval Europe, during the Autocratic colonization periods, anytime humans exercised dominion over other people, the result was a substantial loss of lives. Monarchies wage wars far more easily than Aristocracies, and in turn, Aristocracies wage wars more easily than Democracies. The reason is simply that a Monarch does not need to convince anyone or establish a substantial case for war. Aristocracies need only convince the majority of the few in power. Their case for war needs to be more refined than that of a monarch, especially if the Aristocrats or Oligarchs are elected into their positions. If they inherit their positions, then they do not essentially need an elaborate case for war to be brought to the people. In a Democracy, though, we need only ask: Which sane person would consider war before every other option is exhausted? Democracies are better defenders than aggressors. A Democracy can only engage in war with a majority vote, and the reason for war needs to be justified beyond any doubt. In times of defense, though, democratic armies respond immediately and are far better disciplined. The reasons are that, within a Democratic polity, the people have a duty to defend their city and home. From the ancient Athenian model, we know that when a message was received that Athens would be attacked, the men formed a protective phalanx and organized and mobilized the military before the traditional assembly was organized. In other words, the men manned their positions without any vote and prepared amongst their military for the worst.

While Nationalism serves a purpose in terms of shared military and defense with similar or friendly cities, its role within a Democracy can be seen as redundant. The concern of a Democracy is primarily the city. The City-State model is a democratic model that defines the city as a self-sufficient entity, including its surrounding areas, towns, and villages. Alliances between cities can form leagues. However, as history has shown, these leagues can quickly turn into oligarchies, not simply by a few people controlling one government, but by one city controlling many others.

To some extent, this tradition has remained since the day of the Athenian League, when Athens became the first capital city. This is why it is both difficult and possible for Democracies to operate at the national level. Many people will think of the word 'Nation' as referring to an Ethnos, or the people of a particular ethnicity. The term is used in many ways and with various meanings due to the Autocratic Colonies and their impact on global norms. An Ethnos is a people with a common language, culture, and religion. Some people also consider appearance an important factor, including skin color, hair color, height, and overall appearance. I am not entirely convinced that an Ethnos implies race or some genetic commonness. I do believe, though, that people who behave differently from the common culture and religion and who speak languages other than the common language are prone to isolation and differentiation. The first to attract attention will be those who happen to look different from the majority. Often, those who appear different also stand out more when misbehaving. Appearances are not merely superficial; they are deeply ingrained in many societies. From the way people dress and comb their hair to whether they have a beard. Due to these somewhat trivial and vain aspects of many humans, societies and polities often segregate and differentiate among people. All these things and their personal-level impact will also, to some degree, affect the broader state level. A polity of an Ethnos is a subdivision of the Ethnos, usually based on a geographical separation and, most importantly, an independent government system. There may be many French-, English-, or Spanish-speaking cities that ally based on their common language, faith, and culture, but each of those cities may be a different polity. They may also be different states. The term State, as I mentioned before, implies Kratos, or the region under the rule of a single government. What I am describing here is the city-state. In other words, the City Kratos is the city's government system and its surrounding region. Nations are a collection of Cities, and the Nation becomes the State or Kratos. In other words, the nation may control several other Cities. However, as stated in a city-state model, all cities would require balanced powers. Also, provided the Ethnos is the same, the term Nation is implied. However, when the Ethnos is of a different nature across cities under a single government, we often use the term Empire.

In a world where every city is entirely free, the Ethnos that make up that city may form a League known as an Alliance with other cities. They may collaborate on various projects and coordinate multiple joint ventures. But here lies a problem. If you recall, one of the reasons communal ownership of rural or productive property would lead to arguments is that it would also happen within an alliance. One city will argue who gave the most, who spent the most, who deserves more, and so forth. Some things may benefit one city more than the other, yet require participation from both. This is the problem with Democratic city-states when they form alliances. Yet, there is no reason that the alliance could not be of such a nature that all citizens from all the cities could lead each other in a fair and Democratic government. By doing so, the people are shifting the Kratos from the city level to the national level. This concept is similar to that of Athenian Democracy, which granted the ten tribes or demes of Athens specific rights to participate as a unified people. Similarly, many cities of an Ethnos may choose to form a combined government. Unlike the Athenian democracy, however, it would be difficult to monitor the system to ensure proper voting procedures and that all other procedures were free from corruption. In Athens, all the voters could see the actions of the other voters. But how would the voters of one city truly know what another city has voted? If they rely on a messenger or some system to relay the votes of other cities, then how will the people know the message is true? In Ancient Greece and modern Greece, the term for empire is often

Autocracy. The reason the term 'Empire' is often used to describe an Autocracy is the state's centralized rule. Rather than looking, as we did previously, at how many people form a government relative to the number of citizens, the same method can be applied to the number of cities or polities that form the central body that controls the broader state. If one city governs many cities, it is an Autocracy. If several cities rule over many more cities, it is an oligarchy. If all cities within a defined state have equal voting rights, presence, and participation in government, then they would be democratic states. The latter is fictitious, as it cannot possibly occur honestly. Autocracies were the only forms of government in human history to form empires.

In a philosophical context, the term Kratos implies the center of authority and power. In a Demo-cracy, the suffix -cracy or Cratos (Kratos) is formed by the people. The Kratos, or epicenter of ruling power in a state or polity, can shift. It can be with the population, a few individuals, or a single person. It can also be one city leading many cities, which can be seen as an Oligarchy or Autocracy. It can be an Oligarchy in the sense that the few of one city (even if it is the entire population) are leading the entire populations of other cities. It can also be seen as an Autocracy if we count the number of cities that form a power to rule over the others. In the example I gave, it would be one city ruling over many cities. Also, it was mentioned earlier that the Autocratic colonies distorted some views of what a nation is and what an empire is. Nation implies an Ethnos, yet the Autocratic Colonies are made up of many Ethnicities. The term "Empire" usually refers to the subjugation of foreign cities and their populations by a different ethnic group. But in one former autocratic colony that existed in my time, the people created a state that they called a nation. However, this nation is composed of many ethnicities that arrived primarily as migrants. It also has over a hundred cities. It defies the concept of a City-State; it is hardly a Nation or a polity composed of a single ethnicity. Yet, by its sheer size and diversity, it represents an empire formed by migration rather than conquest. It has filled its population by allowing migrants to enter from many parts of the world. By doing this and encouraging it, the transformation of what may have been a nation became an Empire within the definitions used here and by others in the past.

This rather excessive discussion of nationalism serves a single purpose for my argument: nationalism can lead to significant decay in how effectively a Democracy operates, yet it can also offer some benefits in terms of unity. We are often hesitant to change, and many people are cautious about accepting others' claims as true due to nationalism. This is why it is essential for any polity attempting to establish Democracy to also promote equal status, value, and recognition for all citizens within a state. If the starting population is made up of racially diverse people, then that diversity should be part of the identity of that Democratic state. But isolation, hurting, or cleansing a population for the sake of developing a "pure" Nation is very far removed from Democratic ethics. In particular, the ethics we discussed relate to the importance of individual freedom. This is why I mentioned the legacy of Ancient Greece, since it is probably the most enduring and significant historical example of how Nationalism can do two things: save people and destroy them.

Regarding my original point about the harmony of classes within a polity, I thought it would be best to clarify that the polity, its structure, alliances, and all related aspects needed to be defined. There is no use in discussing the classes within a democratic society, balancing them, and achieving harmony between them if the idea we have of a democratic state is not uniform, at least in this regard. What kind of Democracy could we call a situation where one city enslaves and makes workers of another city? Would such a city be called an ally or some part of a league, or would it be an occupied and controlled city? We, therefore, could not satisfy the formation of a suitable philosophy if these matters were not clarified. This is especially true, given the fine line between truth and lies. We know that Nationalism and Nations can be beneficial; perhaps even empires can be, but the Democratic League or Alliance requires allied city-states, not nations. A Democracy, furthermore, can't have numerous cities sprawled with one nominated as its capital. The reasons for this may not seem immediately clear, as we are so accustomed to seeing the opposite, and many of us have grown accustomed to the view that the bigger the union, the better the government systems and the people's lifestyle. However, in a democratic league, the same condition is achieved by a single city dominating others.

Within a City-State and a Democratic State: Some may argue that everyone will strive to acquire as many assets and as much wealth as possible. That may be true in a society that prioritizes the importance of having money and wealth. However, if society is balanced, people will be drawn to the things they enjoy most, and with sufficient incentive, will achieve the most and best during that period of their lives.

In a better society, there needs to be harmony and cooperation among all classes. Aristotle, Plato, and many of the great minds, including most of the idolized heroes of Ancient Greece, despised wealth. Idolization was seen as a good indicator of how poorly the mind was functioning. A person preoccupied with collecting shiny stones, metals, badges, team-colored scarves, memorabilia, wealth, and money can hardly be considered as intelligent as one seeking the truth. But by the same token, do not underestimate the fact that Greed can manifest in many intelligent ways. A person who is Greedy for knowledge and selfish in its application to make money is also unethical. What good is it for a person to study the doctoring of humans and not apply that knowledge? In the past, those who practiced medicine or the giatric discipline tended to rely on people in nursing, remedies, and medicines. Their job was to use all their skills to treat the ill. Often, Christ is called by many names, and the Healer was one of them. He washed the leprosy off the bodies of the afflicted and demonstrated that cleanliness can treat many diseases.

Also, what good is a person as a philosopher if they have not shared their knowledge with others? Even if the truth can never be achieved, and even at the risk of ridicule, a person who has a philosophy should not be selfish enough to keep it to themselves. It serves no purpose to do so. In a similar way, those who read many books and information but keep it all to themselves without any benefit to society or those around them are also greedy.

We should not target merely the wealthy and expect to take their possessions to benefit the workers, farmers, agrarians, professionals, technicians, educators, or soldiers. The same way that a farmer's produce should not be taken from them, an educator's voice should not be silenced, or the worker left to do nothing, or the weapons taken from the soldiers. All parts of society require a balance for a government system to operate properly. That balance can only be achieved by attending to moderate laws and moderate ways of expressing ideas. Ethical ideas should be favored over unethical ones. So that society can function in a fair and just manner.

As we noted previously, communism upset the balance among the five classes in society as much as capitalism did. There is often a tendency, with change, to gravitate towards the most extreme or radical ideas. A balance is not achieved in a society until an extreme has been experienced. Because the merchant class is the only class to control both the incentive to work and all aspects of society, it is often given a special place within the framework of government. But it is no different from any other class within a society. If we give too much power to the soldiers, for example, then the polity will endure through a militant life. If we give the soldiers too little power, they may even desert their posts. If we give too much power to the workers, they will want all that the rich have without working. If we give too little power to the workers, they will be used till they are nothing more than slaves. If we give too much power to the farmers, they will exploit and dominate all the other classes. If we do not give farmers enough power, there may not be enough food to feed the city. All the classes, if not balanced within a polity, will create problems. This is most certainly true of the Merchant class and of how capitalism and communism attempted to manage a state's economy. With capitalism, merchants began to influence all the other classes and to subdue them by manipulating the incentives people had to work. In Communism, the oligarchy failed to distribute wealth evenly, resulting in a nation plagued by poverty.

A Democratic State, to create a balance between the classes, must recognize the classes in the first place. Then, each class must be treated with caution so that each class performs its intended role for the polity, but not beyond that role. If a government is a Democracy, as we have described, there is little need to encourage the merchant classes, as was done under capitalist ideology. In a true democracy, the freedom of the merchants is, by default, existent, as is the freedom of all the classes. However, unlike capitalism, the government controls all matters and affairs that impact the city and state. Therefore, if exploitation is a concern, the issue will be raised and judged by the people. For a Democratic government to succeed, it must be the wealthiest entity within a given polity. The government should be seen as the most powerful and authoritative entity within a polity. If any controls or regulations are to be imposed, they will come from the government, which is representative of the will of the people. Many people fear that, because all authority in a Democracy is held by the people, whichever class has a majority in an assembly will also govern. If that majority are workers, then the wealthy fear losing their assets to the whims of the majority. However, this should not be the case if people have reserved certain property rights, as we mentioned earlier. Since the rich fear the judgment of the poor, the poor tend to feel underrepresented at democratic assemblies because they often have to work every day. The worker would need a provision in law allowing them to attend an assembly. If not, then the assembly will become dominated by those who do not need to work. Laws must not only reflect the interests of the wealthy and their property but also facilitate the process by which the poor can govern themselves. Without such incentives and legal support, the assemblies may well turn into not a majority of workers but of the wealthy and unemployed. Farmers, soldiers, and all classes require provisions to ensure that each class is represented in a Democratic assembly. While we say that Democracy implies that the People have absolute power over government, the reality is that a government is led by those willing to participate. This creates a certain problem regarding attendance at several classes. For farmers, the hardest time to attend will be when they need the most work, such as sowing crops or during harvest. For soldiers, there may be a need to exclude them from legal courts and requirements while they serve, so they can fully participate as soldiers without hindrance to their duty. But when they are soldiers by choice and remain soldiers, will they be perpetually exempt from civil law? If so, is it not evident that the soldiers will have the power to do as they wish within a society? Therefore, even in the military, laws and regulations must apply to ensure fair class and civic representation. The commander of a single command can fill the assembly with soldiers, who can then become the majority within it. It is, therefore, fair that the service of the military is temporary for the majority of people. During that temporary service, they are withheld from attending the assembly and partaking in any other civil duties. This, as in Ancient Athens, should be no more than two years of mandatory training as part of the process to attain citizenship. Those who want to make a career out of military life cannot be forbidden from attending the Assembly since what they say is of great importance. However, swaying the number of people attending an assembly would require cautious monitoring.

A society that grants too much freedom to military commanders will have a powerful army willing not only to defend but also to prey on the weak. It is like the hunter and the fighter seeking out the weak and carefully laying traps for the stronger. I have spoken little of the technical class and the Tradesmen, but they are obviously as important as the rest. These classes should not allow priests and other professions to gain too much sway in an assembly. If they use words to frighten and sway the votes of those attending, it may not be entirely justified. In some cultures, some holy men call for the destruction of other people. If they are given too much voice and sway, and if they are given too much respect, then they can use that power not for God but for their own benefit. To tame the Priests would require that they not speak as priests in an Assembly but as men devoted to God. So that they may speak and express their opinions if they desire, but not curse all those who vote against their wishes. For such curses may take hold in the minds of many and force their vote to favor the bias of their priest.

It is, therefore, of paramount importance never to let any class become more influential than any other, and that even the lowest-thought individuals must have an equal right to express themselves as the highest-thought individuals. This is the beauty of Democracy: equality is not just in the laws, but in the cultural equal rights of all citizens to make those laws, to judge and enforce them.

For such a psyche to exist amongst all citizens, they must embrace each other as being on the same side and aspiring to a common cause. If the decline of Empires has caused the path of Nationalization, caution must be taken to ensure that those nations do not form empires again. For a true Democracy to exist, the city-state is the core and highest form of government. Understanding a world where no matter where we go, if a single city were to become a Democracy, it would be surrounded by entities far greater and more powerful than itself. A democracy could not exist in that environment. It would be like a fertile seed falling upon a dry rock, but the chances for it to sprout are small. But with faith in that seedling we call Democracy, it can grow, even on that dry rock, because our tears and prayers will water it.

For a Democracy to exist in such a harsh environment would indeed require a miracle. However, if neighboring cities of the same ethnicity form a league, their unity can be potent and work effectively together. As mentioned earlier, a pure city-state is the best Democracy. But in realistic terms, one city is very limited in what it can defend against. It is essential to ensure the longevity of the democratic city; a league should be formed with those considered neighbors, friends, and people of the same ethnic background. Competition will arise, and no city will be able to supply equal shares of everything common to them. However, as long as half of what they keep for themselves is shared and accessible to the other cities, they are truly united. If each city forms a board of administration to coordinate and collaborate on matters of mutual importance, then that board must also be democratic. It must be elected by sortition and composed of members from each city, and its task must be limited to administering, not making laws, regulating, judging, or enforcing them. Such a board, to serve common purposes, must have two components to operate democratically. Each city must appoint, by random lot from a pool of randomly selected individuals, those who fairly represent the city's suburbs, districts, villages, and towns. As the Bouli in the assembly was conducted, so will the administrators organize themselves. So, within a city divided into ten or twelve districts, each will take a turn leading the administration during the year. Among the leading parties, they will hold a vote to select 10 members from a pool of 100 in one district to lead. Based on the Athenian constitution, in addition to those randomly chosen to lead, ten will be randomly selected to serve as administrators, along with ten from each of the other districts. These administrators will be assigned duties by the person whose turn it is to lead that month. It is similar to the Bouli of the Assembly, but does not have the same scope. They will rotate positions and ensure that all districts have led the administrative body, but their scope will be limited to administering the common cause of the League of Cities.

They may, in the process of their duties, raise issues for consideration by the Assembly through the Bouli of the Assembly. The Inter-Polity Administrators will be aides to the Bouli and the people. In this way, many cities can align while remaining independent, sharing common interests and responsibilities. In terms of the military, each city should have an army made up of all its citizens. The active army will always be composed of young people aspiring to citizenship and their trainers, as we have already mentioned, who will serve for no more than three years, with two years spent in active military service. Of this total number of candidates, half should be pledged to common military operations with other cities. However, there is a problem with leading a combined army without a unified leader. This, therefore, should be left to vote amongst the elected generals of each city so that each city has its turn to appoint a general to lead the common army. But in times of War, the people will always follow their leader with greater trust than that of another city. So, while there may be a common General and a common military, that General can not give orders directly to any city's remaining army without first consulting with the Generals of each city. In this way, a board is formed among the Generals, who will find a resolution to the issues they face out of the people's sight. With this system, the faults of previous attempts at democracy may be rendered void, since the greatest problem was the difficulty of working together against a common aggressor. That, with the modification described, would allow two to exist. One army serves all the cities and is partly composed of soldiers from them, while another army serves the city of its origin. At least half of the people applying for citizenship in a city per year should be recorded as eligible for service. After serving their city as local guards and the local army for the first two years, the same soldier will serve a further single year with the common military. On some occasions, it will be their General in charge of their common military. At other times, it will be from another city. In this manner, the aim is for a third of each city's total military to be included in the combined common military. Alternatively, if the total training period is only two years, they will serve only one year as guardians of their city before serving the second year in the common military. The latter method provides half the city's available military population for common military service.

Common military activities for defense would include peacetime operations, patrols, relief efforts, and emergency plans, as well as counter-espionage and other forms of protection. It would be unethical and non-democratic for any Army to attack any other city. We know that, despite how much wars are disliked and how much we wish they could disappear, the steadfast reality of humanity to this day is that war remains a perpetual curse. To break that curse requires far braver people than those who die in wars. It is almost guaranteed that anyone who opposes the norm—the very concept that fuels the coffers of kings, queens, oligarchies, bankers, and financial merchants—is most definitely doomed. War is a reflection of aggression. Many people within polities break out into fits of rage. They fight with fists in the streets and vocalize profanities at others. This aggression, this rage, exists for the most part where words have failed. Aristotle highlighted the difficulty of being mad at the right person for the right reason, at the right time, and in the right way. Doing that is indeed difficult for many people. That is why our unethical selves create unethical polities that, in turn, create unethical governments, and these unethical governments, in turn, handle other governments, polities, and people in an unethical manner. The extreme of their actions is merely an extension of the thugs in the streets who demand what they wish to take. That is humanity; that is the so-called Glory of modern wars. A group of blinded children gathered by autocrats and oligarchs and sent to war. A war, might I add, benefits only those who sent the youth to their demise. Not their families, or their neighbors, not even the polity to which they belonged, but those that sent them to war. This is the nature of war in the era in which I write this. A side effect of a barbaric world that, for instance, had a small sparkle called Democracy and civilization, but to use those words to describe any polity today makes liars of all those who dare.

As stated earlier, moderation is the most crucial aspect to consider in a well-functioning government system. A government system must, to the best of its ability, personify a moderate system in all its methods, laws, judgments, and enforcement. Moderation, temperament, and a sense of non-extremism are hard to find within an enraged polity. Much as it is hard to find sanity amongst the mad. Yet when moderation is replaced with extremism, madness prevails over sanity. This is a continual dilemma of humanity. For many generations, people have had wars in the name of almost everything conceivable. Warriors and governments have often used religion to persuade people to fight. Money has been paid to people to fight. All forms of incentives have been used to rally people. But none are more convinced of imminent death than the ones who fight for an ideal.

Moderation, fairness, and equal representation are needed for the five classes of society to balance. A symptom of corruption within a Democracy begins with the loss of that balance. Much like the sniffle of a person's nose indicates a cold is on the way, so too, a Democracy will know it has become infected when the Democracy begins to favour one class over another, one group of people or an individual over the majority. This is why balancing the classes must be inherited from a polity that is moderate and tempered, rather than one willing to cause harm or throw the balance in its own favor.

11. Variations of government

"Placing a prefix before the word Democracy, such as a Direct Democracy, is an oxymoron. There is only one entity that can be called a Democracy."

We have spoken at length about the importance of harmony and balance among the classes in a Democratic polity. We have also discussed how the economic model can become skewed to the point where it favors certain social classes. This was highlighted through reference to the economic models of Communism and Capitalism. Historically, economic policy has a significant impact on how governments make decisions, affecting not only the economic model but also all facets of society. In the past, especially when more of the world was not under imperial exploitation, governments operated differently. Ultimately, humanity has been limited in exploring different government models, with only a few instances of experimentation. The Athenian Democracy was one such experiment that many would consider a success despite its ultimate conquest.

In the literature of my time, authors often suggest that there were many more variations of Democracy, Oligarchies, and Monarchies than those mentioned so far. To keep the field interesting and active, political scientists often enjoy inventing new words and redefining existing ones. Now that we have a solid basis for our three categories of government, I think it is appropriate to acknowledge some of these variations. These variations of government should not be considered philosophically correct categories or types, but rather as phrases or terms that have become so popular that the uneducated and the majority may come to recognize them.

Initially, let us clarify some issues regarding how the term 'Democracy' might be used. There is only one type of Democracy, as stated; Democracy represents the better form of a Pleistarchy. The vast majority of variations or governments calling themselves a form of Democracy are, in fact, not true democracies. To create confusion, there is now a myriad of false Democratic government types, and to lend them some kind of authenticity, they often categorize the only true Democracy as just another amongst many. There are Liberal Democracies, Militarised Democracies, Despotic Democracies, Representative Democracies, Direct Democracies, Indirect Democracies, and so forth. Perhaps the most critical aspect of this philosophy is the distinction between direct and indirect democracy. We will begin with the distinction between direct and indirect democracy, since indirect democracy, or indirect government, is the most prevalent worldwide.

The Democratic system referred to throughout this philosophy is sometimes referred to as a direct democracy. Using a prefix like "direct" in front of the term democracy is an oxymoron. It is a redundant phrase. As we have thoroughly investigated, democracy can only be directly controlled by the people. All other instances of it are a reduction to the quality of that definition. Let us look at the distinction between Indirect and Direct governance. At least in that way, we can begin to fathom the extent to which Indirect forms of government can manifest.

11.1 Representative Democracy

If a person gives his vote to another through a proxy, it does not constitute a transfer of opinions, deductions, or decisions. A person able to vote and decide on behalf of another citizen simply has two votes: his own and that of the citizen they represent or have been authorized to act as a proxy for. If an individual can effectively convey their opinion to a proxy, and then the proxy, in turn, represents that opinion, then some merit could be attributed to the system. Yet when such a proxy representative arrives in government, how could they relay everything that is before them to their client or source? Even if the representative had prepared what to say and how to vote on behalf of their client when they arrived at the assembly, they could no longer communicate with them, ask for their opinion, or debate the matter, nor could they pass on all the information at hand to the client. If the citizens are not present at the meeting themselves, it is akin to having a jury where people at home cast their votes without listening to any evidence or the discussion that follows.

A representative government can never truly represent anyone other than the individuals who participate in it. Therefore, the premise of an Indirect Democracy, much like any Indirect Government, is that the people do not directly partake in the operation of government and that others represent them. If that is so, then the power of the people is distilled to those who control their votes within the government. Therefore, Indirect Democracy is not a Democracy at all. It is a form of Oligarchy. Indirect Democracies have manifested in several forms throughout the world. The republic or representative forms of Government are the most popular Indirect Democracies and tend to predominate worldwide. Of course, the term "Indirect Democracy" merely hides the true nature of the government model. An indirect Democracy is nothing more than a mask for an Oligarchy to wear and use against the people.

Republics are said to have emerged through Democratic institutions. The evolution or devolution of a republic began with allowing absentee voting. This meant a person unable to attend a meeting could send their son or another individual to represent them. Strictly speaking, this was not allowed during the

Democratic years of the Athenian Democracy. When a citizen could not attend an assembly, they forfeited their chance to attend and had no alternative action other than attending the following assembly. However, the collapse of any system begins with bending its rules. There are reasons rules are established, but given enough time, few people will be aware of them. Who amongst the Athenians would allow the son of an absent citizen to represent his father? To those at the start of the Athenian Democracy, none would. But a century later, people bent the rules that preserved their system and its integrity. Perhaps it was something difficult to monitor and police. By allowing representation for absent members, possibly by other family members, the absentee proxy vote became its own system. It was the basis for the republic that would follow. An act of seeming good can corrupt an entire system. During Ancient Athenian times, the main pervasive issue was absentee proxy voting.

It is worth noting that, historically, Democracy has led to Oligarchy, and Oligarchy has led to Democracy. Democracy is such a fragile thing. It is often transformed into an oligarchy because some individuals consistently seek to establish control or gain more power for themselves. The power-grabbing behavior often created a flux between an Oligarchy and Democracy. Never has a Democracy been reduced to an Autocracy directly.

It was not long after the emergence of the Athenian Democracy that the Roman Republic appeared. Plato in Sicily became a political prisoner for teaching about Democracy. It was not so much his ideas that landed him a comfortable prison within the castle walls, but rather his views came during a period of unrest. Yet, over time, the Greek cities in Italy began to shift towards democratic governments, despite the opposition of the elite and wealthy. It was, in many ways, seen as a compromise to create a Republic. A system that allowed the elite in power and those without power to work together. The Republic was founded on the principle that citizens would trust other individuals (the elite) to express their views to the assembly. Of course, it was merely a system to converge the interests of the extremely powerful and wealthy. The average citizen likely had little to no understanding of the political affairs unfolding within the assembly, senate, and the government system as a whole. The Roman Republic lasted for a considerable period.

As with all systems, they gravitate and fluctuate towards certain modes of operation. Augustus turned the Republic (an Oligarchy) into an Autocracy, being the first to be considered an emperor of the Romans, although this was disputed. It is not hard to see throughout the history of Rome that a Democracy can lose its power when the people become decadent and rely on others to operate a government for them. This decadence led to a few people ruling over the majority of Rome. Finally, the few families that controlled the Roman government were replaced by dictators and other autocrats. Systems based on republics often fluctuated between pseudo-representative oligarchies and dictatorships, as well as other forms of autocratic rule. Absolute monarchs also arise from such systems, but to a much lesser degree. It could even be said that the founders of Rome on the hill of Palatino were autocrats. Furthermore, the generals or the soldier class often usurped the autocratic position. Just as democracy fluctuated between democratic and oligarchic forms, the republic fluctuated between an oligarchic and autocratic form.

Let us clarify one more thing: many people perceive the Republic system as a form of Democracy rather than an Oligarchy. A Republic is perhaps one of the better forms of an Oligarchy and is often referred to as an Aristocracy. Yet, the Republic system is often referred to as a Democracy or a Representative Democracy. Unfortunately, a Representative Democracy is neither representative nor a Democracy. We have already stated the reasons why, but to elaborate further, the term Kratos means the holding of power. In the term Democracy, the suffix -cracy is derived from kratia or kratos, meaning the holding of power.

When examining the scenario of Representative Government, we need only ask where the power lies before and after the citizens' vote. If the power available to the citizen is only the ability to vote for who holds power, then that is not a Democracy. Voting for someone to vote on your behalf in government is not the same as voting on who will be president, or secretary, or what actions will be taken within government directly. Sometimes, republics hold referendums when a topic becomes too contentious and affects a large number of people. They did it when they crucified Christ, and Pontius Pilate said, "I wash my hands of sin," and gave the vote to the ecclesiastical hierarchs and the people. At first glance, voting by referendum may seem like a democratic process. The problem is that the people never set the question that was brought forward in the referendums. So, as you can see, voting on who supposedly represents us gives power to the individual who represents us. It can never be a case where the power or kratos is both with the people and elsewhere. Either the people hold power over the government, or the government holds power over them.

Suppose a young person, unaware of how honey is extracted from hives, is approached by another individual to perform the task. In that case, we expect that the person making the request would also instruct the person appropriately. If the young man is stung during his foolish attempts, are we to blame the bee, the youth, or the man who set the task? To whom was the power, authority, worthiness, or exousia to perform a particular duty? The Exousia, the authority and power, is derived from the man asking for the job to be done. Exousia is more than just the power. It is the derived substance or outer formation of power. It was under another's instruction that the young man met his match with the sting of the bees. Therefore, power is a measure of those capable of attaining actions. In a democratic system, exousia — power, authority, and worthiness — is found in the people. In other types of systems, power may be held by an oligarchy, an aristocracy, an Autocracy, or a Monarchy. The extent to which one perceives power is debatable. What most people imagine as power, or more specifically as some form of holding power in government, varies. Some people are content to believe in illusions, and others are never satisfied until the truth is known. In any case, it is the holding of power that is important to operating a Democracy. Therefore, the spring or source of empowerment must be with the people for it to be called a Democratic condition. If the source of empowerment comes from a minority, it is an Oligarchy; if it comes from a single source, it is an Autocracy.

For instance, many argue that a representative will cast votes that exercise the power and authority of the individual or citizen they represent. Many people further argue that not only is a representative exercising the authority of the citizens they represent, but that the citizens also maintain the authority to change their representative. Alone, such arguments are superfluous in the sense that they state the obvious: that a citizen has given a representative the authority to act on their behalf for a duration of time. However, governments that promote such a system often imply that it is a form of democracy. Some people seem content to let others handle the political agenda, while they can focus on their daily business. In any case, the vote alone does not define the individual's power. The vote is only an extension of the individual's power. In a Democracy, voting is mostly used to decide upon actions and court decisions. In any form of elected government, the vote often comes down to choosing who will represent the citizens. It could be argued that citizens maintain authority over their representatives; however, from a pragmatic perspective, the so-called representatives exercise authority over the citizens.

In most cases, it is not a personal matter, such as the Athenian absentee proxy vote, which utilized relatives or friends to convey a vote or participate in the assembly. Modern representative governments often form parties and groups that enter the political arena as a union of representatives with a common agenda. That common agenda is between the representatives and not the citizens they represent. Once the citizens use their vote to elect a representative, the exercise of power returns to a neutral state until the next election.

Imagine a scenario where we place a group of people and two feeding troughs in a cage. Each trough had two different foods, and the people in the cage were deciding which of the two they should eat. They could cast a vote between them and decide which of the foods to eat. If the people resolved all the matters that affected them, then we could assume they lived in a democratic state. But even still, they do not have a choice of which food to place in each trough. The power they have ends where they no longer have physical control or the ability to operate their affairs. In this case, the hold of their power is limited within the cage. But what if they voted for a group of people to manage their food and relied on the elected group to make decisions on their behalf? The outcome is almost identical, except that the elected group could decide on either option without the direct say of anyone in the cage. In other words, we should not limit any government by labels; the reality is what we endure as humans. If freedom is lost, it makes little difference how the internal political structure operates. Freedom with a Democratic system amounts to much more than a Democracy limited by a cage or by an Oligarchy or Monarchy that confines it.

When we speak of Kratos, Power, and Authority, they can mean many different things to people. It is, therefore, important to clarify these terms more than what has already been mentioned. The definition of Democracy is the holding of power by the people. Therefore, Kratos and Power are entwined in the definition. Holding power must mean directly holding power, as was the case in the Athenian model. If holding power is indirect, then it is no longer a case of holding power but substituting the holders of power from the people to the governors. Power, on the other hand, is a little more complex to define clearly. Power is a fluctuating and perceptive thing.

Reputation, affluence, and other things associated with an individual's status are related to how power is perceived. During the Byzantine era, there were many Monarchs, Autocrats, and Emperors. One of the punishments they devised was to scar the faces of other relatives or potential heirs to their throne. Scarring the face was seen as reducing the capacity for others to follow them. Perhaps there is some merit in this, as humans tend to follow, if necessary, the fittest and what they perceive as the most capable. A bright, clean, well-presented individual who also radiates leadership, skill, intelligence, and knowledge is often followed more easily than the opposite, a dirty individual who appears like a beggar. Even Jesus Christ and his disciples maintained a high degree of hygiene despite their poverty and rejection of material wealth. It has been made apparent throughout the ages that cleanliness is important. So when we say power, it is not a simple noun; it is a descriptive word, perhaps an attribute that describes an energy source. The sense of power being a real and tangible object comes from the ability to apply energy and initiate action. It describes how people perceive the source of dynamic energy. If the energy is applied with great force or momentum, then the power is considered great. In a political sense, power can be popular among peers.

In an assembly, individuals are all made aware of the agenda that they contributed to setting, and then they listen to arguments against and for the situation at hand. They can also speak and ask questions; after a long investigation and understanding of the issue, they cast a vote. In that context, the power is not in the vote but in the attendance, participation, and expression of the individual through the vote. All these things identify the power or source of power as it stems from a citizen.

Voting is merely a method to quantify the discussion points raised during the meeting at the assembly. It is an indicator or measure of the deductions made at an assembly. The vote is not, in itself, an expression of power. It is the right to vote, and it is the attendance and participation that express power. In other words, we must examine the energy source before the action to determine if power truly resides with the person and if it has been effectively utilized.

Regarding proxy voting or any form of representation, the person has given another the right to attend, participate in, and vote on their behalf in the assembly. In some systems, a board of Oligarchs may consider the votes of a broader circle of Oligarchs, tiered into upper and Lower Assemblies or councils, but not necessarily consider their votes. The size of Oligarchies can be very large, but the proportion of those operating governments remains consistent with the few operating governments on behalf of the majority.

Then, we may ask if anyone can truly be represented. Everyone is unique, and our abilities, knowledge, skills, wisdom, and everything that defines us will vary. When we educate children, we do not send them to one teacher. We prefer many teachers, each with something new and different to teach. The importance of knowledge cannot be left to one person to teach. No one retains all the information in the world; therefore, to learn, people must interact with many different individuals. Learning can be a social occasion as much as it can be a private one. However, those who have had many teachers and attended many schools tend to have a better temperament and knowledge, and thus operate as better individuals and citizens in society. It is also why a Democracy works well because a Democracy led by any of the five classes, for example, would be very specific and narrow in its views and become unfavorable to any of the other classes. A government led exclusively by farmers, financiers, merchants, workers, technicians, professionals, and highly educated people all have merit when combined, not when one group leads the others. Every layer and part of a polity can express its view within a Democracy. The opinions of carpenters, nurses, waste collectors, tax collectors, soldiers, and people from various occupations, as well as knowledge and wisdom, contribute piece by piece to form a bigger and more balanced system. If decisions were left to those operating banks or financial institutions, then wouldn't we expect that all their deductions would be biased to what they know? Just as much as when workers speak, would they not seek to lighten their burdens and form biased opinions in their favor? All these things contribute to and illustrate the importance of variation and balance within a democratic assembly. That variation and balance make it possible for everyone to represent themselves to the best of their ability.

I am not referring to legal or court proceedings, where the allowance of a representative to co-work in delivering a case in court may be considered acceptable. Mutes, individuals who are deaf or have some other disability, may be seen as needing representative help, but these would be the exception rather than the norm. Yet all this depends on how the courts are arranged and designed. It is beneficial to have the input of more knowledgeable and capable people, which is even expected in an assembly. If the subject is shipbuilding, we expect the shipbuilders to provide advice, not the bakers or legal consultants. Similarly, certain circumstances necessitate the input of specialized knowledge. Likewise, in courts, it would be expected that people with specialized knowledge would help facilitate the legal process fairly for the sake of justice.

A court is not the entire government's legislature or administrative executive. The Judiciary may be operated by a jury and a panel of professional jurors, but those standing before the Jury are not in power. The Jury is in power. It is, therefore, acceptable to have representatives in that case to facilitate justice. But for a Juror to take an absence and have another take their place by proxy has essentially taken away their power to partake in the Jury. The accused or those involved with the case would need to question the formation of the jury. Therefore, it is clear that while representation is required to facilitate a process known to a few specialists, the process of decision-making should never be left in anyone else's hands. The concept must permeate the entire system, not just at the Assembly or legislature.

Many representative governments attempt to portray the power to vote for an Oligarchy as the fundamental right of each citizen. Ironically, they do not empower the people; the people empower themselves to vote and give away their votes. A representative government relies heavily on persuading the people to vote for the few who lead them. In some places operating a representative government, only positive votes are counted, so if the people cast a blank or alternative vote in protest, their vote is not counted. Additionally, the methods used for voting are often intentionally designed to dissuade any form of unrest within the populace. In some cases, soft government gives people a certain degree of freedom, and as long as the perception of that freedom exists, whether it is real or not, it matters little. That is why voting is often used by soft Dictatorships, where people have the right to vote and, for some reason, perpetually vote the same person or group into power.

In other countries, a similar method is also employed. Still, it is divided into a Didymus (twin) competitor system or pluralism, resulting in the same outcome, regardless of which of the two or several parties enters government. If the people approach systems like these to establish a Democracy, however, the system will be turned against the people. These systems are Oligarchical, and the entire system's construct is to preserve and keep the power of the Oligarchy. Some countries refer to this type of system as a restricted Constitution. There is nothing essentially wrong with such a restricted constitution. Even in Athens, the most serious crime was attempting to corrupt or undermine the democratic nature of the government. In the same way, Oligarchies will defend themselves through a similar constitution as do Autocrats.

It becomes evident when we consider many of the systems in the world and how they operate that voting to elect a representative is essentially not the same as voting in an assembly or as part of a jury. However, a form of voting is often found in places with Representative governments to solve various public issues. The process is called a Referendum, which refers to the people's vote. Establishing a government that operates almost exclusively with referendum votes is theoretically possible. Yet, the process has a fundamental flaw in that the majority of power is retained by those who set the referendum questions. The agenda is limited, and the questions are predetermined, not by the people, but by a separate entity, and they cannot be changed or discussed. For example, while the nation must decide on war or a serious security issue, the people are given the chance to decide on daylight saving time. Almost trivial problems are commonly used in referendum votes, while serious matters are often handled behind the scenes.

The power source in a Democracy is the individual, but it is a soft power, unlike Autocracies and Oligarchies. It is soft because the voice of one person is seemingly powerless alone. Yet the majority voice has the greatest power over any other. Within a Democracy, all voices are a power of their own, but the unity of the majority creates the ultimate political power. The source of action comes from the net result of all the people or citizens. While referendums can be likened to direct democracy, they invite those outside the government—the people—to vote. The voice and power of the people, if kept outside of government, have little effect when sporadically or even methodically granted the opportunity to vote on a set of questions. Referendums eliminate the discourse, discussion, and participation between other citizens before voting. Many governments forbid discussing the matters being voted on at the venues where the votes are held.

The reasons they often give are tangential to the reality. For instance, they may claim to keep the votes unpersuaded and uncoerced; yet, without discourse or discussion, a significant part of the democratic process has been taken away.

No matter how we try to justify the term 'Representative Democracy,' the ultimate conclusion is that no such system exists. Sometimes, we struggle to represent ourselves accurately; how can anyone truly represent another individual? How can a system operated by an elected Oligarchy be called Democratic? It reminds me of a debate I once had with an individual who resides in a Constitutional Monarchy. He said that the Monarch merely serves a Ceremonial role. I asked him if perhaps we should establish a Ceremonial Democracy. Despite all the evidence and indicators, some people seem unbothered by differentiating truth from falsehood. Many reasons exist for accepting falsehoods over truths. Some people, for the sake of a greater cause, nationalistic bias, convenience, diplomatic, or any other reason, will gravitate towards not accepting the full truth. This, however, is a philosophy, and those biases are not present. As already stated, a Republic or Representative Democracy is neither Representative nor Democratic.

Most of our time has been spent analyzing various representative government systems, as they were largely formed at the time of writing this. Many people still refer to them as democracies, even though some constitutions formally founded nations as democracies, yet operate as oligarchies. It is essential to emphasize that there is only one form of democracy. As we have discovered through philosophical and historical analysis, of all the systems at our disposal, Democracy is the best of them.

11.2 Other Government Variations

Other forms of government that arise from time to time are called Kleptocracy or Plutocracy. Kleptocracy means the power is in the hands of Thieves. Although this differs from Plutocracy, which refers to a condition where the wealthy hold power, both terms refer to a skewed economic bias. Since stealing material implies gaining material, both Kleptocracy and Plutocracy are often used as synonyms. The difference is subtle but important. Usually, in a Kleptocracy, the leaders do not necessarily have to have excessive wealth. For instance, if someone is starving and hungry and elected to be a leader, they will first want to satisfy their hunger.

Meanwhile, a well-fed and complacent leader will not have much need to satisfy their hunger. A Kleptocracy usually arises when new people enter an Oligarchy and seek to profit from their roles. A plutocracy typically occurs when the established and extremely wealthy use their wealth to enact laws and systems that protect their wealth. These terms are not categories of Government but subcategories that describe how the three types of government operate. Usually, they are descriptive of Oligarchies and Autocracies.

This same idea extends to situations when the clergy or priests operate a government, often termed a Theocracy or Clerocracy. The fact that the few within a Theocracy are priests or religious clergy does not change the fact that a Theocracy is an Oligarchy. If one priest ruled the government as a Monarch or Autocrat, then such a system is still a Monarchy or Autocracy, but is operated by the Clergy or priests. There are many other names for various forms of Government, and as I have suggested, most are a form of Oligarchy or Monarchy.

12. Synopsis

"...the education and information we have in our lives is not devised to deliver the truth."

Most people intrinsically hope that one day, humanity will inherit the earth through the path of the meek. The term meek means to be humble and in servitude towards a higher being that most of us know as God. Meek, to the secularists or even atheists, tends to infer those bound by morals and good faith towards their fellow human beings. The inheritance of the earth shall not come by the formation of armies and the conquest of neighbors, nor will it be through the bloodshed of others. It has become the universal hope of humanity that a revolution will transform society: from the bad to the good, from lies to truth, and from unrighteousness to righteousness. From the earliest writings, humanity has sought a better way of life, happiness, and prosperity. Yet none of the government systems can offer that prosperity and happiness to everyone. A majority can bring those things to fruition through a Democracy. That is not to say that a minority couldn't achieve the same things on behalf of the majority. Self-governance will not make everyone happy; some individuals will likely complain about their responsibilities. However, self-government through a democratic system is the one thing that Democracy offers that other systems do not. It is a component of our free will and, hence, our freedom.

If the people sought a democracy, they would face many obstacles. For the people to inherit the Earth, they must have the voice and power to do so. It is this matter that has held people back from achieving anything. Consider for a moment that the ancient Athenians and the Hellenistic people are among the few who attained and maintained a Democracy for a respectable period. In irony, the start of the Democratic Revolution in Athens relied on the elite and influential families to support the idea that no elite, oligarchs, or autocrats should rule over the people. A Democracy requires those with power and those without to unite, which is rare and difficult to expect. In addition, the classes that make up society can skew power from one group to another, and we often struggle to balance that power. In Athens, every male was required to serve in the military throughout his productive life. It was their way of balancing the military's power over the entire system. But in a world filled with wealthy merchants, they create a power of their own that can be equal to or more powerful than the military alone. So often, we see both being classes that define authority and power. A Democracy to work requires the classes to be balanced and fair. If one group or some groups become overly powerful, they can upset the mechanism by which any government operates. Even the government has a role and can't be an overbearing power. Otherwise, it is an ochlocracy or some lesser form of government.

Democracy places the entirety of political power and authority in the hands of the people. Yet even when the people are in such a position, maintaining it is the most challenging task given to any government and people. There are always those with power and money to sway the meek and meager. Often, resistance to the influence of the wealthy and powerful seems futile, as their influence seduces many away from a democratic system. People think they are fools for not benefiting in that moment when they have the opportunity. Tyranny does not always rely on force, power, or harsh or draconian tactics. As always, tyranny in the modern age is well equipped with all manner of persuasion, seduction, and force. Education becomes a process for assimilating the pleistos (majority rule). Wealth and money can become so highly desired that people often forfeit their freedom in pursuit of them. It is these incentives that make people work. Currency is one of those things that is frequently used to control people.

Even if the people were educated enough to establish a Democracy, it would not be given to them. There is no government willing to release its grip unless it is challenged, fought, and conquered by the same people it has ruled over. An internal struggle is often fought with words, not weapons. Seemingly, a change such as the one described will result in many physical wars. One would need to argue the value of such wars, and it is within that evaluation that we find disunity, contradiction, and division. We all have an opinion, and we can't all agree on the same thing at the same time. Even if the truth is generally agreed to, other biases manifest and prevent it from being realized. Logic and education go some way towards establishing a Democracy, but it is life experience that brings an understanding of the system and its value.

If we believe that, one day, humanity, in its meekest form, not wild, rebellious, and anger-filled, but ethical and righteous, will inherit the earth, then there is no other system to achieve this. Democracy is the only system that inverts the pyramids of power, placing the average human at its pinnacle and its base simultaneously. Democracy can't guarantee that a war will be waged only when the people deem the correct reasons for it, at the correct time, against the correct target, and in the correct manner. No system can guarantee these things. However, one could argue that a mistake like war is more than likely to be declared on our behalf, as history has shown. The prevention of war is not guaranteed, but it is more likely to be realized by Democratic people.

Unlike Socrates and Plato, who proposed that there is no perfect system, I can't conclude the exact same. While democracy is one of two significant manifestations of a Pleistocracy, the other being an Ochlocracy, the latter indicates that even democracy can be easily corrupted and ruined. Socrates and Plato were indeed correct in their views that no system is perfect. However, Democracy is the best choice we have of all systems, provided it remains ethical and pure and does not degenerate into an Ochlocracy. If it remains a Democracy and does not become controlled by some angry mob or by elitists, then it offers much more than any other system. While the Democratic system can offer us a solution for the future, many questions remain. A person may wonder whether democracy is worth fighting for. If the will of the people leads them to battle, will a Dictator be propped up in the end on their behalf? Numerous historical instances demonstrate that ousting a government often leads to the emergence of a similar ruler, leader, or system. Only during the bloody revolutions from the early 1700s to the mid-1800s across the globe did we see some reasonable change from monarchy to aristocratic or republican rule; yet they remained choked by the same oligarchies. Humanity as a whole is cautious not only with its own lives but with the prospect of supporting a futile battle. Each location on Earth has its own unique political issues. War to achieve Democracy seems ironic to some, but it is testified throughout our history that rebellion and internal wars are the only methods by which a system can change. Yet throughout our history, people have died only to replace one oppressor with another. These factors make us hesitant to initiate such a movement. If the movement prospers, then there are always a few poised to take control of what the people start. Yet, knowing all these things, I still believe we should not leave Democracy on the shelf, as Plato and Socrates concluded. Democracy is a viable solution to most of the problems faced by other forms of government. But the manner to achieve it is through a peaceful union between those with the power and those without it to form a Democracy. Peacefully acquiring a Democratic system takes time, but it is the only tested way. As already stated, the elite of Athens facilitated the establishment of the democratic system.

History has a way of hiding specific laws from us, but we have reached an age where even minor infractions can be considered a crime. By this, I mean that it is no longer, as Plato once paraphrased, the case that a wise man does not necessarily need to read or recite the law to know it. There are indeed many wise laws, such as not stealing, not murdering, and not destroying what others have. Yet today, some laws protect everything except the individual's freedom and rights. For instance, there are laws to protect workers, but no laws to protect citizens. There are fines for parking a transport vehicle in certain areas, but there are no guarantees of freedom to place it wherever one wishes on public property. The laws of the past are entirely different in nature than those of today. Today, the laws, if applied all at once to all of humanity, would make all of them criminals. When a system has reached such a stage where the freedom of people no longer exists, in that case only, would any people consider war to be an option? Many, in small groups, retaliate and form outlaw organizations, and some even organize outlaw businesses. But these entities are an overly reactive symptom of oppressive law. The people involved with such organizations are often worse than their oppressors, and their business is almost always tied to things that are prohibited by the authority of the state. So then, caution must be taken that a reaction to oppression is not done through a minority outlaw and renegade band. Instead, there is a need to formulate a process for restoring or creating a Democracy and fair democratic laws.

The fight – or willingness to enter battle – for the Democratic ideal is also linked to situations in which people want to stop another empire, to cut down the powers of the greedy who manipulate markets and buy cities like the poor buy food. It is a preemptive strike—or perhaps a reactive battle—against world domination or a similar agenda to bring the world under one government. The enemies of a Democracy are the sprawl of big, powerful, overbearing entities that seek nothing more than to enslave and subdue entire nations and cities of countless numbers across the globe. Even Athens, at the height of its democratic institutions, betrayed its principles of Democracy when it subdued its neighbors through power and forced them to pay tribute. It was one of the primary reasons for the Peloponnesian Wars between Sparta and the Athenian League, which lasted for twenty years.

Even if a Democracy exists, it can't be a system of many cities controlled by one city, but rather a league of independent cities. Yet we know that when a city oppresses another, it can manifest as a warring entity. The United States of America once had many independent cities. The Northern Union was a union under the force of military and political maneuvering. The Union eventually subdued the independent and southern cities that had joined a defensive league against the North's military might. Rome, when it began subduing cities, propelled itself into dominance over many cities and suppressed many people to build an unsustainable empire. Athens and its league defeated Sparta but lost to Rome. The recurring theme or story is that an oppressive military may devour the Democratic freedom of independent cities.

In some cases, when an Ochlos is replaced by a Monarchy or Aristocracy, it can be justified since an Ochlos is like a mob. Who is to judge an Ochlos, the few or the majority? Sometimes things require change, and if that change is needed within a short period, war is often used. The concept of Democracy, therefore, may seem doomed as an ideal. A simple matter of war and military strength perpetually eliminates it. However, the League of Nations, which operated independently from 1920 to 1946, spanning World War II, managed to thwart a single-backed nation's attempt to dominate many other cities and nations.

Many also argue today over the aftermath of what the world has come to know as the Autocratic Colonization period. It was a period when autocrats sought to conquer or control lands beyond their national boundaries. Arguably, from the fall of Constantinople through to the early twentieth century, the world endured one of the most horrid periods in human history, far worse than the madness of medieval wars. I wish to provide a list of well-known genocides, attempted genocides, and the mass murder of human beings, but I omit them because I am not certain if all that is reported is, in fact, true. But certainly, of the ones I have investigated, many did occur.

Let us now look at the case for War again. If war is what a nation wants, then the Autocracy and Oligarchy are the best suited to that desire. All they need to do is convince half the people that there is a reason to go to war. If they control the media and all forms of information, then they can easily control the lies that people believe. They can blame the economic collapse on aliens, fictitious entities, or other nations and ethnicities. War is ultimately the reason why so many autocracies and oligarchies exist. It is easier to send people's children into war if the parents and children have no say in the matter. This is why there are no Democracies today, or at least at the time I write this. They have all collapsed, and cities now exist under massive government entities. These empire-styled entities are guarded by some of the most horrific and barbaric weapons humanity has yet to devise. It is ultimately fear that prevents people from speaking against the norm. They can't be blamed. It is much better to be silent than to be a fool who speaks the truth in public, and even greater is the fool who writes it down. But if truth is never spoken and never written, then there will never be anything founded upon the truth. A perpetual lie will exist to keep people subservient and oppressed. It, therefore, is easy to see that if the people wage war, it is the Autocracy and Oligarchies that will have the advantage.

They will win any physical war, as they have throughout the Revolutionary period and throughout all of human history.

In Plato's Allegory of the Cave, he suggests that our knowledge of the world is limited to our perception. Consequently, our knowledge and information are skewed through that limited perception. People have disputed the relevance of such an allegory. Yet not long ago, I noticed that people of various generations shared only what was written in the newspaper, spoken on the radio, and shown on television. My grandmother's remedies are lost. As with generations that followed, the people's memories were filled with clear images of various news, political, and technological events. It seems that Plato's allegory of the cave was not entirely wrong when considering humanity as a whole and its behavior. The allegory of the cave is not difficult to understand, but because it was an example, many disputed its literal meaning instead of grasping its implied message. For clarity, I will provide a translated excerpt of it here:

"… "Next," said I, "compare our nature in respect of education and its lack to such an experience as this. Picture men dwelling in a sort of subterranean cavern with a long entrance open to the light on its entire width. Conceive them as having their legs and necks fettered from childhood, so that they remain in the same spot, able to look forward only, and prevented by the fetters from turning their heads. Picture further the light from a fire burning higher up and at a distance behind them, and between the fire and the prisoners and above them a road along which a low wall has been built, as the exhibitors of puppet shows have partitions before the men themselves, above which they show the puppets." "All that I see," he said. "See also, then, men carrying past the wall implements of all kinds that rise above the wall, and human images and shapes of animals as well, wrought in stone and wood and every material, some of these bearers presumably speaking and

others silent." "A strange image you speak of," he said, "and strange prisoners." "Like to us," I said; "for, to begin with, tell me do you think that these men would have seen anything of themselves or of one another except the shadows cast from the fire on the wall of the cave that fronted them?" "How could they," he said, "if they were compelled to hold their heads unmoved through life?" "And again, would not the same be true of the objects carried past them?" "Surely." "If then they were able to talk to one another, do you not think that they would suppose that in naming the things that they saw they were naming the passing objects?" "Necessarily." "And if their prison had an echo from the wall opposite them, when one of the passers-by uttered a sound, do you think that they would suppose anything else than the passing shadow to be the speaker?" "By Zeus, I do not," said he. "Then in every way such prisoners would deem reality to be nothing else than the shadows of the artificial objects." "Quite inevitably," he said. "Consider, then, what would be the manner of the release and healing from these bonds and this folly if in the course of nature something of this sort should happen to them: When one was freed from his fetters and compelled to stand up suddenly and turn his head around and walk and to lift up his eyes to the light, and in doing all this felt pain and, because of the dazzle and glitter of the light, was unable to discern the objects whose shadows he formerly saw, what do you suppose would be his answer if someone told him that what he had seen before was all a cheat and an illusion, but that now, being nearer to reality and turned toward more real things, he saw more truly? And if also one should point out to him each of the passing objects and constrain him by questions to say what it is, do you not think that he would be at a loss and that he would regard what he formerly saw as more real than the things now pointed out to him?"(Plato, 1969, 7.514a - 7.515d)

Humans are limited in what we know because the education and information we receive in our lives are not designed for the sole purpose of delivering the truth. All facets of modern life have become institutionalized, and people feel uncomfortable when the institution fails to provide what they are accustomed to. Most of these things are luxuries that are not necessary altogether, yet they seem to appease most people. These things of appeasement can be technological products or what has now become almost essential, like hot water within each home. Apathy, decadence, sloth, and laziness are all a part of institutionalized people. They perceive apathy, decadence, and sloth as signs of happiness and contentment. It feels to them like an elevation from the primal life or the primitive existence we expect in nature. Yet, even in that primitive environment, these luxuries could be attained without relying on others.

In some cases, such as with particular forms of technology, it is impossible to produce without dedicated equipment and other advanced technologies. It is, therefore, these technologies that create the case for losing self-sufficiency and submitting to them for their benefits, without much attention to the long-term impact. The long-term impact is the institutionalization of humanity. If we travel anywhere in the world, we will find that every society has a set of normal modes of life. In some remote societies, people may live in huts in the jungle, and we notice that their huts are all similar. Likewise, all the houses in any city adopt a particular style considered normal, and any variations, if any, are usually historical. So, it becomes clear that a degree of institutionalism is derived from the people. How else could such conformity exist in the absence of any law imposing it? However, it must be made clear that while no law demands a particular home to be built in a particular way, those who build it have all been educated by the same institution. It is this conformity among professionals that creates a body, or soma, of similar-minded people. In other words, while many criticize Plato's allegory of the cave, he is being subtle by raising the idea that our education and our knowledge form the foundations of our actions, and by limiting, censoring, or somehow skewing, obscuring, or perverting the truth of such knowledge, it also corrupts our actions.

The issue I have raised is not entirely new. It has appeared sporadically in modern art. Perhaps the most iconic and popular film adaptation of this book to date depicted the nuances of institutionalization. Many also depict the problems of oppressive rule by the minority, the creation of a pseudo-world that institutionalizes the people. People living in such systems are unable to know freedom or slavery or to distinguish truth from lies.

Many people think they are happy and content because they have what they want in life. Yet what they want is not really their own choice. They believe that as long as enough money is generated to meet their needs, wants, and desires, they will be content. The complexity of society does not guarantee the same prosperity for its children or their grandchildren. Therefore, they do what they think is best for the moment. They believe money is the key to happiness, and many strive to make it. Unfortunately, a system only requires a fraction of people to be satisfied, just enough to make the rest feel like they can achieve the same.

A system that facilitates people with qualifications also has a few problems. We see so many people living in deluded bubbles, thinking they deserve their languishing incomes because of some idea that the paper that recognizes their learning process grants them that right. Degrees, diplomas, and similar qualifications not only create a division of economic affluence but also divide some people based on some pretense of worth or social status. Doctors are considered more valuable than cleaners, even though they are both essential. The evaluation of doctors has been a persistent phenomenon throughout history, and, as described, can manifest as a form of worship. This power comes not merely from money, but from the status that doctors hold in most societies. We must then understand that society is complex and that balancing the classes and people's power is a perpetual task that must be monitored and adjusted over time. Otherwise, we end up with one class being of more value and happier than another.

In all institutions where specialization and tertiary education are most employable, there is a tier of financial affluence to accompany the caste of intellect. People considered the most intelligent tend to earn the most, while those considered less intelligent tend to earn the least. Of course, many people are unsatisfied with the prearranged situation and seek to traverse between the classes. A forty-year-old man with numerous years of experience may feel disgruntled to see a twenty-year-old earning more than he takes home to his family. There are many more scenarios, of course, where some people may feel a form of injustice. This is why competition is very high, and people resort to many atrocious things. Some people at the bottom of the socio-economic scale do not necessarily feel content because they are ultimately as intelligent as those earning more. The result is crime, but more correctly, it is the equalization through self-administered justice. This form of justice is, however, very dangerous in the hands of those without wisdom or who are not as intelligent as they wish they were. Often, what is perceived as justice—taking from the wealthy—raises concerns about the methods used. Many innocent people die in the process of self-administered justice.

Additionally, rather than addressing the ideology that is the root of the problem, they resort to theft and robbery, creating anarchy and chaos, all for their own personal benefit, albeit without any meaningful purpose. The Outlaw culture evolves through cultures that allow an increasing number of intelligent people to live in poverty. Let's examine places around the world that are reported to have the highest levels of organized crime, or at least systemic crime. They are also places where a large number of intelligent people live in poverty, without access to mechanisms that can improve their economic conditions.

Organized or systemic outlaw organizations and groups are feared entities in any society. Furthermore, the organization of the poor is something every Oligarchy and Monarchy fears. If these outlaw groups were truly organized with the intent to address the problems that led them to the wrong side of the law, they would no longer be Outlaws, bandits, or gangsters, but freedom fighters.

It is fair for me to conclude that Democracy has flaws, as does any and every other system. Also, if a system change were truly sought, it would require the right timing, place, and organization. The time for change is when enough people wish for it. That number is sometimes the majority, but they can be voiceless and powerless. This is why people need to understand that the only way to control an army, a police force, and a government is to defeat the army, the police, and the government. Even with democracy in place, there will be many attempts to curb the system in favor of various groups. So even in places like Egypt, where people rallied and protested for Democracy in 2013, they managed to replace one dictator with another. They targeted only the government, not the military or the police. This is why people must be cautious not to be coerced into actions that benefit others. Instead, the people must systematically dismantle the system from all avenues, taking control of existing political and military seats of authority. Otherwise, rallies and public protests merely annoy the surrounding birds. Change means unseating the positions of power and authority and replacing them cautiously. I am not prescribing to do so, of course, but if it is to be done, it should be done properly. Many places erupted in democratic protests between 2008 and 2014 against their governments, and yet none succeeded.

In retrospect, and consequential to any attempt to change authority, Democracy can degrade into a lynch mob or ochlocracy if the people are not cautious. Some have often remarked to me, saying that I place far too much faith in the uneducated and poor, implying the majority of people. But I believe we are all equally worthy of everything life has to offer. I believe that with the truth, no matter which caste or mould others try to force us into, we are essentially the same. Given some basic education, most of us have an ethical foundation sufficient to support a Democracy.

It is fair to say that, as already stated, there is an off chance that Autocracies or Oligarchies might present themselves in their finest form. But alas, the truth is that they are the least likely to be fair and just. They are the most prone to wage war and cause mayhem at the expense of other people's children. Autocracies and Oligarchies are intrinsically unable to sustain themselves without enormous skewing of resource ownership. The only way they can keep power is to ensure they own the largest army and police force and are equipped with the best possible weapons. This is mandatory for any system where, in proportion, the top few per cent rule the entire population. While there is no perfect system, as Plato, Socrates, and even Aristotle agree upon, I accept that of all the systems, the finest is our beloved Democracy. Yet, unlike the other systems, it is the most difficult to begin, sustain, and maintain. There will always be someone who wants to control everything for their own benefit. The dictators, kings, monarchs, and autocrats want to diminish Democracy to become a toy for their wealth and pleasure. There will be people who degrade the value of democracy and try to diminish it into an Ochlocracy. There may also be intrinsically good people, but they may be selfish individuals, and in the process, cannot decide on anything that benefits others and everyone.

At this point, my philosophy is complete, and I hope I have answered as many questions as possible about the topic as I initially intended. I would now like to express some thoughts as if we were sitting together and sharing them: It is democracy that will allow the meek to inherit the earth. No Monarchy, Aristocracy, or Autocracy, Oligarchy will ever represent us. How, then, can some believe that we should mimic the Kingdom of God on Earth and have a representative of God walking amongst us?

Believing in our God means believing that we have the God-given right to live our lives freely and happily, in peace, and with love towards each other. When some people heard, "On earth as it is in Heaven," they began to recreate what they envisioned as the Kingdom of God on earth. But God did not want us to mimic him, to install man-gods or elevate people to positions of power. We know this because his name is Emmanuel, the God among us. He is neither above nor below but by our side. Yet, the opposite is what humanity has done and continues to do.

When I saw firsthand the impact of pyramidal structures in my personal life, the lives of those closest to me, and the lives of people in general, I began to realise that pyramidal structures had affected us since birth. We have lived, and continue to live, lives that depend almost entirely on the guidance of the pyramidal structures and the oligarchy at their apex. The reasons that my brothers suffered and that I, too, suffered were the same. The stories may be different, but the root cause was the same. Some say that money is the root of all evil, but this also implies that those who control the money are at the root of all evil. It makes one wonder: if people control the treasury, will they, too, be the root of all the evils that emerge in their society? From all walks of life, the pyramidal structures dictate the steps in our lives.

The church, the people, the government, my life, and all the things I had thought of culminated on the day I began writing this book. I began to see the nature and evil that reside within pyramid structures, not merely in government but also in churches and other similar institutions. To me, the Tower of Babel was not only a story in the Bible, but also a representation of how people with complex and problematic issues continually attempt to elevate themselves into positions of power, prestige, and wealth. The process they undertake causes an enormous number of injustices before they reach their target. It is these individuals who cause others to suffer. It is ultimately the reason why so many people affected by these pyramid builders would rather divide or separate, hide, and display escapist behaviors. Drugs, alcohol, immersive arts, and all forms of things are used to escape the brutality of the reality around them. Yet many believe change is to come from within such systems.

We all reside within the energy that will define humanity's future. The actions we take reflect our ethical stature, and it is upon those ethics that all our actions and those of future generations shall be founded. If we act righteously and morally, as our society defines these, then the foundations we lay will promote the same in the future. We should not be like those who run from the lepers but take the cloth and wipe the disease from them, just as we will wipe the lies and deceit from within society with philosophical truth. Do not seek Kings to rule over our cities, for you will be condemned. Do not seek leaders to lead, but lead each other hand in hand. Do not oppose authority with swords and weapons, but do not deny what you believe either. As Saint Kosmas once said, when they ask to take your guns, keep two so that you can give them one while you keep the other. Some believe that freedom can only be achieved by war. It may seem to be the only way for a government, an army, and a police force to be overpowered and controlled by the people. Believing that protests or marches can be effective without weapons is, sadly, a side effect of propaganda. Admittedly, though, with enough people coordinated, they can be armed with nothing more than their bare hands. Such coordination requires trusted leaders who will not exploit the people's fight and install a system that serves their own interests.

All of humanity can work together to make a difference. All of humanity can make a wonderful world. It is our destiny to claim this earth again; do not let anyone convince you otherwise. Perhaps we must go through far worse before we achieve the final resting place within a Democratic and peaceful world. Perhaps the time and place are not in this generation. Perhaps some places can implement a Democracy, while it will take others longer to achieve it. Humanity can work together, but we all need to understand that Democracy is only a mechanism for solving the world's problems. It will ultimately be the people and what they believe that will manifest into the laws and behaviors of their Democracy.

Democracy, as I have told you, is not a perfect system, but with good, ethical people, they will form an ethical government. An ethical government will treat neighboring and other governments ethically. So, it is we who must improve first before we lay any foundation. A weak foundation, or one with flaws, will cause problems for anything built on it. That is why the start of everything I have mentioned here rests with us. The path ahead requires people to learn what democracy is to become ethical and good people.

We, the people, have an obligation to educate ourselves on these democratic principles and to ensure that we discuss, debate, and develop our philosophies that align with the truth. That is your purpose, as it is mine. I have shared this philosophy with you to rekindle your interest in the timeless topic of Democracy. It is now your responsibility to ensure that our children understand in detail what freedom and democracy are. It is up to you and your children to educate yourselves so that ethical freedom and ethical democracy are one day inherited by our progeny. Of all the tasks set before any parent, you owe us and your children, or children to be, the right to know the truth.

I have, to this point, evaded describing the world around me in detail, but I will give you an image of a world we must change. These so-called nations and empires that dot the world are not formed through the power of the people. They are, for the most part, an investment of some minority. One minority owns one particular nation, and another minority owns another. They create a world that herds humans into cities like cattle or sheep. We are brought from the paddocks into their pens. When they set up mining operations, you see them build the same infrastructure as they would when planning a city or town. Water supplies, roads, housing, and all other forms of infrastructure are developed for the workers. You see, if we spend all day looking for water and food, we have little time to do anything else. When the chore of finding water and food is eliminated, people have what they think is free time. But because someone gave that water and food—or at least provided access to it—they also own that free time. They own it because they will ask for payment for that water and food in some way. That payment will eventually require people to work. Not surprisingly, the same people who provided the infrastructure also provided the work. It is like giving someone something for free initially, then slowly making them do things for it, and eventually, their need for it enslaves them. This world I live in has no polity formed by the people. We live in a dynamic array of minorities and their investments. But when we try to escape and live our own way, with only the shirts and clothes on our backs as our possessions, they will come and try to take those too. They will take them in a myriad of ways, by force or otherwise. But it is in their power to arrest, harm, and imprison anyone who dares defy the authority over them, even by walking out and settling a part of nature on their own. In other words, you do not have to do anything wrong to be guilty in a world where you are powerless and part of someone's investments. We cannot even escape it; believe me, I have tried, as many have before me. Houses were positioned on the beaches near my home by those seeking to escape this very thing. Within a generation, those in power removed them and their possessions from their location. Others had their property confiscated, and some, whom we call the indigenous people, suffered much worse.

So then, do you want someone else to establish a democracy for you? Know that others seek to make investments and to put you and your children in them to build their dreams. Will it be a democracy that you establish? Be strong, intelligent, and brave. Men truly need to learn how to be soldiers, and women need to learn how to support those soldiers. But soldiers are more than killers; they symbolize a way of life. This way of life means being able to survive with only our clothes on our backs. It is an autonomous and self-reliant way of life. It is very different from the one most people are accustomed to. A soldier will find water, food, and shelter to sustain their survival. But men who are unable to do these things will be waiting for others to do them for them, and what they receive will not be the same.

It is similar to the crops harvested by others who are in business to sell them. They are not interested in the flavor, taste, or texture of their crops. They care only for whatever may affect their sale of it. They will harvest large, tasteless crops because these will bring them greater profits. They will harvest crops before they have matured, so they last longer on the shelves and in storage, but they will not harvest them when the crop has ripened and developed all its nutrients and flavors. They will make and process things with the same view of profit and sales. So then, your liberty comes from unshackling yourself and others. If you try alone, you will fail. You can grow your food, be a survivalist, and do all the things you think are making you free. But you will never be free until you have the power to change the laws, write them, debate them, and pass them into action. Freedom only comes when the people share the same understanding and the same capacity to act.

This is why Democracy, like many other things reliant on education, is destined to fail within systems developed and controlled by a minority unwilling to relinquish their power. The city you live in is a plaything of a minority, an investment, a toy that they use to attain their satisfaction. They model and design their cities to the best of their ability, but the designs have numerous intrinsic shortcomings. But they are few and unable to discern everything that affects these cities. Therefore, ultimately, it is the people who pay the price for all their whims and mistakes. This is the world I face today.

The world I wanted relies too much on the ability to bring people to the same order without the trickery that prevents them from establishing a Democracy. You see, if people are reliant on money, those who have it have power over those who don't. A person reliant on money is like a bird free to fly anywhere and eat whatever they like, but, like us, they are easily fooled when food is given to them for free. They will stop searching for the things we provide them, and, in turn, they will slowly lose their freedom without realizing it. How, then, can one man free an enslaved people? They cannot! How can they be free? Only a minority with the knowledge, support, and power can give them the knowledge, support, and power. There must be a handful of people with the power to create the things needed to free the people. This is to make the circulation of money and currency fall into the hands of those who seek freedom instead of those who seek to satiate their greed, to give positions of power to those with the people at heart and interest. To project the skills needed to operate a democracy onto those who can and will most likely pass them on. Without such people, our democracy and our vision of it would be nothing more than a fantasy. People can never have a revolution to take power; they must enter the system and use their power wherever they can to the people's advantage. In doing so, the system slowly matures and becomes partitioned. On one end are the investors, in the middle are the governors, and on the other end are the people. Eventually, however, it is the people who will be the governors, and by doing this, they become the investors and then establish their democracy.

Commonly, people think we have progressed and moved on from old subjects, such as democracy. Within this frame of thought, as Socrates highlighted, do we move on with all the knowledge of the past? Or do we choose which to keep and which to throw out? Or perhaps we have no choice; we simply forget some technologies and gain others. Would there be anyone who knows how to hand-weave a fine silk shirt anywhere today? Or is that technology lost as certainly as that of making a catapult or ballista? What about the old herbal medicines? It wouldn't take much to re-learn them. But that is what would be needed: re-learning. It is one thing to make an object or material and another to do it well. Quality depends on skill, and skill can only be developed by practicing the tasks that comprise it. So, too, the skills of governance can be lost over time, just as academic languages and history, and most things of the past, seem to be eventually forgotten. Therefore, it is our obligation and onus to perpetuate the knowledge of what a democracy is.

References

Aeschin. (1919). Against Timarchus. In: Harvard University Press.

Aristotle. (1944a). Athenian Constitution (H. Rackham, Trans.). In: Harvard University Press.

Aristotle. (1944b). Politics (H. Rackham, Trans.). In: Harvard University Press.

Australian Bureau of Statistics. (2015-2016). *Household income and wealth*. https://www.abs.gov.au/

Herodotus. (1920). The Histories (E. A. D. Godley, Trans.). In.

King John, & Nobility, T. (1215). Carta Libertatum (The Charter Of Liberties) Of King John. In.

Marx, K., & Engels, F. (1955). *The Communist Manifesto* (S. H. Beer, Ed.). Appleton-Century-Crofts Inc.

New Testament. (2023). KJV New Testament. https://www.profitisilias.com.gr/

Pertusi, A. (1976). *La Caduta di Costantinopoli: Le testimonianze dei contemporanei*. Fondazione Lorenzo Valla. https://books.google.com.au/books?id=N-kTAQAAMAAJ

Plato. (1969). Republic (P. Shorey, Trans.). In: Harvard University.

Rousseau, J.-J. (1754). A Discourse Upon the Origin and the Foundation of the Inequality Among Mankind. In *Discours sur l'origine et les fondements de l'inégalité parmi les hommes*.

Septuagint. (2023). Old Testament. In.

Smith, A. (1976). *An Inquiry Into the Nature and Causes of the Wealth of Nations* (R.H.Campbell, A. S. Skinner, & W. B. Todd, Eds.). Oxford University Press.

The West Australian. (24 December 1932). PROPERTY MARKET. *The West Australian (Perth, WA: 1979-1954)*, 10. http://nla.gov.au/nla.news-article32586068

Thucydides. (1906). The History of the Peloponnesian War (R. Crawley, Trans.). In.

Xenophon. (1921). Hellenica (C. L. Brownson, Trans.). In: Harvard University Press.

End Notes

This book is a revised second edition of the original book. The revisions have focused on condensing the phrasing, correcting grammatical mistakes, and improving the text's overall readability. Although expanding and explaining certain things better was tempting, the book has been left as close to the original as possible. Due to the rephrasing, the book is now approximately 30 pages shorter. Nothing was subtracted; instead, some additional sentences, grammar corrections, and rephrasing resulted in the changes. There is still more work to be done, but it is a very polished version and much easier to read than the first edition.

Democracy: Demokratia is a bold philosophical work with ancient roots used to expose modern distortions of democracy. Drawing from classical philosophical thought and contemporary ethical insight, the author challenges readers to rediscover democracy not as a system of governance, but as a moral commitment to truth, political participation, and human dignity. With clarity and conviction, this book exposes the creeping influence of an oligarchy and calls for a renewed civic spirit grounded in justice and collective responsibility. A timely and timeless work, Democracy: Demokratia is both a warning and a guidepost for those who still believe in the power of the people.

About the Author

Tim Damianidis is a philosopher, ethical risk consultant, and author whose work bridges ancient democratic ideals with the urgent moral questions of our time. In Democracy: Demokratia, Tim reclaims the soul of democracy from its modern distortions, tracing its roots to ancient classical thought while confronting the oligarchic tendencies of today.

The author has worked in numerous businesses at almost all levels and spoken on a wide range of platforms.

www.ingramcontent.com/pod-product-compliance
Lightning Source LLC
LaVergne TN
LVHW012338100826
845148LV00018B/2708

9781763743151